Mixed Faith and Shared Feeling

Mixed Faith and Shared Feeling

Theater in Post-Reformation London

Musa Gurnis

Published in Cooperation with
Folger Shakespeare Library

PENN

UNIVERSITY OF PENNSYLVANIA PRESS

PHILADELPHIA

Published by
University of Pennsylvania Press
Philadelphia, Pennsylvania 19104-4112
www.upenn.edu/pennpress

Printed in the United States of America on acid-free paper
1 3 5 7 9 10 8 6 4 2

Library of Congress Cataloging-in-Publication Data
Names: Gurnis, Musa, author.
Title: Mixed faith and shared feeling : theater in post-reformation
    London / Musa Gurnis.
Description: 1st edition. | Philadelphia : University of Pennsylvania Press,
    [2018] | Includes bibliographical references and index. Identifiers:
    LCCN 2017052154 | ISBN 9780812250251 (hardcover : alk. paper)
Subjects: LCSH: Theater—Great Britain—Religious aspects—
    History—16th century. | Theater—Great Britain—Religious
    aspects—History—17th century. | Theater audiences—Great
    Britain—Religious aspects—History—16th century. | Theater
    audiences—Great Britain—Religious aspects—History—17th century. |
    Theater and society—Great Britain—History—16th century. | Theater
    and society—Great Britain—History—17th century. | English
    drama—Early modern and Elizabethan, 1500–1600—History and
    criticism. | English drama—17th century—History and criticism.
Classification: LCC PN2590.R35 G87 2018 | DDC 792.0942/09031—dc23
LC record available at https://lccn.loc.gov/2017052154

To Wayne Jordan, my fellow practitioner in the Paradise School,
for showing me that theater exists to transform audiences
and
to Atticus Zavaletta, my brother in Christ,
for pointing out that the Reformation was when
religion got queered

CONTENTS

Introduction   1

Chapter 1. Mixed Faith   10

Chapter 2. Shared Feeling   38

Chapter 3. In Mixed Company: Collaboration
in Commercial Theater   67

Chapter 4. Making a Public Through *A Game at Chess*   89

Chapter 5. *Measure for Measure*: Theatrical Cues
and Confessional Codes   122

Epilogue: Pity in the Public Sphere   151

Notes   161

Bibliography   219

Index   245

Acknowledgments   255

Mixed Faith and Shared Feeling

Introduction

This book is a cultural materialist study of the mutually generative relationship between post-Reformation religious life and London's commercial theaters. Early modern English drama is shaped by the polyvocal, confessional scene in which it was embedded. Yet theater does not simply reflect culture. The representational practices of the theater business *refract* the confessional material they stage. Early modern plays draw contradictory scraps of confessional practice together in powerful fantasies that reconfigure existing structures of religious thought and feeling. These performances do not evacuate religious material by bending it. Nor do they offer audiences a simple psychological escape from the realities of confessional conflict into a power-neutral space of free play and fellowship. What post-Reformation English theater did was involve mixed-faith audiences in shared, imaginative processes that allowed playgoers to engage with the always-changing tangle of religious life from emotional and cognitive vantage points not elsewhere available to them. Recent scholarship on the relationship between commercial theater and post-Reformation culture moves beyond a binary model of Catholic and Protestant religious difference, toward a fuller recognition of the diversity and complexity of confessional positions available to early modern English people. However, this rich critical conversation remains limited by a tendency to focus on single authors, particularly William Shakespeare, and on individual strands of the broader confessional culture.[1] In contrast, *Mixed Faith and Shared Feeling: Theater in Post-Reformation London* shows how industry-wide, representational practices reshaped the ways ideologically diverse Londoners accessed the mingle-mangle of religious life across the spectrum of belief.

The long aftermath of the religious upheavals of the mid-sixteenth century cannot be understood through attention to any one confessional group in isolation. As Ethan Shagan writes, "English Protestants and Catholics [of varying stripes] defined . . . their identities . . . in response to their ideological opponents, allowing for a remarkable degree of cross-pollination of ideas, imagery, and texts across confessional divides."[2] The subcultures of puritans, church papists, Laudians, recusants, ardent conformists, and converts were entangled and mutually defining. These lives cannot be understood either in crude, block categories or as idiosyncratic snowflakes of private faith, but only as embedded in the densely woven fabric of mixed religious discourse and practice through which they were made. Particular confessional identities developed in relation to a larger and always-changing religious matrix. However, the heterogeneity of these confessional positions should not be mistaken for protomulticultural, Erasmian toleration.[3] The reality of religious diversity existed in constant tension with the shared belief that there could only be one true faith. Confessional factions sought the power to define and enforce orthodoxy with a ferocity commensurate with the stakes—life and death in this world and the next. Yet Protestant hegemony was internally contradictory, changing, and contested. Dominant versions of English Christianity were displaced not only through direct religious opposition but also indirectly through the countless jostlings of alternative, often muddled, everyday confessional practices. Post-Reformation religious culture was produced collectively and chaotically, by diverse agents from endlessly reappropriated materials.

So too was commercial theater. Plays were made by mixed-faith groups of creative professionals responding to industry trends with the resources available to them. Author-focused projects implicitly assume that the ideological imprints of individual playwrights are extractable from the larger processes of creative production. Others ascribe the confessional complexity of the drama to the complexity of the broader religious culture, passively recorded in particular plays. Throughout this book I will be arguing that this is not how theater works. The confessional dispositions of individual playwrights do not always correlate with the religious leanings of their plays. This is true of single authors (who even alone write in dialogue with other playwrights, companies, and audiences), but all the more obviously so in the common case of multiple authorship. As I show in Chapter 3, confessionally mixed groups of players and playwrights cobbled together commercially viable drama from the representational tools at hand. The conventions of genre and characterization, the structures of audience engagement, and the capacities of stage space and costume all exert their own influences. The cultural products of this complex and highly contingent system are seldom coherent expressions of anyone's individual faith. Commercial plays do not transmit religious matter intact. The business and formal pressures of theatrical mediation reshape confessional content. The multiagential processes of creative production exceed the ideological control of any one person or discourse.

The post-Reformation landscape offered the stage rich material, but the confessional terrain did not simply transpose its existing features onto plays; theater recontours the religious ground it represents, by drawing alternative routes of thought and feeling for mixed-faith audiences to travel. The fundamental contention of this book is that theatrical process lures playgoers astray from their everyday religious orientations. In Chapter 1, I demonstrate the confessional diversity of post-Reformation playgoers at some length, in order to counter the usual, often implicit, assumption that theater audiences were uniform, orthodox groups of Church of England Protestants. Yet my purpose in showing examples of the complex and varied religious lives of known playgoers is not to suggest that these individuals' responses to plays were narrowly or directly determined by their respective confessional identities; rather, these identity positions are points from which to measure the kinds of imaginative stretching elicited by theatrical effects. The orchestration of audience response is not experientially or ideologically totalizing. It was rarely directed toward changing opinions on matters of religious controversy. However, commercial theater did enable ongoing, collective, emotional experimentation with alternative religious perspectives.

The shared, affective thinking structured by performance pulled different religious groups into a mixed-faith public. Whatever the long-term, historical aftereffects of the emergence of this cross-confessional theater public, playgoing was not a secularizing activity for early modern Londoners themselves. They remained enmeshed in the religious culture of the period in which they actually lived. Neither was the general function of commercial drama to produce the merry, protoecumenical, English good-fellowship that appears in some parts of some plays. Nor was theater the handmaiden of Protestant hegemony. Rather, playhouses were spaces of virtual experimentation with changing structures of religious thought and feeling. Theater gives cultures, as Steven Mullaney writes, "a means of thinking about themselves, especially when confronting their more painful or irresolvable conflicts and contradictions." In the multidirectional, uneven, and massive transformations of the long English Reformation, theater was "an affective technology . . . an especially deep, sensitive, and probing instrument, as theater tends to be in times of crisis."[4] The impact of this collective, cross-confessional, affective thinking on early modern religious life was indirect but profound.

Post-Reformation theater's polyvalent religious experiments do not point forward in a teleological narrative of disenchantment or "Anglican" triumph. But this does not mean that theater does not effect cultural change. It is precisely in the multiple, erratic, exploratory, imaginative shifts structured by performance that the stage does its ideological work. Cultures, as Raymond Williams clarifies, are processes, not static things:

> A lived hegemony is always a process. . . . It is a realized complex of experiences, relationships, and activities, with specific and changing pressures and limits. In practice, that is, hegemony can never be singular. Its internal structures are highly complex. . . . [Moreover], it does not just passively exist as a form of dominance. It has continually to be renewed, recreated, defended, and modified. It is also continually resisted, limited, altered, challenged, by pressures not all its own. . . . The most interesting and difficult part of any cultural analysis . . . is that which seeks to grasp the hegemonic in its active and formative but also its transformational processes.[5]

The continual reiteration on which dominant structures of religious belief depend is never self-identical, and never uncontested. Cultures reproduce themselves and change through repetitions that are never the same. As many cultural materialist and new historicist scholars of the 1980s and 1990s recognized, "colluding" or "contesting" are inadequate categories to describe these ongoing, multiple, and entangled processes of cultural reproduction and mutation.[6] Accordingly, I attend less to moments of direct religious opposition than to a more slippery set of confessional experiences orchestrated by theatrical devices: unlikely sympathies, arousal, uncertainty. Commercial plays did not generally change people's doctrinal beliefs—nor did they seek to—but the conventions and pleasures of theater could loosen existing religious structures and wiggle them into other shapes.

This is possible because people too are cultural processes, as Judith Butler observes. Like gender identity, religious identity is not a thing but a "stylized repetition of acts through time."[7] The confessional lives of individual audience members should be thought of not as static facts but as practices. Religious selves are not discrete, coherent, ideological units. Rather, these identities are constituted and continually recalibrated through their interactions with confessional culture. This ongoing process of reinscription and change is always at work in even the most inane daily activities. But early modern theater offered groups of diverse individuals special license, as well as the imaginative tools, to encounter their world differently than they did in everyday life, to feel their culture from other perspectives. Theater gave Londoners, across the spectrum of belief, particularly capacious and flexible forms of mental and emotional access to the tangle of post-Reformation life. However intangible their impact on the outside world, these virtual, emotional, and mental experiments are themselves small, embodied, cultural transformations. While flickers of feeling (especially in response to something fictive, not even real) may seem insignificant, such experiential micromovements are the most basic unit of ideological reproduction and change.

Representation itself is a social process. This is most overtly true in the case of theater, where the real-time interactions of live actors and audiences are the very medium. (As Peter Brook writes, "A man walks across a stage and someone else is watching him, and this is all that is needed for an act of theatre to be engaged.")[8] Theater is a relationship between performers and audiences that unfolds over time. In my close readings, I stress the phenomenology of performance, and the dialectic between stage and playhouse, because it is in these temporal and relational dynamics that it is easiest to see how theater works as a mechanism of cultural adaptation, rather than as a repository of discourses. Post-Reformation culture, the Londoners who lived it, and the plays they collectively made are all interlocking processes; and my purpose is to show the enmeshed workings of the gears that connect and move them.

The drift over the last decade toward readings in which plays simply register historical conditions is now being countered by a renewed emphasis on theatrical form—originally so crucial to the cultural materialist and new historicist project. The goal of this work was always to track living relationships between a society and its fantasies, not to spot discourses in texts as if pinning and labeling butterflies. While the newer critical moniker "historical formalism" usefully marks its affinities with new historicism and distinguishes itself from belle-lettrism,[9] I retain "cultural materialism" in order to mark emphatically that my goal is not just to juxtapose literary texts and historical conditions in a way that richly describes both, but rather to show the active role of representation in the ongoing making of the world. The term stresses continuity with the insights of revisionist Marxists of the 1970s and 1980s (particularly Louis Althusser, Pierre Macherey, Fredric Jameson, Terry Eagleton, and Williams) regarding the transformative cultural work enabled by the semi-autonomy of literary form. It maintains that representation is not merely reflective but constitutive, and it takes up the challenge of understanding the complicated ways that people and their societies make each other through language, with the belief that this model of culture is also why our own scholarly and pedagogic work matters.

Attending to such critical lineages enables genuine methodological growth, instead of pendulum swings by which merely reflective readings of texts are replaced by merely contextual treatments of history. "What will come after historicism?" is a question that misunderstands the methodology it looks to replace. The basic premise of cultural materialism, and of revisionist Marxism generally, is that the world as imagined and the world as lived create and constrain each other continually. To adapt the old "Mother Russia" joke: we can never be done with this dialectic, because it is never done with us. Understanding the always-changing, cultural feedback loop through which individual subjects and societies form each other is difficult, unending, and vital critical work. At its fullest, cultural materialism articulates a dense, formative matrix of human experiences, expressions, and activities in the world. It is a methodology adept at showing dynamic relationships between seemingly disconnected areas of social practice and culture. By insisting on the entanglement of the past and present, it demands continual methodological revision: "It is the eternally vigilant prophet proclaiming the relations between the tasks of the immediate present and the totality of the historical process."[10]

Now, while we are watching the fire sale of the humanities in a university system that runs on the exploitation of an adjunct precariat, is a particularly suicidal time to abandon a methodology devoted to analyzing the relationships between social conditions, and the forms of knowledge production and cultural expression that subtend and change them. A country that elects a billionaire, reality television star as president cannot dispense with Marxist cultural studies. Creeping neoliberalism teaches us to assume that critical paradigms have built-in obsolescence after which they need replacing or rebranding. Looking for the "next thing" turns a capacious way of seeing the ongoing process of collectively making and being made by the world, into a "thing" that has outlived its market value. It is not progress to pursue a theater history that ignores social history, or to embrace pseudomaterialist criticism that describes "stuff" rather than social relationships.[11] Cultural materialism is not an emaciated ghost, shuffling toward the dustbin of criticism. We need this politically useful, intellectually flexible, and profound way of looking at the mutually shaping relationships between humans, language, and the world.

In the chapters that follow, I flesh out the claims I have been making in this introduction, showing by close engagement with dramatic texts and performance practices how early modern theater drew mixed-faith playgoers into new relations with a complex religious culture. Refuting the common assumption that audiences consisted of conforming Church of England Protestants, Chapter 1 illustrates the confessional heterogeneity of theatergoers, through representative examples of the complex and changing religious lives of about seventy known playgoers. This sample presents a far more diverse set of confessional characters than previously has been imagined in playhouses.[12] Alongside various kinds of fellow Protestants, and assorted types of Catholics, puritans attended the commercial theaters throughout the period. I demonstrate this fact—and discuss the critical persistence of the false notion that godly people hated plays. The religious position of individual playgoers informed, but did not narrowly determine, their responses to theater.

In Chapter 2, I argue for theater's capacity to restructure playgoers' experiences of confessional material. Early modern commercial drama fostered imaginative flexibility. Audiences were initiated in the pleasures of generic variety, experiments with staging conventions and genre, and the proliferation of dramatic subjects and perspectives available in the entertainment market. The emotional and mental elasticity cultivated by this theater culture extended to playgoers' experiences of dramatized religious material. Recent work on theatrical response emphasizes uncued audience behavior and diverse appropriations of the drama.[13] This scholarship tends to pit agential, individual playgoers against the supposedly totalizing force of stage spectacle. Yet the usual dichotomies drawn between active and passive, emotional and critical, individual and collective reception, are inadequate to describe the complex and fluctuating mixtures of these elements of response orchestrated by theatrical process. To illustrate how theatrical pleasure can reorient playgoers' experiences of confessional content, I turn to a group of plays from the early 1620s that capitalize on popular interest in the Spanish Match. Unlike the rigid, oppositional religious binary into which *A Game at Chess* interpellates its audiences, other Spanish Match plays, such as *The Noble Spanish Soldier*, *The Spanish Gypsy*, and *Match Me in London*, invite more ideologically supple forms of identification and delight.

In contrast to work that seeks to identify the religious affiliations of individual playwrights, Chapter 3 focuses on mixed-faith collaboration. Religious differences among playhouse colleagues were common, and they had varied and unpredictable effects. Turning to a subgenre of stage hagiographies, I show how basic conditions of dramatic production, such as collaborative authorship, as well as the pressures of dramatic trends, generated confessionally hybrid plays. For example, the popularity of Falstaff led to the incorporation of the jolly English—and Catholic—thieving priest Sir John in the godly play *Sir John Oldcastle*. Playwrights with antipapist sentiments but expertise in the subgenre collaborated on a script sympathetic to the eponymous Catholic martyr, *Sir Thomas More*. Even in a genre that fosters plays with explicit religious loyalties, the working practices of the theater business produce mixed ideological formations.

In Chapter 4, on Thomas Middleton's 1624 topical allegory *A Game at Chess*, I attend to the confessional and political work of surveillance in which the play enlists audiences. In contrast to existing criticism that focuses largely on identifying references to historical people and events, I show how the play's structures of address and spacialization exercise theatergoers' faculties of religious and political discovery, interpellating a Protestant collective out of a mixed-faith crowd. *A Game at Chess* does not simply publicize political and religious content but rather engages playgoers in the collective activity of being a confessionally and politically discerning public.

In Chapter 5, I take Shakespeare's *Measure for Measure* as a case study in the capacity of theatrical process to shift habits of religious thought. The play inducts its mixed-faith audiences into a Calvinist hermeneutic of social and spiritual judgment, leading confessionally diverse playgoers to make assumptions on cultural grounds as to characters' election or reprobation. Yet *Measure for Measure*'s reversals of plot and affect disrupt the predestinarian framework of thought and feeling that it initially asks mixed-faith audiences to adopt. Through such basic dramatic devices as soliloquies and dramatic irony, *Measure for Measure* activates—and unsettles—one of the most deeply entrenched practices of Calvinist culture. The play offers spectators of varied confessional identities (those for whom predestinarian theology was anathema, as well as those who lived its pressures daily) a multidimensional experience of the internal instability of a dominant religious paradigm. *Measure for Measure* offers mixed-faith audiences shared predestinarian feeling. It allows intimate access to the interiority of a puritan hypocrite and possible reprobate, and it asks playgoers of various religious affiliations to suspend judgment on Angelo's soul.

In the epilogue, I explore the theater's distinctive role in early modern public formation. Unlike Habermasian print publics centered on rational-critical debate, drama offered a different kind of encounter with matters of religious controversy. For example, John Ford's 1630 *'Tis Pity She's a Whore* recasts the tension of a Caroline controversy between Laudians and Calvinists, as to whether the Church of Rome was the Antichristian Whore of Babylon, onto the star-crossed romance of incestuous lovers, allowing audiences a more emotionally layered experience of a divisive religious issue. Early modern commercial theater was a public-making forum, but one in which feeling was a central, and essential, tool for collectively reimagining post-Reformation culture.

CHAPTER I

Mixed Faith

The early modern commercial theaters drew confessionally diverse audiences. Despite increasing attention among scholars of the drama to the diversity and complexity of post-Reformation religious life, it remains common practice to refer to these audiences simply as "Protestant."[1] This shorthand is useful insofar as it registers the large numerical majority of conforming members of the Church of England, as well as that institution's claim to national hegemony. However convenient, the term risks homogenizing the de facto pluralism of the post-Reformation religious scene, erasing Catholic factions, and eliding the changing and internally contested nature of English Protestantism itself. This chapter shows that a far more diverse set of confessional characters filled the playhouses: hot, lukewarm, and cold statute Protestants; recusant, church papist, and militant Catholics; avant-garde forerunners and Laudians; converts and serial converters; the conflicted and the confused.

The varied confessional filters through which people experienced these plays exceed taxonomy. Religious identities—then as now—are more than the box one might tick on a census. They consist not only of consciously held beliefs but also of doubts, automatic devotional habits, unorthodox longings, curiosities, residues of rejected ideologies, and degrees of fervor. "Believers," as Judith Maltby observes, "are rarely theologically consistent."[2] Confessional positions are relative: one man's conforming Church of England Protestant is another's church papist. They are situational, subject to alteration over the course of an individual's life through conversion, experimentation, or wavering commitment. It was also possible for a person's religious orientation to remain constant while the social meaning of that position changed, as was the case for many Calvinists during the Laudian ascendency who found themselves relabeled as "puritans," or for English Catholics at varying moments of relative toleration or persecution. Moreover, religious identities are constantly recalibrated in response to changing institutional, social, and devotional stimuli: a woman might be a differently interpellated religious subject when attending Church of England services in the morning than when she is speaking with a puritan neighbor in the afternoon or lying awake, afraid of death, at night. Religious identities are not so much something one *is* but rather something one is constantly *doing*. This is not to say that post-Reformation English people did not hold strong and sincere beliefs, or that confessional labels did not have real social and spiritual consequences; rather, like all discursively produced subject positions, confessional selves are shifting composites of mixed cultural materials. Peter Lake aptly calls post-Reformation religious life "a number of attempts, conducted at very different levels of theoretical self-consciousness and coherence, at creative bricolage."[3] Religious identities, in other words, are like gender identities as described by Judith Butler: "The very multiplicity of their construction holds out the possibility of a disruption of their univocal posturing."[4] These heterogeneous threads not only constitute religious identities but also contain the possibilities for their reconfiguration. The variety, complexity, and mobility of playgoers' confessional positions should deter us from a default assumption that audiences' responses to theater were ideologically coherent or orthodox.

While religious differences did sometimes generate contrasting experiences of particular plays, the variegated confessional identities of individual playgoers did not delimit their possible responses to theater in narrow or predictable ways. People also felt things in theaters not easily aligned with their belief systems. In Thomas Cartelli's words, "The playgoer may . . . entertain responses that would seem decidedly abnormal outside the theater": thousands of committed Christians dared God out of heaven with the atheist Tamburlaine.[5] As Susan Bennett observes, the process of reception "acts bi-directionally."[6] Particular confessional positions form part of the interpretive frameworks that create the play in varying shapes in the minds of playgoers. But spectators too are reshaped, however imperceptibly, by the dramatic fantasies that they absorb. Theatrical process can orchestrate responses that jostle spectators into emotional perspectives and mental experiences that fall outside the orbit of their real-world religious beliefs. This is one of the basic reasons people go to plays: to feel, imagine, and occupy subject positions differently than they do in real life. Theater's particular capacities to generate shared emotion, and structure collective attention, could pull diverse audiences into temporary, cross-confessional communities. To adopt playgoer John Donne's phrase, in the theaters, "these mixed souls [do] mix again."[7]

My claim is not, however, that the playhouses promoted protosecular religious toleration, or Erasmian good fellowship. If confessional differences were sometimes subsumed, displaced, or reconfigured in shared dramatic fantasies, the result was not the consolidation of a distinctly via media theater culture. Both the extant body of drama and the material practices of the theater business that produced it are far more confessionally polyvocal. The playhouse was a space of "suspended belief," where the indirection of dramatic fiction allowed theatergoers more license to imaginatively experiment with the possibilities, and emotionally wrangle with the problems, of post-Reformation life. The commercial theaters offered their mixed-faith audiences sophisticated *techne* for collectively thinking and feeling through the densely layered palimpsest that constituted their religious world. The records left by this shared daydreaming about the endlessly reappropriated cultural materials of the holy are characterized not by the clear triumph of one ideological position (for example, minimally doctrinal, decently ceremonial, proto-Anglican, or protosecular Church of England Protestantism) but rather by the complexity of the drama's refractions of London's diverse religious cultures. The confessional impact of the practices of the commercial theater business is difficult to specify, but this does not mean that religious discourses, or their enmeshed embodiments (people), were unchanged by the vivid, unruly refashionings of mixed-faith materials on offer in the playhouses. The usual absence of immediate, easily identifiable, social consequences to theatrical performance does not mean that plays do nothing. Early modern drama's influence on London's religious culture was multivalent, contradictory, and often subterranean. Theater's capaciousness as a form of social thought and emotion, its distinctive facility to both accommodate multiple perspectives and focus collective attention, made it a medium well equipped to engage with the complexities of post-Reformation life. The commercial theaters gave confessionally diverse Londoners somewhere to be shaken by the ground moving beneath them, to feel the tremors of tectonic shifts, whose ultimate direction was unknown.

In the playhouses, ideologically divided crowds processed the seismic instability of post-Reformation confessional culture together. Sir Humphrey Mildmay, an avid theatergoer with some Catholic leanings, recorded frequent trips to the playhouse in mixed-faith company. Sir Humphrey saw *Volpone* accompanied by his godly brother Anthony, who was a "great opposer . . . of Popery" and would later serve as jailor to King Charles I, along with their cousin Sir Frank Wortley, who would become an enthusiastic officer in the King's army and pen a defense of the episcopacy.[8] This ordinary occasion—when a crypto-papist, a puritan, and a pro-episcopal loyalist sat together, watching a play written by multiple convert Ben Jonson while he was still Catholic, with puritan actor John Lowin in the title role—demonstrates how thoroughly confessional heterogeneity permeated the production and reception of commercial drama. In Chapter 3, I discuss the complex and unpredictable effects of mixed-faith collaboration among actors and playwrights within theater companies. Here, the crucial point is not simply the fact of these playgoers' confessional diversity but also the flexible imaginative engagement with London's mixed religious culture enabled by the process of performance.

For example, early in *Volpone* Nano the dwarf and Androgyno the hermaphrodite entertain their employer with a rhyming exposition of the transmigrations of the soul of Pythagoras, which initiates the audience in the pleasures of transformation that are central to the play. While *Volpone* generally keeps religious issues peripheral, here they are underscored. Nano and Androgyno's repartee begins with the question:

How of late [hast thou] suffered translation
And shifted thy coat in these days of reformation[?][9]

The ensuing back-and-forth traces Pythagoras's soul's journey through the bodies of a "reformed . . . fool," a Carthusian monk, a lawyer, a mule, a puritan, and a hermaphrodite. This tour de force of doggerel includes four lines of antipuritan satire. It would be po-faced and tone-deaf to assume that Sir Humphrey Mildmay, Sir Anthony Mildmay, and Sir Frank Wortley each found the antipuritan jokes funny or not funny in direct proportion to his real-world opinion of the godly. The jaunty couplets, the erratic "tumbling" meter, the range of subjects satirized, and the atypical physicality of the speakers themselves all give the zanies' routine a sense of comic overflow that orients audience attention to the movement between forms of identity. The logic of the joke is accretive, accelerating slippages of confessional selfhood, chaotically mixed with transformations of other kinds—between sexes and between species. The cumulative energy of the "transmigration" encourages growing laughter across particular confessional jabs. In performance, the function of the zanies' skit is not to divide playgoers along sectarian lines but to involve everyone in the quasi-erotic gratifications of variety and change. This kind of ideologically unruly grafting of religious culture and theatrical form permeates the extant corpus of early modern drama. In the playhouses, mixed-faith audiences shared theatrical experiences that transmogrify religious categories.

The real-world religious positions of audience members were part of the generative, confessional polyvocality of the commercial theater scene; yet these identities did not rigidly predetermine how people felt watching plays. Theater happens in the oscillation between "audiences" (actual groups of diverse and complex living people) and "the audience" (that imagined collective elicited in performance).[10] Meanings are not produced solely by the ideological disposition of spectators, nor solely by the experiential impact of theatrical process, but by their mutual interaction. The varied, complex, and changeable confessional positions of playgoers, to which I now turn, do not fix limits to imaginative responses to theater but rather mark starting points from which to measure the possible imaginative and emotional distances traveled in the two hours' traffic of the stage.

Mixed Audiences, or, People Are Different

Here, I illustrate the confessional diversity of early modern commercial theater audiences, using as examples the religious lives of about seventy known playgoers.[11] Obviously, this tiny sample cannot give us any statistical information about the confessional demographics of audiences. It is estimated that at least fifteen thousand people attended the theaters weekly: totaling as many as a million visits a year, on average, over the nearly seventy years between the construction of the first, purpose-built playhouse in 1576 and the closing of the theaters in 1642.[12] Even assuming that the confessional breakdown of the playgoing public reflected that of London, religious historians are rightly cautious when making demographic claims about confessional groups. The legal requirement of church attendance made sincere conformity often indistinguishable from its tepid simulation, and nonattendance could indicate anything from Catholic recusancy, to puritan sermon gadding, to an irreverent preference for the alehouse.[13] Moreover, because confessional nomenclature was relative and often polemical, we cannot treat the religious subcategories used by contemporaries as neutrally descriptive.

That having been said, the shifting size and visibility of particular confessional groups has been widely canvassed. As Patrick Collinson summarizes, "Historians continue to disagree over the extent to which the English people took the new religion to heart and became more than what contemporaries called 'cold statute Protestants.' But it is now generally accepted that by the end of the [sixteenth] century the English nation was Protestant in the sense that (except for a repressed minority) it was no longer Catholic."[14] Maltby describes committed conformists or "Prayer-Book Protestants" as "nothing other than a minority, though a significant minority, on the religious spectrum."[15] The godly too were a minority, though one that also claimed for itself a normative role in the national Church.[16] Puritanism bled into a wider Calvinist culture.[17] London's active puritan underground fostered the "miscegenation" of familist and antinomian ideas with more mainstream strands of puritan thought.[18] An "avant-garde conformist" minority appeared even in the midst of the broad "Calvinist consensus" of the late Elizabethan and Jacobean Church.[19] This group's emphasis on ceremony and its movement away from Calvinist, predestinarian theology would gain traction in the Caroline Church with the rise of William Laud.[20] Catholicism persisted in England, both through the survival (or mutation) of traditional devotional habits and through the efforts of post-Tridentine missionaries.[21] Estimates vary, but recusant Catholics may have accounted for as little as 2 percent of the population of London.[22] Beyond this visible sliver of engagés lay a larger number of committed Catholics, who avoided persecution through occasional conformity. Without windows into men's souls, these strategic schismatics blend into a broader group of conforming parishioners with conservative, religious tendencies, whom hotter Protestants also described as "church papists."[23] While complaints about widespread religious ignorance and indifference were often polemical, there is also evidence of subdoctrinal, popular Pelagianism ("Be good, and you will go to Heaven"), as well as more actively irreverent, or irreligious, behaviors and attitudes.[24] Alongside these competing and overlapping confessional cultures, there existed a muddily subconfessional, perhaps even sub-Christian, world of folk belief and magical practices.[25] The religious spectrum was broad, and the positions people occupied along it were often slippery. "Orthodoxy," or religious normativity, was contested and elusive territory.

If, as Alfred Harbage asked, we imagine the motley crowd pouring out of the Globe, we can never know how many in that audience were Catholic, or puritan, or converts, or had avant-garde attitudes toward ceremony. Then again—because confessional difference was often invisible but existed in every socioeconomic class, among both men and women, and in every age group— neither could they.[26] (For this reason, debates about the class and gender composition of London theater audiences are not immediately relevant to this study.)[27] Our inability to recover specific statistical information about the religious sympathies of playgoers, despite our awareness of the reality of confessional diversity, puts us in something like the position of audience members themselves, whose perceptions of the size and activities of both their own and other confessional groups could be highly subjective. Religious heterogeneity was greater than the sum of its parts. The confessional lives described next index the variety, complexity, and mobility of religious positions that audiences brought to plays. Collectively, they suggest the endlessly revisable possibilities of a mixed-faith culture.

Playgoing Puritans

The notion that puritans were en masse fundamentally opposed to theater has persisted despite repeated debunkings.[28] As George Walker in his 1935 biography of puritan playgoer Richard Madox points out, "It is a modern fallacy that Puritans were enemies of the drama."[29] Unquestionably, some godly people rejected theater, not only because of its immoral subject matter and dissolute crowds but also because of its association with Catholic or residually popish ceremony. Certainly, the accusation of antitheatricalism was a common trope of antipuritan polemic. Nevertheless, antitheatricalism was not so widespread among the godly as to eliminate puritans from theater culture. My purpose here is to refute the tenacious falsehood that godly people were, by definition, enemies of theater, as well as to identify the underlying assumptions that keep this an intervention that must be repeated each time as if from scratch.

Several recent books, most notably Jeffrey Knapp's *Shakespeare's Tribe: Church, Nation, and Theater in Renaissance England* and Alison Shell's *Shakespeare and Religion*, reassert the view of a London theater scene grounded in a via media religious culture, in which the godly had little to no part.[30] In Knapp's *Shakespeare's Tribe*, early modern English theater is Erasmian, that is, minimally doctrinal and broadly inclusive—but separate from the world of puritans. He writes, "The godly in churches, the good fellows in alehouses and playhouses: these were the rival camps."[31] Unfortunately, this influential book repeatedly misidentifies divisive polemic that claims for itself the privileged position of moderation, as evidence of Erasmian toleration—which it is not.[32] In other words, Knapp not only (like many others) ignores or minimizes evidence of puritan theater people; he homogenizes a wide range of real confessional differences among theatergoers and practitioners into an undifferentiated ecumenicalism. As the last thirty years of revisionist scholarship debunking the Whig narrative of the English Reformation as the successful installation of an anodyne, via media Anglicanism suggests, Knapp's account does not accurately describe the diversity and complexity of post-Reformation confessional life.[33]

Shell offers an erudite version of a similar argument. She recognizes some forms of confessional diversity in the playhouses, affirming that "audiences were not homogeneous," but also restates a qualified version of the familiar claim that "[puritans] stayed away from the theatre." Shell goes so far as to suggest that "a typical London audience of the early seventeenth century [pre-1620s] might have contained, relative to the city's population in general, a disproportionately large number of those who consciously recoiled from Calvinist doctrine."[34] This is an astonishing claim, since these decades are widely identified as a heyday of the Calvinist consensus, when anti-Calvinist innovations to doctrine and ceremony were still in a nascent stage of development. "Calvinist doctrine" was no fringe of radical religion, as one might suppose from Shell's speculation here; rather, it was the theological core of the Church of England, as well as a pervasive part of post-Reformation popular culture. The archbishop of Canterbury was Calvinist, as were the many ordinary people who enjoyed godly broadsides and providential monster pamphlets. Essentially, Shell here acknowledges the continuum between puritanism and broader Calvinism, but she does so to reposition Calvinism itself as marginal rather than mainstream. To the contrary, if early Jacobean Calvinists had avoided plays, the theaters might have closed for lack of bums on seats. In short, both Knapp and Shell continue to treat positive forms of puritan engagement with drama as exceptional, rather than normal, and privilege semi-Pelagian, conforming, Church of England Protestantism as central to the theater culture. That is, these books resurrect an old narrative that ties (especially Shakespearean) drama to a merry old, doctrinally unfussed, sensibly Anglican England.

We know, however, that Parliament's initial decision to close the theaters in 1642 had more to do with crowd control than with the spiritual threat of idolatrous spectacle.[35] We know that not all puritans were antitheatricalists, and not all antitheatricalists were puritans.[36] We know young John Milton liked going to plays.[37] Yet the received narrative—that while earlier sixteenth-century English reformers, such as John Bale and John Foxe, embraced playing as a means of spreading the gospel, their puritan successors from the 1570s onward rejected theater as idolatrous—remains largely intact.[38] However, Scott McMillin and Sally-Beth MacLean have shown that, in spite of some emerging criticism of playing within the puritan movement, godly statesmen Sir Francis Walsingham and Robert Dudley, Earl of Leicester, formed the Queen's Men touring company in 1583 to disseminate hot Protestant values.[39] Michael O'Connell has demonstrated that Philip Henslowe was producing plays about Protestant heroes that targeted a puritan audience into the early 1600s.[40] Margot Heinemann has identified godly investments in the drama as "evidence . . . [that puritans] must have been in the audience" through the 1610s and 1620s.[41] Martin Butler has proved that puritans attended private playhouses in the last decade before the theaters' closing.[42] Together, these accounts demonstrate a sustained puritan presence in the early modern theater scene. Why then are puritan playgoers still widely regarded as unicorns: elusive creatures that either do not exist or, if real, are so rare that no one is sure they have seen one?

The expectation of a stark antipathy between godly people and theater people produces interpretive habits that confirm this foregone conclusion. It is common, indeed almost "common sense," to point to the many plays containing antipuritan satire as indicative of a broad hostility between the theaters and the godly. However, this satire is often surprisingly affectionate toward its targets, and it has usefully been read in the context of more local conflicts, rather than as evidence of total war.[43] Moreover, early modern plays are also full of anti-Catholic satire; yet few critics, if any, suggest that therefore most Catholics were enemies of theater generally. To the contrary, it is far easier for scholars to imagine English Catholic people attending plays, even when so many of them have papist villains, because of the strong connection between Catholicism and theatricality. This associative link, powerfully described by Huston Diehl and others, did affect the experience of theater (and of visual and material culture generally) for English people across the confessional spectrum in multiple ways.[44] "Catholic theatricality" was a strong and pervasive discursive formation. However, it did not prevent all godly people from attending plays. The idée fixe that the playhouse was too popish for puritans to stomach generates scholarly practices that erase evidence of godly theatergoing. For example, Shell interprets in opposite ways similar calls from puritan and Catholic divines for the faithful to avoid the theater: as signs of godly absence and of Romanist presence. Why is the same type of evidence treated as descriptive in the former case but prescriptive in the latter? This interpretive discrepancy is an object lesson in the ways the expectation that we will not find puritans in the playhouses can keep us from seeing them there.[45]

In part, the continued critical reluctance to imagine godly people inside theaters rests on the mischaracterization of puritans as pleasure-hating outsiders. Although puritans habitually identified themselves as a beleaguered minority for theological reasons, as Collinson has shown, they were "not alien to . . . the English Church but [represented] the most vigorous and successful of religious tendencies contained within it."[46] Nicholas Tyacke and others have demonstrated how doctrinal consensus, and a shared sense of religious purpose, united English Calvinists who were otherwise divided on issues of Church ceremony and organization. Until the Laudian ascendency, the Calvinist consensus meant that the difference between Protestants and puritans was largely one of degree, not kind.[47] For much of the period, the godly were like other Church of England Protestants—only more so—and the distinction between them was subjective. Part of the difficulty in discussing the relationship between puritans and theater is the highly relative nature of the confessional label itself.[48] Playgoer Benjamin Rudyerd describes himself as "zealous of a thorow reformation," but he understands this as a mainstream position.[49] He objects to Laudian, ceremonial innovations and the recasting of devout Protestants as dangerous radicals: "They have so brought it to passe, that under the Name of Puritans, all our Religion is branded."[50] Simply put, modern scholars should not be more convinced that "puritans" avoided plays than early modern people themselves were certain, or in agreement, as to whom that term actually described.

The fluidity of puritanism as a category (subject to both change over time and conflicting applications) is apparent in the Protestant religious writer Richard Baker's defense of the theater. Rejecting William Prynne's antitheatrical tract, Baker writes, "(What *Puritans* may do, I know not but) I verily think, scarce one *Protestant* will be found to take his part."[51] Here, Baker categorizes antitheatricalism as puritan. However, we should not simply reproduce this polemical conflation.[52] Rather than maintaining a clear division between moderate Protestants who enjoy theater and radical puritans who reject it, Baker's pamphlet itself blurs these distinctions by invoking the puritan Francis Walsingham's support of plays: "Who hath not heard of *Sir Francis Walsingham* an Eminent *Councellour* in *Queen* ELIZABETH'S *Time*, famous for his . . . *Piety* in advancing the *Gospel?* yet this was *the Man* that procured the *Queen* to entertain *Players* for her *Servants*; and to give them *Wages* as in a just *Vocation*? And would he ever have done this, being so *religious* a Man, if he had thought *plays* to be *prophane*[?] . . . And now, me thinks, I have said enough in *defence* of *Plays*."[53] This paragraph opens the tract, framing Walsingham's approval as the first and last word on the religious acceptability of plays. Baker presents Walsingham, who supported both the puritan cause and players, as a normative, nostalgic figure of Protestant piety, in order to position Prynne's antitheatrical tract as "puritan" extremism. Curiously, Baker asserts Walsingham's perfect Protestantism through positive terms of godly piety, emphasizing his commitment to an evangelical, preaching ministry ("advancing the *Gospel*") and using a puritan-inflected idiom ("to give them *Wages* as in a just *Vocation*"). Baker's appropriation of godly Walsingham against godly Prynne demonstrates the degree to which the distinction between puritan and Protestant was in the eye of the beholder, as well as the diversity of thought among the godly regarding theater.

English Protestantism encompassed a range of positions on the role of the visual and material in religious worship that did not neatly correspond to particular attitudes to theater. For example, Stephen Gosson's 1582 tract *Playes Confuted in Five Actions* attacks theater with a hot Protestant aversion to images. Yet Gosson himself was a ceremonial conformist; he used the Book of Common Prayer, wore the surplice, and made the sign of the cross at baptism.[54] The contrast between the puritan tone of Gosson's tracts and the conforming style of his churchmanship demonstrates that attitudes to the visual in religious ceremony and in art did not always match. Some hot Protestants were iconophobic, but generalized antipathy to visual and material culture was far from standard among the godly. It is a mistake to think that people who strongly rejected "popery" in the English Church were therefore averse to plays, even when they made polemical connections between popish ceremony and theatrical artifice. To the contrary, the incriminating taint of theatrical popery could be used to advance a puritan agenda in ways that did not imply a wholesale rejection of plays themselves. For example, godly theatergoer and satirist Samuel Rowlands attacks the surplice by comparing it to a stage costume:

> The gull gets on a surpliss
> With a crosse upon his breast.
> Like Allen playing Faustus,
> In that manner was he drest.[55]

Rowlands uses the accusation of theatricality to raise a puritan objection to popish vestments, yet his memory of a specific costume, actor, and role suggests a pleasurable engagement with the play.[56] Early modern London was not divided between prayer book Protestants, whose moderate views on ceremony enabled the uncomplicated enjoyment of dramatic spectacle, and precise extremists, whose zealous commitment to reformed worship precluded theatrical pleasure. In fact, it was possible for godly people to separate the negative association between theater and popery from their attitude toward actual plays.

The diary of theatergoer and puritan preacher Richard Madox demonstrates the ability of the godly to reject excessive materiality and spectacle in religious worship but still attend the theater. In 1582, Madox kept a journal of time spent in London while waiting to set sail as chaplain on a trade ship to the Moluccas, a position he received on the recommendation of that champion of puritan clergy, Robert Dudley, Earl of Leicester, and which the zealous Madox understood as an opportunity for evangelization.[57] The London diary records both the details of a sermon, which "shewd . . . God is always with us and therefore we need no ymage," and a trip to the playhouse. There is no indication in the diary of a sense of contradiction between attending a sermon against the use of images in worship and watching a play. In both entries, the preacher seems to be sightseeing. Madox writes, "We went to the theater to se a scurvie play set owt al by one virgin which there proved a fyemartin with owt voice so that we stayed not the matter."[58] Part of his description suggests possible moral disapprobation—the play is "scurvie."[59] But this remark is a far cry from the heated denunciations typical of antitheatrical polemic, and we should not extrapolate from it a general antipathy to theater because of Madox's religious orientation. Furthermore, the reason Madox gives for leaving the play is not moral but aesthetic, the performer's being "with owt voice." The description of the player as a "fyemartin," or "freemartin"—a sterile female calf with partly male anatomy—may refer not so much to the actor's transvestism as to the vocal failure of a boy player going through puberty.[60] In any case, Madox's disappointment itself shows the expectation of pleasure.

Madox and Rowlands were not the only puritans who enjoyed theater. In practice, the godly attended plays alongside their less zealous neighbors. Butler has already demonstrated the substantial presence of puritans in late Caroline playhouses such as Blackfriars. These playgoing puritans included Sir Thomas Barrington, who supported nonconforming clergy; Sir Thomas Lucy, who was praised for godly piety; and Mary Rich, Countess of Warwick, whose religious devotion is celebrated in a biography by the puritan divine

Samuel Clark. Godly Bulstrode Whitelock was such a habitué of Blackfriars that the house musicians struck up a tune he had written whenever he walked through the door. Sir Edward Dering, who as member of Parliament introduced the Root and Branch Bill proposing the abolition of the episcopacy, also frequented the theater—even on the Sabbath. That Butler can locate these godly individuals in the privileged audiences of the Caroline playhouses demonstrates both how embedded puritanism was within the English establishment and "how false it is to conceive of puritan feeling as being in a state of intransigent hostility towards the theatres in the 1630s."[61]

Other playgoing puritans further demonstrate that a zealous commitment to reform in Church worship did not necessitate a rejection of theatrical spectacle. In a 1659 speech to Parliament, godly moderate Henry Cromwell (son of Oliver) compares his own political fortunes to the temporary elevation of the clown Christopher Sly in *The Taming of the Shrew*, recalling the performance in detail and without disapprobation.[62] Theatergoer and later parliamentarian army officer Captain Charles Essex kept a nonconformist chaplain.[63] Moderate puritan Richard Newdigate frequented both godly sermons and Jacobean playhouses.[64] Sir Robert Rich, Earl of Warwick, attended plays in the public theaters in the 1610s and later supported the separatists who decamped to Massachusetts.[65] His brother Henry Rich, Earl of Holland, took in *Henry VIII* at the Globe in 1628, while part of a puritan court faction.[66] Rich's unlicensed chaplain, John Smith, a man who mocked Laudian bishop (and fellow playgoer) Richard Corbett's inability to preach, declared in 1633 "that he loved the company of players above all, and that he thought there might be as much good many times done by a man hearing a play as in hearing a sermon."[67] Not all puritans perceived a conflict between their religious beliefs and enthusiasm for plays.

Godliness was an ongoing process. People's religious leanings and attitudes to theater were subject to alteration. While he did ultimately reject theater, the puritan diarist Richard Norwood also describes an earlier period of his life when he felt the alternating pulls of religious fervor and worldly attractions such as plays. Like many in the period, Norwood's religious life was full of change. However, Norwood's later convictions do not negate his previous experience of wavering between godly piety and the appeal of the stage.[68] The former puritan and future royalist William Prynne, in the course of rethinking his political and religious alignments in the 1640s, also recanted his earlier attack on the theater, *Histriomastix*, for which he had lost his ears. "It is no disparagement for any man to alter his judgement upon better information," Prynne writes, declaring "that Playes are lawfull things."[69] Prynne's changes of heart show the value of looking at religious positions not as static and discrete entities but as entangled strands of a broader mixed-faith culture.

No One Is Normal

In the theaters as in local parishes, the zealous mixed with other members of the national Church. If we do not presuppose a normative, proto-Anglican via media in conflict with a puritan fringe, we can better understand the rival ceremonial and doctrinal tendencies within the Church of England, competing for centrality in a large, shared tent. Just as "puritan" was a capacious and contested term, used to describe individuals with significantly different ideas about ceremony, ecclesiology, and art, so too was the pseudoneutral category of religious "moderation" itself fraught and contentious. Ethan Shagan observes that "the golden mean was not merely a point on the spectrum but a condition of authority," and he rightly warns against "allowing historical categories of debate [such as moderation] to masquerade as scholarly categories of analysis."[70] For example, playgoer Bishop Joseph Hall's suggestively titled *Via Media* (ca. 1626) was not the irenic olive branch it rhetorically presents itself to be, but rather part of the Calvinist pushback against emerging, Arminian works of controversy.[71] To the playwright and future clergyman John Marston, Hall was a "devout meale-mouth'd Preceisean."[72] To his more radical fellow theatergoer, and 1642 pamphlet war adversary, John Milton, Hall's defense of the episcopacy was an endorsement of "plaine Popedom," and Hall himself was guilty of "lukewarmenesse . . . [cloaked] under the affected name of moderation."[73]

While claims to religious moderation were often confessional land grabs in disguise, there were playgoers who sought to negotiate the religious landscape, both doctrinally and interpersonally, in ways that were genuinely conciliatory toward other confessional groups. Although theatergoer John Newdigate III came from a godly family, he also maintained friendships with Arminians.[74] Protestant playgoer Francis Bacon laments in a 1609 letter to his close friend, and fellow theater enthusiast, Catholic convert Toby Matthew "that controversies of religion must hinder the advancement of sciences."[75] Lucius Cary, Lord Falkland, scion of a mixed family, and center of a skeptical, Erasmian group of intellectuals, praises latitudinarian questioning as the path to religious truth: "I cannot see why he should be *saved*, because, by reason of his *parents* beleife, or the Religion of the *Countrey*, or some such *accident*, the *truth* was offered to his understanding, when had the *contrary* beene offered he would have received that."[76] Pacifist playgoer James Howell called for mutual restraint in religious conflict: "Good Lord, what fiery clashings have we had lately for a *Cap* and a *Surplice!* [What] bloud was spilt for ceremonies only . . . for the bare position of a *table!*"[77] However, efforts to carve out more conciliatory positions were sometimes difficult to sustain in the context of confessional conflict. Howell was accused of lukewarmness and timeserving.[78] Tolerant Cary was so grieved by the escalation of religious and political factionalism into outright civil war that in 1643 he committed battlefield suicide, saying that "he was weary of the times."[79]

Even discourses and practices that established common ground among English Protestants (such as anti-Catholic prejudice and the shared liturgy) also marked fissures. Until the Laudian recuperation of the Roman Church as a true Church, English Protestants were broadly united by patriotic anti-Catholicism. As Christopher Hill says, the long Reformation "sublimated and idealized" English nationalism.[80] For example, the overwhelming majority of his fellow playgoers would have applauded William Lambarde's staunch commitment to a Protestant England. Lambarde's Anglo-Saxon scholarship recovered historical foundations of English Protestantism; in Parliament in the 1580s, he made a bold attempt to prevent the possibility of a Catholic English monarch. His academic and political efforts epitomize a widely shared sense of national Protestant identity.[81] However, it would be a mistake to treat popular, anti-Catholic nationalism as straightforward evidence of Protestant unity. Although the pope presented a common enemy against whom intra-Protestant groups could join in opposition, the perceived threat of popery within the Church—in myriad forms, from the episcopacy, to the surplice, to altar rails, to set prayers, to superstitious parishioners—was a major locus of internal division.[82] For example, playgoer Lionel Cranfield's ornate, private chapel would have satisfied Laudians devoted to the "beauty of holiness," but been seen by the godly as dangerously popish.[83] English Protestants generally agreed that popery was bad, but they fiercely disagreed as to what popery was.

Playgoer and prayer book Protestant Lady Anne Clifford represented a "significant minority [of] committed conformists" whose faith was embedded in the liturgy of the established Church.[84] During the interregnum, Clifford continued to use the proscribed prayer book, although to do so put her in danger: "She had in the worst of times the liturgy of the Church of England duly in her own private chapel . . . though she was threatened with sequestration."[85] Clifford's loyalty to the set prayers of the English Church defies what Maltby identifies as the "[false] assumption that non-conformists took their faith more 'seriously' than men and women who conformed to the lawful worship of the Church of England."[86] But standards of conformity were shifting and contentious; the prayer book itself was a mixed-faith document.[87] Religious normativity was a moving target. Despite his self-presentation as an exemplar of orthodoxy, Bishop John Overall's enthusiasm for ceremony and aversion to Calvinist doctrine were decidedly avant-garde for the Jacobean Church. Yet Overall's visitation articles, establishing rubrics of conformity, would become the model for at least twenty other sets of articles used—albeit, still controversially—by Laudian divines in the later 1620s and 1630s.[88]

Moreover, even pious, conformist theatergoers such as Clifford were immersed in a broader, mixed-faith culture. Clifford's eulogist praises her ability to sift "controversies very abstruse," recalling how "she much commended one book, William Barklay's dispute with Bellarmine, both, as she knew, of the popish persuasion, but the former less papal; and who, she said, had well stated a main point."[89] Julie Crawford has shown how Clifford, in her struggle to claim property from her husband and the King, drew on models of political resistance from puritan texts.[90] This does not mean that Clifford was secretly inclining to either Catholicism or puritanism. The point, rather, is that even firm conformists did not live in an orthodox bubble, untainted by contact with the broader religious spectrum.

The long Reformation embroiled everything it touched in the unstable processes of cross-confessional appropriation. For example, theatergoer Richard Brathwaite's *Spiritual Spicery* (1638) includes an anodyne Protestant autobiography, alongside translations of devotional material by Catholic theologians. Similarly, in the same year he published his famous appraisal of contemporary dramatists, Church of England deacon Francis Meres also translated the work of the Spanish, Dominican mystic Louis de Granada.[91] These men were not crypto-Catholics. Brathwaite asserts the orthodoxy of "[extracting] flowers from Romish authors," by labeling anyone who objects "a rigid Precisian."[92] It was common for committed Protestants to draw on Catholic devotional texts. The Jesuit Robert Parsons's *Christian Directory* was adapted by the Calvinist Edmund Bunny into *A Book of Christian Exercise*, one of the most frequently reprinted books in Elizabethan England: Clifford read both Bunny's version and Parsons's.[93] People across the spectrum of belief productively engaged with texts and practices coded as belonging to other confessional groups, often repurposing these cultural materials for radically different ends.

Catholics, Church Papists, and the Curious

English Catholicism was not simply a monolithic other, against which various English Protestants defined their own identities; this internally diverse, master category offered rich devotional and cultural resources to its various adherents and sympathizers.[94] Although anti-Catholic prejudice was rife— playgoer John Melton describes Catholics as "blood-sucking antichristian tiraunts"—even committed Protestant audience members were capable of a more open range of attitudes toward Catholic people and Catholic culture.[95]

Early modern English Protestants sometimes flirted with Catholicism without actually converting. As Shagan points out, "[Dabbling] with Roman books and services [was] part of the normal spectrum of English religious activity . . . [comparable to] experimentation with illicit substances . . . in the modern world."[96] For example, Sir Humphrey Mildmay was born into a family with an impeccable puritan pedigree, but he seems to have been attracted to Catholic devotional practices.[97] His diary shows him lending part of a Douai Bible, that is, the Catholic translation of the Bible into English.[98] As shown earlier, there were certainly steadfast Protestants who owned and read Catholic books. But Sir Humphrey's diary also records him performing "the Spaniards discipline" before bed, a reference to the Spiritual Exercises of the Spanish Jesuit Ignatius of Loyola, and it makes frequent invocations of the Blessed Virgin Mary.[99] Collectively, these practices suggest Sir Humphrey was inclined toward the Roman Church. Yet, in the midst of legal difficulties in 1648, he made a formal statement denying the charge that he was ever a recusant or held Catholic sympathies.[100] We cannot gauge precisely the strength or exact nature of Sir Humphrey's attraction to Catholicism. Then again, this might have also been difficult for Sir Humphrey himself. He falls somewhere in the gray region occupied by English Protestants who felt drawn toward devotional practices too popish for the established Church, but not so strongly as to prompt conversion. Similarly, theatergoing courtier Sir John Harington seems to have harbored Catholic sympathies; he supported toleration for members of the Roman Church, and his epigrams are peppered with pro-Catholic arguments and devotional references.[101] Harington's self-description as a "Protesting Catholick Puritan" at the opening of his *Tract on the Succession to the Crown* testifies to his sense of his own mixed identity and "epitomizes his interest, quintessentially post-Reformation, in how conflicting religious positions can cohabit."[102]

As with intra-Protestant struggles over nomenclature, defining who was Catholic was a matter of debate among contemporaries, and it continues to pose methodological problems for historians. Earlier Catholic historiography's emphasis on recusancy has been enlarged to include a broader range of forms of Catholic practice by Alexandra Walsham's work on church papistry and Haigh's attention to the conservative religious habits of ordinary people.[103] Both those committed Catholics who avoided persecution through occasional conformity and others whose devotional tendencies leaned toward traditional religion, but who may not have described themselves as members of the Roman Church, were labeled by various kinds of Protestants as "church papists." English Catholics were divided among themselves as to their religious obligations. Although strategic conformists were often criticized by their recusant coreligionists as "schismatics" who had abandoned the Roman Church, this group in fact played a crucial role in sustaining an English Catholic community.[104] Playgoer John Davies of Hereford was Catholic, but he attended Protestant services; he was married and buried in the Church of England.[105] Davies of Hereford may have wished to retain the social benefits of parish life and participate in Christian community with neighbors.[106] As Walsham writes, "Living in frosty isolation from people who were in principle agents of heresy and the devil, but in practice friends, acquaintances, and relatives, was largely an impracticable polemical ideal."[107]

Faithful English Catholics sought various ways to balance their spiritual commitments against the economic, social, and political costs of practicing an illegal religion.[108] Even for privileged Romanists, the steadfast recusancy demanded by polemicists was difficult to maintain, and many Catholic casuists included exceptions permitting conformity in pastoral literature. As Protestant playgoer John Earle mocks, "A Church-Papist is one that parts his religion betwixt his conscience and his purse."[109] Playgoer Sir John Davies of Oxford (not to be confused with his eponymous coreligionist mentioned previously) for a time refused to attend Church of England services. However, while Davies of Oxford continued publicly to embrace the Roman Church, he also made concessions to the Protestant state. In 1610, when considering whether to restore Davies's blood nobility after his involvement in the Essex rebellion, Parliament carefully parsed the mixed signs of his resistance and accommodation. As they saw it, Davies was "halted between two opinions."[110] He was more willing than previously to attend Protestant services, but he continued to evade communion by pretending to be out of charity with his neighbors. This common ruse of church papists, and his equivocal answer when asked if he would see a Church of England minister, led the bishop of Asaph to conclude that Davies was one of those "obstinate resolved papists [who] do come to church to save the penalty . . . and yet rest their conscience on not receiving communion."[111] But where Asaph saw an entrenched religious position, Lord Zouche saw confessional movement in Davies's new outward conformity and was "hopeful of his coming."[112] Zouche was encouraged by Davies's willingness to take the oath of allegiance, and he observed a difference among Catholics whereby, "though at the first, few recusants would refuse it, now almost none will take it."[113] What constituted adherence to the Roman Church was a matter of external, as well as internal, debate.

English Catholics were divided among themselves regarding the conflicting allegiances claimed by the monarch and the pontiff. After the pope's 1570 bull declaring Elizabeth a heretical monarch and licensing her assassination, English Catholics were dogged by versions of the "bloody question": If Spain invaded to re-Catholicize England, for which side would you fight? Challenges to Catholic patriotism were sometimes posed explicitly by an interrogator, but doubts about papist loyalty were often implied, or taken for granted, as in the popular saying "English face, Spanish heart."[114] The religious and political contradiction lived by English Catholics generated both a body of resistance theory and defenses of Catholic loyalism.[115] For some, attending Protestant services was a meaningful and voluntary act of political obedience. For other Catholics, conformity was duplicitous, and loyalty was best demonstrated by the open profession of their faith. Theatergoing Catholics included both Sir Charles Percy, a likely participant in the Gunpowder Plot, and William Parker, Baron Monteagle, who revealed his coreligionists' terrorist conspiracy to the Privy Council.[116]

"We know that most of the principal Catholicks about London doe go to plays," writes theater buff and Catholic priest Father Thomas Leke.[117] The Romanist upper classes served as an important resource for their coreligionists in post-Reformation England.[118] These pillars of "seigneurial" Catholicism supported their community by harboring illegal priests, making sacraments available, employing (or converting) Catholic servants, setting visible examples of recusancy, and participating in international Catholic networks.[119] However, English Catholicism was far from a "top-down" phenomenon. Many tradesmen, students, yeomen, servants, and apprentices actively supported Romanist networks, hiding priests and circulating Catholic texts and devotional objects.[120] In London, Catholics of all ranks had some degree of access to sacraments through foreign embassies and the townhouses of Catholic nobles, such as Montague House in Southwark, as well as in prisons such as the Clink (both close to the Globe).[121] Often, Catholic inmates were allowed to gather together, and free Catholics were permitted to visit prisons for spiritual succor. On one occasion in 1602 when pursuivants did raid the Clink, they found "nearly forty laypersons, mostly women and poor people" about to celebrate Mass.[122] There was an active Jesuit enclave in Jacobean Clerkenwell, ministering largely to the same demographic of working people that made up the audience of the nearby Red Bull Theater.[123] The Inns of Court afforded a semiprivate space for Catholic ritual, as well as a steady constituency of student playgoers.[124] Holborn was known as an area with a high concentration of Romanists.[125] Fleet Street, which had a similar reputation as a Catholic neighborhood, was a short distance from the Salisbury Court, St. Paul's, and Blackfriars playhouses.[126]

Both upper-class and ordinary English Catholics practiced a form of religion very different from that of their late medieval ancestors. As Lisa McClain writes, "Catholic goals changed—from maintaining strict adherence to pre-reform or Tridentine practices . . . to finding ways to duplicate the *functions* of traditional or Tridentine practices while reinterpreting the *forms* such practices might take."[127] Because of the obstacles to receiving sacraments, the circulation of books and manuscripts in Catholic circles took on greater importance. The poetry of Romanist playgoer William Habington appears in a collection compiled by a Catholic woman. Post-Reformation English Catholicism, too, was a religion of the word.[128] In London, the public execution of Catholic martyrs galvanized sympathetic communities of witnesses.[129] The devotional life of English Catholics was often piecemeal, idiosyncratic, and flexible, cobbled together from occasional sacraments snatched when they could be had, news and consolation from local networks of fellow believers, pastoral literature, and private meditation, often involving repurposed objects or spaces.

In place of the visible, corporate community of the faithful, so powerfully described in Eamon Duffy's account of the late medieval Church, later English Catholics faced the isolation of practicing an illegal, minority religion.[130] But both recusant and conforming Catholics found ways to sustain their spiritual lives within the strictures of Protestant society. As John Bossy observes, "The features of pre-Reformation Christian practice to which conservatively-minded people held most strongly were those which . . . belonged to a region of private social practice which in effect lay outside the field of legislation"—such as fasting.[131] Devout Catholic convert and enthusiastic playgoer Elizabeth Cary herself fasted during Lent ("living almost wholly . . . on nettle porridge"), but she also served meat for Protestant family members and guests. Her table was confessionally mixed in both food and talk. She describes meals with her children and their Oxford friends, "conversing freely . . . [about] religion [with] those very capable on both sides."[132] For Cary, the goal was to reconcile those around her to the Roman Church, but she understood the conviction of conversion as emerging from uncertainty and open dialogue.

Conversion and Mixed-Faith Families

Religious lives were changeable. But conversion was not a simple flip from one ecclesiastical monolith to its opposite. As Michael Questier observes, "It is a misreading to see the English Reformation just as a struggle between two tightly consolidated blocks, Roman and Protestant, facing each other across a deserted religious no-man's-land with a few isolated and lack-lustre nonentities [moving] between the two positions."[133] Religious "start" and "end" points could themselves be unstable composites. Even those who professed throughout their lives the same faith into which they were born also wavered and experimented, under often conflicting pressures of family and education, internal conscience and external law. All post-Reformation English people lived in conditions of at least potential convertibility. Playgoing clergyman John Gee became an anti-Catholic polemicist only after his budding interest in the Roman Church led him to the so-called fatal vespers, the 1623 disaster in which overcrowding at a Catholic service caused the building to collapse, killing ninety-five people. Gee's providential escape (and subsequent interrogation by the archbishop of Canterbury) led him to recommit to Calvinism. The minister's account of how he came to be at the deadly Catholic gathering is instructive: "I was the same day in the fore-noone at the Sermon at *Pauls-Crosse*: and lighting vpon some Popish company at dinner, they were much magnifying the said *Drury*, who was to preach to them in the afternoone. The ample report which they afforded him, preferring him far beyond any of the Preachers of our Church, and depressing and vilifying the

Sermons at *Pauls-Crosse*, in regard of him, whetted my desire to heare his said Sermon: to which I was conducted by one *Medcalfe* a *Priest*."[134] Gee's report gives a glimpse of an urban religious culture in which it was possible for a Church of England minister to hear the Calvinist Thomas Adams deliver an open-air sermon before thousands at Paul's Cross in the morning, and attend a clandestine Catholic service conducted by the Jesuit priest Robert Drury for a packed crowd of three hundred in a room at the French embassy that same evening.[135] Gee's cross-confessional gadding demonstrates the polyphony of the discursive field that post-Reformation Londoners negotiated daily.

A similar sense of malleability, and the contingency of multiple religious influences, characterizes the autobiography of theater enthusiast (later turned amateur actor and playwright) Arthur Wilson, who describes himself as "such Waxe in Religion, as was apt to take any Impression."[136] Wilson was apprenticed to fellow playgoer John Davies of Hereford, "who being also a Papist, with his Wife & Familie, their Example & often Discourse gave Growth to those Thrivings I had. So that, with many Conflicts in my Spirit, I often debated which was the true Religion."[137] Later apprenticed in another papist household, Wilson continues to question and dispute: "Finding no way fitter to discover the Truth than to search into it, & being always in Argument against them, I went under the Notion of a Puritan; but God knowes, it was rather out of Contention than Edification: for indeed I was nothing."[138] Afterward, "out of the Societie of Papists" and serving as secretary to tepid presbyterian Robert Devereaux, third Earl of Essex, he writes that he "became a confirmed Protestant: but found nothing of the Sweetnes of Religion."[139] His piety deepened later in the employ of puritan playgoer Robert Rich, Earl of Warwick, who maintained silenced ministers: "Now Preaching, the true Glasse of the Soule, discovered more unto mee that I had formerly seene; & good Men, by how much they were eclipsed by the Bishop's, did privately shine the brighter."[140] Wilson's later-life, godly, presbyterian commitments are evident in the disparaging treatment of the episcopacy in his *History of Great Britain*.[141] On one hand, there is a clear trajectory in Wilson's life from youthful dalliances with papistry to mature puritan devotion. However, it is also apparent that his taste for cross-confessional discussion did not evaporate with his turn toward godly piety. In later years, Wilson struck up a friendly acquaintance with the Catholic priest Father Weston: "Being familiar with him, I askt him many Questions, which are *Arcana* among them; & he was ingenuous to me in discovering the Truth."[142] Wilson's interests in both religious dialogue and theater were lifelong and compatible.

In the process of conversion, spiritually turning toward God (*metanoia*) and changing denominations could be entangled in various, complex ways. For playgoer and Catholic priest Father Augustine Baker, a horse-riding accident immediately set his mind on higher things ("*If ever I git out of this danger, I will beleive there is a God*"). Yet his denominational conversion came later in an intense burst of prayer and reading.[143] Sometimes piety and confessional commitment grew together: playgoing clergyman Peter Heylyn moved from an initial reluctance to study theology under the influence of his "zealous Puritan" Oxford tutor, through a growing love for the English Church that awakened skepticism toward Calvinist thought, to a career as a Laudian polemicist.[144] These examples illustrate differences not only in the content but also in the experiential process of religious change. Baker's first conversion is an event, and his second the product of a concentrated period of reflection, whereas for Heylyn religious change was a gradual, long-term evolution.

Spiritual conversions did not happen in splendid isolation from worldly concerns. However, Questier rightly points out that it is reductive to speak of people simply subordinating their consciences to better their careers or avoid persecution. More often, "when political and religious motives were both engaged in the mind of the individual convert they were maintained in a constant tension."[145] For example, theatergoer Christopher Blount was educated by William Allen himself, but in 1585, he abandoned his faith and helped Francis Walsingham embroil Mary, Queen of Scots, in the manufactured conspiracy that led to her execution. Blount's apostasy seems to have been driven initially by worldly considerations, whether for political advancement or to protect his Romanist family from persecution. Yet his subsequent years of dedication to Leicester (under whose command he served in multiple, Protestant military campaigns); his marriage to Leicester's widow, Lettice; and his ill-fated loyalty to Leicester's stepson, Robert Devereux, second Earl of Essex, suggest a factional commitment beyond shallow careerism.[146] Confessing at his trial that he supported Essex because the earl had promised "toleration for religion," Blount refused to speak with a Protestant minister before he was beheaded, declaring, "I die a catholic," but adding the oddly *sola fide* qualification, "Yet so, as I hope to be saved only by the death and passion of Christ, and by his merits, not ascribing anything to mine own works," followed by a request for intercessory prayer from the gathered witnesses.[147] The theological irregularity of Blount's death speech, as well as the complex intersection of political, personal, and religious ties that brought him to the scaffold, demonstrates the conflicting pressures that simultaneously shaped confessional lives.

Public conversions were fodder for polemic. Because both Protestants and Catholics agreed that one sign of the true Church was that its numbers were ever increasing, gains and losses on both sides were widely publicized. In 1637, Lady Newport's public appearance at the Cockpit, immediately after her scandalous conversion to the Roman Church, contributed to rising alarm about prominent Catholic conversions at court.[148] Perhaps few defections to the Roman Church were as embarrassing to the Church of England as that of playgoer Tobie Matthew, the son of the archbishop of York. Matthew's autobiography describes a series of efforts by Protestant divines to reclaim him, culminating in what can only be compared to a modern-day intervention: "There came by accident, if it were not rather by design, a kind of . . . little College, of certain eminent clergymen . . . into a good large room of the house . . . with [my parents and] many others of their great family . . . to persuade me [to] return to my former religion."[149] This was not a success.

Theater buff John Harington observes that, "[although] brothers and brothers, fathers and sons, husbands and wives [differ] one from another in opinions and beliefs, [yet] many times as myself have seen [they] live in house and bed and board together very lovingly."[150] Yet, as the archbishop's mixed-faith household demonstrates, cross-confessional relationships could be intimate without being easy. Catholic convert Matthew's mother was "more fervent toward the Puritanical sole-Scripture way." He recounts passive-aggressive exchanges of concern for each other's spiritual well-being: "She would be telling me often how much she prayed to the Lord for me, whilst I, on the other side, would also . . . let her know whatsoever I conceived to import her for the good of her soul."[151] In a culture where religious pluralism was widely considered an offense to God, and a danger to society, these acts of pious harassment could be understood as gestures of Christian love or "charitable hatred."[152] Early modern English people were capable of maintaining close ties with individuals who held beliefs they strongly rejected, yet religious differences could still strain personal relationships.

Converts and others whose personal lives were strongly marked by conflicting religious influences could retain (sometimes in indirect forms) aspects of abandoned belief systems, or the experience of religious change itself. Playgoer and dean of Saint Paul's John Donne was born into a family of fervent Catholics descended from Saint Thomas More himself, but he converted to the Church of England around 1600. The complexity of Donne's life, poetry, and prose have led critics to identify in them concealed beliefs as varied as crypto-Catholicism and crypto-Calvinism. But Molly Murray argues persuasively that Donne was a sincere convert who returns to the paradigms of conversion—irresolution, perplexity, change—as a language in which both to seek and to keep hidden those parts of religious life that are beyond articulation.[153] Donne's gift for thinking in paradoxes was exceptional, but he exemplifies a state of lived contradiction that was common among mixed-faith people.

Ungodly, Occult, Foreign, and Urban

Not all playgoers approached spiritual life with equal seriousness. Religious differences could be of temperament as well as kind. The parishioners of Giles Saint Cripplegate complained of their ungodly curate Timothy Hutton, who let bodies pile up unburied in the churchyard, refusing to leave the Fortune to perform his office until the play was done.[154] Playgoing courtier, amateur playwright, and Restoration theater manager Thomas Killigrew was noted for his "profain or irreligious discourses."[155] Killigrew's theater-bug sister Elizabeth (later mistress to Prince Charles) was similarly described as "very vain and foolish."[156] Playgoer Henry Skipwith was implicated in the Castlehaven trial as an accomplice to crimes so depraved they were considered godless.[157] Theater enthusiast Nathaniel Tomkins's support for his patron Laud's program of decent ceremony in worship did not prevent him from selling "diverse vestments and other ornaments" of Worcester Cathedral to be used as "Players Capps and Coates."[158]

The religious spectrum was also striated with beliefs about the supernatural that did not neatly map onto particular confessional positions. While some folk beliefs were contiguous with residual, late medieval, Catholic lore and apotropaic practices, it is a mistake to think that only papists, or those sympathetic to traditional worship, believed in magic. Protestants too engaged with the occult. Playgoing conjurer Simon Forman's clients were drawn from across the confessional spectrum.[159] As Keith Thomas has shown, many forms of superstitious activity—such as fortune telling, divining the location of lost objects, using love charms, and more—were a fairly ordinary part of the way mixed-faith English people made sense of the supernatural.[160]

Londoners were also exposed to Continental Protestants, as well as members of non-Christian religions. These more exotic expressions of faith were interpreted through the prism of internal debates among English Christians, but they also pointed outward, offering alternative perspectives on English religious life. Of the total foreign population of Elizabethan London, about half belonged to French and Dutch Reformed Churches.[161] Shakespeare's landlords were French Huguenots.[162] Puritan playgoer John Greene attended sermons at churches belonging to London's smaller Spanish and Italian Protestant communities.[163] Many of these immigrants were refugees from Catholic persecution. Although they were subject to xenophobic hostility, their presence also fostered international Protestant solidarity. The godly looked to stranger churches as a "Trojan horse" that might import more fully reformed worship.[164] Recognizing that stranger churches were a resource for puritans (or "nurseries of ill-minded persons to the Church of England"), Laud in the 1630s attempted unsuccessfully to suppress them.[165] In addition to the congregations of these Reformed Protestant Churches, there were some members of a more distant Christian cousin, the Greek Orthodox Church. Ignorant of the importance of iconography in Orthodox worship, English Protestants, and particularly puritans, embraced Greek and Armenian believers as allies against Catholics and Muslims.[166] Non-Christian faiths were similarly interpellated into English confessional conflicts, often without regard for their actual theologies or practices. English Protestants largely misrepresented Islam as a form of idolatrous paganism associated with Catholicism. Popular lore about Judaism was similarly deployed in conflicts between English Christians: puritans were mocked as "Jews" for their allegedly hyperliteral and legalistic treatments of scripture. However, there were small numbers of real Muslims and Jews in London, as well as many merchants and sailors who had direct (if fuzzy) knowledge of their faiths.[167] For many English people, rumors of circumcision, the power of the Ottoman Empire, and the potential seduction of Islam were threats to Protestant identity.[168] Yet, as Corinne Zeman observes, "elements of Islamic culture—including religiously inflected objects, such as the turban—were often folded into the fabric of cosmopolitan life in London."[169] Though space precludes a fuller discussion of foreign influences, domestic confessional conflicts were connected to a broader world of religious difference.

London was a mixed-faith clearinghouse: the hub of national and international confessional networks circulating books, rumors, objects, and people. While religious diversity existed all over England, the mixed strands of post-Reformation culture converged in London with particular density. Hearing different preachers was an attraction for both tourists and city dwellers; public executions for religion were more frequent in London, and they could draw larger crowds of witnesses. As seen in Gee's day of Calvinist and Catholic service hopping, the city made a range of confessional experiences easily available. Rapid urban growth enabled mobility and anonymity that likely made conformity more difficult to enforce. Population density drew different confessional perspectives together cheek by jowl. More than this, the city offered a special, capacious instrument for collectively sifting and imaginatively reconfiguring the mixed-faith culture in which all Londoners were immersed: the commercial theaters.

Shared Theatrical Experience of a Mixed Religious Culture

Though constrained by the social conditions of their production, fictions also shift the boundaries of a culture. Doubtless there were some ideological ne plus ultras beyond which individual playgoers could not emotionally travel. But these imaginative limits were not uniform or orthodox. Because confessional lives themselves were mixed and fluid, it is unreasonable to assume that these identities narrowly or rigidly predetermined audience reactions to theatrical fantasies about religion. This is especially true insofar as "theatrical experience is . . . generally far more permissive than our socially regulated experience of everyday life."[170] While theater did not happen in splendid isolation from real-world, ideological commitments, the imaginative technologies of the early modern English stage facilitated flexible engagements with a heterogeneous, religious culture. In the next chapter, I explore the capacity of dramatic technique to structure collective encounters with post-Reformation religious life. The orchestration of shared playhouse experiences that imaginatively blur, shuffle, contort, or otherwise reshape existing ideological formations was a crucial mechanism through which early modern commercial theater regenerated, and transfigured, the mixed-faith culture that fed it.

The theater's ability to lure playgoers into other pleasures and subject positions is evident in the story of the playgoing Venetian ambassador Antonio Foscarini. While in London, Foscarini made frequent trips to the low-rent Curtain to stand in the yard "incognito." On one occasion, when the actors invited the audience to name the next day's play, "he actually named one. But the crowd wanted another and began to shout *'Friars, Friars.'* . . . So loosening his cloak, he began to clap his hands just as the mob did and to shout, 'frati, frati.' As he was shouting this the people turned to him and, assuming he was a Spaniard, began to whistle [menacingly]. But he has not given up visiting the other theatres."[171] The animosity of the crowd at the Curtain makes Foscarini's desire to join with them all the more important. The ambassador abandons his own choice and embraces the wishes of the playgoers around him. Although we cannot with certainty identify the play, just as presumably Foscarini could not at the time, it would have been reasonable for the ambassador to have guessed that "*Friars*" contained antipapist material.[172] Yet he claps and shouts along. Playhouse experience could gather mixed-faith audiences into fleeting communities of thought and feeling. As Francis Bacon writes of theater, "The minds of men in company are more open to affections and impressions than when alone."[173]

CHAPTER 2

Shared Feeling

The mixed-faith audiences that filled early modern London's commercial playhouses responded to live theater in ways that were not always aligned with—or the outcome of—their individual beliefs. Sophisticated and ever-evolving theatrical techniques invited playgoers to pretend: to imagine different versions of the world, to fantasize beyond their ordinary ken, to entertain alternative perspectives of thought and feeling. Plays allowed confessionally diverse audiences to mentally and emotionally traverse the shifting ideological landscape with greater imaginative license than was afforded in many spheres of religious life. This is not utopian transcendence: London commercial theater over the seventy-five years before the English Civil War did not erode sectarian differences, or foster a general playgoing culture of Erasmian toleration. But plays in performance did temporarily focus the attention and energy of mixed-faith audiences into shared daydreams whose relations to real-world confessional politics were often productively oblique. Plays mediated religious discourses through theatrical devices that were no great respecters of doctrinal integrity but were effective in shaping audiences' engagements with the drama.

Plays bound religious content to theatrical forms that had the power to prompt reactions that might contradict playgoers' actual theological commitments. To say that dramatic effects shaped much of how mixed-faith audiences experienced plays does not mean that theater coerces playgoers into ideologically and emotionally uniform responses. Charles Whitney mischaracterizes critical attention to the formal orchestration of theatrical experience as a paradigm in which "the text or performance constructs audiences who perceive largely with innocent eyes from an abstract subject position."[1] My point is not that theater erases religious identities but rather that theater creates a generative misalignment of real-world confessional positions and the confessional worlds of plays. My interest is in the kinds of conceptual and affective movement—even if it is only a temporary shifting of entrenched positions—produced when people with diverse beliefs respond together to a reimagined version of their shared, mixed culture.

Theater ventures beyond the boundaries of everyday life.[2] While religious differences did not disappear at the playhouse door, many plays depend, sometimes as a basic condition of their intelligibility, on the willingness of theatergoers to imaginatively embrace religious frameworks that they would reject outside the playhouse, or to dwell in stage moments that muddle confessional categories. Richard McCoy rightly emphasizes the difference between the demands of religious faith and the conditional "faith" elicited by theatrical illusions.[3] The miscalibration between the ideological positions of audience members and theater's refracted images of religious life made it possible for playgoers to experience their mixed confessional culture from other vantage points. Or, put differently, it was the semiautonomy of dramatic fantasy that made it a productive interlocutor, not merely a parrot, of confessional culture. Commercial theater permitted the "suspension of *belief*," by which I mean that plays ask their mixed-faith audiences to process religious activities, objects, and subject positions differently from how they otherwise might in church, or at an execution, or during a theological debate.[4] While antitheatricalists insisted on the moral and physical dangers of playgoing, there was also recognition that because theater is fictive, it operates with different interpretive protocols and consequences. As Philip Sidney puts it, "The Poet . . . nothing affirmes and therefore never lyeth."[5] In other words, plays allow confessionally diverse spectators to believe in religious counterfactuals—to feel them *as if* real—without having to avow them as true.[6] Commercial theater offered post-Reformation Londoners shared, vicarious experiences that cross confessional boundaries. These collective theatrical fantasies were not an escape from religious culture but rather a means of affective experimentation within it.

Early modern drama gave spectators the license to cognitively and emotionally invest in scenarios and subjectivities far removed from their own identity positions. In this chapter, I outline ways the representational practices of the theater business cultivated the imaginative elasticity of audiences. While many of the examples do not pertain to religious culture per se, they do demonstrate broader conditions of reception conducive to flexible engagements with religious culture. *The Late Lancashire Witches* (1634) offers a specific instance of theater's capacity to reconfigure mixed-faith playgoers' experiences of topical religious material. An eyewitness account of the play demonstrates how theatrical pleasure could displace confessional agendas. Yet the most extensive evidence of such imaginatively elastic, theatrical encounters with confessional material are the very scripts that structure these experiences. Plays orchestrate collective thought and feeling. However, responsive audiences are not passive victims of stage spectacle: reception is an active process.

The embodied, affective, and cognitive responses of audiences are the locus of theater's ideological work. Culture is made and remade in the playhouse through gasps, tears, and snorts of laughter. Ideology is always lived; and the virtual experiences of playgoers are a particularly malleable site of reinscription and change. In closing, I show how a subgenre of Spanish Match plays from the 1620s capitalizes on the widespread fear among Protestants of a marriage alliance with Spain, yet also recasts these anxieties into more emotionally pliable fantasies. Unlike the rigid, religious binaries into which *A Game at Chess* interpellates its mixed-faith audiences (discussed in Chapter 4), the confessional transpositions seen in such plays as *The Spanish Gypsy* (1623), *The Noble Spanish Soldier* (1622), and the (1623) revival of *Match Me in London* are more characteristic of commercial theater's mediation of post-Reformation confessional culture. While these Spanish Match plays do reinforce anti-Catholic tropes, they also offer unexpected pleasures, as well as opportunities for identification with unlikely characters, that allow affective movement within and around the dominant paradigm in which papist Spain is the implacable enemy of Protestant England.

Cultural Pressures and Theatrical Process

My goal is to articulate the dialectic between post-Reformation English society and its dramatic fantasies; that is, to show mutually constitutive exchanges between the religious lives of early modern Londoners and the confessional worlds imagined in the commercial theaters. The methodological risk of emphasizing the broader cultural pressures that informed playhouse experience is the elision of the reciprocal impact of theatrical process (and vice versa). Some recent scholarship ascribes shared playhouse responses primarily to discursive influences, such as humoral theory or the doctrine of Eucharistic participation. Other criticism emphasizes the crucial agency of disparate audience members in creating theatrical events and their meanings, stressing the diversity of playgoers' interpretations and uses of theater.[7] This book insists that broadly collective audience responses were structured most immediately (that is, most directly during the time of performance) not by external cultural frameworks but by theatrical effects. Of course, the worlds imagined inside the playhouse are never separable from the world outside its walls.[8] However, tracking their mutual entanglement depends on the recognition of the distinctive, representational aptitudes of theater.

We lose an invaluable archive of human experience if we look only at the ways plays are socially conditioned by early modern conceptions of emotion and not at how plays themselves produce feelings in the social exchange among actors and audiences. For example, Allison Hobgood's claim that the "most determinative factor" in the interactions between early modern players and their playgoers was humoral discourse homogenizes all plays into manifestations of "the two primary resources [of theater:] . . . the early modern cultural script about the communicability of passions . . . and, second, the playgoers who materialized that cultural script."[9] Doubtless, humoral theory affected some of the ways early modern people understood emotional interactions, including those in the theater. However, the limitation of this model is that it makes the resources of actual play scripts merely instrumental to a preexisting and unchanged "cultural script." Steven Mullaney rightly cautions against an overliteral projection of humoral discourse as an etiology of playhouse passions: "In a phenomenology of historical or theatrical emotions, it might be tempting to limit evidence to the explicitly articulated, reported, or theorized. If we do, however, are we producing a history of emotions or a history of ideas about emotions? Aren't we confusing evidence with the explicit as well as the extant? . . . [Instead, we must] embrace formal literary and theatrical analysis as a useful tool for the study of early modern emotions, not merely in terms of what characters and plays say or explain or represent but also, and more crucially, in terms of what theatrical performance makes happen in and with its audience, beyond the discursive and mimetic dimensions of the stage."[10] The emotional responses of playgoers are not simply products of preexisting, historical paradigms of affect but rather are molded and mobilized by the specific and changing stimuli of performance. Plays do not just describe the passions stirring elsewhere in a culture; they make their own, often more unusual or supple, structures of feeling.

More germane to the religious concerns of this book is Anthony Dawson's account of theatrical experience as characterized by a shared sense of "eucharistic participation."[11] While Dawson recovers a feeling of playhouse collectivity in the period that bore affinities to communion, the conceptual scale at which Dawson examines audience engagement is difficult to reconcile with the local effects of particular plays. It may well be the case that religious communion subtends the practices of theatrical reception in a diffuse but powerful manner. However, neither humoral contagion nor Eucharistic participation can be taken either as a descriptive model or as a direct cause of unified playhouse response. Dawson's depiction of playhouse communion is largely dependent on a structural comparison between the relation of actor to role and the dual nature of Christ. Put bluntly, I doubt many people were strongly affected by theories of Christic hypostasis when Ned Alleyn was stalking the stage as Tamburlaine in red, velvet pants. The dynamic between actor and role is indeed a crucial aspect of performance (especially for a famous actor like Alleyn, who specialized in a type); and 2 *Tamburlaine* does have a communion scene that envelops playgoers (when their proxies, the scourge's sons, dip their hands in his blood). The problem is that these more immediate, theatrical *technes* of complex personation and audience involvement are subsumed under a broader discourse of "communion." The collective responses of mixed-faith audiences are not mystical unions but shifting convergences of feeling and thought induced by the shared apprehension of specific stage effects.

My point is *not* that extratheatrical, cultural frameworks do not also shape the reception of plays. Much important work, such as Dawson's on communion, has demonstrated the influence of contiguous or analogous discourses and social practices (including, among others, spectacles of royal power, dissection, traditional festivities, fairs and markets, civic entertainments, executions, bearbaitings, medical theories of vision and the humoral body, sermons, and iconoclasm) that together overdetermined the basic conditions of behavior and perception fundamental to early modern theater. Ongoing scholarship that articulates such formative cultural pressures is vital to our understanding of the period in general, and to its drama. However, my priority here—which I understand to complement rather than to contest such work—is to stress how theater reconfigures the religious discourses it absorbs, and reshapes the ways mixed-faith audiences experience them.

Theatrical Cultivation of Imaginative Competencies

The repertory and representational practices of the commercial theaters encouraged mixed-faith audiences to approach plays with a flexible mentality. Whereas the focus of theater historians from Alfred Harbage onward has been the preexisting "mental composition" of audiences (that is, the intellectual and social experiences that playgoers took with them into the playhouse),[12] my interest is in the imaginative competencies developed by theater itself. As Jeremy Lopez writes, "Companies built and maintained followings by continually increasing the demands on their audiences' attention, thus creating audiences that could handle those demands."[13] Early modern commercial theater developed new genres and dramatized an unprecedented range of subjects. The constant influx of new plays did not just cater to audience tastes but created them. Regular theatergoers were exposed to many different kinds of drama, and people often visited the playhouse without knowing what would be performed.[14] Audiences were asked to make quick emotional shifts between generic registers, "mingling Kings & Clownes [in] mungrell Tragy-comedie."[15] Early modern plays regularly contain multiple representational levels, such as inset masques and dumb shows.[16] They toy with generic expectations (as in *King Lear*'s counterfactually tragic ending), and they disrupt basic conventions of staging (as in Edgar and Gloucester's climb up the cliffs of Dover). The drama habitually asks its audiences to adjust their perceptions during performance, and by doing so to deepen their theatrical competencies. Early modern playhouses were places where people could acquire new ideas and accumulate vicarious experiences. The drama disseminated elite and emerging bodies of knowledge to a broad audience, thus facilitating critical habits of political thought, social skills for urban life, and "mind-travelling" to foreign lands.[17] Early modern commercial theater was an experimental and world-expanding medium. It cultivated mental and emotional elasticity that carried over into audience engagements with stage treatments of confessional culture.

Theatrical representation changes its objects and the viewer's relationship to them. The resources of stagecraft gave theatergoers special kinds of emotional and imaginative access to confessional activities and subjectivities. To use a familiar example, *Hamlet*'s pacing, costume, language, and use of stage space call on largely Protestant audiences to imaginatively and emotionally take the possibility of purgatory seriously, even though reformers tended to treat it as an absurdity.[18] Perhaps some Protestants did watch *Hamlet*'s act 1, scene 5, thinking, "This ghost is popish nonsense." However, such a response would have very little to do with the actual scene unfolding onstage, "whose lightest word / would harrow up thy soul."[19] Plays ask audiences to "go along with" the action on stage: this could lead anywhere.

Thomas Wright's *Passions of the Minde in Generall* (1604) illustrates the transformative potential of emotional expression and exchange. As an example of the principle that like attracts like, Wright tells this story: "*Alexander* asked a pyrat that was taken and brought before him, How he durst be so bold to infest the seas, and spoyle the commerceries? he answered, That he played the pyrat but with one ship, and his Majestie with a huge navie: the which saying so pleased *Alexander*, that he pardoned his life, and graunted him libertie: *so much could the similitude of action transport the kings affection.*"[20] Wright's point is that the similarity between the two men breeds sympathy between them. However, the story is memorable precisely because of the obvious difference between the imprisoned, one-ship pirate and his interrogator, the conqueror of Persia. Rather, it is the pirate's metaphor that makes "similitude" where there was none. Just as the pirate's figurative speech creates a new imaginative and emotional bond between himself and his observer—one that crosses the actual social divide between them—so too, early modern commercial theater possessed devices for characterization and audience engagement (for example, soliloquy, costume, and plot twists) capable of reconfiguring the imaginative status of dramatis personae or events, as well as their relationships to the audience.

While it is important to track affinities between clusters of social experience and dramatic fantasies that seem geared toward those real-world perspectives, we cannot presume to know the limits of the interests and pleasures of particular demographics of theatergoers. Roslyn Lander Knutson wisely observes, "Audience taste is difficult to verify, being not necessarily as tied to class as scholars of a former time liked to assume."[21] The same is true of gender. For example, Andrew Gurr and Karoline Szatek argue that around the early 1610s the King's Men began adding plays featuring strong women to appeal to a sense of gender solidarity among female playgoers.[22] While this is entirely plausible, it does not mean (nor do they claim) that compelling female characters did not also draw sympathy from male playgoers. Henry Jackson describes a 1610 performance of *Othello* that "brought forth tears," especially at the sight of "that famous Desdemona killed before us by her husband, [who] acted her whole part extremely well, yet when she was killed was even more moving, for *when she fell back upon the bed she implored the pity of the spectators by her very face.*"[23] The very specificity of Jackson's memory of Desdemona's dying gesture and expression registers the empathetic attention elicited by the actor's skill. Commercial theater offered playgoers intimate engagement with characters, and imaginative investment in scenarios, far removed from their own life experiences: watching a king of England wake up in a cold sweat, or witnessing the tragic unraveling of an interracial marriage.

Nor, I am arguing, were theatergoers' delights welded to their religious identities. Early modern people were sometimes curious about matters that lay beyond whatever their contemporaries, or modern academics, assign as their sphere: Wright describes men who will "wrangle about matters exceeding their capacitie, as a Cobler of Chivalrie, [or] a Tailor of Divinitie."[24] Theater was a form of virtual experience that could expand playgoers' frames of reference and foster new modes of thought and feeling. As with class and gender fantasies, confessional fictions on stage elicit similar extensions of imaginative and emotional faculties into different cultural terrain.

Though it does not record a real audience's response to an actual play, Barnabe Riche's pamphlet *Greenes Newes both from Heaven and Hell*—written by a playwright, in the voice of another playwright, and featuring a stage clown—nevertheless illustrates the potential of live performance to shake up fixed religious positions. In hell, the ghost of Robert Greene finds a papal legate, newly arrived to conspire with Lucifer, and "a most abominable company of Popes, Cardinals, Bishops, Pryors, Abbots . . . for the better establishing of the Kingdom of *Antechrist* [in] *England*."[25] The pope's representative has no sooner finished speaking:

> But in comes *Dick Tarlton*, apparrelled like a Clowne, and singing this peece of an olde song.
>
> *If this be trewe as true it is,*
> *Ladie Ladie:*
> *God send her life may mend the misse,*
> *Most deere Ladie.*
>
> This suddaine jest brought the whole company into such a vehement laughter, that not able agayne to make them keepe silence, for that present tyme they were faine to breake uppe.[26]

The English Protestant clown Dick Tarlton cracks up the whole popish, Antichristian convocation. The interruption of seditious, Romish scheming is temporary ("for that present tyme"), but it still ruptures confessional animosity with comic energy.

Coming out of nowhere in the narrative and breaking the prose with verse, he formally, as well as diegetically, interrupts their plotting. Tarlton's jest also derails the narrative's running anti-Catholic satire, shifting the tone away from confessional invective. In other words, both the audience in the story and the audience of the story are jostled out of binary, oppositional, religious positions by a singing clown.

Plays Are Not Tracts

The more entertaining aspects of a play often derail the possibility of didacticism, or doctrinal clarity. When plays answer back to early modern religious life, they do not always teach lessons but sometimes speak gibberish, or cry, or make a joke. However, modes of expression that cannot be summarized in statements are still part of the dialogue between theater and confessional culture. Peter Lake offers an invaluable account of how London commercial theater created a public engaged with the political and religious problems of their time.[27] In recognizing the socially shaping work of audiences' mental engagements with plays, Lake takes the political efficacy of theater more seriously than many literary critics. By close reading plays in their entirety (rather than in discursive snippets), he recovers sequential, theatrical experience as a social process. Yet if Lake's correction to new historicism's abstract understanding of power is a more fine-grained account of the immediate political and religious contexts of plays, conversely, scholars of the drama can bring to this conversation a more nuanced picture of theatrical form and the cultural work it does. Lake's close readings largely stay on the level of plot, attend primarily to "high" politics, and limit the responses of playgoers to cognitive judgments. But theater is not simply a narrative of the actions of elites presented for analysis. It is a subtler and more complex series of interactions and pleasures, capable of indirect engagements with *longue durée* shifts, as well as more explicit forays into topical issues. Without question, early modern playgoers did watch plays "for use" in making sense of the dangers and possibilities of their religious and political circumstances, or for moral application in their personal lives. Nevertheless, theater offered pleasures other than instructions for living, imaginative challenges beyond the examination of court politics. As Stephen Gosson complains, "Sometime you shall see nothing but the adventures of an amorous knight, passing from countrie to countrie for the love of his lady, encountring many a terrible monster made of broun paper, [and returning unrecognizable except] by a broken ring, or a handkircher, or a piece of a cockle shell, *what learn you by that?*"[28] The familiar binary Gosson draws here between pleasure and profit is a false one. Our shared interdisciplinary project must be to connect archival and formal specificity, high and cultural politics, as well as the cognitive and emotional work of audiences.

Nathaniel Tomkyns's eyewitness account of an August 1634 performance of *The Late Lancashire Witches* at the Globe shows how even an overtly topical play could baffle attempts at application.[29] The play dramatizes the alleged occult shenanigans of four women from Lancashire recently incarcerated in London on charges of witchcraft. Because the testimony that condemned them had since been recanted, it was unclear at the time of performance whether the accused would be pardoned or punished. The affair divided both popular opinion and the Privy Council between believers in the supernatural and skeptics—including the archbishop of Canterbury, William Laud. The case was a religious and political hot potato that passed through several courts. Eventually, without any final determination made as to their guilt or innocence, the women were sent back to Lancashire, where they died in jail.

The King's Men capitalized on the topicality of *The Late Lancashire Witches*;[30] however, rather than offering a judgment as to whether the women were guilty, the play parodies the question.[31] Opposing views as to the reality of witchcraft are continually expressed back to back, and several characters reverse their opinions to comic effect. The braggart Whetstone's tales of witchcraft are dismissed as his usual lies. When the magic he boastingly describes is shown onstage, it is funny both because his improbable fibs turn out to be true and because, through their association with Whetstone, the supernatural tricks seem phony. One of the running jokes of the play is that witchcraft is shown primarily as the cause of everyday, embarrassing "Crosses":[32] impotency, bastardy, bad luck hunting, getting beaten in a fistfight. As the witch Meg herself points out, regarding the inversions of social hierarchies through sorcery that put unruly women above their husbands, and make children and servants overly bold with their parents and masters:

But that's no wonder, through the wide
World 'tis common. (C4v)

The effect of coding magic as a convenient excuse is that the tricks happening almost continuously in front of the audience seem as much a shaggy-dog story as actual enchantments. Witchcraft is often a dirty joke: Mrs. Generous is turned into a "jade" with a bewitched bridle and "ridden hard" (G4r). When the women are apprehended and patriarchal order restored, all their respectable interrogator wants to know are the dirty details: "And then [the devil] lay with thee, did he not sometimes? . . . —and how? and how a little? was he a good Bedfellow?" (L3r). Keeping the question of the witches' guilt or innocence open is crucial to the "game" of the play. The running gag of *The Late Lancashire Witches* is the simultaneity of these mutually exclusive possibilities. The play's comedy depends on sustaining a religious question; it does not encourage spectators to take a stance in the debate. That would ruin the joke.

Because of its explicit topicality, eyewitness Tomkyns "expected . . . [a] judgment" in the play regarding the question of the women's guilt, or a moral "application," but he finds neither. Tomkyns's correspondent, Sir Robert Phelips, would likely have been keen to hear any theatrical commentary on the issue decoded, since his father had been Speaker of the House of Commons when it passed the witchcraft law with which the women were charged. The newsletter begins with an attempt to make politic observations on the play as a social event in London, but it primarily records its physical comedy. Magic tricks flout Tomkyns's best efforts to be edified. Similarly, Simon Forman's detailed, eyewitness accounts of William Shakespeare's plays garnish a dominant interest in striking stage moments with sprigs of application.[33] Since Tomkyns's description of live performance is less frequently discussed than Forman's, and because the number and vivid physicality of the special effects demonstrate my point, I quote the passage in full:

> Here hath bin lately a newe comedie at the globe called *The Witches of Lancasheir*, acted by reason of the great concourse y[e] people 3 dayes togither: the 3[d] day I went with a friend to see it, and found a greater apparance of fine folke gent[men] and gent[weomen] then I thought had bin in town in the vacation: The subject was of the slights and passages *done or supposed to be done* by these witches sent from thence hither and other witches and their familiars; Of ther nightly meetings in severall places: their banqueting with all sorts of meat and drinke conveyed unto them by their familiars upon pulling of a cord: and walking of pailes of milke by themselves and (as they say of children) a highlone: the transforming of men and weomen into the shapes of severall creatures and especially of horses by putting an inchaunted bridle into ther mouths: their posting to and from places farre distant in an incredible short time: the cutting off a witch-gent^{woman's} hand in the forme of a catt, by a soldier turned miller, known to her husband by a ring thereon, (the onely tragicall part of the storie:) the represent-

ing of wrong and putative fathers in the shape of meane persons to
gent[men] by way of derision: the tying of a knott at a marriage (after
the French manner) to cassate masculine abilitie, and y[e] conveying
away of y[e] good cheere and bringing in a mock feast of bones and
stones in steed thereof and y[e] filling of pies with living birds and
yong catts &c: And though *there be not in it* (to my understanding)
any poeticall Genius, or art, or language, or *judgment to state o[r] tenet
of witches (w[ch] I expected,) or application to vertue but full of ribaldrie
and of things improbable and impossible*; yet in respect of the newnesse
of y[e] subject (the witches being still visible and in prison here) and in
regard it consisteth from the beginning to the ende of odd passages
and fopperies to provoke laughter, and is mixed with divers songs and
dances, it passeth for a merrie and ex[c]ellent new play. per acta est
fabula. Vale.[34]

Tomkyns's description captures the kind of fantasy and physicality that Gosson rejects as a gratuitous distraction to theater's more serious, didactic purpose, even down to the recognition-by-token device in the severed hand of
Mrs. Generous. However, the fact that *The Late Lancashire Witches* proposes
no "tenet of witches" does not mean that its entertainment value makes it irrelevant to public discourse on the topic: the "newness of the subject (the
witches being still visible and in prison here)" is still a large part of the appeal
of the play, even though it "consisteth [of] . . . fopperies."

While larger confessional conflicts over traditional festivity and the enforcement of conformity hover at the edges of the comedy,[35] the play maintains no clear position in these broader debates. One of the stage tricks in *The
Late Lancashire Witches* is the supernatural flight of the servant Robin to the
Miter tavern in London for wine for his master, who, "since hee was last at
London and tasted the Divinitie of the Miter, scarce any liquour in Lancashire
will go downe with him, sure, sure he will never be a Puritane, he holds so
well with the Miter" (E2r). The joke is about boozing, but the religious associations of the pub's name are developed enough to glance at Laud. This reference is not a coded message so much as a wink. The magical jaunt to the Miter
runs irreverent, frenetic rings around a complicated set of real-world religious
conflicts. *The Late Lancashire Witches*' absurdist nose-thumbing at serious
controversies is itself an important form of religious and political expression.
The play's "improbable and impossible" stage tricks allow its mixed-faith audiences to take pleasure in suspending the question of whether the magic

was "done or supposed to be done." The play's comedy is too imbricated in the debate surrounding the so-called witches to be considered escapist. However, it allows audiences divided on these debates to share an alternative attitude toward the question, to approach a fraught, religious issue with greater imaginative and affective license. Rather than a release from religious politics, the play offers a giddy, double vision, in which sorcery is real and not real, the witches are socially disruptive and harmless, and confessional differences are recalibrated to pub preferences.

Tomkyns's first-person account is a compelling piece of evidence, unusual in the specificity with which it connects cultural context, stage effects, and audience response. It shows that even plays whose commercial and artistic success depended on their explicit engagement with topical religious material did not always transmit identifiable stances on these matters to their audiences. Important as this document is, we do not need Tomkyns's direct testimony that the play contains no "judgment . . . of witches" to know that this is not a didactic play making a sustained, serious case against either sorcery or superstition but is instead a comedy in which the central conceit is the inability to separate magic from hoax. That evidence is in the script. Undeniably, Tomkyns's extensive description of props and effects not included in the stage directions points up the limitations of play texts as records of performance. Nevertheless, the premise of the script and its punch lines structure and mobilize the physical comedy. *The Late Lancashire Witches* orchestrates not a resolution but a ridiculous encounter with a religious impasse. We erase a crucial form of public engagement with confessional life if we look to plays only for the kind of "position taking" elicited by works of controversy and ignore the subtler, stranger, but equally strong processes of collective thought and feeling orchestrated by early modern commercial drama.

The Orchestration of Active Reception

Plays were considered to be working when they gathered playgoers' imaginations. The idea that plays move their audiences as a group from one mood or mode of thought to another is implicit in early modern theater's frequently noted connection to oratory: the art of swaying a multitude.[36] Skillful players were praised for their ability to focus an audience's attention. "Sit in a full Theater," writes Thomas Overbury, "and you will think you see so many lines drawne from the circumference of so many eares, whiles the [Excellent] Actor is the Center."[37] As Matthew Steggle demonstrates in detail, the mark of a successful comedy was loud, theater-wide laughter, and a good tragedy was one that made the crowd weep.[38] In other words, the basic, declared goal of early modern stagecraft was to guide collective audience experience.

Implicit in plays are processes of shared perception and feeling. While external evidence of playgoer behavior can seem more empirically sound than the internal evidence of plays, it is also more limited. Unattached to a specific dramatic moment, Overbury's description of the magnetic actor only tells us that a good performer can engage a crowd. Plays offer more detailed maps of thought and feeling. Playwrights used generic cues hoping to elicit particular reactions, and, as Lopez points out, "for a device to become conventional it must be functional."[39] Scripts, and the staging practices they index, structure audience response. Even though they exclude the very things that constitute theater—live bodies, contingency, and physical staging—play scripts remain the richest and most extensive records of early modern English playhouse experiences. Nor has this archive been mined to exhaustion, especially as current scholarship attends to only a fraction of the extant corpus of early modern drama. Scripts are admittedly, as Richard Preiss objects, only a partial record of one half of a conversation, and as such omit the voices of live audiences.[40] Yet these incomplete transcripts are full of speaking silences.

To value scripts in this way is not to privilege text over performance, or to reify fantasies of authorial control over the distributed agency of the playhouse. A script is not a prison house but a spine that enables movement. Play scripts are synecdochical for live performance, a suggestive piece that conjures something larger than itself. In synecdoche, the part does not "stand in for" the whole in a mimeographic fashion, like an architect's blueprint blown up in scale on a projector. "Think when we talk of horses, that you see them," is not a prescriptive instruction but an open invitation. The "imaginary forces" of audiences that piece out vasty fields of France within the wooden *O* are always bigger and wilder than the scripts that set them to work.[41] Preiss imagines an oppositional relationship between scripted drama and audience interactivity: "not 'partnership' but competition."[42] But scripts are not the disciplinary machinery of authors intent on a territorial battle for control of the stage against a distracted multitude who come to the playhouse solely to watch themselves act up. It is true that early work on audience response to early modern performance, such as Jean E. Howard's *Shakespeare's Art of Orchestration*, tended toward a more coercive vocabulary in which stage effects "force" or "compel" particular responses from spectators. Yet, rather than harp on thirty-year-old diction choices that have since been abandoned by How-ard herself—and by most others who are interested in the effects of plays on the people who watch them—it seems more productive to me to develop the methodological insights of reader-response-derived performance criticism into the intimate relationship between theatrical technique and audience experi-ence.[43] For example, although *Shakespeare's Art* prioritizes the craft of the au-thor, Howard's early recognition of scripts as shaped by and for a fuller field of performance practices anticipates the expanded understanding we now have of theatrical agency as distributed across the playing system as a whole.[44] Per-formance is a river that no one steps in twice. However, reader-response-based criticism's attention to scripts as agents and archives of the unfolding of audience experience over time makes it well equipped to examine the cultural processes enabled in live theater.

Certainly, early modern theatergoers sought forms of gratification unre-lated to the performed script. Preiss, Paul Yachnin, and others offer compel-ling accounts of the opportunities playhouses afforded for individual social performance.[45] People went to the theater for many perfectly good, nondra-matic reasons: to sightsee, to sell or steal things, to cruise for sex, to flaunt their clothes and wit. Playgoers could be fractious, resistant, and sometimes more interested in themselves than the stage. But this does not preclude more receptive playhouse moods. Audience members could revel in their own ac-tivities independent of the drama, and also enjoy being moved as a group in harmony with a play. Robert Shaughnessy describes actor-audience interac-tivity in the reconstructed Globe as a process of "entrainment," defined in communication studies as the phenomenon in which "two or more individu-als lock into each other's rhythms of, for example, movement, speech, and ges-ture."[46] In the context of theatrical reception, this does not mean marching in lockstep. Shaughnessy records divided responses among different demo-graphics of playgoers, as well as strong feelings of playhouse-wide connected-ness. Modern actors often describe Globe audiences as a "sea of faces."[47] The metaphor captures the simultaneously synchronic and multidirectional qual-ity of theatrical response. The shared visibility among audiences and actors produces eddies, as well as waves, of emotional contagion. Actors and audi-ences share always-changing oscillations of feeling and attention. But while the rhythms of performance move the playhouse, actors also experience their audiences as too vast and protean to control. Entrainment is a complex and mutual process: not hypnosis.

The orchestration of collective and ideologically elastic audience experience is not an oppressive form of "mind control."[48] Some recent work seeks to "restore power . . . to early modern spectators" by prioritizing "uncued audience agency."[49] Hobgood objects to conceptualizing theatrical experience in terms of drama's impact on playgoers and "rejects an incapacitating docility [implicit in the term] 'reception.'"[50] This is a gratuitously convoluted way of thinking about theater, predicated on a narrow definition of agency. Responsiveness is not mindless submission but a necessary contribution to performance. To say that much of an audience's interaction with a play consists of loosely collective reactions to things happening on stage is not to treat playgoing "as if [it] were primarily a form of discipline"[51] but simply to recognize that shared experience is a basic pleasure and raison d'être of theater.[52]

Shared responses are never identical. As Whitney rightly notes, "A collective roar, sigh, or wave of laughter in the playhouse may be generated by many diverse, individualized inflections of feeling."[53] No two people, even those who occupy similar social positions, will ever perceive, judge, and remember a play in exactly the same way.[54] Rather, by collective responses I mean emotions, thoughts, and somatizations sharing a family resemblance, incited by the simultaneous perception of theatrical effects.[55] Orchestrated, shared experiences may be ambiguous or conflicted. Collective responses are entangled with the process of the play's unfolding over the time of performance. However, they do not necessarily cumulate into one shared interpretation or "takeaway" opinion of the play as a whole. Collective playhouse experiences may have different implications for spectators depending on their social circumstances. The corrupt but beautiful femmes fatales of Jacobean tragedy described by Huston Diehl may send a shiver through the whole theater, yet the shared desire and repulsion provoked by the stage embodiment of the Whore of Babylon could have different aftershocks of meaning for Calvinist, Catholic, and Laudian playgoers.[56] The dramatic organization of confessionally fluid, collective experience is not totalizing. Plays do not summon into being ideologically uniform audiences. However, they do make the same virtual experiences available to everyone in the theater, even if participation asks of them different kinds of mental stretching. Orchestration draws thousands of simultaneous, individual, imaginative extensions into the experimental, social space of shared fantasy.

The active reception of theater takes many forms. While recent criticism productively attends to more conspicuous forms of audience participation,

playgoer agency is not limited to its most literal, visible, and individual manifestations.[57] It is not only through uncued behavior that theatergoers contribute to the coproduction of meaning and pleasure in the playhouse. N. R.
Helms writes, "Though spectators may seem to do nothing [but] . . . attend
to the business onstage, their minds are always busy."[58] As Keir Elam describes,
plays begin and end in negotiations between performers and their audiences.[59]
Anticipated audience responses shape the play from its conception. Playgoers
make commercial theater possible by turning up and paying. Actors adjust
their delivery depending on audience reactions during performance. Most im-
portantly, audiences imaginatively create plays as they watch them. Plays exist as the assemblage of the experiences of audience members. Matteo Pangallo
dismisses "the idea of the theatrical consumer becoming a producer" as an
exhausted "critical commonplace," and he turns his attention to overt forms
of audience agency instead of the "merely imaginative."[60] The direct ways in
which playgoers revised plays discussed by Pangallo were indeed an important form of theatrical participation. But there is nothing "mere" about the
collective imaginings of thousands of people.

Antitheatricalists as well as defenders of the stage describe theater's capacity to transform audiences en masse, both when plays fulfilled the amelio-
rative moral function ascribed to them in classical dramatic theory and when
they went dangerously awry.[61] These accounts not only share an awareness that
playgoers as a group are affected by performance (for better or worse); they
also understand being moved by a play as a form of activity. Thomas Heywood praises the ability of dramatic examples of warriors to rouse like bravery in theatergoers: "What English blood seeing the person of any bold English
man presented and doth not . . . *pursu[e] him in his enterprise with his best
wishes*, and as being wrapt in contemplation, *offers to him in his hart all pros-
perous performance* . . . so bewitching a thing is lively and well spirited action,
that it hath power to new mold the harts of the spectators and fashion them
to the shape of any noble and notable attempt."[62] Here, playgoers are engrossed
("wrapt" and "bewitch[ed]") but also exercise their imaginations energetically
("offer" and "pursu[e]"). They receive and are shaped by the pressures of the
play ("new mold[ed]"), but in a way that makes them active (ready for any
"notable attempt"). For Heywood, dramatizations of English heroes elicit a
kind of mental support or accompaniment. Stage action and audience imagination blur together: the spectator's wishes "pursu[e in the] enterprise." "Pros-
perous performance" happens simultaneously in the fiction of the play, on
the stage, and in the playgoer's heart.

For opponents of theater, the problem was precisely this kind of collective emotional participation. Anthony Munday writes that playgoers "al by sight and assent be actors. . . . So that in th[e] representation of whoredome, al the people in [their] mind[s] plaie the whores."[63] Plays change spectators into inner performers. Stage representations are inseparable from playgoers' "minds' play." For both Heywood and Munday, theater affects playgoers as a group: even the most virtuous spectator could be corrupted by licentious theater, just as even a coward could be emboldened by stage heroics. In other words, early modern theorists of performance observe that audience members do not maintain their individual, preexisting, inward dispositions intact for the duration of the play: "all the people" are affected by what they see. However, these mentally receptive audiences are not submissive lumps but imaginatively active partners in the creation of the play.

Debates about audience activity tend to propose binary alternatives: either rowdy or docile, either individuals or a group, either critical or feeling. The presumption is usually that there is a correlation among the former and latter sets of terms: that critical thought is limited to individuals, and more likely to be expressed through self-separating behavior such as interruption; whereas collective playhouse experience is understood as uncritically immersive, emotive, and passive. These are false assumptions. A quiet audience is not necessarily a passive one. Vocal playgoers are not always resistant. Immersive spectatorship can exercise critical faculties. Individual and collective playhouse experiences are not mutually exclusive.[64] Theater is not a zero-sum game in which either agential, individual playgoers run roughshod over the play and players or the force of "spectacle" batters a homogeneous blob of audience into "complacent" submission.[65]

The cumulative evidence shows a variety of audience behavior, from rapt attention to backchat to boredom to violence. While it is important to recognize a broader difference between the polite customs of modern theatergoers and the generally more participatory range of practices available to early modern audiences, the relative frequency of attentive or disruptive behaviors in London commercial playhouses cannot be determined, given the limitations of the extant body of contemporary descriptions of playgoing. In any case, it is the wrong question. Knowing the things audiences did in playhouses does not necessarily reveal how they experienced theater. While some forms of playgoer expression are unambiguous (for example, throwing eggs at actors), it is not always possible to know what inward states are indicated by audiences' outward behavior.

Expressions of emotion that modern playgoers might find irritating may rather for early modern theatergoers have enhanced the performance. For Preiss, audible crying disturbs the play: "The convulsive weeping of even one spectator, let alone hundreds, can be a loud and distracting business."[66] However, in Thomas Nashe's vivid description of collective audience response to Talbot's death in act 4, scene 4, of *1 Henry VI*, mass weeping does not detract but rather contributes to the scene's effect: "How it would have joyed brave *Talbot* . . . to thinke that after he had lyne two hundred yeares in his Tombe, hee should triumphe againe on the Stage, and have his bones newe embalmed with the teares of ten thousand spectators at least (at severall times) who, in the Tragedian that represents his person, imagine they behold him fresh bleeding."[67] Heywood records audiences responding to the scene collectively and emotionally, but not without agency, and not in a way that diminishes the play's effects. The group response elicited by Talbot's death transforms the scene from a representation of lost futurity to the restoration of a heroic legacy in the present.

In the play, as Alexander Leggatt points out, "the Talbots' deaths . . . truly constitute an ending. After this, not only is the English cause . . . doomed, but Talbot and his son are forgotten."[68] The script stresses the loss of Talbot's line. His son John Talbot appears only briefly, for the sole, dramatic purpose of dying with his father in battle. The play underscores the extinction of their family. Talbot laments, "In thee thy mother dies, our household's name."[69] John Talbot's bravery establishes him as a true heir: "An if I fly, I am not Talbot's son" (4.6.2243). But the promise of patrilineal succession is confirmed only when precluded: "If son to Talbot, die at Talbot's foot" (4.6.2245). Their deaths follow fast on each other. Together they exit to battle, Talbot urging his son to "fight by thy father's side . . . let's die in pride" (4.6.2248–49). A skirmish follows, immediately after which John Talbot's corpse is brought onstage, and Talbot dies just fifteen lines later. Talbot's last words—"Now my old arms are John Talbot's grave" (4.7.2284)—register a generational collapse. The script shows the end of Talbot, both his death and the loss of his legacy.

But the weeping of playgoers changes the play. Live audiences resurrect and "new embalm" Talbot. Their responses not only affect the emotional event in the theater but touch even the dead person played on stage: "How it would have joyed brave *Talbot* . . . after he had [lain] two hundred years in his tomb." As Rebecca Schneider describes the affective labor of historical reenactment, "The *stickiness* of emotion [drags] the temporal past into . . . [the] present."[70] The live, wet "teares of ten thousand Spectators" revivify Talbot's historical corpse "fresh bleeding." His affective reanimation in the present compensates for the loss of futurity scripted into the scene. Repeated performance gives Talbot the posterity the plot denies.

Here, the emotional responses of audiences revise the play not by displacing or destroying it but in collaboration with the script. Powerful as the implied, Pietà blocking is, the Talbots' death is not simply a sad, static tableau but an interactive process of feeling. The playwrights use a technique that I call "audience priming": the script prepares playgoers for a dramatically climactic response by placing a small-scale version of an emotional situation immediately before the big scene. This is often done through a reported speech or minor character. This device is not just a thematic doubling. What makes it effective is the temporal build. The death of a minor character, John Talbot, affectively attunes audiences for the death of the play's hero; Talbot's mourning for his son models audiences' sorrow for him. In practical terms, it gets their bodies ready to cry on time. That is useful in this scene, because playgoers are asked to make a rapid, emotional transition from the adrenaline of stage combat to grief at Talbot's death. Priming an audience, like priming a gun or a pump, is partly a physical preparation. Yet spectators are not simply having their tears jerked. Audience priming is a complex, recursive technique of deepening feeling; it is outward moving, self-replicating, an extension seeking further extension.[71] Their weeping is a supplement as Jacques Derrida describes it: "The supplement adds . . . and makes. . . . Its place is assigned . . . by the mark of an emptiness."[72] It fills and changes an incomplete emotional structure.

Similarly, early modern theatergoers might not necessarily have found it distracting if some spectators shouted during a performance. Instead of indicating the atomization of the audience into individuals, whooping and heckling could have contributed to a group sense of investment and immediacy. To draw a modern-day comparison, for many moviegoers, yelling at the screen is a sign of absorption rather than opposition, and it especially intensifies the enjoyment of particular genres (action and horror), even for those who themselves are quiet.[73] In his defense of theater, Heywood describes an action scene, in which "[soldier] and horse even from the steeds rough fetlocks to the plume of the champions helmet [were] together plunged into a purple Ocean," that would make any playgoer "hugge his fame, and *hunnye* at his valor."[74] Heywood's whinnying spectator is not detached or interrupting. He is the soldier's horse. By this, I am not saying that Heywood is describing an audience member imitating actual horse noises. However, in comparing the spectator's

cheering to neighing, Heywood conceives of playgoer vocalization as something absorbed into the fiction during performance. The same is true of
somatized, emotional response: the playgoer mentally "hug[s]" the valiant
soldier, just as onstage the steed and champion are tightly joined, "together
plunged" from hoof to plume. These playgoer reactions participate in the mar-
tial world of the play. In short, we cannot assume that we know what playhouse noises or actions early modern Londoners would have considered truly
disruptive, and what may have been incorporated into the performance event.

Furthermore, I suspect that playgoers who did behave badly (whatever
that actually meant) were unlikely to bring the whole imaginative enterprise
to a grinding halt. Even extreme examples of theatrical disruption could
continue to interact with the fiction in performance:

> *Fowler* you know was appointed for the Conquering parts, and it be-
> ing given out he was to play the Part of a great Captain and mighty
> Warriour, drew much Company; the Play began, and ended with his
> Valour; but at the end of the Fourth Act he laid so heavily about him,
> that some Mutes who stood for Souldiers, fell down as they were dead
> e're he had toucht their trembling Targets; so he brandisht his Sword &
> made his *Exit*; ne're minding to bring off his dead men; which they
> perceiving, crauled into the Tyreing house, at which, *Fowler* grew an-
> gry, and told 'em, Dogs you should have laine there till you had been
> fetcht off; and so they crauled out again, which gave the People such
> an occasion of Laughter, they cry'd that again, that again, that again.[75]

The story ends suspended in the crowd's repeated demand for the improvised
joke, but the performance itself did not. "The Play began, and ended with his
valor," in spite of the corpsing in act 4. "Recovering" the thread of action and
the attention of the crowd from disturbances contingent on live performance
is as basic an acting skill as memorizing lines. More to the point, it would be
a mistake to think of the event described here as entirely "stopping" or "step-
ping outside" the play. Even though the plot is interrupted, and the conventions of theatrical representation are visibly not working, and the performance
genre has changed from action to clowning—nevertheless, even here there is
creative seepage between the fiction of the play and the flap in the playhouse.
Even from the beginning the boundary is blurred: the crowd does not come to
watch the character within the drama but to see the actor Fowler play the type
of "conquering" role for which he was famous. The extras break character

because Fowler's personation of a warrior is so lifelike: their prop shields tremble with real fear. The star so terrifies his onstage observers that they pretend to die before he can pretend to kill them. This is acting: to strike viewers without touching. The personae of the "great captain" and the leading man bleed together. So do fictional place and theatrical space: he exits brandishing his sword, not minding "to bring off" (the stage) "his dead men" (the characters). Fowler's haughty disregard for his fellow actors is continuous with a "conquering" disdain for slain enemies. He commands the "[mute] dogs" to crawl as imperiously as Tamburlaine lashes the vanquished kings that pull his chariot. It is unclear how far afield of the imaginative world of the play this interruption to the scripted action actually goes. The playgoers shouting "that again" are not impeding the performance so much as including themselves in a game among the actors, which itself echoes and elaborates (and ultimately is reintegrated into) the dramatic fiction. That is to say, plays do not usually break if dropped: they bounce.

Plays are only destroyed or undermined by vocal and physically active audiences *if* we think of plays as self-contained mimetic units. However, early modern scripts are not closed in this way but instead open the dramatic fiction out to a broader field of performance. Erika T. Lin aptly calls attention to the disjunction between the aesthetics of tragedies and the jigs routinely attached to them.[76] Moreover, theatrical performance does not stop at the edge of the stage. As Mullaney writes, "It extended beyond the acting space or scaffold to take place in and with the audience, its necessary participant and dramaturgical collaborator."[77] William N. West describes early modern theater as "encompassing" audiences, "so that their experiences and responses become part of the play."[78] To adapt the axiom of the Prague formalists, the playhouse makes everything in it a sign. Scripts in performance do not simply create fictions on stage. They make apertures between the world of playgoers and the world of the play.

Early modern drama is full of what I call "open scenes" that depend on the collaboration of the playhouse as a whole in the creation of theatrical effects. *Othello* riles up the crowd with its sing-along English drinking song, making the audience itself part of the illusion of a wild party in Cyprus. Thomas Middleton's *Roaring Girl* transforms the faces of playgoers into a picture gallery, incorporating audiences into the architecture of the imagined house. So easily in so many plays, real theatergoers flesh out fictional multitudes, or groups of observers, invoked by extension as a "band of brothers" or included as "pale and trembling mutes or witnesses" to the act. Audience contributions to the performance event need not be loud or literal to be powerful. Playgoers might offer a kind of attention (whether silent or not) in which Desdemona's unexpected breath—"O"—is a coup de theatre.[79] Francis Bacon compares the effect of actors on audiences to the movement of "the bow to the fiddle."[80] Although active in different ways—one striking, the other resonating—both are necessary parts of the same creative instrument.

Case Study: Playing on the Spanish Match

Any critical project that seeks to connect historical change and representational process is an attempt to leap between two moving trains. Yet this is necessary work, because it is through such jumps—back and forth, instant by instant, continually, and in every area of human activity—that cultures and subjectivities make each other. In theater, a social art in which anything can be anything else, these synapses fire with particular freedom: a puritan's arousal at the Whore riding a prop dragon, an Arminian's surprise at a predestinarian plot twist. A play is not a "thing" but a volatile nexus of interactions between people and the possibilities of their culture. As Mullaney writes, "The play is not embodied on the stage . . . such embodiment is a process rather than a presentation, and it takes place within the architectonic sociality of the playhouse."[81] Post-Reformation culture was continually re-created through the lived experiences of believers, and with particular flexibility through the virtual experiences of mixed-faith audiences.

The reiterative and adaptive nature of genre allows it to explore multiple variants of a cultural problem. *A Game at Chess* (see Chapter 4) was part of a larger vogue for plays set in Spain or dealing with the Spanish Match in the early 1620s. This dramatic fashion reflected, but also helped shape, how early modern Londoners thought and felt about this crucial matter of public interest. The Spanish Match subgenre flourished in part because the issue was of current concern, but it was also popularized by the repertory practices of theater companies. The King's Men (KM) and the Lady Elizabeth's Men (LEM) in particular offered competing Spanish plays that cultivated an appetite for drama on the subject that was likely profitable for both companies.[82] These include *The Spanish Curate* (1622 KM), *The Changeling* (1622 LEM), the lost play "The Spanish Duke of Lerma" (1623 KM), *The Spanish Gypsy* (1623 LEM), and the lost "Spanish Viceroy" (1624 KM), among others. Whereas the stagecraft of *A Game at Chess* produces tub-thumping ideological clarity that divides its audiences largely along denominational lines, the dramatic techniques of other Spanish Match plays generate more confessionally fluid fantasies that gather their mixed-faith audiences in shared imaginative and emotional exploration.

Theater helped condition the terms in which popular audiences conceived of Spain. I do not mean this subgenre "convinced" audiences that Spain was bad. While they do reinforce existing anti-Catholic and anti-Spanish stereotypes, these plays also involve forms of transposition and indirection that twist familiar narratives and fears into less recognizable forms. Dominant ideology reproduces itself through repetitions that are never self-identical. The reiterations on which hegemony depends are always (even if imperceptibly) changing. This constant process of re-creating the social world reinforces existing structures but also revises them. Representation changes a culture the way that waves redraw the shoreline that contains them over time.

For example, many Spanish Match plays feature disastrous weddings. Yet, while the trope perpetuates the social anxiety of which it is symptomatic, each theatrical variation modifies its precise emotional and ideological contours.[83] The plot of Thomas Dekker's *Noble Spanish Soldier* (1622) revolves around a fatal marriage contract: the foreign Florentine queen and the Spanish lady Onaelia claim competing engagements to the King. The play closes with the King poisoned at an unlawful wedding. It opens with a heavy-handed display of Spanish monarchical pomp and popish ceremony: *"Enter in Magnificent state, to the sound of lowd musicke, the King and Queene, as from Church, attended by the Cardinal [and court]."*[84] To similar ideological effect, Cold War action movies and contemporary political thrillers attach signs of Russian and Arabic culture (respectively) to sinister generic cues. The scene that follows deepens the atmosphere of lurid, Romanist intrigue: *"A Table set out cover'd with blacke: two waxen Tapers: the King's Picture at one end [a dagger stuck in it], a Crucifex at the other,* Onaelia *walking discontentedly weeping to the Crucifex"* (2.1.s.d.). This is laying it on thick. The mise-en-scène is composed of Catholic devotional objects: tapers and a crucifix (considered idolatrous by many Protestants because they showed Jesus' body, not purely the symbol of the cross).[85] The altar is black. The Spanish monarch's portrait, stabbed with a knife, emblematizes the deadly nature of image worship. Onaelia herself exemplifies a dramatic convention in which, as Diehl has shown, seductive but deadly women embody the spiritual dangers of the physicality of Catholic worship.[86] Diehl attends to the emotional contradiction of iconoclasm for Protestants, so libidinally manifest in Jacobean sex tragedies: attraction to something that therefore must be destroyed. But how did Catholics themselves experience the (always entangled) demonization and eroticization of their religion? It would be naïve to assume that Romanist theatergoers were simply offended by persistent vilification of the Whore on London stages. Desires and identities are formed in complicated relations to stereotypes. People internalize hegemony in strange ways. In the scopophilic regime of revenge tragedy, Catholic femmes fatales occupy a position like the lethal beauties of film noir. Just as Protestant playgoers felt the allure of papist ceremony through seductresses such as Vittoria Corombona, so too, Catholics could experience some of the sinister sexualization of their faith through the theatrical orchestration of a Protestant gaze.[87]

Conversely, by positively coding the eponymous hero's stereotypically Spanish bravado as honorable valor, *The Noble Spanish Soldier* makes available to English playgoers an exhilarating identification with a distinctively Spanish style of military violence. Balthazar is praised by all for his bravery in battle, particularly against Moorish enemies, establishing the Catholic soldier as a defender of Christendom generally. His heroic masculinity is heavily inflected with stereotypically Spanish bombast. He regales the King with a description of battle: "To that heat we came, our Drums beat, Pikes were shaken and shiver'd, swords and Targets clash'd and clatter'd, Muskets ratled, Canons roar'd, men dyed groaning . . . there heads were tost like foot-balls; legs and armes quarrell'd in the ayre . . . thus write I mine own story, *Veni, vidi, vici*" (1.1.86–98). If such rousing forms of address were able, as Heywood claims, to "new mold the harts of spectators . . . [to] any . . . notable attempt," here the rousing, collective, and affective enterprise into which English audiences are drawn is Spanish, Catholic conquest.

Match Me in London, a 1611 city comedy by Dekker, was revived by the Queen Anne's Men in 1623 to cash in on the dramatic trend because of its Spanish setting.[88] The plot follows Tormiella, who marries shopkeeper Cordolente for love. Though nominally Spanish, the hero is coded early as an English Protestant. In the first scene, when their elopement is discovered, their trusty servant feeds the metatheatrical red herring to her outraged father and jilted fiancé: "'Tis some English man has stolne her" (7). Later, the apprentice praises him—"There's not a Diego that treads upon *Spanish* leather goes more upright upon the soles of his Conscience, then our Master does"

(14)—calling attention to his reformed faith and difference from his nominal countrymen. The lecherous King of Spain pursues Tormiella, overlaying the imperial aggression of Catholic Spain onto a city comedy preoccupation with the sexual predations of courtiers on citizen wives. The bawd who attempts to corrupt the teetotaler shopkeeper's wife plies her with wine: "I'll give you the best in Spain" (22). When Tormiella refuses, she is chided as a "puritan foole" (24): citizen and hot Protestant resistance are folded together. Court gossips describe her as a "pinnace" facing an "Armada" (35). The King attempts to force Tormiella into a bigamous second marriage. The climactic scene opens with ominous ceremony: *two Fryers setting out an Altar*" (72). Cordolente's attempt to stop the proceedings is quashed. But a deus ex machina special effect—"*it Thunders and Lightens*"—providentially interrupts the tragic wedding: "Heaven came its selfe downe, and forbade the Banes" (73). *Match Me in London*'s rom-com resolution that reunites the godly, citizen lovers also benignly resolves the Spanish Catholic threat.

Mark Bayer wrongly asserts that the play's connection to the Spanish Match would only have been intelligible to the upscale crowds at the Cockpit, and would have been "lost on an audience of apprentices [at the Red Bull, who instead] could plausibly view the same play as an exoneration of their own dogged work ethic."[89] First of all, it is well documented that Londoners of all social classes were keenly interested in the Spanish Match.[90] The more serious problem is Bayer's failure to recognize the playhouse as a place where people can have experiences that exceed the boundaries of their own lives.[91] Moreover, Bayer's reading artificially separates theatrically interwoven discursive strands. This play does not stage two different dramas for two different audiences: one a pro-citizen, anticourt rom-com for illiterate artisans, and the other a commentary on Anglo-Spanish politics for informed elites. Shopkeeper hero Cordolente is figured in terms of English Protestant masculinity, and the Spanish king's erotic aggression is presented as the intrusion of tyrannous court power into citizen domestic space. These two cultural stories unfold through the same experiential processes; their meanings are entangled.

The revival of the 1611 city comedy in the context of the match remaps tensions between citizens and courtiers onto the conflict between England and Spain: an ad hoc business decision with an interesting ideological by-product. The villain besieging the chaste wife of a shopkeeper embodies both royal power and Spanish danger. This conflation of Spanish and monarchical tyranny in the play's 1623 reprisal anticipates the logic of the 1643 parliamentarian pamphlet *The Game at Chess*, which polemically recasts King Charles in the role formerly occupied by the King of Spain in Middleton's play. Yet *Match Me in London* is in no way "making the case" for the later parliamentary position. Rather, the dramatic fiction floats a possible ideological configuration into the sphere of the thinkable, one that will increasingly accumulate cognates and gain traction in changed political and religious circumstances.

The Spanish Gypsy (1623), by Middleton, William Rowley, John Ford, and Dekker, also engages heightened contemporary emotion around negotiations for the match; the play both consolidates dominant anxieties and offers a pleasurable alternative fantasy of Spanish marriage. The romantic plot, pastoral trappings, and comic structure of *The Spanish Gypsy* invite audience members opposed to the actual match to enjoy an imaginary version of the interfaith union. Set in Madrid, and peppered with references to the unpopular wooing expedition that drew Prince Charles and Buckingham away to the Spanish court at the time of its first performance, one plot follows a family of gypsies who sing and tumble through the play. Among this charming band of vagabonds is Preciosa, a beautiful young gypsy repeatedly presented in terms reminiscent of the infanta.[92] Intertwined with this blossoming romance is the play's rape plot. *The Spanish Gypsy* opens with an attack on a Madrid street. Clara identifies her rapist by a crucifix, a sinister, papist variation on the recognition-by-token device. This material made the play anti-Spanish enough to be reprised at court on November 5, 1623 (the anniversary of the Gunpowder Plot), following Charles and Buckingham's October return from Madrid after negotiations for the match had soured. Yet the play intersplices the tragic threat of Spanish rape with a pastoral experience of cross-cultural marriage. The generic fluidity among the pieces of this collaboratively authored play enables ideological movement between scenes.

In act 4, scene 1, the nobleman Don John is sworn in as a member of the gypsy band, before being handfasted to Preciosa. As was widely feared of Charles's potential marriage to the infanta, the hero's conversion is a necessary condition of his engagement (albeit a temporary one; at the end of the play, it is the bride who abandons vagabond life). The ceremony that turns Don John into a gypsy has Catholic monastic overtones ("Close this new brother of our order"), but mainly it celebrates the gypsies' festivity ("Dance, sing") and pastoral purity ("Flowre bancks . . . to be thy bourd").[93] Not only is Don John's conversion presented as entry into a merry green world, but the ceremony that binds him to Preciosa (the infanta figure) is imagined as the idyllic consecration of innocent love:

> Set foote to foote, those Garlands hold,
> Teach him how, now marke what more is told;
> By crosse Armes the Lovers signe,
> Vow as these flowers themselves entwine,
> Of Aprills Wealth building a throne
> Round; so your love to one or none,
> By those touches of your Feete,
> You must each night embracing meet;
> Chaste how e'er disjoyn'd by Day,
> You the Sun with her must play;
> Shee to you the Marigold
> To none but you her Leaves unfold;
> Wake shee or sleepe, your Eyes so charme,
> Want, woe, nor weather doe her harme. (F4v)

The vow describes their union as chaste, floral, and mutual. Bestowing on the bride an apotropaic blessing typical of an epithalamion poetically legitimates the wedding contract. This scene is designed to generate delight, to give the audience pleasure. The deictic phrases "those garlands hold" and "these flowers . . . entwine" indicate prop floral garlands, common decorations at early modern English weddings.[94] The internal stage directions "now foot to foot" and "cross arms" draw Don John and Preciosa closer together. The mise-en-scène—young lovers embracing, entwined with flowers—positions playgoers as sympathetic witnesses to the handfasting ceremony. This lush and lovely gypsy wedding orchestrates an emotional community of well-wishers to the couple out of its confessionally diverse audiences, despite the fact that most Protestant playgoers would find the real-world corollary of the onstage romance repugnant, and despite the play's intermittent returns to a plot in which Spanish marriage is rape.

The Spanish Gypsy and A Game at Chess are both topical plays; however, in contrast to the overt religious and political commentary of Middleton's allegorical drama, the oblique incorporation of the Spanish Match into The Spanish Gypsy produces a more ideologically wayward fantasy. In both the handfasting scene in The Spanish Gypsy and the deceptive mirror scene in act 3, scene 3, of A Game at Chess, Middleton uses an aurally distinctive rhyming tetrameter to give the ceremonies an air of Catholic enchantment.[95] The two incantations also share similar anaphoric invocations: in *The Spanish Gypsy*, "By crosse Armes, the Lovers signe" and "By those touches of your Feete"; in *A Game at Chess*:

> By her fair and fruitful love,
> By her truth that mates the dove.[96]

The generic differences between the two scenes (one showing a true romance, the other Antichristian deception) make the tetrameter function in tonally opposite ways. Yet the very fact that this shared linguistic marker of Catholic magic can produce opposite emotional effects in different dramatic contexts shows the flexibility with which the theater can reconfigure existing tropes to give audiences altered experiences of confessional discourses. *The Spanish Gypsy*'s benign version of a charmed Catholic wedding was staged at a time when the match was still an alarming possibility, whereas its more sinister doppelgän-ger in *A Game at Chess* appeared after the alliance with Spain was no longer a real threat.[97] This contradiction between dramatic fantasy and cultural cir-cumstances highlights the distinctive work that theater does. The pastoral romance of *The Spanish Gypsy* is not reflecting reality, or escaping it, or argu-ing for an alliance with Spain; rather, it opens alternative channels for the col-lective affective negotiation of the religious and political landscape. Ideology is never only what is consciously avowed, or imposed from above, or possible to state as a claim. Rather, it is the totality of half-articulated thoughts, emo-tions, habits, inklings, erotic investments, curiosities, and confusions that con-stitute the lived world. The constant and collectively experienced reassemblage of these shreds and patches was the business of early modern London's com-mercial theater.

CHAPTER 3

In Mixed Company: Collaboration
in Commercial Theater

Plays for London's commercial theaters were produced by mixed-faith groups of skilled professionals. Contrary to Jeffrey Knapp's mischaracterization of "theater people" as Erasmian "good fellows"—protoecumenical, minimally doctrinal Christians whose Pauline openness put them above the confessional fray—plays were, in fact, made by contributors occupying a wide range of particular and complex religious positions.[1] These ideologically mixed networks of playwrights, actors, impresarios, and censors generated dramatic "mash-ups" of the variegated religious culture from which they drew. In this chapter, I demonstrate the range of religious positions of theater practitioners, highlighting examples of mixed-faith working relationships. Whereas much work on religion and early modern drama has sought to connect the confessional worlds of plays with the confessional lives of their authors (particularly in the case of William Shakespeare), I argue that the distribution of agency, at all stages of the creative process, engendered plays that are often difficult to align with the worldviews of individual contributors. The ideological outcomes of the processes through which multiple authors cobbled together commercially viable drama from various scraps of religious culture and theatrical memes for mixed-faith performers to interpret were varied, unpredictable, and beyond the control of any one artist. Collaboration among theater practitioners, working in response to changing trends in the entertainment business, produced surprising amalgamations of post-Reformation, religious shrapnel. First, I outline some of the common, collaborative working conditions of the early modern entertainment business. Then I show the confessional diversity of the human (and nonhuman) resources of the most prominent and successful theater company in Jacobean and Caroline London: the King's Men. Finally, I turn to two examples from a cluster of hagiographical plays to show some of the industry-wide pressures that shaped theatrical mediation of religious content. *1 Sir John Oldcastle* and *Sir Thomas More* demonstrate the potential of the collaborative business practices of the commercial theaters to imaginatively dislocate and reconfigure existing structures of ideology.

Distributed Creative Agency

The theater business, as Roslyn Lander Knutson points out, was not governed by interpersonal conflicts. Industry-wide commercial strategies and trends shaped company practices. (If Jonson's murdering a member of the Admiral's Men did not stop the company from paying him to cowrite, evidently his Catholicism was not a career deal breaker either.)[2] As in guilds, theater professionals maintained working relationships with colleagues who held different religious beliefs.[3] Certainly, habits of thought and expression of particular playwrights are visible across the corpus of their work. However, in the experiential unit of the play in performance, the stylistic and ideological imprint of an individual biological person is never manifest in splendid isolation.

First of all, even a playwright with an uncommon degree of artistic mastery, career security, and creative control, such as Shakespeare, who was a sharer in the Lord Chamberlain's and King's Men and worked mostly alone, still wrote within and against existing conventions, in response to other playwrights, and in relation to the vicissitudes of the entertainment business. Bart Van Es shows how Shakespeare's plays are tailored to the specializations of his company's actors, in ways that shape characterization and interactions among dramatis personae.[4] Playwrights and groups of playwrights were sometimes commissioned by companies to produce plays on current subjects. Even when writing on spec, playwrights developed scripts that would be attractive to companies looking to capitalize on theatrical trends. In this way, crucial aspects of play scripts—such as their topic, genre, setting, style of dialogue, stage business, and character types, as well as the size and number of parts—were all hugely influenced by the basic conditions of company organization, and by changing fashions.[5]

More than half of all plays for the English commercial theaters were written collaboratively. Cowriting happened in a range of institutional and interpersonal circumstances.[6] Clumps of playwrights sometimes worked together repeatedly in "syndicates," and sometimes changed partners. These groupings might be of their own choosing, or put together by a company manager. Playwrights divided composition into units of variable size. Individual contributions were not always separable into discrete plotlines; one writer might insert a speech or dialogue in another's scene. Additions and changes were sometimes made later. Plays that stayed in the repertory over long periods of time were refreshed to stay current.

Multiple playwrights creating a viable play work differently together than alone. Playwrights' individual contributions to a script were mutually entangled. As Jeffrey Masten writes, "Collaboration in early modern English drama was [not] merely . . . a more *multiple* version of authorship. . . . Collaboration is . . . a dispersal of author/ity, rather than a simple doubling of it."[7] Playwrights might alter their own habits of plotting, characterization, and dialogue to accommodate the contributions of others. While playgoers could recognize, and take pleasure, in identifiable authorial voices, these distinctive, rhetorical modes were not tethered to the individual authors who developed them. Others might adopt a set of formal tics. A stylistic personality is not coterminous with a person. "Marlowe" wrote far more plays than Marlowe did.

Scripts designed for the playhouse were crafted again through performance. Characterization, pacing, emotional emphases, humor, and innumerable other crucial effects are largely determined by actors' delivery. Star performers with substantial and well-known repertoires of roles might carry aspects of one character into another. Clowns inserted their own dialogue. Even when scripted, clowns were often well-known personalities with distinctive shticks. As Richard Preiss writes, "[The clown] was always understood to be playing himself."[8] Rehearsal processes could affect the dynamics of a scene. Audiences sometimes called for revisions.[9] Scripts were also mediated through the technical constraints and affordances of physical staging: the playing space, as well as available props and costumes, could import confessional valances that may or may not align with the ideological bent of the script.[10]

My claim is not that individual creative agents in the theater business did not have religious commitments that they brought into their art, or that their personal confessional tendencies were so highly mediated that they never appear in plays in any recognizable form. No. Theater people did not check their religious identities at the door when they engaged in this business enterprise. However, the confessional predilections of individual playwrights manifest in their collaborative work in widely varying degrees of clarity and consistency. Sometimes, plays for the commercial theaters bear confessional markings that

Figure 1. Ledger stones for John Fletcher and Philip Massinger, who coauthored plays for the King's Men, in their parish church, a short distance from the Globe. Photo by Nick Waplington, by kind permission of Southwark Cathedral.

correlate with the ostensible religious beliefs of some of their makers.[11] But not always. A play is a conglomerate unit of expression of multiple creative agents, whose individual religious intentions, as well as unconscious leanings, may affect the performance in ways that are powerful *because* they are indirect or contradictory. The question is not whether there are any links between (a) consciously held beliefs, (b) the erratic fractals of religious ideology as lived experience, (c) artistic intentions, and (d) artistic productions. These are all deeply connected, though through circuits more resembling perpetual motion machines than straight lines. The challenge, rather, is to map the various, complex ways that creative professionals enmeshed their skills and perspectives to meet market demands, with widely divergent ideological outcomes. In this project, there are two desiderata: first, that the confessional identities of individual, creative agents are themselves understood as social processes, not fixed things; and second, a recognition of the constitutive pressures of theatrical form. As Jeremy Lopez writes, "The centrifugal movement toward form is as likely to send ragged pieces of content flying as it is to smooth their edges and keep them in orbit around an authorial center of gravity."[12]

The King's Men: Human and Nonhuman Actors

A great deal of scholarly attention has been paid to the question of Shakespeare's religious identity, and its relation to the plays he wrote. This ground is so well covered that it is unnecessary to rehearse the matter here.[13] More to the point, the focus on Shakespeare's personal faith—or on the individual beliefs of any one playwright—obscures the pervasive practice of mixed-faith collaboration. Working relationships in the theater business made strange religious bedfellows. Succeeding Shakespeare as house playwright, John Fletcher developed cross-confessional writing partnerships with Francis Beaumont, and later Philip Massinger.[14] Fletcher was the son and grandson of godly Protestant ministers, whereas Beaumont was the scion of a devout, recusant family.[15] Yet contemporaries praise the seamlessness of their cowriting, describing the duo as "twin-stars . . . Whom oft the Muses swaddled in one sheet."[16] Massinger too may have been Catholic. In any case, he embraced ritual and physicality in mourning rites in a way that his collaborator did not. The whopping sum of two pounds was paid for ceremonial extras at Massinger's funeral, while Fletcher was buried in the same churchyard for the relatively low supplementary fee of twenty shillings, which paid for only "an afternoon's knell of the great bell."[17] In Southwark Cathedral, their cenotaphs lie side by side. But on the Globe stage a short distance away, these mixed-faith collaborators were entangled.[18]

Just as the religious affiliations of individual audience members did not narrowly circumscribe their responses to plays, so too, the confessional positions of individual theater practitioners did not always correlate with their contributions to the creative process. The ideological tensions within early modern plays are not produced simply by the involvement of multiple artists, as if the religious valences of their artistic input were determined solely by their various confessional lives. To use Masten's terms, the religious worlds of plays are created not by a doubling of creative agency but by its dispersal (or rather, its distribution). My goal in showing some of the confessional diversity within the company is to mark points from which to measure the ways in which the specific resources, contingencies, and processes of theatrical production could reassemble the diverse religious perspectives that creative professionals brought to their work.

As the confessional positions of theater people did not always dovetail with their art, extrapolating biographical claims from the religious tendencies of plays is dangerous. For example, Lisa Hopkins's inaccurate assertion that John Ford was Catholic is largely predicated on the perceived "baroque" aesthetics of his plays.[19] In fact, Ford, who contributed several successful plays to the King's Men's repertory, including *The Broken Heart* (1630), was a pious Protestant committed to Calvinist theology.[20] Ford's 1620 prose tract, *A Line of Life*, voices a reformist rejection of ceremonial accretions in worship ("derivitive depravation"), and a desire to return to early Christianity's "primitive puritie."[21] Ford rejects "puritan" as a term of abuse, in order to rebuke those who ridicule the godly:

> The mockers of th'elect and holy,
> . . . .
> Despising Preachers, and nicke naming those
> With malice whom the holy ghost chose.[22]

These lines express support for an evangelical ministry, defend hot Protestants against their nicknaming enemies, and also designate the godly as elect. Though Ford would dislike the label, this anticeremonial, pro-preaching, double-predestinarian Protestant could easily be termed a puritan.

Godly affiliates of the King's Men, such as Ford, were not aberrations. Puritans were part of company life. Caroline actor Eyllaerdt Swanston "profest himself a Presbyterian."[23] He performed a number of key roles for the King's Men, including Othello, Bussy D'Ambois, and Richard III, and often represented the company in business dealings.[24] The presbyterian actor is remembered nostalgically in the Restoration as part of a lost generation of excellent players: "'Tis impossible that [actors now] should do any thing so well as I have seen . . . *Swantted.*"[25] The puritan John Lowin's career as a principal actor and sharer in the King's company spanned from 1603 to 1642.

The religious lives of theater professionals often stood at oblique angles to their work. Edward Alleyn was famous for playing Marlovian atheists, but in private life he served in parish offices, and his charity founded the College of God's Gift at Dulwich. The King's Men player Lowin sought to reconcile his theatrical work with his commitment to a godly life in the 1607 tract *Conclusions upon Dances.*[26] Though far from the sweeping antitheatricalism of some other puritans, Lowin advances his discussion of the spiritual dangers of dancing in godly terms. The actor draws his evidence entirely from scripture, and praises the rigor of a Calvinist theocracy: "The prohibition of *dances* in *Geneva* [was necessary] because of the great abuses of them. . . . Is not this [example] a sufficient argument, to proove such an action to be good?"[27] Lowin does not address the case of theatrical dancing specifically, although perhaps its categorization as a form of "honest recreation" is implicit in the fact that the author identifies himself as an actor: "Written by J. L. Roscio."[28] On the other hand, Lowin declares, "the greater part of . . . Dances used *everie where, in these dayes* [are] profane," and therefore irreconcilable with proper devotion. This godly man, so intent on the distinction between vain entertainment and celebration compatible with piety, also "used to act, with mighty Applause, *Falstaff.*"[29] It is impossible to know how Lowin himself processed the incongruity of being a puritan actor playing a puritan caricature. Perhaps he unproblematically classified the fat knight's irreverent physicality as exempt, because it belongs to dramatic fiction, and as such theoretically serves a didactic purpose. Perhaps Lowin's profession was a source of unresolved, spiritual anxiety. Or perhaps the pamphlet represents "an essay in personal clarification . . . an exercise bent on vindicating the author . . . [as a] godly player."[30]

Nathan Field, who was a star performer in the King's Men from 1616 to his death in 1620, similarly insisted that his calling was compatible with godly piety. Yet Field performed in plays that set the stage and the brethren in stark opposition; most notably, in the scene in *Bartholomew Fair* in which a puppet refutes the antitheatrical tirade of the puritan caricature, Zeal-of-the-Land Busy. Field specialized in romantic leads, and he held a position second only

to Richard Burbage among players in the company. He was the son of the
presbyterian firebrand John Field, who in 1583 describes the collapse of the
Paris Garden, in which many were killed, as a "judgment of God" for the sin
of bearbaiting on the Sabbath, and warns that "the *Theater*, the *Curtin* and
such like, one day those places wyl like-wise bee cast downe by God himselfe &
with them a huge heape of . . . prophane persons utterly killed & spoyled in
their bodies."[31] In 1616, rejecting his father's position on the theater but laying
claim to a godly spiritual identity, the famous actor self-consciously adopts
the language of the brethren to challenge his parish preacher's condemnation
of players:

> Beare wittnes with me, O my Conscience, and reward me, O Lord,
> according to the truth of my lipps, how I love the Sanctuary of my
> God; how I have . . . indeavored to study Christ and make sure of
> my election; how I reverence the feete of those that bring clad tid-
> ings of the Gospell, and that I beare in my soule the badge of a Chris-
> tian practise to live the lief of the faithfull, wish to dye the death of
> the righteous, and hope to meet my Savior in the clouds. If yow mer-
> veyle, sir, why I beginne with a protestacion soe zelous and sacred, or
> why I salute yow in phrase soe confused and wrapped . . . [it is
> because] yow have been late pleased, and that many times from the
> Holy Hill of Sion, the pulpitt, a place sanctified and dedicated for
> the winning . . . of soules, to send forth . . . uncharitable and unlim-
> ited curses of condemnations, against that poor calling it hath
> pleased the Lord to place me in, that my spirit is moved; the fire is
> kindled and I must speake; and the rather because yow have not
> spared in the extraordinary violence of your passion particularly to
> point att me and some other of my quality, and directly in our faces
> in the publique assembly to pronounce us dampned, as thoughe yow
> ment to send us alive to hell in the sight of so many wittnesses.[32]

Field pointedly uses locutions ("truth of my lips") and the apostrophic address
("O my Conscience") commonly associated with zealous preaching. But this
is not Jonsonian parody. Field is defending his soul. He professes his Christian faith with godly emphases, expressing assurance of his election, and his
commitment to an evangelical ministry. He challenges the minister Thomas
Sutton's position on scriptural grounds, declaring there to be no condemna-

tion of playing "in Godes whole volume—which I have studied at my best parte."[33] The theatrical metaphor for immersive Bible reading is an assertion of religious legitimacy. Field is aware that Sutton will perceive a contradiction between his occupation and the puritan rhetoric of his remonstrance ("you marvel [at my] zealous . . . phrase"). Field's point is that he too has a right to this pious language. Field wields the terms of puritan critique against his opponent, accusing him of "ungodly" impiety for arrogating a judgment that belongs only to God by presuming to know who is damned: "How ungodly a speech it is in a publik pulpitt to say that he maynteynes those whome God hath damned. . . . Truly, sir, in my religion it is daungerous . . . [to call] the poore members of Christ dampned."[34] Field's closing sentence reverses Sutton's accusation that actors are reprobates, and instead claims for himself, and his fellows, a place among the brethren: "Holding it for a generall maxime that the sclanders of the wicked are approbations to the godly."[35] The conflict is not between a puritan antitheatricalist and an antipuritan actor but between competing definitions of godly belonging.[36]

Multiple convert and King's Men affiliate Ben Jonson was the nexus of a mixed-faith milieu.[37] Jonson skewered the brethren onstage, but he had no problem drinking with them.[38] "Son of Ben" Thomas May's 1645 pamphlet, *The Character of a Right Malignant*, advances puritan arguments through the form of a Jonsonian character sketch.[39] Of the "malignant," a term of abuse for Royalists, May writes, "Hee is one that professes love to the Protestant Religion; but hatred to all that Party . . . which maintaine it. . . . He calls those hypocrites, who lead a godly life."[40] Puritan poet Samuel Rowlands was part of Jonson's circle of regulars at the Mermaid tavern. The playwright's influence is evident in Rowlands's satirical epigrams on urban fashions and foibles.[41] By contrast, boy player and company sharer Richard Robinson, who was celebrated by Jonson for his female roles, had more ceremonial confessional leanings.[42] In 1641, Robinson signed a testimonial defending the orthodoxy of bowing at the name of Jesus and the use of altar rails.[43] Not only were his associates a mixed-faith group, Jonson's own theatrical work intersects with his religious life with different degrees of intensity and directness. The strategically veiled engagement with the persecution of English Romanists in *Sejanus* speaks to and from Jonson's own position as a Catholic more immediately and coherently (indeed, conspicuously enough to be censored) than *Volpone*'s idolatrous adoration of his gold relates to the playwright's actual Catholic worship.[44]

The physical resources of staging carried confessional associations from their past lives outside the theater, as well as from their use in other plays. As Elizabeth Williamson writes, "When [religious] objects are translated into the public theatre, either directly or indirectly, they necessarily take on new meanings, but their old ones are not always expunged."[45] Like the mental resources of artists, the ideological baggage of these materials could be reconfigured through the process of theatrical production. The idol in *Sejanus* was a company prop recycled in a variety of theatrical and religious contexts that resonate with and modify each other.[46] Williamson describes the King's Men's tomb property as an "affective technology," capable of producing a range of emotional effects through its association with "a set of practices that are both religious and theatrical."[47] In concert with creative professionals, these non-human and nonintentional actors helped shape the confessional valences of plays. Paul Yachnin rightly insists "not only on the social agency of the playwright, players, playgoers, and readers, but also the social agency of the texts, textual bits, props, and costumes" to organize and change the social processes happening in the playhouse.[48] The case study that follows illustrates some of the ways these mixed-faith resources interacted in the daily operations of the theater business, producing ideologically flexible fantasies.

Merry Martyrs

Theater companies acted as creative units, but they were also subject to larger-scale industry practices and trends. Elsewhere, I describe how the perceived possibility of religious change attendant on the Elizabethan succession crisis wrested a subgenre of Protestant martyr plays away from the triumphalist teleology of their source material in John Foxe's *Acts and Monuments.*[49] However, this representational shift was not produced solely by the pressures of a historical moment of heightened religious contingency. The creative mechanics of theatrical production were also a force of ideological dislocation. Here, I highlight how the everyday, ad hoc operations of the theater business—playwrights working in syndicates, specialization, cluster marketing, character-based spin-offs, generic duplications of hits, and players changing troupes—generate surprisingly inclusive, nostalgic representations of English Romanists in two martyr plays: one celebrating the eponymous protopuritan martyr, *1 Sir John Oldcastle*, and the other a hagiography of the Catholic saint, *Sir Thomas More.*

Staged in 1599 by the Admiral's Men and written by Michael Drayton, Richard Hathway, Anthony Munday, and Robert Wilson, *1 Sir John Oldcastle* announces its hot Protestant agenda explicitly from the beginning. The opening declares the play a refutation of the representation in Shakespeare's *1 and 2 Henry IV* of the Lollard martyr Oldcastle as the debauched, self-promoting coward renamed Falstaff. Lollardy was understood as a historical precursor to puritanism.[50] The prologue praises the godly martyr:

> It is no pampered glutton we present,
> Nor aged counsellor to youthful sins:
> But one whose virtues shone above the rest,
> A valiant martyr and a virtuous peer.[51]

The script marks Oldcastle as a protopuritan. His worship is described in terms of zealous, voluntary religion. The Lollards meet in "secret conventicles . . . spurning at ceremonies" (A4v–B1r). Bishops are bad guys bent on tyrannically persecuting Oldcastle over "only . . . conscience for the Gospels sake" (H1v). The play *1 Sir John Oldcastle* is about puritan, political loyalty. Oldcastle is three times accused of involvement in acts of sedition, but each time publicly exonerated. This repeated plot cycle occasions lengthy articulations of loyal, godly dissent.

This explicit and pervasive, hot Protestant agenda aligns roughly with the known religious proclivities of two of the playwrights. In 1591, Drayton published a collection of hymns "for the solace and comfort of the godly."[52] Wilson may be the "R. W." who wrote the 1591 anti-Catholic tract *Martine Mar-Sixtus*.[53] In 1586, he worked as a messenger for Robert Dudley, Earl of Leicester, then leading a military campaign in the Low Countries in the name of international Protestant solidarity. In contrast to these hotter Protestants, Munday spent the late 1580s shutting down presses publishing presbyterian polemic in the Marprelate Controversy. The writing team of Drayton, Hathway, Munday, and Wilson was not selected to write *1 Sir John Oldcastle* because of their shared religious commitments. The group was an informal jobbing syndicate that also worked together on such historical plays as "Owen Tudor" for the Admiral's Men that season.[54]

In spite of the declared ideological opposition of the prologue, the Admiral's Men benefited commercially from the similarity between the rival plays. As James Marino demonstrates, "Part of the play's value [to the Admiral's Men at the Rose] lay in its proximity to the Chamberlain's Men at the Globe."[55]

The Admiral's Men were using two common business strategies, as identified by Knutson, to their advantage: cluster marketing and character spin-offs.[56] Philip Henslowe's company profited from being close (both physically and stylistically) to their competitors. In Marino's words, "The Rose *Oldcastle* was intended for Falstaff's audience, the playgoers who were now frequenting Southwark and the neighborhood of the Globe."[57] The Admiral's Men reproduce much of the Chamberlain's Men's stage business. Oldcastle's bluff servingman, Harpoole, forces the Bishop's disrespectful minion to swallow the summons he delivers, just as the soldier Fluellen in *Henry V* makes the braggart Pistol eat his leek. King Henry and the thieving priest Sir John share a half coin as a token of recognition, as when in Shakespeare's play Harry gives Williams his glove. In both plays, King Henry coolly confronts conspirators Cambridge, Scrope, and Grey. In developing these theatergrams, the company satisfied and cultivated a particular set of audience tastes.[58]

If *Oldcastle* is a religious rejection of the antipuritan satire embodied in the fat knight, it is also a Falstaff spin-off. The Admiral's Men follow the common business strategy of importing popular characters, or their ersatz twins, into new plays. The Admiral's Men shift the confessional markers of Shakespeare's play, reinventing the puritan Sir John Falstaff/Oldcastle as Sir John of Wrotham, a Catholic priest. On one level, their Sir John is a walking anti-Catholic satire, a proverbial "Sir John Mumble-matins." A highwayman and whoremonger, he refers to thieving and lechery in terms borrowed from Catholic religious practice. His "benefices" are the roads he robs (F4r). The woman he pimps is his "poore mans boxe" (F1r). He calls his whore his "chappel of ease" (C4v). As a parody of popery, Sir John complements the announced, hot Protestant agenda of the play. However, while *Oldcastle*'s title role offers an object lesson in godly loyalty, its Falstaff figure also inserts into the play a merry, nostalgic representation of English Catholicism. Despite being characterized through the tropes of anti-Catholic polemic, the figure of Sir John participates in theatrical fashions that include him in the community of Englishness. The tropes of merriness and hospitality in *Oldcastle*, which recuperate space for an identity that is both Catholic and English, are largely lifted from generic cognates of the play. This demonstrates how the recycling of theatrical material to capitalize on current dramatic fashions could divert even the most explicit of religious agendas.

The play's open accommodation of the Catholic priest in its staging of the merry English past is established as soon as the character introduces himself:

For kinde sir John of *Wrotham* honest Jacke

. . . .

I am not as the world does take me for;
If ever woolfe were cloathed in sheepes cote,
Then I am he, olde huddle and twang, yfaith,
A priest in shew, but in plaine termes, a thiefe,
Yet let me tell you too, an honest theefe.
One that will take it where it may be spent.
And spend it freely in good fellowship. (B3r–B3v)

The anticlerical satire cedes to tavern camaraderie in the space of a few lines. *Oldcastle*'s treatment of Sir John shares in the vogue for nostalgic representations of a "merry" English past. He is repeatedly hailed in the idiom of good-humored fellowship: "a good honest merry priest" (C4r), a "good fellow" (F2r), "the madst priest that ever I met with" (D1r). Like "mad" Simon Eyre of Thomas Dekker's *Shoemaker's Holiday*, a nostalgic comedy also staged in 1599 and set in the reign of good King Harry, Sir John is one of the lads. He personifies an old, lost, merry world of fellowship and hospitality, a cultural fantasy that at the end of a decade of dearth and inflation was being eagerly consumed by patrons of the commercial theaters.[59]

In the godly play *Oldcastle*, a theatrically and financially crucial character is both Catholic "them" and English "us."[60] Sir John and the Lollard servant Harpoole recognize each other as part of a community defined by old-timey hospitality:

> *Sir John:* Give me thy hand, thou art as good a fellow, I am a
> singer, a drinker, a bencher, a wencher, I can say a masse,
> and kisse a lasse. . . .
> *Harpoole:* Well said mad priest, weele in and be friends. (D1r)

In this scene, a Catholic priest and a puritan walk into a bar, fight over a girl, and make up over a beer, embedding mad wag Sir John in English, alehouse *communitas*. His comic version of Roman priesthood—"say a mass and kiss a lass"—offers audiences a "cakes and ale" version of England's Catholic past.[61]

King Harry too recognizes Sir John as a stouthearted English subject. In *Oldcastle*'s version of the scene in *Henry V* in which the King in disguise meets common soldiers, Harry and Sir John play a merry game of dice.[62] Harry starts the game inviting all company as equals and sends expressly for Sir John:

> Al friends at footebal, fellows all in a field,
> Harry, and Dicke, and George, bring us a drumme,
> Give us square dice, weele keepe this court of guard,
> For al good fellowes companies that come.
> Wheres that mad priest ye told me was in Armes,
> To fight as well as pray if neede required? (F3v)

Harry's speech promises the hearty, egalitarian, masculine fellowship that in Shakespeare's play is deployed to consolidate a "band of brothers" across the national and class divides of the English army. This scene performs similar work, smoothing over religious differences by including the Catholic priest in Harry's festive fellowship.[63] Sir John joins the group, confident of his belonging: "Edge ye good fellows, take a fresh gamester in" (F4r). When Harry recognizes the "lusty thief" who robbed him by the gold coin they broke between them, Sir John begs for his life, protesting, "Ye have not a taller man, nor a truer subject to the Crowne and State than Sir John of Wrootham" (G1v). When Henry pardons him, the priest swears, "My Liege, if ye have cause of battell, ye shall see Sir John of Wrootham bestirre himself in your quarrel" (G1v). Sir John's integration into a discourse of hearty, English masculinity allows him to claim a place as a loyal subject despite his criminal activity, or rather despite the Catholicism for which his criminality is the sign.[64] In *Oldcastle*, the recycling of theatrical tropes of merriness and hearty masculinity allows Sir John the priest to model a position that is both Catholic and English. These depictions counter the ideological work of other scenes in *Oldcastle* that explicitly present the Roman clergy as disloyal usurpers of royal prerogative.

The connection between Sir John Falstaff and Sir John of Wrotham intensified in 1602, when the clown Will Kemp migrated to the Worcester's Men, who acquired the script when they took up residency at the Rose. Kemp had played Falstaff for the Chamberlain's Men. He was a famous and popular performer with a well-known persona. The script already overlaid Wrotham with Falstaff before Kemp took over the character. When the priest mugs the King on the road, Harry references the Gadshill robbery in *1 Henry IV*: "Wel, if thou wilt needs have it, there tis: just the proverb, one thiefe robs another, where the divel are my old theeves, that were wont to keepe this walke? Falstaffe the villaine is so fat, he cannot get on's horse, but me thinkes Poines and Peto should be stirring here abouts" (F2r). In the ensuing friendly exchange between the Catholic thief and his royal mark, Sir John again references his counterpart in recounting that Harry himself "once robde me before I fell to the trade . . . when that foule villainons guts, that led him to all that rogery, was in's company there, that Falstaffe" (F2r). These stage moments point up the correspondence between Wrotham and his generic double.[65] As Gina Bloom, Anston Bosman, and William N. West write, "Intertheatricality foregrounds how performances relate to one another, presenting a form of citationality that is not allusive, in the sense that it does not point back to past performances. Instead intertheatrical citationality thickens present performance by mediating it with other performances."[66] In this sense, Falstaff is not a figure that Sir John of Wrotham references but a dimension of his persona.

With another performer in the role of Wrotham, name-checking Falstaff connects the characters while offering a playful challenge to the alternative version available at the Globe. However, having the same clown play both roles changes the intertheatrical relationship between them. Kemp folds the two characters together. With him playing Wrotham, the crucial effect is that his body makes the two Sir Johns (in an obvious way, yet one that is difficult to theorize) the same person. The King puts pressure on the physical identity of Sir John when he recognizes him as the robber:

> There was a thiefe, in face much like Sir John,
> But t'was not hee, that theife was all in greene,
> Met me last day upon Blacke Heath, neere the parke,
> With him a woman . . .
> . . . .
> . . . Sir John, the thiefe I meane,
> Tooke a just hundreth pound in gold from me. (F4v–G1r)

Harry's clarification of the confusion between the two Sir Johns—"the thief I mean"—points up the interchangeability of the characters, especially since the job description fits them both. The lines "much like . . . but not he" flirt with the near identity of the roles. The suggestion is that the only thing that distinguishes the characters is a green suit.[67] The King's inspection guides metatheatrical attention to the player's person. When Kemp plays Sir John, the convention that differentiates characters by costume breaks down because audiences can recognize the actor's face and body as the fat knight's. The comic tension is no longer the similarity between the Falstaff and Wrotham: with Kemp the joke is that they are the same.

However, the effect of shared personhood between the two Sir Johns is not produced in a direct, unmediated fashion by the actor who plays both. The Catholic priest's physicality was modeled on Falstaff's before Kemp took over the role. Wrotham's entrance armed and ready to fight reproduces Falstaff's appearance on the battlefield. Dressing "the mad priest . . . in arms" was more likely motivated by a desire to reinforce the resonances between the two plays than to present a hearty embodiment of Catholic loyalty; nevertheless, that is precisely the ideological by-product of this costuming decision. The *Oldcastle* script gives its Sir John a companion, "Doll," a woman who is not so much an independent character as an instrumental character supplement who condenses Wrotham's connection to Falstaff through her parallel to Doll Tearsheet. More to the point, Sir John's physicality in *Oldcastle* is mediated not only through Drayton, Hathway, Munday, and Wilson's imitation of the Chamberlain's Men's play but also by Shakespeare's own adaptation of Kemp's preexisting identity as a solo performer. Describing the ways Shakespeare tailored characters to the members of the company for which he wrote, Van Es writes, "Kemp arrived with an existing on-stage persona. . . . Above all it is Kemp's physical capacity, his strength and energy, [his prodigious stamina], that comes through from the record. . . . Kemp presents himself as the spokesperson and embodiment of a plain, pleasure-loving Englishness."[68] Kemp's physicality and good-fellow affect run before his body into the Admiral's Men's script, via Shakespeare's, before he catches up with himself in the Worcester Men's production, accruing Falstaff along the way.[69] Styles of physicalization, as well as styles of writing, were shaped collectively by the processes of theatrical production.

Part of the refutation of *1 and 2 Henry IV*'s slander on godly Oldcastle is to displace Falstaff's hypocrisy, criminality, and debauchery onto the Catholic Wrotham; yet the generic overlap between the two merry, English thieves erodes the religious difference between them.[70] Falstaff and Wrotham are never put in opposition in the way the prologue sets godly Oldcastle against his antipuritan doppelgänger. Much of the theatrical pleasure of *Oldcastle* rests in the overlay between the Sir Johns. This is especially true as Sir John of Wrotham picks up Falstaff's language of grace and redemption, as well as his hearty sociability. "Live and repent, and prove an honest man," King Harry charges him, and asks the companionable group onstage: "My lords, will you be his sureties?" (G1v). Their goodwill models an extension of faith from the audience—not an expectation that he will stop stealing, but an emotional apprehension of the character's general social and spiritual redeemability. At the end of the play, when charged by a justice, "You have bin lewd, and many yeares / Led a lascivious unbeseeming life," the old, merry thief echoes Falstaff, swearing, "Oh but my Lord, he repents, Sir John repents, he will mend" (K4r). His use of the third person invokes "Sir John" as a figure larger than himself. The same kind of comic excess and *communitas* that in Shakespeare's play carves out a space of grace and social inclusion for the hypocritical sinner Falstaff also characterizes Wrotham. In *1 and 2 Henry IV* and *Oldcastle*, financially savvy personations of merry good fellows occasion the inclusion of an antipuritan caricature and an anti-Catholic parody in the community of English Christianity—"in Arthur's bosom"—despite these plays' more overt, ideological work.

Similarly, in *Sir Thomas More*, popular theatrical tropes of merriness and hospitality recuperate the Catholic saint into a community of English, Christian fellow feeling. While the dates of the play's first composition and revision are contested, its "trendiness index" supports John Jowett's argument for an initial script in 1600, locating it among cognate plays about Protestant martyrs such as *Oldcastle* (1599), *Thomas Lord Cromwell* (1600), and *The Famous History of Sir Thomas Wyatt* (1602), as well as plays celebrating London citizen heroes, such as *The Shoemaker's Holiday* (1599).[71] The fact that critics have questioned so strenuously whether this play was performed at all is symptomatic of the ways in which expectations of the past affect the interpretation of evidence.[72] Instead of assuming that *Sir Thomas More* would have been abandoned by the company on the grounds that its sympathetic treatment of a Catholic martyr would put them in danger of punishment, we should consider it more likely that the theater business operated as it usually did. Munday was a seasoned playhouse professional and former government agent—someone with expert knowledge of both theatrical expression and the repressive apparatus of the state—who clearly wrote the original script thinking that the subject matter, delicately handled, could be licensed. He was right: the censor Edmund Tilney did not ban this play. He gave specific instructions for revision, on the understanding that an edited version would eventually be staged. The company followed his instructions for reforming the script.[73] The bottom line is that no company would spend money on revisions to a play they did

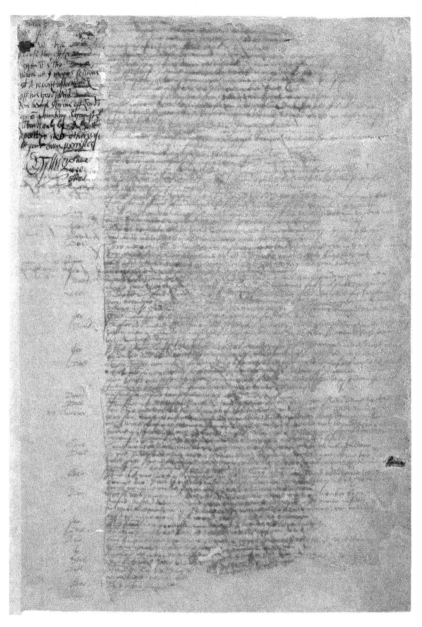

Figure 2. The censor Edmund Tilney's specific instructions for revision: "Leave out the insurrection wholly and the cause thereof, and begin with Sir Thomas More at the Mayor's sessions, with a report afterwards of his good service done being Sheriff of London upon a mutiny against the Lombards—only by a short report, and not otherwise, at your own perils." *The Book of Sir Thomas Moore*, by Anthony Munday, Henry Chettle, Thomas Dekker, Thomas Heywood, and William Shakespeare, Harley MS 7368, fol. 3r, British Library.

not intend to perform. In this case, an absence of evidence of performance is not evidence that the play script would be nervously discarded after paying for rewrites addressing the specific objections of the censor. The expectation that a play about a Catholic saint would not have been performed before largely Protestant audiences obscures the many ways that *Sir Thomas More* was business as usual, produced through the same multiple agencies as other plays, and recycling popular tropes.

Susannah Brietz Monta's insightful discussion of *Sir Thomas More* usefully locates the play in the context of its hagiographical sources, as well as Protestant accounts;[74] these give conflicting interpretations of the historical More's mirth at his execution as, respectively, a sign of his holiness and the truth of his martyrdom or as a mark of his folly and deluded faith. Monta argues that since the theological content of More's religious resistance is never explicitly stated, his laughter is "opaque" and the question of his sanctity is left open to either interpretation. The problem with this is that while Monta attends to the discursive contexts in which the historical More's humor was understood, she neglects the theatrical conventions that shaped mixed-faith playgoers' shared experiences of the saint in the playhouse.[75]

Merriness and hospitality are central to the play's nostalgic presentation of More as part of a charitable English past. More's jests "punch upward, not downward," as modern comics say. Audiences meet him playing a practical joke on a blowhard Justice that spares a thief from execution. "Well, Master More, you are a merry man," his target concedes, after having his own pocket picked as lesson against lecturing crime victims (2.1.184). More's humor is not folly; he closes the scene with the adage, "Wisdom still [keeps] the door" (2.1.197). His wit is recognized by other characters as socially corrective, virtuous, and, later in the play, as a sign of spiritual peace. Hospitality or "housekeeping" in *Sir Thomas More* is presented in terms of traditional, open-door charity distributed by great lords, a form of public assistance often lamented as having declined since the Reformation.[76] Like Oldcastle, who "keepes good beefe and beere in his house, and every day feedes a hundred poore people at's gate" (C2v), the Catholic martyr's charity to the poor is a constant refrain. More jokes he has been England's "poorest chancellor," going broke from buying such "commodities" as "crutches . . . and bare cloaks, / For halting soldiers and poor needy scholars" (16.46.51, 55–56). His porter praises his open-house charity: "Ye have [not] many lord chancellors comes in debt at the year's end, and for very housekeeping!" (15.18–19). In *Oldcastle*, the conspirators' refusal of the Lollard martyr's hospitality marks them apart from the community of

English good fellowship, which encompasses godly Oldcastle, royal Harry, and papist Sir John, by setting their "Businesse" of treason against the loyal martyr's invitation to "be mery" (E1r). Similarly, in *Sir Thomas More* hospitality is a force of social cohesion. The rioting Londoners listen to More because of his charity to the poor: "Let's hear him. 'A keeps a plentiful shrievaltry" (6.51). His argument extends to foreign immigrants the principle of keeping open house. He calls on his audience to imagine themselves as "strangers [in a nation that] Would not afford you an abode on earth . . . spurn you like dogs" (add. 2.146, 149, 151). In this scene, More's reputation for generosity, and defense of hospitality to strangers, turns rebellion to loyal obedience. His gracious entertainment of the Lord Mayor and other city worthies consolidates bonds among citizens. More's egalitarian good cheer extends from the virago, rabble-rouser Doll Williamson to courtiers, to citizens, to actors, and to his servants, who all lament their master's death "fellow-like . . . co-partners of one woe" (15.60).

As More moves toward his martyrdom, the emotional effects of his constant merriness shift. His jailor interprets his sustained good cheer as a sign of spiritual peace in the face of death:

> And your fair patience in imprisonment
> Hath ever shown such constancy of mind
> And Christian resolution in all troubles,
> As warrants us you are not unprepared
> . . . .
> In life and death, still merry Thomas More. (16.7–10, 22)

Contrary to Monta's claim that the play leaves More's spiritual state indeterminate, audiences' emotional interpretation of More's death is strongly guided. The play's praise for his exemplary life and death is virtually univocal. While many try to convince More to change his decision, no character articulates a clear, negative assessment of his spiritual condition to counter the play's relentless modeling of sympathetic response to the martyr, particularly in the succession of mourning loved ones and old acquaintances that greet More on his way to death. Protestant emissary of the court Lord Shrewsbury is confident he will see More in heaven, "God send us merry meeting" (14.52). Even his jailor "weeps" (17.13.s.d.). As More ascends the scaffold, he expands the fellowship that surrounds him outward to the audience: "The higher I mount the better I can see my friends about me" (17.61–62).

Deprived of office, imprisoned, and sent to execution, More repeatedly charges friends, family, and others around him not to cry for him. An expurgated passage crystallizes the opposition that runs though the end of the play, between worldly tears and More's holy mirth. The saint soliloquizes:

Yet, seeing both are mortal—Court and King—
Shed not one tear for any earthly thing. (13.64)

That Tilney cut this explicit articulation of the dichotomy between Catholic More's spiritual joy and the earthly punishments of the state suggests the radical potential of this emotional position. Despite the censor's edits, More's heavenly laughter—and his refusal of tears for worldly suffering—remains the central framework through which the play presents More's death. The execution scene elicits compassion from audiences, though not through simple "mirroring" of the protagonist's emotional state. The contrast between More's good humor and the mourning of those around him separates him from both his onstage and playhouse witnesses. This "affective irony," as Steven Mullaney terms configurations in which "what the speaker feels is precisely *not* what we feel," does not alienate viewers (in the sense of creating antipathy) but rather draws audiences closer in a kind of "inverted sympathy."[77] The gap between the saint's cheerful fortitude and spectators' sorrow makes More's interiority inaccessible, not in the sense of being indeterminate but because it places him on a separate plane untouched by human tears. Instead of the doctrinal affirmation Monta seeks, this estrangement effect creates experiential evidence of More's sanctity. The confirmation of the truth of More's martyrdom is dependent not on a verbal declaration of his religious beliefs but on playgoers' affective responses.

While many have speculated that Shakespeare harbored some degree of Catholic sympathy, his mixed-faith collaborators on the script are unlikely candidates as coauthors of a play about a Catholic saint. In 1606, Dekker gives the character of an English Romanist as follows:

Envies heart and Treason's head,
For, *England* bout the neck hee clips,
And kisses. But with *Judas* lips.[78]

Henry Chettle was a conforming member of the Church of England who, in a 1603 pamphlet, praises Queen Elizabeth for "establish[ing] the true . . .

Religion in this land . . . [without] multitudes of idle superstitions."[79] Thomas Heywood, in a verse history of English monarchs, commemorates Elizabeth:

> She did the Gospel quicken, and confound
> *Romes* Antichrist.[80]

Munday in the early 1580s worked as a pursuivant for the notoriously sadistic torturer Richard Topcliff. Having spent time in the English College in Rome, either as a student or a spy, he informed on his Catholic countrymen, including the martyr Edmund Campion. Munday likely seized the hagiographical source material for the play during a raid on the lodgings of the saint's grandson, also named Thomas More. These anti-Catholic positions are a far cry from the play's presentation of More as "the merriest councillor of England" and a "sweet soul to live among the saints" (15.40, 11.66).

Like the *Oldcastle* writing team, these playwrights became involved with *More* not because of their religious beliefs but because of their expertise with similar plays.[81] Shakespeare had a decade of successful English history plays behind him. Heywood had recently written the citizen-centered history *Edward IV*. Dekker produced similar effects of merriness and hospitality in *Shoemaker's Holiday*. Heywood and Dekker both contributed to the martyr play "Lady Jane."[82] Munday worked on the martyr play *Oldcastle* and the mid-Tudor *de casibus* drama "Cardinal Wolsey," as well as two Robin Hood plays that nostalgically invoke an English past of good fellowship. It was common practice for playwrights to develop dramatic lines, working on generically similar plays or producing duplicates and spin-offs of their own work.

Munday is the immediate common denominator between the two martyr plays. To sum up, he was a Romanist seminary student, and a priest-hunting pursuivant; More's theatrical hagiographer, and the persecutor of his descendants; an author of a propuritan play, and an agent in the state's crackdown on Martinist presbyterians; an antitheatricalist, and an actor. Munday's religious identity, and its relationship to his theatrical work, was complicated. He lived in the contradiction between his complicity with state-sponsored, religious violence and his collaborative work on ideologically flexible drama.[83] Yet Munday is not an exception so much as an exaggerated, representative example of the ordinary operations of the theater business. The threads of confessional possibility and cultural expression that knot so densely in Munday also weave through the lives of his mixed-faith colleagues, constraining and enabling their shared, imaginative work.

CHAPTER 4

Making a Public Through *A Game at Chess*

Thomas Middleton's *A Game at Chess*, a topical allegory performed by the King's Men over a nine-day run in August 1624, centers on unmasking the Spanish Jesuit plot for world domination. "Discovery" and conspicuous secrecy saturate the action and dialogue. Yet discovery is more than the theme the play represents, and it is more than a matter of identifying topical references. "Discovery" is the process of performance, a continuous activity involving the play's audiences. *A Game at Chess*'s stage techniques enlist a confessionally wide swath of Protestant audience members in the keen-eyed detection of Jesuit and Spanish deceit while marking out Catholics—not only onstage but also in the playhouse—as targets of investigation. In this chapter, I show how the play exercises the theatrical competencies of Protestant playgoers in order to engage their confessional and political discernment. *A Game at Chess* entrains and extends audience perceptions of stage action into extradramatic, partisan surveillance. In eliciting the self-conscious participation of playgoers in religious and political discovery, *A Game at Chess* offers an unusually overt example of the socially constitutive character of the shared imaginative processes of live theater.

In contrast to criticism that maintains *A Game at Chess* undoes its own religious binaries, I insist the play interpellates a Protestant collective intent on the discovery and persecution of a Catholic minority.[1] Arguments for the play's ideological ambivalence rest on the false assumption that the representational license, and economic pressures, of commercial theater made it an inherently "postconfessional" mode of public formation. However, the fact that early modern drama recirculated religious material more playfully than sermons or pamphlets, and drew a mixed-faith clientele, does not mean that all plays are confessionally neutral. Representational complexity and ideological ambiguity do not always go hand in hand. As seen in the case of *A Game at Chess* (or in the case of Leni Riefenstahl's *Triumph of the Will*), a great deal of sophisticated artistry can harden the crudest and most murderous belief systems.[2] Many commercial plays consolidate Protestant hegemony. The crucial point is that such dominant, cultural structures are not static things that are merely described in plays but rather are continually remade through the social processes of representation. *A Game at Chess* does not simply reflect the religious and political climate at the time of the play's run but through the process of its performance helped create the brief moment of intra-Protestant solidarity that followed the collapse of the Spanish Match, a proposed marriage alliance between Prince Charles and the Spanish infanta. Whether they invite confessional curiosity or incite sectarian violence, plays are not passive receptacles of existing ideology but are instead semiautonomous instruments for the reorganization of public feeling.

As multiple extant reports from contemporaries indicate, *A Game at Chess* orchestrated broadly aligned responses from subgroups of Protestants. The play gathers Protestant factions in the large tent of the "White House" by addressing its diverse playgoers as one half of a religious binary, and by engaging that imagined collective in the shared work of surveillance. The monolithic Protestantism invoked in the play should not be mistaken for a fixed, a priori social reality but rather recognized as contingent not only on historical context but also on its cultural representation. Of course, the play does not summon into being a uniform religious group. Theater is not ideologically totalizing. The large and detailed archive of audience responses shows that while *A Game at Chess* consolidated Protestant sentiment, it also prompted divided responses from various Catholic subgroups, with some perceptions shared across the spectrum of both Churches. The fact that *A Game at Chess* actually endangers Catholic people, by instructing the Protestant crowd to seize on papists exiting the playhouse, sets a constraint on the degree to which theatrical feeling can be shared across the Catholic-Protestant divide. Yet, even with the threat of physical violence, some Catholic playgoers took pleasure in an alternative experience of the play, in which papist villainy registers as political savvy. These multiple extant reactions to *A Game at Chess* show the complex ideological architecture that is formed through the intersections of preexisting identity positions and the imaginative processes of performance. These responses demonstrate the capacity of live drama to both gather and divide feeling within a mixed-faith audience. They illustrate the interwoven pulls of cultural perspective and theatrical pleasure that are the warp and weft of playhouse experience.

Obviously, *A Game at Chess* did not produce a social moment of intra-Protestant reconciliation by itself. Other forms of cultural expression drew Protestants together in 1623–24, including the street celebrations welcoming home Prince Charles. Godly polemicists adopted an amenable tone. Puritan Thomas Scott wrote in praise of his previous factional enemy, the Arminian George Villiers, Duke of Buckingham: "Who did not [before] expect his suddain withering againe with wishes? But now who doth not look upon him as upon an Oake or Cedar sound at the heart, like to last long and be profitable to the upholding of Church and State."[3] The frontispiece of godly Scott's *Vox Dei* shows Buckingham destroying "faction." The collapse of the Spanish Match fostered conciliatory feeling among Protestants: "The King and the people goe all on and together . . . as the like hath not been seen these many yeeares."[4] The fact that this sense of relative harmony among English Protestants cannot be taken as a normal state of affairs is evident from prior and ensuing factional conflict.[5] Yet this brief time of intra-Protestant solidarity was not due to the changed circumstances of international diplomacy alone but was also produced by the ways early modern Londoners themselves narrativized this new set of religious and political conditions. Ordinary people were responding not just to events but also to other popular responses. While the play was, of course, not the sole force affecting religious and political public sentiment at this time, the imaginative work of the stage helped assemble confessional feeling. The distinctive theatrical techniques of *A Game at Chess* orchestrate the attention of theatergoers into collective Protestant vigilance. More than simply recording the religious climate, the play's imaginative process had a visible cultural effect.

Contemporaries recognized the impact of *A Game at Chess* as a public event. Playing over nine days to a capacity of three thousand playgoers, *A Game at Chess* could have been seen by as many as twenty-seven thousand people, more than one-tenth of the population of London.[6] As one letter writer reports, "I doubt not but you have heard of our famous play of Gondomar, which has been followed with extraordinarie concourse, and frequented by all sorts of people old and younge, rich and poore, masters and servants, *papists and puritans*, wise men et[c] churchmen and statesmen . . . and a world besides."[7] The fact that so many people saw the play within a short period of time could have expanded a sense of simultaneous social experience beyond the playhouse, creating a feeling that *A Game at Chess* was "something happening" not just in the theater but also in the city. Simply the fact that this was a break from normal repertory practice called attention to the play's daringly explicit treatment of religious and political content, generating buzz among theater-goers: "The Players looseth no tyme, nor forbeareth to make haye while the Sunn shineth, acting it every day without any intermission and it is thought they have already gott neere a thousand pound by it."[8] Not simply about current events, the play itself was news. So many records of playgoers' responses to *A Game at Chess* exist because it was so widely discussed. Manuscript presentation copies of the play were in demand before it finished its run.[9] *A Game at Chess* focalized a short honeymoon period among English Protestants; its imaginative structure extends from the stage through the playhouse and helped shape broader public feeling. Because of its demonstrable impact, *A Game at Chess* offers a concentrated example of the culturally formative work of shared theatrical experience.

Scholarship on *A Game at Chess* has largely sought to identify the real historical people and events represented by particular chess pieces and plot points, or to trace the play's polemical print sources.[10] In other words, critics have focused on *A Game at Chess*'s religious and political content: what the play says, not what it does. Relatively little attention has been paid to the religious and political effects of the play's form.[11] In contrast, my interest is not so much in the play's didactic lessons (which are obvious) as in the dialectic interactions with playgoers through which these lessons are produced. Scholars have misrecognized the theatricality of *A Game at Chess* as crowd-pleasing entertainment, irrelevant to its religious and political substance.[12] The focus on identifying allegorical figures has sometimes made the theatrical texture of *A Game at Chess* into a discardable husk: the "vehicle" of metaphor in the narrowest sense, something merely carrying, rather than creating, meaning.[13] Yet the process of the play's performance is itself politically and confessionally formative. As Raymond Williams writes, "We cannot think of communication as secondary. We cannot think of it . . . as something that happens after reality has occurred; because it is through the communication systems that the reality of ourselves, the reality of our society, forms and is interpreted."[14]

Contemporaries who recorded performances of *A Game at Chess* recognized that it put *arcana imperii* on stage more explicitly than any other play in the period. However, the topic of the play—the recently collapsed negotiations for a marriage alliance between England and Spain—was already widely canvassed in pamphlets, sermons, and other popular media. *A Game at Chess* did not disseminate new religious and political information. Ordinary Londoners were already familiar with the play's key points: that the match had been recognized as a Spanish Catholic scheme to control and convert England but was no longer a live political issue; that Jesuits were sneaky, and Spain remained dangerous; and that the architect of the failed alliance, former Spanish ambassador Count Gondomar, was a Machiavel with an anal fistula. Yet reports of the play register a feeling of immediacy ("they show to the life") and a vivid sense of uncovering ("the whole Spanish busines is ripped up to the quicke").[15] This qualitative experience of seeing religious and political machinations exposed is generated partly by the revealed content of *A Game at Chess*, but also crucially by its theatrical form. The process of revelation orchestrated by dramatic technique entrains playgoers to think and feel as a public. As Paul Yachnin writes, "To be a member of a public is not only to take a lively interest in . . . [matters of] religion, but also to cultivate an awareness of oneself engaging with others publicly in cultural work and social action."[16] *A Game at Chess* is a "public event" not only because of the secrets of state it presents to the audience, or the size of the crowds it drew, but also because the play's formal unfolding engages playgoers in the activity of being a politically and confessionally discerning public.

The Topical Context and Allegorical Identifications

The subject of *A Game at Chess* was unmistakable to contemporaries: "[It] describes Gondomar and all the Spanish proceedings very boldly and broadly."[17] The play dramatizes the recently failed negotiations for the wildly unpopular proposed marriage between Prince Charles and the Spanish infanta. During the previous seven years of diplomatic talks toward the possible union, it was James I's hope that an alliance with Spain would resolve the conflict with the Hapsburgs in the Palatine, thus restoring the exiled "Winter Queen" Elizabeth Stuart to the throne of Bohemia.[18] England's activist Protestant wing opposed James's pacifist plan and advocated war with Spain in cheap print and from the pulpits throughout the early 1620s, prompting two ineffective royal proclamations forbidding discussion of the issue. The pro-war, anti-Spanish pamphlets, such as Scott's *Vox Populi* (1620), that continued to circulate in spite of state censorship provided much of the source material for Middleton's play.

To the horror of most English Protestants, in February 1623 Charles and the Duke of Buckingham traveled to Spain disguised as "Jack and Tom Smith" to woo the infanta in person. It was widely feared that Charles would not return alive. Negotiations in Madrid were a fiasco. Neither side was willing to breach the impasse on the two key issues in question: restoration of the

Palatine and toleration for English Catholics. Interpersonal conflicts soured diplomatic talks. In order to leave Madrid without incident, Charles agreed in bad faith to all the Spanish conditions.[19] Once safely back in England, Charles and Buckingham reversed their former position, joining the anti-Spanish, pro-war faction at court. The official and widely accepted version of events, peddled by Buckingham on their return, was that, all along, "the journey was a desperate stratagem for opening James' eyes to the Spaniards' true intentions."[20]

On October 5, 1623, huge crowds of Londoners flooded the streets, ringing bells and pulling down wooden signs for bonfires, to welcome Prince Charles when he returned from Madrid, still single and still Protestant.[21] This massive enthusiastic outpouring of popular support signaled the beginning of a short honeymoon period among English Protestants, following what was understood as Charles's providential deliverance from Catholic Spain's clutches. The minimal punishment the King's Men received for *A Game at Chess*'s illegal representation of living monarchs on the stage demonstrates the permissive and confessionally conciliatory atmosphere of August 1624. One contemporary observes that had the players "donne [this] last yeare, they had everyman been hanged for it."[22] As others have recognized, *A Game at Chess* was far from a piece of "opposition drama."[23] My point is to stress the role of the play's theatrical form in helping to consolidate shared Protestant feeling.

The message of *A Game at Chess* was clear: "The descant [is] *that the* Jesuits mark is to bring all *the* Christian world under Rome for *the* [spirituality] & under Spayn for *the* temporalty."[24] The play's stark moral, religious, and political commentary is blatant in the allegorical frame: a chess match in which English Protestants are white and Spanish Catholics are black. Three interlaced plots repeat one basic story: deliverance from the threat of Charles's marriage to the infanta and conversion to Catholicism. In the first story arc, the White Queen's Pawn (a pious, Protestant "Everywoman" or, more abstractly, the true faith of the Church of England) is tempted to convert, then threatened with rape, by the Jesuit Black Bishop's Pawn. When she attempts to expose the truth to the court, she is prevented by a Black House conspiracy but redeemed by a clever trap laid by the White Knight (Charles) and White Duke (Buckingham), who are not fooled by the deceit. In the next sequence of action, the Jesuitess Black Queen's Pawn shows the White Queen's Pawn an image of her promised husband in a deceptive magic mirror, thereby luring her into a false marriage contract with the Jesuit Black Bishop's Pawn, disguised as a gentleman. However, the Jesuitess contrives a bed trick for her own pleasure, allowing the White Queen's Pawn to escape with her chastity intact. Finally, in the third plot arc, the White Knight and White Duke travel to the Black House, feigning friendship as a ploy to expose the Spanish Jesuit plot for world domination—just as Charles and Buckingham claimed they had embarked on the wooing expedition to Madrid in order to thwart the Spanish court's duplicitous dealings. As Jane Sherman observes, "Middleton used the pawns' plot to tell, far more candidly, the *same* story [as the White Knight and Duke's] plot."[25] While the White Knight and White Duke's journey to the Black House maps most literally onto a specific sequence of diplomatic events, this episode mentions neither conversion nor marriage, whereas the dangers of these potential transformations are central—and reinforced by being conflated—in the White Queen's Pawn's story lines.[26] As a contemporary observes, the play "give[s] several representations under different names of many of the circumstances about the marriage with the Infanta."[27]

Historical personages of the Black House are individuated far more explicitly than White House pieces, making them the primary targets of scrutiny. In other words, the play only registers in passing the English court intrigues, and intra-Protestant tensions, that have often preoccupied critics. Rather, the representational resources of *A Game at Chess* are deployed in a sustained burlesque of Jesuits and the Spanish.[28] This formal emphasis shaped audience experience. That is, contemporaries understood that *A Game at Chess* devotes its energies primarily to skewering Catholic Spain by satirizing its individual representatives. As a Spanish embassy official complains, "They hardly shewed anything but the cruelty of Spain and the treachery of Spaniards, and all this was set forth so personally."[29] Nearly every contemporary commentator identifies Gondomar, the Black Knight, as the central role, several referring to the piece simply by his name.[30]

The caricature of the Spanish ambassador struck observers as an unusually specific impersonation: "They counterfeited his person to the life, with all his graces and faces."[31] To make the imitation of the former ambassador more overt, the company bought Gondomar's own clothes for the player's costume, as well as his infamous litter, and reproduced his notorious "chair of ease"—the latter two both specially designed to accommodate his anal fistula. The second most frequently identified figure is the turncoat Fat Bishop as multiple convert Marc Antonio de Dominis, a role assumed by the clown William Rowley, a key performer in the company. In short, the King's Men devoted significant stage resources to foregrounding Black House targets, and this emphasis is reflected in the records of audience reception. By comparison, the White King's Pawn and White Duke speak fourteen and thirty-six

lines, respectively, but these figures have attracted disproportionate critical attention.[32] Yet the primary theatrical thrill *A Game at Chess* offers audiences is
not determining whether the White King's Pawn stands for Tobie Matthew
or Lionel Cranfield. Doubtless, parsing these finer points of court politics was
of interest to some playgoers; as one remarks, "Every particular will bear large
paraphrase."[33] Yet the kind of decoding that has preoccupied scholars faced
with a page of speech headings in chess shorthand (WK, WKn, WKnp, WKp,
BB, BBp) is not the same interpretive activity in which the play in performance
engages theatergoers. The attempt to fill in all parts of the allegory with equal
precision distorts one of the play's most crucial and sustained effects: zoom-
ing in on the personal satire of Spanish Catholics while leaving in soft focus
tensions among Protestant factions. The central imaginative work of *A Game
at Chess* is not to involve audiences in elaborate rounds of pin-the-historical-
tail-on-the-allegorical-donkey. The identifications that matter are clear. The
pleasure of the play in performance is the excess of representational labor that
goes into its tub-thumping, ideological clarity. *A Game at Chess* directs the
attention of playgoers to track imbalances of religious and political knowledge, both on stage and in the theater. The game it asks audiences to play is
less often "Who is who?" than "Who knows what?"

The Game of Discovering the Obvious

Knowledge is the site of contest between England and Spain in the play. Unlike its closest formal analogue, Thomas Dekker's religious and political allegory *The Whore of Babylon* (1606), in which papist henchmen with knives
and guns make repeated attempts to kill Elizabeth I, Middleton's *A Game at
Chess* figures Catholic menace not in terms of violence but as secret machinations. When Gondomar, the Black Knight, discusses the possible military conquest of England by Spain, he does not talk about actual fighting but gives an
unsettling description of his espionage:

> I . . . *learned* the depth
> of all their channels, *knowledge* of all sands
>   and rivers, for invasion properest
> A *catalogue* of all the navy royal
> . . . .

The *number* of the men . . .
         for the *discovery* of the inlands,
Never a shire but the state *better known*
to me than to her . . . inhabitants. (4.2.62–70, italics mine)

The danger to England is not the size of the Spanish army but the extent of the Spanish ambassador's information. The allegorical frame thickens the emphasis on espionage, since chess was understood as an elite game of strategy that developed skills of statecraft.[34] Spanish villains in *A Game at Chess* carry not weapons but letters of intelligence. Secrets are key to religious conflict in the play. As the Jesuitess puts it, "Knowledge is a mastery" (4.1.43). The Jesuit Black Bishop's Pawn's primary strategy to ensnare the pious, Protestant White Queen's Pawn is to learn her "privat'st thought that runs to hide itself / In the most secret corner" through confession (1.1.123–24). In this story line, as in those that follow, the control of knowledge has religious and political stakes. More to the point, the mastery of secrets in *A Game at Chess* is not simply the subject of the plot but a theatrical process that involves the whole playhouse.

From the induction, Protestant playgoers are enlisted as active, partisan participants in the geopolitical and eschatological struggle for knowledge that is the subject of the allegory. Their playhouse perceptions are part of the game. Ignatius Loyola's deictic opening line collapses the dramatic place of the play into the real English (or "Anglo") space of the theater: "What *angle* of the world is *this*?" (induction, line 1, italics mine). Looking out at the mixed-faith audience, he integrates them into the play as a uniformly Protestant group: "I can neither see [nor smell] . . . any of my disciples" (induction, lines 2–4). Loyola's speech engages Protestant audience members' penetrating sight in the religious and political conflict staged in the play. Spectators' eyes are a system of national defense. As Loyola explains, the reason swarms of Jesuits have not "made dark the land [of England]" is that "Here's too much light appears shot from the eyes / Of truth and goodness never yet deflowered" (induction, lines 7, 9–10). In allegorical terms, the upshot is that England is not Catholic because it is Protestant. However, Loyola's "here" is the theater, and "the eyes of truth" are the eyes of the playgoers looking back at him. The mutual visibility of direct address in the induction establishes a dynamic in which spectators' piercing sight affects the game. The audiences' visual policing is what keeps the Jesuit locusts out of the playhouse, and out of England.

It is rarely difficult for playgoers to see what nefarious schemes against Protestant England are hatching in *A Game at Chess*. To the contrary, Black House characters announce the secret plot for Spanish and Jesuit world domination at every possible opportunity. Within the first hundred lines of the first scene, when asked by the White Queen's Pawn what Jesuits do all day, the Black Queen's Pawn informs her outright that they "principally aim at . . . universal monarchy" (1.1.52, 51), elaborating that Jesuit spies lurk "in many courts and palaces," reporting back "important secrets" (1.1.53, 60). Black House pieces in *A Game at Chess* reveal their own secrets so compulsively that Gondomar cannot even hide an erection:

> Venery!
> If I but hug thee hard I show the worse on't. (5.3.126)

The interpretive challenge is not discerning an ambiguous danger but keeping abreast of the play's techniques of highlighting the obviousness of the Spanish Catholic threat.[35]

Audiences are repeatedly shown conspicuously hidden arcana. In scene 2.1, Black House characters read aloud letters from a neatly labeled "cabinet of intelligences" before destroying the evidence to avoid detection (2.1.88). Here, Protestant playgoers are given knowledge that is pointedly inaccessible to their White House counterparts. The cabinet is brought onstage and the filing system described in detail. Audiences watch Black House figures rifle through the bundles, reading aloud at random the details of various nefarious plots. This fantasy of total access ends with the direction to "scorch me 'em soundly burn 'em to French russet and put 'em in again . . .'twill mock the adversary strangely (2.1.216–18). Tauntingly burning the letters just past legibility emphasizes the secrecy of what the audience has seen, making playgoers' theatrical experience fill the gaps left by the more limited awareness of White House figures in the play.

Similarly, references to the "great work" of Spanish Jesuit world domination that recur throughout the dialogue are heavy-handedly framed. Placement as the first lines of the Black Knight's first entrance underscores the baldness of his declaration of progress on the plot for world conquest:

> So, so,
> The business of the universal monarchy
> Goes forward well now. (1.1.242–44)

Like the lab mice in the children's cartoon *Pinky and the Brain* who doggedly "try to take over the world" each night, the script returns to this refrain a few lines later when the Black Knight asks the Black Bishop's Pawn for an update:

> But what for the main work, the great existence,
> The hope monarchal? (1.1.290–91)

The display of letters of intelligence about to be made illegible and the continual declaration of conspiracy both make secrecy conspicuous. Alan C. Dessen describes such devices as "theatrical italics" that heighten audience attention.[36] In *A Game at Chess*, playgoers' pleasure is often less about getting the joke and more about getting how blatantly the joke is staged. The Protestant audiences' task of monitoring the Black House baddies is not so much hard as hypertheatrical.

Characters sharing the stage in *A Game at Chess* almost never possess equal knowledge. The continuous activity with which the audience is charged is to track imbalances in levels of awareness, so that the keen-eyed Protestant collective in the playhouse maintains the dominant perspective. Asides are the primary device through which the play engages theatergoers in tracking gaps in knowledge. Asides are delivered most frequently, though far from exclusively, by Black House pieces. As Jeremy Lopez points out, "[When] information comes in the form of asides [it can make] the character's duplicity more evident."[37] Often, the play presents competing, or "contrapuntal," asides that invite "an active quest for a point of view more comprehensive than the limited . . . perspective[s] onstage."[38] Sometimes, these asides are juxtaposed so that characters from the Black and White Houses express conflicting views, as when the White Bishop's Pawn and Black Knight's Pawn enter in succession from their opposing houses and each assess the scene they observe: the Jesuit's attempt to convert and seduce the White Queen's Pawn. In speeches marked by anaphora and parallel phrasing, the White Bishop's Pawn expresses confidence in her pious chastity, whereas the Black Knight's Pawn casually assumes her corruption (1.1.195–210). There is no ambiguity as to who is good and who is bad. Yet the heavy-handedness of the counterpoint elicits heightened attention. These addresses ask playgoers to adopt a self-conscious, master perspective that encompasses, and can toggle between, conflicting positions onstage. The challenge for audiences is not to discern subtleties but to keep up with the representational work of belaboring the obvious. As Lopez puts it, "Surprise is . . . beside the point: [the effect is] to make you aware of what everyone else is missing, and to make you feel as a result that you are getting everything."[39] The mental activity engaged is not simply to follow the intrigues of the plot; rather, the play's complex structures of layered address cultivate audiences' attention to their own attention.

Characters in *A Game at Chess* repeatedly observe and assess each other in asides that compete for dominance. One affordance of the "early entrance," as Dessen describes the device, is that "figures . . . can size up a situation before others onstage are aware of their presence."[40] At the Black Knight's first entrance, he criticizes the Black Bishop's Pawn, who is at work on the unsuspecting White Queen's Pawn, calling attention to the shift in his own acting when the Jesuit's notice prompts him to change his demeanor:

> He spies me now, I must uphold his reverence,
> Especially in public. (1.1.267–68)

By playing up to the audience his own distance from the false display of piety that he and the Jesuit are performing for the benefit of the clueless Protestant Everywoman, he highlights the three layers of awareness onstage, and the power relations they structure, among the Black House superior, his lackey, and their dupe.

Sympathy for the Machiavel; or, The Affective Limitations of an Anal Fistula

For almost the entire play, Gondomar is the character whose privileged knowledge gives him mastery over others onstage, putting him in a position of intimacy vis-à-vis the audience. As in the scene described previously, his asides circumscribe and dominate others. Gondomar is a stage Machiavel in the tradition of Richard III, a charming monster who lets the audience share in his secrets and in the pleasures of his histrionic manipulations of others. *A Game at Chess* spotlights the chief schemer's usual mastery of knowledge when the Black Knight alone detects that the Jesuitess's feigned support of the White Queen's Pawn is really another plot against her. He crows:

> Did I not say 'twas craft and machination?
> I smelt conspiracy all the way it went
> Although the mess were covered, I'm so used to it. (3.1.241–43)

However, at the end of the play Gondomar's position is reversed. The play reconfigures the structure of dramatic irony to give White House characters the upper hand at the Black Knight's expense. The Machiavel's defeat is metatheatrical, accomplished by undermining his mastery not only in the plot but also in performance.

In his first appearance onstage, the Black Knight announces that he achieves his religious and political schemes through his magnetism as a performer, and he cautions audiences not to be taken in by his skill as an entertainer:

> And what I have done, I have done facetiously,
> With pleasant subtlety and bewitching courtship,
> Abused all my believers with delight;
> They took a comfort to be cozened by me.
> To many a soul I have let in mortal poison
> Whose cheeks have cracked with laughter to receive it;
> I could so roll my pills in sugared syllables
> And strew such kindly mirth o'er all my mischiefs,
> They took their bane in way of recreation
> As pleasure steals corruption into youth. (1.1.257–66)

The first thing the Black Knight tells audience members about himself is that laughing along with him will deceive and destroy them when they are most enjoying it. Gondomar's metatheatrical warning takes up the common trope in antitheatrical writing of denouncing the stage as a dangerously delicious drug.[41] Stephen Gosson compares the theater to "the deceitful Phisition [who] giveth sweete Syrropes to make his poyson goe downe the smoother."[42] The antitheatricalist laments that audiences "are so asotted with these delightes . . . and drunken with the sweetnes of these vanities."[43] Associating himself with the dangers of the stage, the Black Knight correlates positive audience responses to him as a performer with the success of his religious and political machinations—again collapsing the game between playgoers and actors into the game played onstage.

Like Richard III's withered arm, the script's persistent reference to Gondomar's anal fistula is a device that regulates playgoers' pleasurable intimacy with the silver-tongued Machiavel. Despite Gondomar's boast that his "leaking bottom" has not kept him from being "often tossed on Venus' seas," the gross-out factor has a distancing effect (2.1.173–74). The use of the fistula to

THE SECOND PART OF VOX POPVLI,
or
Gondomar appearing in the likenes of
Matchiauell in a Spanish Parliament,
wherein are discouered his treacherous & subtile Practises
To the ruine as well of England, as the Netherlandes.
Faithfully Tranflated out of the Spanish Coppie by a well-willer
to England and Holland.

Simul Complectar omnia

Gentis Hispanæ decus

Printed at Goricom by Afhuerus Jansf.
1624. Stilo nouo.

Figure 3. Count Gondomar, the Spanish ambassador, with his infamous chair and coach, both specially designed to accommodate his anal fistula. Thomas Scott, *The Second Part of Vox Dei* (London, 1625), Folger Shakespeare Library.

alienate audience affiliation from Gondomar is most explicit in the scene featuring the "chair of ease"—the King's Men's reproduction of the special seat designed with a hole to accommodate the discomfort of the ambassador's anal complaint. It is clear from a contemporary woodcut that this piece of furniture was visually identical to a privy.[44] Scott describes Gondomar's "chaire" as "the true sworne brother, or at least the nearest kinsman that might be to a close stoole."[45] The phrase "chair of ease" points to the synonym for a privy, "house of easement."[46] Critics have noted the prop's importance in terms of intensifying the personal satire of the ambassador, but they have not explored the effects it produces as part of the scene in which it is introduced. Gondomar's fistula chair is not a one-off visual gag that identifies and insults the ambassador and then becomes a mere background object. To adapt Anton Chekhov's maxim that when a gun is introduced into a play it must be fired, I propose that when a toilet is brought onstage there must be farts. The scene's extended scatological humor undercuts Gondomar's conspiratorial disclosures to the audience, as well as the position of power they give him.

A contemporary reports that Gondomar, "seated on his chair with a hole in it . . . confessed all the treacherous actions with which he had deceived and soothed the king of the whites."[47] This blocking for the long speeches in which Gondomar reveals his villainy, correlates the Black Knight's anal and verbal incontinence. For most of the play, Gondomar controls the stage; here, he cannot control his sphincter. In *A Chaste Maid in Cheapside*, Middleton similarly connects the gossips' unrestrained speech with their leaky bladders. The women cannot keep their secrets, and they leave a puddle of urine onstage.[48] *A Game at Chess* does not relegate the fistula jokes to the realm of abstract insult; rather, the insistent physicality of Gondomar's oozing anus activates the flatulence puns (largely variations on "wind") that fill the dialogue. The Black Knight's Pawn punctuates his master's disclosures with scatological one-liners. When Gondomar declares, "I feel no *tempest*, not a *leaf-wind* stirring / To shake a fault; conscience is becalmed," the servant replies, "I'm sure there is a *whirlwind huffs* in mine, sir" (4.2.38–40, italics mine). The pawn returns to the fistula when he comments on one of the Black Knight's successful plots: "Sure you put oil of toad into that physic, sir," referencing a remedy "very good against evil ulcers" (4.2.76).[49] Gondomar refers to selling the office of "groom of the stool" (4.2.41). These jokes, and the toilet-humor stage business that accompanies them, alienate audiences from Gondomar's "filthy" boasting of his religious and political deceptions.[50] The "chair of ease" scene in *A Game at Chess* makes Gondomar's religious and political disclosures a repellent form of logorrhea.

The Black Knight's Pawn's responses to the Black Knight's flatulence guide the reactions of playgoers. Much of what makes the scene funny is the way Gondomar's oral and anal emissions nauseate his lackey. Immediately after the Black Knight settles onto the privy, ("O soft and gentle, sirrah! / There's a foul flaw in the bottom of my [bum], Pawn"), he observes that his assistant looks sickly: "How now, qualm? / Thou hast the pukingest soul that e'er I met with" (4.2.6–7, 9–10).[51] T. H. Howard-Hill glosses "qualm" as "one stricken by conscience," instead of the more literal meaning of a sensation of vomiting or fainting—obviously appropriate responses to whatever "ease" the Black Knight is giving his fistula. The servant's "pukingest" reactions function as a kind of silent, or gestural, aside to the audience. The pawn does not just model disgust for playgoers. He opens a plane of superior awareness between himself and the audience that Gondomar does not share.

The scene gives the longest and most detailed declaration of Gondomar's plots (including the plan for invasion) and marks a turning point in the audiences' relationship with the Black Knight. In terms of both secrets of state and bodily secretions, it makes public what is most privy. Yet the effect here is that the pleasure of sharing superior knowledge, which Gondomar's earlier monologues and asides invite, is made repulsive.[52] As the Black Knight's Pawn's reactions suggest, this moment of fistula-and-all intimacy creates distance between the ambassador and his confidants, both onstage and in the playhouse. Or, more precisely, Gondomar's anal disclosures make proximity disgusting. Getting up close and personal with the close stool makes quasi-complicit intimacy with the Machiavel too close for comfort. From here to the end of the play, the Black Knight loses his charismatic sway over other characters within the drama, as well as his privileged theatrical position vis-à-vis the audience as the figure most in the know—ultimately finding himself the butt of the joke.

Scholars often inaccurately describe the plot of *A Game at Chess* as culminating in the discovery of Black House treachery by the White Knight and White Duke, in a way that implies these plots are not detected by others in the White House until finally unmasked.[53] Actually, that is not what happens in the play. The difference at the climax is not that all the White House characters are finally aware of Black House duplicity. To the contrary, *A Game at Chess* devotes a whole emotional scene to stressing the White King and White Queen's foreknowledge of the White Duke and White Knight's plan to expose the Black House. This last scene with White House court figures before the final "discovery!" of the Black House insists that the White King is a knowing participant in the plan.[54] This is a massive revision of actual historical circumstances, one that goes far further than Buckingham's own "relation" of diplomatic events in erasing internal conflict among Protestants. By making James in on the plot, the play retroactively denies the existence of a pro-Spanish party within the English court altogether.

The difference, then, in the ultimate scene of "discovery!" is not that Spanish Jesuit deceit is finally recognized by the White House; rather, it is that for the first time in the play, Gondomar is on the business end of the scene's dramatic irony. From the opening of 4.4, in which the White Knight and White Duke establish their scheme to insinuate themselves into the Black House in order to expose Spanish Jesuit deceptions, they control the action and occupy a dominant position onstage through their superior knowledge. For the first time in the play, the scene gives White House pieces the advantage of the "early entrance"; the White Duke assesses Gondomar before he sees them: "Look . . . In yonder smile sits . . . treachery [and] face-falsehood" (4.4.15–16). The climactic scene in the Black court is, in a sense, an acting contest. The White Knight emphasizes that he and the Duke are adopting Gondomar's tactics, "for truth to feign a little" (4.4.16–17). The Black Knight's attempts to ensnare the English heir are again presented in terms of entertainment:

> Can you mistrust
> Any foul play in me [?] . . .
> . . . .
> How often have I changed for your delight
> . . . .
> Into a mimic jester, and become
> . . . .
> a light son of pastime
> a tomboy, a mere wanton?
> . . . .
> I will change
> To any shape to please you. (4.4.20–33)

Describing Gondomar's machinations as amusing performances metatheatrically correlates the Black Knight's charm onstage with his religious and political success. But by the end of the play, the court wit has become a bore. The Black Queen apologizes to her White House guests for the ambassador's long-windedness: "He'll raise of anything" (5.3.55–56). Whereas earlier in

A Game at Chess, the Black Knight's verbal dexterity is a sign of his theatrical and political mastery, here his failed attempts to delight his listeners index his lack of awareness. Audiences' knowledge of the plot puts them in on the joke of the White Knight's laconic replies to Gondomar's waning charm.

The White Knight strings the Black Knight along, feigning faults to elicit declarations of Spanish Catholic villainies. In the climactic entrapment of the dialogue, the White Knight announces:

> The hidden'st venom,
> The secret'st poison: I'm an arch-dissembler sir. (5.3.144–45)

He repeats his declaration a moment later:

> The time is yet to come that e'er I spoke
> What my heart meant! (5.3.147–48)

These lines tease the audience, building attention to their knowledge of the White Knight's deception and pointing up the Black Knight's failure to recognize the impending "discovery!"—even when he is told the White House trick directly. Essentially, the punch line of the joke (that the White Knight is lying to him) has to be repeated three times before Gondomar gets it. This crucial scene hinges on the Black Knight's loss of stage mastery, achieved through a reversal of dramatic irony. The Black House pieces are finally all bagged not because of a diegetic change (characters learning new facts) but because of a theatrical one, in which the audience plays a key role. The awareness that playgoers share with the White Knight and White Duke holds taut the net of superior knowledge that ensnares Gondomar.

However, while the overwhelming majority of records of response identify Gondomar as the primary target skewered in *A Game at Chess*, several contemporaries also register an alternative experience of the Machiavel's engaging duplicity. Florentine ambassador Amerigo Salvetti recognizes the play's focus on the full disclosure of "all the exploits of Gondomar . . . not leaving anything out, . . . [that] would reveal them, so they describe his machinations and falsehoods with so much applause." But Salvetti also arrives at the subversive conclusion that "they cannot tear Gondomar so much by revealing his fashion of dealing, without depicting him as a man of worth, consequently reflecting weakness on those that gave him credence, and that daily dealt with him."[55] Similarly, eyewitness John Holles, Lord Haughton, describes at length the play's "full discovery of all [Spanish Catholic] knaveries," but he also observes that by showing how Gondomar "set the Kings affayrs as a clock, backward & forward, made him believe & unbelieue as stood best with his busines," the play was "no great honor to England."[56] In this interpretation, the play's exposure of Gondomar's manipulations has the side effect of presenting the English king and court as his gullible dupes. Notably, this counter reading is not simply the product of the bias of a particular confessional subset of playgoers. Rather, it is a view available to both the Catholic ambassador and Protestant nobleman. The basis of this alternative experience of the play is not the preexisting ideological disposition of the viewer but the complex pleasures of engagement with the Machiavel that *A Game at Chess* offers.

Protecting the White Queen's Pawn; or, The Spatialization of Awareness

The protective attention of Protestant audiences is enlisted on behalf of the White Queen's Pawn, as playgoers are continually called on to detect dangers of which the Church of England Everywoman is blithely ignorant. In this way, playgoers' awareness is oriented vis-à-vis the pretty face of true religion in a formally elaborate version of a panto "Look behind you!" From the beginning, audience members are positioned as the "eyes" of the Protestant ingénue, not only through the terms of the metaphor but also through their engagement with the stage. A contemporary report conflates the characters of Ignatius Loyola and the Jesuit Black Bishop's Pawn. This suggests that the same actor doubled as Loyola in the induction and as one of his own disciples in the play proper: "[When] St. Ignatius from Hell . . . found himself again in the world, the first thing he did was to rape one of his female penitents."[57] In the induction, the Father General of the Jesuits menacingly addresses playgoers as the "eyes of truth and goodness never yet deflowered," then reappears as the Jesuit, who spends two-thirds of the play trying to deflower the White Queen's Pawn, who represents truth and goodness. The continuity that doubling creates between the two villains connects those they accost: Protestant playgoers and the White Queen's Pawn. Protecting the White Queen's Pawn persists as a primary mental and emotional activity in which *A Game at Chess* involves its audiences.

Much of the play's humor derives from the dramatic irony in the gap between the White Queen's Pawn's perceptions and those of playgoers, wherein she is the naïve, but sympathetic, foil to the audience's more sophisticated awareness. In the opening scene, the innocent White Queen's Pawn fails to recognize the Jesuitess's fake crying as playacting:

> They're tears plainly.
> Beshrew me if she weep not heartily. (1.1.7–8)

The joke establishes that the audience can identify histrionics that the White Queen's Pawn cannot. The theatrical risk that the Everywoman's obliviousness will simply make her a rube is countered by the emotional depth the play gives her, through the backstory of her thwarted engagement to the White Bishop's Pawn and through her interiorizing monologues. The Jesuit's onstage attempt to rape the White Queen's Pawn generates audience sympathy, as does her powerful, and thwarted, denunciation of her attacker before the court:

> Through my alone discovery
> . . . .
> I bring into your knowledge through my sufferings
> . . . .
> The absolut'st abuser of true sanctity
>   can be found
> In any part of the universal globe. (2.2.107, 112–14)

Her metatheatrical "globe" reference anticipates the ways the White Queen's Pawn will, with increasing explicitness, call on Protestant playgoers to extend their vigilance on her behalf beyond the stage, through the social space of the theater itself. The heroine provides a focalizing point that not only orients the Protestant audience's sympathy but also galvanizes their attention to the stage into a form of confessional and political activity.

Much of the danger the White Queen's Pawn faces relates to the way knowledge controls theatrical space in *A Game at Chess*. In the play's opening gambit, the Jesuitess and White Queen's Pawn enter the stage from their respective houses. The Black Queen's Pawn pseudosoliloquizes her grief at seeing such a beauty damned as a heretic. Pretending to think herself out of earshot, the Jesuitess speaks to be overheard, until the White Queen's Pawn enters her range of address. Even if the White Queen's Pawn does not physically move, she still has been lured "closer." It is as if the Black Queen's Pawn lays the space of earshot like a trap that she tricks the White Queen's Pawn into entering by pretending to be herself outside it. Throughout the play, the Jesuitess has an especially masterful relation to space, which corresponds to her privileged knowledge.[58]

Because asides affect the relationship between stage space and imagined place—opening a plane of shared awareness between the character speaking and the audience, one that is separate from other characters nearby—they have serious implications in the action of the chess game, in which pieces are taken by proximity.[59] This dangerous closeness is achieved in the play not by frontal assault but by catching someone unawares.[60] Characters are "taken" in the sense both of being gulled and of being seized simultaneously. For example, the spatial stakes of awareness create tension in the scene in which Gondomar delivers a forged letter from the pope, tempting the archbishop to revert to the Roman Church (a stage moment illustrated in the quarto engravings).[61] Onstage, as soon as the characters are close enough for the Fat Bishop to take the letter from Gondomar's hand, de Dominis insists the Black Knight keep away and references the threat to himself as a chess bishop:

Pray keep your side and distance. I am chary
Of my episcopal person. (3.1.26–28)

In this instant of dangerous proximity, the balance of knowledge and power shifts. It is when the Fat Bishop is physically close enough to take the epistolary bait that he falls for the Machiavel's trick. Similarly, the duplicitous White King's Pawn switches to the Black House by conscious choice, without immediate punishment; but he is "bagged" at the very moment he is tricked by the Black Knight's double cross.[62] Even the crudest slapstick sequence of chess play hinges on uneven stage knowledge. The White Pawn sneaks up on the Black Jesting Pawn ("Were you so near? I'm taken"), only to fail to "look well about" himself, and thus be "snapped too" by a Second Black Pawn (3.3.9, 29, 31). In this play, a lapse of attention will "firk" you.

A Game at Chess activates the affordances of theatrical space in the contest to master secrets. It is likely that the Globe's stage was painted as a chessboard for the run of the play. Though it cannot be assumed to directly record a stage picture, the title page illustration in both Q2 and Q3 shows the Black Knight and Fat Bishop standing with a chessboard at their feet.[63] More persuasive is the eyewitness description that "the whole play is a chess board"— not a chess game but a chess*board*—which appears just before another visual observation about costume.[64] Since *A Game at Chess* was performed in a run

Figure 4. The Black Knight and Fat Bishop stand over a chessboard, illustrating a moment of dangerous proximity in the script. Gondomar entices multiple convert Marc Antonio de Dominis back to the Roman Church with "a letter from his holiness." Warily taking the bait, the Fat Bishop tells him, "Keep your distance." Title page of *A Game at Chess* (1625), STC 17884, copy 1, Folger Shakespeare Library.

of nine consecutive days, a checkered stage would not have affected the performance of other plays in the repertory. Black-and-white squares could have been painted with relatively little time and expense. A seasoned and inventive theater company such as the King's Men might seize on this representational opportunity, even though it was not a known practice in the commercial theaters. Painting the stage black and white is no stranger, or more innovative, than writing a script in which the characters are pieces of a board game. While we cannot know for certain that it was done, painting a checkered stage is a feasible choice, suggested by the basic conceit of the script, related visual material, and an eyewitness report.

A checkered stage could have several effects beyond enhancing the chess allegory and the binary effect of the costuming. While the painted stage still allows fluidity of location from scene to scene (with action unfolding in the court, a street, a room, and so on), in a larger sense, playing the chess game on a chessboard collapses the difference between theatrical space and dramatic place. The checkered stage traps the characters on the board.[65] At times in the play, characters move like chess pieces (as when the White Queen's Pawn's and Black Queen's Pawn's entrances imitate a typical opening gambit); however, the range of implied action in the script makes it unlikely that the blocking imitated a chess match in a consistently schematized way. Yet a chessboard stage keeps the spatial quality of the game present, even when the blocking is not explicitly framed as a chess move. As Gina Bloom points out, the theatrical incorporation of board games attunes spectators to "spatial skill[s] of placement and positioning."[66] In this way, the chessboard underfoot could add latent menace to such moments as the Jesuit's elaborately narrated, slow, and lascivious first approach to the White Queen's Pawn, in which her obliviousness makes her vulnerable to his encroachment.[67]

The play makes complex metatheatrical demands on playgoers' ability to read theatrical space in order to protect the White Queen's Pawn. The Jesuitess begins to entrap the White House Everywoman in a bogus marriage contract with the Jesuit Black Bishop's Pawn, disguised as a gentleman, by showing her the man she will marry in "a magical glass" (3.1.330). The mirror trick around which the con revolves asks playgoers to read the conventions of staging through a hermeneutics of suspicion. This is a crucial sequence of theatrical interpretation, as the exact nature of the Jesuitess's scheme has not yet been revealed. The audience knows the Black Queen's Pawn is hatching "a new trap / for [the White Queen's Pawn's] more sure confusion," and that her plans involve the Black Bishop's Pawn: "I'll bring him strangely in again" (3.1.238–39,

3.1.207).[68] However, in contrast to the many Black House plots described in detail throughout the play, these are the only two lines establishing her ruse before it unfolds. In other words, the magic mirror scene is one of the few moments in this otherwise compulsively explicit play in which the action on stage is actually ambiguous. Playgoers are heavy-handedly reminded that they are watching a deception, but they must work to determine its nature. This perceptual challenge hinges on a tension between the magical illusion and the alienation effect of its staging.

Here is what happens in the script. Having gained her trust by speaking against the Jesuit's rape attempt before the court, the Black Queen's Pawn offers to show the White Queen's Pawn her future husband in a magic mirror. The women exit; after a forty-line exchange between three comic pawns, they reenter and summon the fiancé by magic. The Black Bishop's Pawn appears disguised as a gentleman, then exits. Every modern editor of *A Game at Chess*, from R. C. Bald to Gary Taylor, has assumed that the Black Queen's Pawn and the White Queen's Pawn resume the scene with the Jesuitess using a handheld mirror to conjure the suitor, who appears behind the White Queen's Pawn, so that she sees his reflection.[69] However, the two Queen's Pawns are already standing alone onstage, making it unnecessary to exit and reenter to introduce a handheld prop, as the Jesuitess could simply have it with her. Breaking up the scene unnecessarily in such a way would run counter to what Dessen calls "the principle of dramatic economy."[70] The short exchange that intervenes is not crucial to the play. It does not affect the plot, and the characters do not appear again. It is omitted in two of the formal manuscript presentation copies.[71] This bit of comic business exists to give the White Queen's Pawn and the Black Queen's Pawn time to exit and reenter—but for a different theatrical effect.

I propose alternative blocking, in which the Jesuitess and the White Queen's Pawn reappear in the discovery space and, from there, looking *outward* through the opening of the discovery space (as if it were a wall mirror that they were looking *into*), summon the suitor, who appears *before* them on the main stage (not *behind* them, as he would be in an actual reflection). This configuration has dramatic precedent. John Kuhn outlines a theatrical tradition, beginning with the Admiral's Men in the late 1580s and early 1590s, of using the discovery space as the location for extended scenes of conjurations, as in *Doctor Faustus*, or as the place from which characters use a supernatural object to see action played out on the thrust stage, as in *Friar Bacon and Friar Bungay*, in which students watch their distant fathers duel through a magic mirror. The device persists through later plays, such as *The White Devil*, in which the Conjuror uses an enchanted object to show Bracciano the deaths of his wife and rival, enacted on the main playing space.[72] This staging is as easy to execute as that which has been previously assumed, but it creates a more complex stage picture.[73] Instead of using a handheld mirror to see the reflection of someone actually behind them, the two women pawns see the illusion *through* the front opening of the discovery space while looking *at* the opening as if it were a wall mirror: creating a contradiction between diegetic and theatrical optics. The dialogue supports this blocking. The Jesuitess's deictic first lines on reentry establish the space as integral to conjuring the vision:

> *This is the room* he did appear to me in;
> And look you, *this the magical glass* that showed him.
> (3.3.1–2, italics mine)

There is no need for a handheld prop, since the actors can create the impression of a wall mirror in the empty architectural frame simply through their gaze and gestures. The stage directions also imply that the mirror functions as a fixed feature in the space, not as a moveable object. The Black Bishop's Pawn in disguise *"presents himself before the glass"* (3.3.52.s.d.).[74] Using the convention of the discovery space as a supernatural vantage point stresses the magic of the Jesuitess's trick. The fact that the magic mirror contradicts the natural laws of optics creates a visual tension between stage space and imagined place. The challenge for playgoers is to read the mechanisms of staging, to see through the enchanted spectacle.

When the Jesuit passes across the thrust stage *"in rich attire,"* the audience does not know whether the actor is doubling as another character in a different costume or the same character is wearing a disguise (3.3.52.s.d.). Not until the last line of the scene ("She's caught, and which is strange, by her most wronger") are playgoers told that the magical fiancé is really the Jesuit rapist (3.3.71–72). While the exact nature of the trick is unclear, audiences are aware that the White Queen's Pawn is being deceived. This is obvious both because the Black Queen's Pawn is a baddie and because the White Queen's Pawn is falling for it. She eagerly accepts dubious proof of the mirror's efficacy: "'Twill satisfy me much" (3.3.22). The chromatic irony of the Black Queen's Pawn's declaration, "My truth reflects the clearer," signposts that the glass is as false as she is (3.3.36). Here again, the White Queen's Pawn's lack of circumspection elicits compensatory, heightened attention from the audience.

The magical display engineered from the discovery space is stagey.[75] The invocation of the specter in the White Queen's Pawn's name lasts for fourteen lines (compared to six and four lines, respectively, for the unsuccessful "test calls" in the names of the Black and White Queens). Anaphora links eight lines of the invocation; a pentameter couplet caps and elongates the preceding te- trameter.[76] In other words, the Black Bishop's Pawn's entrance is heavy-handedly signaled. This rhetorical elaboration suggests either a strong spell or a conspicu- ous cue—or both. The Jesuitess stage-manages the supernatural effects, calling attention to the music that by convention accompanies an apparition:

Hark, how the air, enchanted with your praises
And his approach, those words to sweet notes raises. (3.3.50–51)

She refers to the Black Bishop's Pawn as a "shadow," punning on specter and actor (3.3.55). The Jesuit appears on the main stage at the tense intersection of the White Queen's Pawn's deluded gaze and the audience's more discerning sight line. If she sees a new suitor in a magical vision, the audience can also see a performer walking across the stage in different clothes.[77]

The magic mirror scene creates a sense of slowness to foreground and elon- gate the challenge of perception for audiences. The Black Bishop's Pawn en- ters and "*like an apparition presents himself*" (3.3.51.s.d.). This phrase does not describe his costume (the stage direction separately specifies "*rich attire*") but indicates a spectral manner of movement, conventionally slow or stately. In the Rosenbach manuscript, a drawn line separating the direction "*stands be- fore the glasse*" from "*then exit*" indicates an acting beat.[78] As he departs, the White Queen's Pawn pines, "O let him stay a while, a little longer!" suggest- ing that the Black Bishop's Pawn leaves the stage slowly enough to string along her desire for his lingering (3.3.52). This suspended scene of seeing draws out the audiences' mental work.

The religious stakes of this problem of theatrical interpretation (disguise or different character) are clarified in the scene that immediately follows. Here, a lackey of the Black Knight recognizes the Jesuit in disguise as a gentleman:

Black Knight's Pawn: 'Tis he, my confessor! He might ha'
     passed me
Seven years together, had I not by chance
Advanced mine eye upon that lettered hatband,

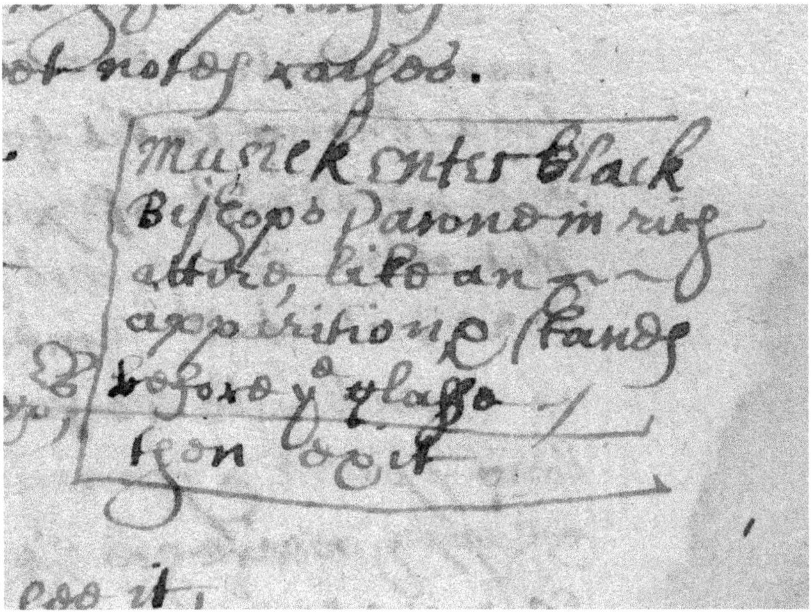

Figure 5. Stage directions from the Rosenbach manuscript of *A Game at Chess*, describing the movements of the Jesuit in the magic mirror scene: "Musick Enter Black Bishop Pawne in rich attire, like an apparition, & stands before the glasse. / then exit." The underscore line indicates an acting "beat." MS V.a.342, Folger Shakespeare Library.

> The Jesuitical symbol to be worn
> By the brave collegians by consent.
> 'Tis a strange habit for a holy father,
> A president of poverty especially;
> But we, the sons and daughters of obedience,
> Dare not once think awry, but must confess ourselves
> As humbly to the father of that feather,
> Long spur and poniard, as to the alb and altar,
> And happy we're so highly graced to attain to it.
> [*To him*] Holy and reverend!
> *Black Bishop's Pawn:* How hast found me out?
> *Black Knight's Pawn:* O sir, put on the sparklingest trim of glory,
> Perfection will shine foremost, and I knew you
> By the catholical mark you wear about you,
> The mark above your forehead. (4.1.1–17)

The Black Knight's Pawn declares the same difficulty in recognizing the Jesuit *"richly accoutred"* that both the White Queen's Pawn, and audiences, experience in the preceding scene.

However, the aside also points out that the Black Bishop's Pawn's disguise only makes him all the more a Jesuit, since such subterfuges are their common practice:

> Some of our Jesuits turn gentleman-ushers,
> Some falconers, some park-keepers, some huntsmen;
> One took the shape of an old lady's cook once. (4.2.53–55)

The holy father hiding in plain sight is one of a number of Catholic insinuations into everyday English life the play exposes. The Spanish have tricks to "convey White House gold to our Black Kingdom / In cold baked pasties," and to smuggle religious objects "in rolls, tobacco-balls . . . by one i' th' habit of a pedlar" (4.2.50–51). Identifying the priest passing by on the street models for Protestant audiences the detection of papists in public that they themselves will be called on later to perform in, and beyond, the theater. The sign by which the Black Knight's Pawn recognizes his confessor recirculates real-world advice about "how to kenne or smell a Priest." In one of the play's source pamphlets, John Gee writes, "If, about *Bloomesbury* or *Holborne*, thou meet a good smug fellow in a gold-laced suit, a cloke lined thorow with velvet, one that hath good store of coin in his purse, Rings on his fingers, a Watch in his pocket . . . a broad-laced Band, a Stiletto by his side . . . willing (upon small acquaintance) to intrude into thy company, and still desiring further to insinuate with thee; then take heed of a Jesuit. . . . *The Jesuit hath a superlative cognizance whereby they know one another . . . a gold hat band studded with letters or characters.*"[79] Catholic priests in England did dress as gentlemen to allow greater freedom of social and geographical movement, as well as to avoid detection when their spiritual children showed them signs of respect. The play's Jesuit is disguised, just as a real Jesuit would be disguised.[80] This compression of levels of representation folds the extradramatic world into the allegory of the play.[81]

The Jesuitess brings the White Queen's Pawn and the Black Bishop's Pawn together through the manipulation of stage space. Orchestrating the meet-cute between the Jesuit in disguise and the unsuspecting Everywoman, the Black Queen's Pawn speaks to the White Queen's Pawn as if out of earshot of the Black Bishop's Pawn (recalling the strategy of her opening gambit). Yet the two Black House agents clearly work in cahoots, coordinating his actions with her gloss. Exemplary of the way that characters with greater awareness in *A Game at Chess* also master the playing space, the Jesuitess is able to cross from the White Queen's Pawn's imagined place directly to the Black Bishop's Pawn's (addressing them in consecutive lines of dialogue), whereas the Jesuit must exit and reenter to arrive at the White Queen's Pawn's location. When he reappears at her side, they metrically share a line of dialogue, creating dangerous romantic proximity.

Similarly, *A Game at Chess* stages the Jesuitess's bed trick, which spares the White Queen's Pawn's chastity, with unusual architectural explicitness: "Enter BLACK QUEEN'S PAWN as conducting the WHITE to a chamber; then fetching in the Black Bishop's Pawn, the Jesuit[ess] conveys him to another, puts out the light and she follows" (4.3.s.d.). The sexual switcheroo makes the control of stage positioning conspicuous. The Black Queen's Pawn's placement of the other figures in their "chambers" reads as a power move in which the Jesuitess controls the board (as she controls the trick), especially since these spaces likely doubled as the two "Houses" from which the sides enter.[82] When the Jesuitess reveals her successful sexual shell game to the Black Bishop's Pawn, she does so by taunting him unseen from offstage, perhaps using the same space from which she raised the noise that foiled the Jesuit's rape attempt.[83] Even physically absent, the Jesuitess's control of secrets translates to a mastery of the stage.

The resolution of the White Queen's Pawn's plot makes explicit her claim on the protective vigilance of audiences. After the bed trick, the Protestant ingénue meets the Black Bishop's Pawn in his religious garb, thinking he is there to marry her to the gentleman. She rebuffs his sexual advances again and appeals to playgoers to use their "cunning judgments" of the stage on her behalf:

> You should never speak
> The language of unchasteness in that habit;
> You would not think how ill it does with you.
> The world's a stage on which all parts are played:
> You'd count it strange to have a devil
> Presented there not in a devil's shape,
> Or wanting one, to send him out in yours;
> You'd rail at that for an absurdity
>   For decorum's sake then

. . . .
If you'll persist still in your devil's part,
Present him as you should do, and let one
That carries up the goodness of the play
Come in that habit, and I'll speak with him;
Then will the parts be fitted and the spectators
Know which is which. They must have cunning judgments
To find it else, for such a one as you
Is able to deceive a mighty auditory;
Nay, those you have seduced, if there be any
In the assembly, when they see what manner
You play your game with me, they cannot love you. (5.2.16–36)

The White Queen's Pawn's direct plea to audiences involves their judgments
and emotions in the action. Here, the script openly acknowledges the religious
divisions among playgoers. Recognizing the danger that spectators may be seduced by the Black House, the White Queen's Pawn casts the theatrical game
as a battle for hearts and minds. The gap between her knowledge and that of
the playgoers' comes down to a theatrical competency: the ability to read costuming. The White Queen's Pawn cannot see that she is in a play in which
good guys and bad guys are distinguished by their clothes. The joke is that
playgoers can easily "tell which is which," and that the Jesuit in his clerical
garb *is* "in a devil's shape." As with Gondomar's downfall, the White Queen's
Pawn's triumph over the Black Bishop's Pawn is a function of her position in
the scene's double structure of dramatic irony: she does not yet know that the
Jesuit is actually the suitor; but he does not yet know that the woman he had
sex with was actually the Jesuitess. While the Black Bishop's Pawn unmasks
himself as the false fiancé, brags about the bogus engagement, and mocks its
enthusiastic consummation, playgoers maintain a knowledge that protects the
White Queen's Pawn, as if Protestant audiences were the keepers of her deliverance until its revelation.[84]

Lurk for Your Life: Theatrical Surveillance from Stage to Street

A Game at Chess maintains an insistent thinness between the dramatic fiction
and the world of playgoers through its explicit identifications, and its continual

direct address. Particularly toward the end of the play, the symbiosis between stage and playhouse is self-consciously spatial. Bringing Gondomar's litter on-stage complements the theatrical gesture of putting his chair of ease front and center: whereas the privy scene makes something belonging to domestic space public, the litter brings something from the street into the theater. Gondomar's litter was recognizable to Londoners, and it had been the target of popular violence. In 1621, apprentices attacked the ambassador's litter, crying, "There goes the devil in a dung-cart."[85] The play's intervention is to move the litter "from one culturally demarcated zone to another," and this theatrical appropriation changes playgoers' relationship to the object represented.[86] Whereas the real-life, urban protesters were punished (one died from whipping), Protestant playgoers are allowed greater license to subject the litter to their judgments and projectiles. The last line of the play proper, the White King's triumphant call to "welcome our White Knight with loud peals of joy" (5.3.219), recasts audiences as the crowds celebrating Charles's return ten months prior—an urban event in which most playgoers likely participated—fusing the fiction of the play to an extratheatrical, social event.

The ending of *A Game at Chess* charges its Protestant audiences to extend the surveillance of Catholics, in which they have been theatrically en-trained, to the world beyond the playhouse. Reversing the Black House open-ing of the play, the White Queen's Pawn delivers the epilogue:

> My mistress, the White Queen, hath sent me forth
> And bade me bow thus low to all of worth
> That are true friends of the White House and cause,
> Which she hopes most of this assembly draws.
> For any else, by envy's mark denoted,
> To those night glow-worms in the bag devoted,
> Where'er they sit, stand, or in private lurk,
> They'll soon be known by their depraving work.
> But she's assured that what they'd commit to bane,
> Her White friends' loves will build up fair again.
> (Epilogue, lines 1–10)

The White Queen's Pawn asks White House sympathizers to monitor the fa-cial expressions of fellow audience members for "envy's mark," meaning not so much signs of jealousy as those of general ill will. A seventeenth-century essayist identifies the conventional features of this disposition: "I behold Envy (as the Poet describeth her) to have a pale face without blood, a leane body without moysture . . . squint eyes, foule or blacke teeth, a heart full of gal, a tongue tipt with poison, never laughing but when others weep; never sleeping because she alwaies thinketh on mischiefe."[87] That is, Protestant playgoers are instructed to monitor the reactions of fellow audience members for signs of affective alienation: weeping when others laugh, laughing when others weep. The White Queen's Pawn's glow-worm reference carries both the metaphorical sense of a false light and the more practical reminder to look out for the "sparklingest . . . catholical mark . . . the mark [that] shine[s] above [the] forehead," the gold-studded hatband audiences are taught earlier to recognize as a "Jesuitical symbol" (4.1.14–17, 4).[88] These directives activate a latent threat for Catholics that the playhouse could become a place of dangerous exposure. The playgoing priest Father Leke was rebuked by his superior for "appear[ing] in a theater, where multitudes of people see, and beehowld you and most of them scoffers at priests and Catholick religion . . . at a vulgar stage play . . . everyone who will may lay howld . . . every man may be an officer to apprehend."[89] The White Queen's Pawn's instructions are tailored to the space of the playhouse, referencing audience members who "stand" in the pit, as well as those who "sit" in more expensive seats. The epilogue, a formal hinge between the play and the world beyond, redirects the surveillance work of Protestant audiences from the stage, through the playhouse, and out into the city.[90] The play turns Protestant playgoers into pursuivants.

A Game at Chess explicitly encourages the majority of audience members to persecute a minority of their fellow playgoers as they exit the theater. By report, the play seems to have accomplished its declared agenda. A Spanish diplomat writes, "All these people come out of the theatre so inflamed against Spain, that, as a few Catholics have told me who went secretly to see the play, my person would not be safe in the streets."[91] Witnesses record enthusiastic crowd responses: "extraordinary applause," "so much applause," "great applause."[92] Gondomar's replacement writes, "There was such merriment, hubbub and applause that even if I had been many leagues away it would not have been possible for me not to have taken notice of it."[93] The loudness of these collective responses is a rough measure of audiences' experiential cohesion. Yet, as the new Spanish ambassador observes, the play both consolidates and divides audiences: "To the general applause of bad men and to the grief of those whose intentions are sound."[94] *A Game at Chess* produces both a large, rowdy Protestant surveillance team and—given that Romanist playgoers exiting the theater occupy a position like that of supporters of the wrong side in a stadium of football hooligans—exactly the kind of furtive Catholic "lurk[ing]" that Protestants playgoers are taught to police.[95]

Because *A Game at Chess* puts an ideological subset of audience members in physical danger, we might reasonably expect to find harder emotional and imaginative limits to Catholic experiences of the play. This is only partly the case. Among the records from Catholic sources, national loyalties, as well as factional divisions, generate varied responses. While Romanists in general recognized the play as aggressively anti-Catholic, some did not feel themselves to be the sole or primary target. As seen earlier, the Venetian ambassador was able to look beyond the fierce satire of his coreligionists and understand the play as glancing at weaknesses among the English themselves. An English Catholic, Paul Overton, writes to the secular priest William Bishop, bishop of Chalcedon, "Wee have noe stay of persecution, nor is any likelihood yet. . . . At the globe playhouse is dayly presented an odious play against Spaine, but principally Gondomar and the Jusuits."[96] Although Overton frames the play as a "persecution," something damaging for "we" Catholics in general, he also identifies the play's primary targets as Spain, Gondomar, and the Jesuits. This is significant, given that Overton is writing to the bishop of Chalcedon, whose very presence in England represented a victory for the secular clergy in their long-standing conflict with the Jesuit order. If Overton shared his correspondent's loyalties in this internecine struggle among English Catholics, he might well have stood in the theater and been offended by the play as a Catholic; yet he might also have felt that the play was not totally directed against his identity category but rather against a group with which he himself was also in conflict, the Jesuits. Moreover—as in the case of the Venetian ambassador and the Protestant commentator who share a view of the play as uncomplimentary to the English, which is grounded in the formal complexity of Gondomar's rapport with the audience—Overton's take on *A Game at Chess* is not simply an expression of his confessional identity but also reflects the play's own features and stresses. His perception that the play is against Catholics generally, but "principally [against] Jesuits," registers both the play's binary religious logic and its satirical emphasis on the order. The responses of mixed-faith audiences to *A Game at Chess* were determined by the complex interactions of a combination of factors: the ideological positions of individual playgoers, the immediate circumstances of cultural possibility, and the orchestration of shared theatrical experience.

CHAPTER 5

Measure for Measure: Theatrical Cues and Confessional Codes

William Shakespeare's *Measure for Measure* (1603–4) offers a case study in the way theatrical form can orchestrate collective experiences that unsettle play-goers' real-world patterns of confessional judgment. The play interpellates its mixed-faith audiences into a Calvinist hermeneutic of social and spiritual differentiation. Predestinarian snap judgments are integral to the play's intelligibility and its impact for spectators across the confessional spectrum. *Measure for Measure* makes the inner struggles of a puritan hypocrite emotionally available to playgoers with varying degrees of familiarity, and sympathy, with the distinctive strain of reprobation anxiety to which the godly were particularly prone. Having drawn ideologically diverse audiences into a Calvinist interpretive and affective system, *Measure for Measure*'s theatrical reversals make visible and unsettle the very practices of predestinarian judgment that the play initially asks playgoers to take for granted. In so doing, *Measure for Measure* enacts what Raymond Williams identifies as "[both] the active and formative [as well as the] transformational processes" of hegemony.[1] The play asks theatergoers of diverse beliefs to inhabit a world in which the hermeneutic and emotional problems of Calvinism are central; in this respect, it reinscribes dominant ideology. However, *Measure for Measure* does not inculcate mixed-faith audiences with predestinarian orthodoxy; rather, the play entangles both characters and spectators in a Calvinist interpretive net, one that seems all the more knotted and binding the more it unravels around them. The theatrical processes of the play do not affirm the coherence of the spiritual and social hermeneutics of Calvinist culture. Rather, *Measure for Measure* puts theatrical pressure on pre-destinarian judgments. This play does not ask its confessionally diverse audiences to univocally assent to the Calvinist theology that grounds key elements of the plot and characterization; instead, it invites them to inhabit, and to chafe at, that dominant paradigm from different positions within it.

Measure for Measure demonstrates a sustained preoccupation with the central experiential challenge of predestination: the difficulty of knowing the preordained and unchangeable condition of souls, one's own as well as others'. Shakespeare's Vienna is a murky world of misperceptions with mortal consequences. Dead men's heads are indistinguishable. Souls are difficult to discern. The Duke lurks in dark corners disguised as a monk, "contend[ing] especially to know himself" (3.2.226–27).[2] His seemingly saintly deputy Angelo is secretly a corrupt coercer of virgins, an example of "what man may within him hide, / Though angel on the outward side" (3.2.264–65). Full of false appearances, the play continually troubles what characters "think" they "know" in questions of sin and virtue, where the stakes are life and death (5.1.202–3). Claudio, afflicted with "incertain thought," awaiting death in prison for a crime that no one is sure is a crime, cries out, "Ay, but to die, and go we know not where" (3.1.126, 117). Concentrating these broader tropes of indeterminacy in a specific language of grace and reprobation, *Measure for Measure* investigates predestinarian theology, and its attendant forms of cultural judgment, as an epistemological problem.[3]

Moreover, *Measure for Measure* does not simply thematize the indefinite hermeneutics of predestination; it performs them. Leading mixed-faith theatergoers through a series of interpretive bait-and-switches, the play both activates and troubles the common Calvinist practice of making assumptions on cultural grounds as to the election or reprobation of one's own or another's unknowable soul. *Measure for Measure* repeatedly lures its confessionally diverse audiences into adopting predestinarian presumptions that are then undermined. Since *Measure for Measure*'s most prominent potential reprobate is the subject of multiple theatrical reversals of spiritual expectation, the cumulative effect is not to show playgoers' assessments of Angelo's soul to be wrong but to render all such judgments uncertain. In the process of disrupting the quotidian interpretive practices of predestinarian culture, *Measure for Measure* surprises its mixed-faith audiences with a series of soliloquies that invite identification with the internal struggles of a puritan hypocrite. The play does more than reflect the ambiguities of Calvinist doctrine; its basic dramatic devices—plot twists, dramatic irony, and soliloquies—undermine dominant habits of religious judgment and make available unexpected subject positions to playgoers across the confessional spectrum.

Recent scholarship on *Measure for Measure* has tended to focus on the play's engagement with political theology and puritan agendas of social reform.[4] This work usefully demonstrates the play's attention to the issues that puritanism raises in terms of the relationship between church and state. However, it tends to neglect *Measure for Measure*'s related interest in the private, experiential aspects and the more subjective, street-level ramifications of Calvinist doctrine. For example, while Peter Lake's work on *Measure for Measure*'s critique of puritan proposals for moral reform does acknowledge the play's attention to the "affective style" of puritans, his argument nevertheless remains on the level of policy and political theology.[5] Insofar as godly attempts to self-separate from the wicked through social regulation had predestinarian underpinnings, my focus on the difficulty of reading the conditions of souls complements the work of Lake and others who deal with *Measure for Measure*'s engagement with macropolitical questions of Christian justice and godly rule. In closing, I will return to the implications for the state of the spiritual question, How do I know who is saved and who is damned? First, however, I track this epistemological problem as it plays out on the more local scale of interpersonal interactions, subjective judgment, and self-examination. Despite injunctions against it, English Calvinists commonly presumed correlations between the conditions of souls and various markers of cultural identity—from the fervor of one's piety to the style of one's clothes. Through the distinctive capacity of theatrical form to orchestrate loosely collective responses, *Measure for Measure* sets in motion, and unsettles, one of the most ordinary practices of Calvinist culture: (mis)reading the unreadable signs of salvation or damnation in one's own soul or one's neighbors'.

Spectators of the King's Men's play had different relationships to predestinarian culture. Catholics embraced an alternative theology, and social theory, of grace in which salvation was not delivered by divine diktat but as part of a dialogue between creator and creatures that included prayer and works.[6] Predestination was a cornerstone of the doctrinal consensus within the Church of England, yet even as early as the 1590s some avant-garde theologians, such as Peter Baro, were raising palliative, proto-Arminian challenges to the rigid "double decrees" to salvation or damnation.[7] Ordinary Calvinists dealt with predestination with varying degrees of theological sophistication and spiritual seriousness. The possibility of reprobation was not an exclusively puritan preoccupation. Predestinarian thinking (with varying levels of explicitness) was a ubiquitous part of English culture. Given the doctrine's presence in popular media, along with mandatory church attendance, and the high degree of exchange among confessional groups, post-Reformation Londoners of all faith groups had some degree of familiarity with the concepts of election and reprobation, as well as some firsthand experience of how those categories could be deployed in everyday interactions.

Measure for Measure asks its mixed-faith audiences to assume, and to adjust, predestinarian habits of thought and feeling as part of their imaginative participation in the dramatic world. The positions of characters vis-à-vis Calvinist taxonomies of salvation are almost as varied as those of playgoers. However, post-Reformation people did not connect only to the perspectives and experiences of their onstage, confessional counterparts. The play does not offer Angelo's soliloquies of reprobation anxiety exclusively to hot Protestant spectators, nor does it pitch the prayers of the ingénue novitiate solely to those playgoers already sympathetic to intercessory models of forgiveness for sin. Godly characters do not speak in a spiritual code accessible only to a coterie of the confessionally likeminded. Much of what is dynamic about the play—such as the reversals of expectation and shifts in sympathy—hinges on the ability of mixed-faith audiences to adopt, and to revise, confessional assumptions in response to theatrical effects. The act of entering into a fiction in which the codes of legibility and feeling are Calvinist asks different kinds of ideological openness from papists, proto-Arminians, Pelagians, prayer-book Protestants, puritans, and the impious. Yet, regardless of audience members' real-world relationships to predestination, *Measure for Measure* offers all playgoers the chance to participate in a hypothetical world in which a dominant confessional code is provisionally operative, but also subject to reconfiguration through the experiential process of theater.

Interpreting the Unknowable: Predestinarian Culture

Doctrinally, the Church of England maintained that predestination is not a result of divine foreknowledge of human actions but rather proceeds solely from God's will. The elect are not chosen because God foresees they will be good, nor the reprobate rejected because God foresees they will be wicked; such assertions would make salvation the result of works, not grace. Rather, the saved are saved and the damned are damned because God is God.[8] Faced with this difficult doctrine, English Protestants were given conflicting directives. On the one hand, God's judgments were secret and not bound by earthly reason; therefore, human attempts to arrogate knowledge of an individual's election or reprobation were an affront to God's inscrutable sovereignty. Thus, it would be dangerous, as well as uncharitable, to presume that the godly (those who appeared holy, specifically puritans) and the elect (those whom God has actually chosen to save), or the wicked (people who sin) and reprobates (people going to hell), were coterminous groups. As William Perkins admonishes in *A Golden Chaine*, "No man may peremptorily set down, that he or any other is a reprobate. For God dooth oftentimes prefer those, which did seeme to be most of all estraunged from his favor to be in his kingdom above those, who in man's judgement were the children of the kingdom. Hence is it, that Christ saith: *The Publicanes and harlots goe before you.*"[9] On the other hand, it was the serious, perhaps primary, religious duty of every English Protestant to examine his or her soul for evidence of saving grace, and to read the book of the world for marks of divine judgment. So, despite the ambiguity of the signs of election and reprobation, and despite injunctions like Perkins's against making peremptory predestinarian judgments, de facto speculation about souls was a ubiquitous practice.

The Church of England taught that it was indeed possible on earth to achieve a state of faith termed "assurance," a legitimate conviction of one's personal salvation. To count oneself among the godly implied that one had received, or hoped to receive, this sense of assurance. Since fellow feeling with other chosen people was widely recognized as one of the chief signs of election, group and individual godly identity were mutually affirming.[10] However, other English Calvinists often regarded puritan spiritual confidence as a form of false assurance referred to as "security."[11] As one Jacobean sermon warns, "This over-venturous conceite, that heaven is theirs . . . is carnal securitie, not heavenly assurance."[12] George Chapman mocks the godly presumption of salvation and criticizes "bold Puritans (esteem'd elect)."[13]

However, this accusation was not leveled against puritans only by their detractors. The godly themselves, who tended toward heightened self-scrutiny, were more likely to be painfully aware that both the inner movements of piety and the outward signs of a holy life could be misleading.[14] Puritans were particularly concerned with the danger of unconscious spiritual hypocrisy.[15] In *The Mystery of Selfe-Deceiving*, published in eleven editions between 1614 and 1642, Daniel Dyke writes of those who possess only a temporary, not saving, faith: "These men we see go very far, so that, as the *Apostle* speaketh, they are in some sort, *made partakers of the holy Ghost*, they *taste of the powers of the world to come* & expresse their inward grace by outward obedience, bringing forth fruit very speedily, far sooner than others, as the stonie ground is more quick & forward than other soiles. And yet for all this these also, being rotten at heart, are to be ranked in the number of *selfe-deceivers*, as falsely judging themselves to be in a state of grace."[16] One could embrace Christ's word, repent, feel spiritual blessings, live an outwardly holy life, and still be damned. It was possible for a time to delude oneself with the false signs of sanctity or, as Perkins puts it, to "taste" of God's banquet without "feed[ing]."[17] Ultimately, it was understood, the reprobate would return to sin and despair. However, this distinction was complicated by the belief that even the sanctified elect, while they could not finally or totally fall from grace, might continue to struggle with sin and doubt. In other words, even the godliest individuals—whose souls are touched by the gifts of the Holy Spirit, who lead virtuous lives—might one day learn to their dismay that they are, as John Calvin puts it, "not at all superior to devils."[18] "I was troubled againe for I thought I had binne a reprobate . . . and looking upon the grasse my consince tolde me my sinnes were more in number than the speares of grasse. . . . [I was tempted to] drown myself. . . . And my God . . . put into my mind that his mercies were more in number then my sinnes and if I have grace to repent for them, the Lords Name be praised for evermore."[19] Nehemiah Wallington moves from reprobation to grace, from suicidal despair to consolation, within the space of a short paragraph. For him, doubt and assurance are entangled. Wallington's consciousness of "sins more in number than spears of grass" summons his sense of "mercies more in number than my sins." This spiritual vacillation proceeds in part from the fact that the signs of salvation and damnation could be experientially identical. The abject awareness of sin Wallington describes could either be a mark of reprobation, as he initially suspects, or, as he then concludes, the precondition for receiving saving grace. Inversely, a firm persuasion of God's love and mercy could be either what it seems, evidence of election, or its doppelgänger, false faith. Despite the fact that puritan and prayer-book Protestants alike habitually interpreted external signs as evidence of God's favor or judgment, these signals too were uncertain and reversible, since both worldly prosperity and affliction could signal either reprobation or election.[20] Predestination presented English Protestants with a hermeneutic conundrum: the continual pressure to interpret signs that were, by definition, indeterminate.

Warnings in sermons and other religious texts against making overhasty negative predestinarian judgments often appear cheek by jowl beside headier passages casting aspersions on the salvific prospects of those guilty of the sin being censured. For example, the Geneva Bible devotes nearly all the commentary on the book of Job to an extended rejection of condemning as

damned those who suffer afflictions; yet annotations throughout the translation use the terms "wicked" and "reprobate" interchangeably to identify the
many vices and failures through which those eternally rejected by God may
be known in this world.[21] Similarly, in the egregiously mistitled sermon "The
Poore Mans Hope," John Gore acknowledges in passing that he "dare not
say . . . common beggers . . . are *all* the seed of reprobates . . . else God forbid,"
but he immediately proceeds to describe the poor as "children of Beliall,
without God, without Magistrate, without Minister; dissolute, disobedient, and
reprobate."[22] Prescriptive warnings against making predestinarian judgments
should not be taken as evidence that such assumptions were rare; rather, these
cautious disclaimers often appear alongside, and sometimes rhetorically excuse
or enable, the very interpretive practice they disavow.

Reading reprobation in others was as much a form of cultural judgment
as a matter of spiritual vigilance, and it could demarcate a range of religious,
economic, and behavioral battle lines. Sometimes, the vituperative suggestion
of reprobation, with varying degrees of explicitness, was directed against fellow Protestants with a different style of piety.[23] So, puritans might cast aspersions on the salvific prospects of their "lukewarm" neighbors. However, these
less hotly reformed parishioners could in turn be quick to point to the moral
failings of godly individuals as signs of spiritual hypocrisy, the absence of true
saving grace.[24] Protestants disagreed on the degree to which members of the
Roman Church were necessarily damned. Salvation was widely considered impossible for those who, despite the revelation of true religion, remained obsti-
nately committed the Antichristian Whore. Protestant subgroups granted
different exceptions. Godly divines tended to make salvation for papists conditional on their complete ignorance of true religion, whereas Arminians made
broader allowances for sincere Christians within the Roman Church.[25]
Calvinist popular culture offered gleeful images of papists in hell. Yet many
ordinary Protestants tacitly made room for Catholic family members, cowork-
ers, and friends in their heaven. Similarly, while Catholic orthodoxy maintained that salvation was possible only within the Church of Rome, some
papists were capable of more charitable attitudes toward their heretic neighbors.[26] Predestinarian judgments also marked economic conflicts. Sometimes the implication of reprobation was used to vilify the poor, as in Gore's
sermon quoted earlier. But this condemnatory imputation could also be directed at targets higher up the social ladder; popular ballads recount providential judgments signaling the damnation of corn hoarders, enclosers, and
rack-renting landlords.[27] Sometimes lifestyle choices—the kind of sex one

had, or the clothes one wore, or the amount of time one spent in the alehouse—could prompt others, consciously or unconsciously, to group one among the damned. However, determining what behavior constituted a sin grievous enough to count as a sign of damnation was highly relative.

Arthur Dent's *The Plaine Mans Path-Way to Heaven, Wherein every man may clearly see whether he shall be saved or damned*—which went through twenty-five editions between 1601 and 1640, making it one of the most frequently reprinted books of the period—stages a discussion among Protestant speakers that demonstrates the difficulty of spiritually parsing these cultural signs. For example, Dent lists "Pride" as the first of nine "verie cleare and manifest signes of a mans condemnation."[28] The bulk of the section concerns pride of apparel. Asked by the prayer-book Protestant Asuntus, "What say you to these great ruffes?" the godly preacher Theologus replies, "For such things sake the wrath of God cometh."[29] Instead, he praises simple, modest clothes as the outward sign of a true Christian spirit. A less pious interlocutor points out, "One may be proud of plaine apparell."[30] The godly Philagathus crystallizes the problem by asking, "But who shall judge what is comely, sober, handsome, modest, &c? For every man and woman will say their apparell is but decent and cleanly, how gallant, brave, and flaunting soever it be."[31] The point is not that there was one group of people identified as damned by all others, but that the cultural signs of reprobation were varied and relative. To adapt Patrick Collinson's famous phrase, reprobates were half of a stressful relationship.

Although audience members had diverse experiences of predestinarian culture, they were all surrounded by it. Predestinarian thinking, both overt and implicit, saturated English popular media, from Paul's Cross sermons to cheap-print tales of providential judgment.[32] Competing models of salvation did not exist in splendid isolation. Some English Catholics took a positive interest in Calvinist culture. As seen in Chapter 1, papists could absorb reformed tendencies: playgoer Christopher Blount died for the Catholic faith, yet even on the scaffold he prayed to be redeemed by his savior alone, and not his own works.[33] Romanists were capable of a range of relationships to Protestant theology and culture.

We cannot assume that *Measure for Measure*'s complication of predestinarian paradigms spoke only to Calvinists in the audience who lived this theology daily, inwardly, and in their social interactions. Theatergoers were not exclusively interested in, or sympathetic toward, those characters and scenarios that most closely resembled their own religious lives. For papist, lukewarm, and ungodly spectators, the vicarious experience of a puritan's fear of unwitting spiritual hypocrisy may have been compelling precisely because it was unfamiliar. *Measure for Measure* offers Catholic playgoers an insider's experience of a doctrine they rejected; it allows less pious Calvinists access to puritan writhing. The play asks godly spectators to check hardline predestinarian thinking against the more humane voices of sinners such as Lucio, for whom pregnancy out of wedlock is a sign not of damnation but of "blossoming time" (1.4.41), and the bawd Mistress Overdone, who keeps a whore's infant bastard out of charity. *Measure for Measure* invites playgoers across the religious spectrum to occupy the complex dimensionality of predestinarian culture together. The shared experience of the play does not erase differences among mixed-faith spectators. However, the sequential unfolding of theatrical effects synchronizes shifts in individuals' emotional perspectives. In Steven Mullaney's words, "Feelings [are] points of view."[34] *Measure for Measure* rotates the imaginations of confessionally diverse playgoers simultaneously, allowing them to see faith from other affective angles. These changes in emotional perception offer mixed-faith audiences a prismatic experience of religious ideology.

Misreading the Invisible in *Measure for Measure*

Although audiences necessarily make sense of plays through reference to the real world, as Keir Elam notes, "The dramatic world has to be specified *from within*."[35] While most spectators of *Measure for Measure* were Calvinists who embraced, with varying degrees of intensity and clarity, predestinarian rubrics of spiritual and social judgment in their daily lives, it is not the case that these playgoers (and only these playgoers) filtered *Measure for Measure* through this theological lens, simply because that was their normal ideological orientation. Regardless of the degree of knowledge of, or sympathy toward, the problems of Calvinist judgment that mixed-faith playgoers brought with them into the playhouse, *Measure for Measure* asks all theatergoers to invest in a fictional world with predestinarian parameters. Theatrical cues make operative ideological codes. Often, this is not subtle. With comparable bluntness to declarations of place such as "Well, this is the forest of Arden" in *As You Like It*, the opening scenes of *Measure for Measure* locate playgoers in a world divided between the godly and the wicked.[36] Devices as basic as costume create a confessional atmosphere.

Like the recognition of genre, attunement to the religious sensibility of a play is often instant, palpable, and unconscious. With the same immediacy that a stage hung with black prepares audiences for tragic emotion, the opening scene of *Hamlet* summons a world haunted by the affective structures of purgatory (regardless of the ontological status of the actual ghost). Theatergoers do not need to consciously assent to the theology that they imaginatively accept. Theatrical induction into an ideological framework can be powerful, not despite but because of the ways that this acclimation works unconsciously. The theological alignment of a play is not always established primarily through dialogue. Just as a television viewer flipping channels can readily identify a thriller by its soundtrack or a romantic comedy by its lighting, so too the heavy-handed ceremony that opens *The Noble Spanish Soldier* establishes a play world suffused with the dangerous allure of the Roman Whore before anyone speaks a word. The recognition of such cues is visceral. They create expectations not only of plot but also of affect and cultural preoccupation.

The confessional worlds into which theatrical effects interpellate mixed-faith playgoers are not ideologically consistent. For example, *The Duchess of Malfi* features anti-Catholic tropes: a corrupt cardinal, an ambiance of Italianate decadence, seductive but dangerous women, a deadly devotional object, and plenty of deceptive surfaces. Yet it also gathers nostalgic reverence, and a sense of communication with the dead, around a ruined abbey.[37] Cariola's warning against false pilgrimages has force for Protestant theatergoers, despite the Duchess dismissing her as a "superstitious fool," because of its dramatic function: foreshadowing.[38] Here, a simple theatrical cue gives resonance to a religious practice most playgoers would reject as popish hogwash. But an audience member who thinks that these ominous words are nothing to worry about, because pilgrimages are an invalid form of devotional expression, does not know how to watch a play.

In *Measure for Measure*, Calvinist concerns seep into Catholic practices, and vice versa. The play explores the problems of sanctity and social respectability in predestinarian terms; yet this Calvinist cultural idiom is not only polysemous but also in dialogue with Catholic voices.[39] Throughout, the play registers a range of models of salvation. Lucio observes that "grace is grace, despite of all controversy . . . in any language"; the Gentleman adds, "or in any religion" (1.2.22–25, 23). Early modern plays habitually intertwine characters, settings, plots, business, dialogue, and props with different confessional valences. The nonchalance with which the Duke moves from charging his deputy to enforce the laws of a Calvinist theocracy to announcing his intention to disguise himself as a friar—in the space of twenty lines—is typical of post-Reformation drama. For mixed-faith playgoers, ideological incongruity was not the same as fictional implausibility. Audiences were accustomed to adapting to the shifting confessional idiosyncrasies of dramatic worlds. In *Measure for Measure*, the initial judgments of the godly magistrates, their subsequent revision—the dynamic encounter between a novitiate of Saint Clare and a sex-crazed puritan—and the wavering of a godly conscience all involve audiences in a hypothetical religious world that is always changing. In Elam's words, "The possible worlds of the drama are never simple and static states of affairs, but, rather, a complex *succession* of states."[40]

Measure for Measure's manipulation of audience expectation establishes, and then challenges, the presumption of a correlation between one's inward, predestined condition and one's external, social status. In this play, souls cannot be slotted into worldly categories. The godly magistrate may be a reprobate, and the convict in chains may be a man with a well-ordered conscience. Yet conflating godliness and election is precisely the mistake that mixed-faith audiences are initially led to make, the first in a series of predestinarian misjudgments the play invites in order to revise. The "precise" Angelo, as scholars have long acknowledged, would have been recognizable to playgoers as a puritan, one of the godly (1.3.50).[41] He is also introduced in terms that suggest he is—or is perceived to be—among God's chosen. Alongside the obvious connotations of the name Angelo, he is addressed twice in the opening scene in language that evokes election. Within the first twenty lines of the play (and only two lines after Angelo is first named), the Duke announces:

> For you must know, we have with special soul
> Elected him our absence to supply. (1.1.17–18)

Although this statement literally means simply, *I have with special care and all the faculties of mind chosen him to fill my place*, the phrase "special soul / Elected" in a conversation about a man of conspicuous piety attunes listeners to a predestinarian subtext. This resonates a few lines later when the Duke declares to Angelo:

> We have with a leaven'd and prepared choice
> Proceeded to you. (1.1.51–52)

Describing the precise Angelo as the "leaven'd . . . choice" invokes a familiar metaphor used to describe the relationship between true Christians and Christians in name only. It was a commonplace of puritan culture that the Church of England was validated as a true Church by the presence of a godly and elect minority among the unredeemed, imperfectly reformed majority of English Christians, a "saving remnant" often referred to as "the leaven that leavens the lump."[42] Confessionally specific tropes such as this were accessible not only to early modern theatergoers who consciously identified the reference but also those who recognized the gist. The opening scene presents Angelo in terms that establish for mixed-faith playgoers not only his godliness but also the presumption of his election, as well as the correlation of the two. This does more than define one character's confessional identity; it instantiates predestinarian judgment as the operative code of legibility in the world of the play.

The dramatic expectation that godliness indexes election, while wickedness signals reprobation, is solidified in the first two scenes by the contrasting presentation on stage of two visually distinctive sets of characters. In the opening scene, a grave Duke and two godly magistrates discuss how best to enforce the city's strict sex laws. In the scene that immediately follows, profligate gentlemen flout the morality laws in friendly banter with a madam and a sex criminal in chains. Costume likely accentuated the visual contrast between these two groups. Angelo, who takes secret pride in the "gravity" of his "habit" (2.4.9, 15), may have been dressed in a style of plain clothes that would identify him onstage as a puritan, or perhaps he and Escalus simply wore somber robes appropriate to their office. By contrast, the folio's list of characters identifies Lucio as "a Fantastic," suggesting him to be foppishly attired.[43] The fact that theater audiences are habituated to quickly distinguishing heroes from villains, by extrapolating from the details with which characters are introduced, makes the drama particularly equipped to exploit, and to expose, the elision of predestinarian status and its external perception. As the pious magistrates exit the stage and the whoremongers enter, spectators of various faiths likely take for granted that they can tell who is the leaven and who is the lump.

However, having established early the confessional framework operative in the play, the dialogue that follows begins to trouble mixed-faith audiences' shared expectation that implied spiritual groups match visible cultural ones. The libertine Lucio jokes with his companions:

Lucio: Thou art thyself a wicked villain, despite of all grace.
1 *Gent*: Well, there went but a pair of shears between us.
Lucio: I grant: as there may between the lists and the velvet.
    Thou art the list.

> 1 *Gent*: And thou the velvet; thou art good velvet; thou'rt a three-
> piled piece, I warrant thee: I had as lief be a list of an English
> kersey, as be piled, as thou art piled, for a French velvet. Do I
> speak feelingly now?
>
> *Lucio*: I think thou dost: and indeed, with most painful feeling of
> thy speech. I will, out of thine own confession, learn to begin
> thy health; but whilst I live, forget to drink after thee.
>
> 1 *Gent*: I think I have done myself wrong, have I not?
>
> 2 *Gent*: Yes, that thou hast; whether thou art tainted or free.
>
> (1.2.24–40)

Their banter tosses back and forth casual predestinarian speculation. Lucio teasingly calls his friend a reprobate: "Thou art thyself a wicked villain, despite of all grace." Gentleman 1 retorts that if he is damned, he has Lucio's company. But his proverb, equivalent to the modern saying "cut from the same cloth," introduces an image of separation—"a pair of shears between us"—even as it asserts their spiritual sameness. Lucio picks up this suggestion and expands on it to reassert the invisible spiritual divide in terms of visible class difference. His revision of the metaphor makes the split between the regenerate and the reprobate analogous to the cut between "the lists and the velvet": that is, between luxury fabric and disposable scraps.[44] Yet the added clarification, "Thou art the list," itself suggests the possibility of swapping positions. Like the potentially endless, reciprocal children's taunt "I know you are, but what am I?" the Gentleman's riposte readapts the metaphor to reverse their roles. With the threadbare, worn "velvet" now referring to hair loss from mercury treatments, the difference between the saved and the damned is reconfigured, in terms of the less apparent distinction between healthy men and those infected with venereal disease. Lucio's comeback, that the Gentleman sounds like he knows all too well what he is talking about, leaves his interlocutor uncomfortably aware—as Angelo in a more serious register will become later—of having somehow entangled himself in the very sexual and spiritual category he was so insistent to avoid: "I think I have done myself wrong, have I not?" The closing phrase to this exchange, "whether thou art tainted or free," which is differentiated from the preceding dialogue because delivered by a new speaker and punctuated by the arrival of Mistress Overdone, leaves the state of the Gentleman's genitals and soul conspicuously uncertain. The reversibility of predestinarian positions in this flyting match, and the baffling effect of this indeterminacy on the Gentleman, launches the play's running dramatization of the practical impossibility, whether the soul in question is one's own or another's, of telling the saved from the damned.

The distinction between respectable and disreputable individuals—so crisp in the transition between the first two scenes—becomes increasingly blurred. Pompey reports that while all the brothels in the suburbs are to be torn down, those in the city will remain untouched because "a wise burgher put in for them" (1.2.92); in other words, whorehouses are maintained by good citizens. The indeterminacy of the upright and the degenerate introduced in this scene recurs throughout *Measure for Measure* even at the level of the line. The play is full of moral oxymorons such as "sanctimonious pirate" (1.2.7), "devilish mercy" (3.1.64), "notorious benefactors" (2.1.50), "precise villains" (2.1.54), and "damned Angelo" (4.3.123). The earnest, dimwitted constable Elbow delivers a scene's worth of malapropisms that replace respectable words with their dodgy antonyms and vice versa: "profanation" for "veneration" (2.1.55), "cardinally" for "carnally" (2.1.79), "benefactors" for "malefactors" (2.1.51–52), and "respected" for "suspected" (2.1.159–73). Even the name of the executioner, Abhorson, which jams together "abhor" and "whoreson," suggests both "ab [from] whore / whore's son" and "abhors whores."[45] In the comic trial scene, Pompey (a pimp) tries to get Froth (a john) acquitted for whatever obscene act was attempted on Elbow's wife. He beseeches Escalus, "Look in this gentleman's face. . . . Look . . . Doth your honour mark his face? . . . Mark it well. . . . Doth your honour see any harm in his face?" (2.1.145–51). Pompey's spurious defense of Froth is a reductio ad absurdum of the play's central recurring problem: the inability to judge inner conditions by outward appearances.

The question of visible grace emerges also around Catholic Isabella. Lucio the womanizer greets Isabella at the door of the nunnery:

Hail virgin, if you be—as those cheek-roses
Proclaim you are no less. (1.4.16–17)

The lines hover between a physical observation and a spiritual implication: that her ruddy complexion shows her attractive youth, or that her blushing proves her chastity. The Duke at their first meeting takes Isabella's beauty as an outward sign of her inner virtue: "The hand that hath made you fair hath made you good. The goodness that is cheap in beauty makes beauty brief in goodness; but grace, being the soul of your complexion, shall keep the body of it ever fair" (3.1.179–84). The Duke spends most of the play ferreting out secret sins, yet he takes Isabella's soul at face value. While audiences know that the Duke has overheard Isabella defend her virtue, what they see onstage is not so much a response to her argument as a religious version of love at first sight. Given the Duke's later marriage proposal, this spiritual meet-cute has a sexual undercurrent. Suggestions of corruption appear even as the Duke proclaims her chastity. "The hand that made you fair" refers to divine creation but also recalls the art that women use to paint their faces. The "good" that ends the first sentence describes her soul, yet the "goodness" that begins the next sentence refers to the feminine charms that lead to corruption. The wavering between virtue and vice in this anadiplosis is not internal to Isabella but a projection of the Duke's. The problem of moral perception that the pretty novitiate raises for male characters is not the difficulty of seeing hidden corruption but the depravity of their own gaze. Like Angelo, the sight of chaste Isabella makes the Duke think of sin. In his description, Isabella's "complexion" refers both to her character and her face, "grace" carries a suggestion of gracefulness alongside its spiritual meaning, and "fair" means both comely and chaste. These puns consolidate the unity between her outward beauty and her inner virtue. However, the Duke's closing compliment to the purity of her soul ends with attention to her "fair . . . body." The confessor is checking out more than her spiritual health. Just as Angelo's apparent piety covers his attempt to rape Isabella, the Duke's monastic disguise enables covert sexual attention to the young nun in training. Professing to have only the holy thoughts of a man of the cloth allows him to be alone with her: "My mind promises with my habit no loss shall touch her by my company" (3.1.177). With thick dramatic irony, Lucio falsely accuses the ersatz churchman of dishonesty: "*Cucullus non facit monachum:* honest in nothing but in his clothes" (5.1.261–62). Yet the joke—as becomes clear a moment later when Lucio unfrocks the Friar to reveal the Duke—is that in this case, the hood really does not make the monk. The Duke's abrupt declaration of sexual interest in a woman of devout chastity continues the play's unmasking of misleading appearances of sanctity.[46] The problem of discerning souls from clothes and faces is not affixed solely to the puritan Angelo but bleeds into other plots and characters with different confessional coloring.

Nevertheless, Claudio's first lines onstage give this ongoing ambiguation of vice and virtue clear predestinarian implications. Forced by the deputy Angelo to do public penance for his crime, Claudio complains:

> Thus can the demi-god, Authority,
> Make us pay down for our offense by weight.

The words of heaven; on whom it will, it will;
On whom it will not, so; yet still 'tis just. (1.2.112–15)

Directly identified as a scriptural quote—"The words of heaven"—Claudio's lines closely paraphrase Romans 9:15–18, "I wil have mercie on him, to whome I wil shewe mercie: and wil have compassion on him, on whome I wil have compassion . . . he hathe mercie on whome he wil & whom he wil, he hardeneth," one of the key biblical proof texts for the doctrine of predestination. Claudio's point, as is clear from his subsequent exchange with Lucio, is that Angelo is unjustly condemning him arbitrarily as if he were God, whose inscrutable will alone determines election and reprobation.[47] This caustically ironic reference to scripture, delivered at an early moment of heightened dramatic attention (Claudio's entrance under arrest), highlights the gap in Calvinist theology between divine and earthly "judgments"; that is, between God's secret, immutable decrees and imperfect human attempts to imitate his justice. Claudio's first appearance onstage introduces the main plot to mixed-faith theatergoers in explicitly predestinarian terms.

Sympathy for the (Potential) Reprobate

Measure for Measure devotes substantive stage resources to exploring the inner life of a puritan hypocrite and potential reprobate. The theatrical development of Angelo's subjectivity elicits different kinds of ideological and emotional flexibility from theatergoers who occupy different confessional positions. Angelo articulates a spiritual identity that was, for many Protestants, outside the bonds of Christian community. Comparing reprobates to devils, the preacher William Burton instructs his parishioners, "Nay we ought not to pray for all, because all shall not be saved."[48] Yet the same people who may have denied a damned soul their prayers while sitting in their church pews nevertheless could participate in a character's struggle with reprobation in the playhouse. For many from both Churches, the greater leap may have been engaging emotionally with a puritan stereotype. *Measure for Measure* offers intimate access to the interiority of a spiritually and socially demonized figure to theatergoers of all faith positions: papists for whom even the premise of Angelo's crisis was alien, as well as lukewarm Calvinists who experienced through him a more fraught version of the familiar. The ostensible proximity between Angelo's fear of reprobation and godly theatergoers' own experiences of predestinarian culture does not mean that his soliloquies ask less emotional elasticity from puritan playgoers. *Measure for Measure*'s complex development of godly subjectivity calls on some audience members to extend their imaginations across vast religious differences, and on other theatergoers to pivot in their habitual spiritual positions. These are different kinds of ideological stretching, but the unfolding of performance synchronizes and connects them.

Measure for Measure's central plot twist—that the outwardly holy Angelo, the man so pure his "urine is congealed ice," turns out to be a corrupt would-be rapist and potential reprobate—clearly dramatizes the dangers of conflating cultural and (presumed) spiritual status (3.2.106–7). The more emotionally engaging revelation, however, is not that Angelo is wicked, but that his secret hypocrisy is a surprise even to himself. The play prompts confessionally diverse audiences to expect the discovery of the abstemious Lord Angelo's hidden "appetite" at the close of 1.3, when the Duke announces the exposure of Angelo's character as a motive for his monastic disguise, ending the scene with the tantalizing couplet:

> Hence shall we see
> What our seemers be. (1.3.52–54)

The revelation these lines anticipate is the familiar exposure of the base desires of the hypocritically pious that Kristen Poole has shown was a stock feature of stage representations of puritans since the anti-Martinist plays of 1589.[49] However, unlike Malvolio in *Twelfth Night*, who privately indulges in erotic fantasies, Angelo is disturbed to discover in himself a carnal craving. Reversing the expectations of the reversal of expectations—making the holy Angelo not only a hypocrite but an unwitting one—further troubles the ability of mixed-faith theatergoers to read spiritual states through the play's predestinarian hermeneutic. Unexpectedly, *Measure for Measure* unearths not simply the secret sins of a smooth-faced puritan but the inner struggles of a self-deceiver.[50] Angelo is a caricature with tragic interiority. Given the most frequent and most complex soliloquies in the play, this dramatically privileged subjectivity offers confessionally diverse audiences a potentially damned puritan hypocrite as an unlikely figure of identification through whom to explore the primary, experiential problem of predestination: reprobation anxiety.

Angelo's first soliloquy presents his moral crisis in the specific language of reprobation:

> Is this her fault or mine?
> The tempter, or the tempted, who sins most, ha?
> Not she; nor doth she tempt; but it is I
> That, lying by the violet in the sun,
> Do as the carrion does, not as the flower,
> Corrupt with virtuous season. (2.2.163–8)

The image of the carrion and the flower was commonly used in Calvinist tracts to explain why God is not to blame for the sins of reprobates.[51] For example, William Burton's *Exposition of the Lords Prayer* explains the metaphor in the following exchange:

> *Q.* How else can you prove that God is the author of the action, and not of the corruption that is in it?
> *A.* By the very light of nature & common reason. For, the Sunne shineth upon carrion, and it stinketh more than it did before. It shineth also upon flowers, and they smell more sweete then they did before, the Sunne is the cause of their smelling more then they did: but not of the stinking of the one, nor of the sweetnes of the other, for the cause of that is in the natures of the things themselves. So may God be the author of an action and not of the corruption of the action.[52]

Similarly, Gervase Babington, future bishop of Worchester, compares the sun to God, the stinking carcass to a reprobate soul, and sweet flowers to the elect.[53] Like Burton and Babington, Angelo frames the flower/carcass image as an explanation of why the ostensible "cause" (Isabella) is not to blame for sin but simply reveals the inherently corrupt nature of the sinner (himself). The close correspondence between the terms and logic of these texts suggests the elect flower/reprobate carcass metaphor was a commonplace.[54] The suggestion of "carrion" damnation is reinforced a few lines later when Angelo, horrified at his own desires, asks himself, "What dost thou, or what art thou, Angelo?" (2.2.173). Coming just three lines after the image of the reprobate carcass, the move from "dost" to "art" shows the chillingly swift, fallacious logic at the heart of the interpretive practices of predestinarian culture. It indicates a shift from thinking of his lust as an isolated, sinful impulse to considering it evidence of what he "is": damned.

Not only does Angelo against Perkins's warning "peremptorily set down that he . . . is a reprobate," he also expresses an awareness of his particular position as a "white devil" or "self-deceiver," an unconscious spiritual hypocrite. He laments:

> O cunning enemy, that, to catch a saint,
> With saints dost bait thy hook! (2.2.180–81)

Overlaying different confessional traditions, these lines invoke the visions of virtuous women that tested the chastity of desert hermits like Saint Jerome,[55] as well as the sense of "saints" as a synonym for "the godly," suggesting their assurance of election. The speech continues:

> Most dangerous
> Is that temptation that doth goad us on
> To sin in loving virtue. (2.2.181–83)

Together these lines connect the sexual temptation presented by the chaste nun to a more abstract sense in which the love of virtue itself can pose a spiritual threat: the danger of self-complacency. Later Angelo speaks of his "gravity / Wherein . . . I take pride" (2.4.9–10) and decries his apparent virtue as "false seeming!" (2.4.15). Cumulatively, these lines present Angelo's failing as a form of unhealthy, prideful cultivation of things that are in themselves good. This is precisely the trap of "security" that books such as Dyke's *Mystery of Selfe-Deceiving* sought to expose.

Dramatically, the speech encourages mixed-faith audiences to identify emotionally with a speaker who implicates himself as reprobate. It is the first soliloquy in the play, which foregrounds and privileges playgoers' access to Angelo's interiority. Ideologically diverse audiences and Angelo discover his hypocrisy together, aligning their perspectives. The evidence he marshals of his own reprobation is presented rhetorically in ways that stress his flustered vulnerability. "What's this? What's this?" he begins, bewildered by his own lust for Isabella (2.2.163). The quick succession of questions, eleven in twenty-six lines, registers his confusion; thirty-two caesuras mark his fitful agitation; and fourteen extrametrical lines suggest his breathlessness.[56] In contrast to the measured logic with which he publicly justifies his rulings elsewhere in the play, playgoers here see a man rapidly changing his mind. Abruptly, he declares after a caesura, "O, let her brother live!" (2.2.175). His jumbled, non-sequential sentences signal emotional upheaval and loss of control. Overcome, Angelo confesses that the virtuous Isabella "subdues me quite" (2.2.186). The only metrically short line in a speech full of run-ons, the text underscores this admission of defeat with a pause. This beat also accentuates the concluding statement, "Ever till now / When men were fond, I smil'd, and wonder'd how" (2.2.186–87), which not only builds depth of character by divulging Angelo's hitherto blank erotic history, marking a growth in awareness, but also newly includes cold fish Angelo in the community of men who love. At this point in the play, irrespective of their real-world attitudes to puritans, spectators may anticipate not the scene of sexual coercion that later follows but rather an odd couple romance between godly Angelo and would-be nun Isabella, who despite their confessional differences are matched temperamentally in their legalistic thinking and ardent sexual purity. In other words, at this moment Angelo is both the play's potential reprobate and its potential romantic hero.

When Angelo reappears a short scene later, his second soliloquy deepens both confessionally diverse playgoers' awareness of his alienation from God and their sympathetic engagement with his emotional turmoil. He begins bemoaning his inability to pray—"Heaven hath my empty words" (2.4.2)—and describing the affairs of state on which he can no longer concentrate as "like a good thing being often read / Grown sere and tedious" (2.4.8–9), echoing puritan complaints of spiritual dryness, a troubling potential indication of a lack of saving grace. While the soliloquy amplifies the signs that he is not a child of God—he considers adopting "the devil's crest" (2.4.17)—it also intensifies the intimacy of mixed-faith theatergoers' relationship to an emotionally exposed Angelo. By implication, Angelo's opening declaration that he can only offer heaven "empty words" positions playgoers of all religious orientations as privileged auditors of thoughts more personal than prayer, an effect strengthened by the interjection, "Let no man hear me" (2.4.10). The puritan hypocrite uncovered here for mixed-faith audiences is a baffled soul, undone by desire, unable to pray or work, disillusioned with the gap between his public identity and inward sin, and convinced of his damnation. In contrast to Richard III's cheekily cruel declaration of his intent to seduce Anne ("What, I that kill'd her husband and her father?"),[57] Angelo is so overwhelmed by Isabella's impending entrance that he feels faint:

Why does my blood thus muster to my heart,
Making it both unable for itself,

And dispossessing all my other parts
Of necessary fitness? (2.4.20–23)

After a metrical pause, perhaps an implied cue for a moment of wooziness, Angelo describes his heart as like "one that swounds," and the blood that rushes toward it as like "foolish throngs" that block the air by crowding in "obsequious fondness" and "untaught love" (2.4.24, 28, 27). Literally lovesick, Angelo is so overwrought that even his emotions have emotions.

Nothing in this vulnerable soliloquy anticipates the attempted rape and extreme abuse of power in the following exchange with Isabella. Angelo's last explicit comment on Claudio's case, before he attempts to use it to extort sex from the novice nun, implies he will "let her brother live!" Though early in the conversation Angelo suggests exchanging sex for a pardon, this possibility is carefully couched in hypothetical terms: "I'll not warrant that" (2.4.59), "I subscribe not that" (2.4.89), "such a person" (2.4.91), "this suppos'd" (2.4.97). While audience members of all religious positions can see the ugly direction in which the dialogue is headed, Angelo's cagey reluctance to directly proposition Isabella also makes it by no means certain that the interview will end as it does: with Angelo demanding sex by threatening Claudio's death and torture. At least initially, the joke (one not entirely unsympathetic to Angelo) is the awkwardness of his ineffectual attempt to leverage sex from the innocently uncomprehending Isabella. Sharing in the secret of his attraction to her subjectively aligns mixed-faith audiences with Angelo for the first hundred lines of the exchange, before he delivers his ultimatum. The dramatic irony attunes confessionally diverse theatergoers to Angelo's desire and discomfort. This creates not only suspense but comedy, as when Isabella passionately declares that to preserve her chastity, "th' impression of keen whips I'd wear as rubies / And strip myself to death as to a bed / That longing have been sick for" (2.4.101–3), unconscious of the effect of the image of her naked, flagellated, longing body on her interlocutor; or when Angelo responds to Isabella's acknowledgment that she strategically downplays her brother's offense with deadpan irony: "We are all frail" (2.4.121).

Having been led to sympathize with this unlikely figure—the hypocritical puritan and potential reprobate—Angelo's volte-face midscene, from swooning lover to sex "tyrant," confronts mixed-faith audiences with another failure to read inner states (2.4.168). Abruptly shifting the tone of the conversation, Angelo switches from cautious hypotheticals to lecherous imperatives: "Let me be bold" (2.4.132). The startling attack seems to confirm for confessionally diverse spectators what they have been told about Angelo by Angelo himself: he is carrion. His sexual demand is framed in terms that recall a common distinction in Calvinist thought between those who are still "of the corrupted and damned stocke of Adam" and those who are "regenerate in Christe."[58] This theological framework is established in the initial encounter, when Isabella pleads with Angelo to spare Claudio by asking him to remember the redemptive grace he himself hopes to receive from God:

> O think on that,
> And mercy then will breathe within your lips,
> Like man new made. (2.2.77–79)

The phrase "man new made" invokes the process of "regeneration," in which the Holy Spirit works on the soul of the elect to produce a spiritual rebirth.[59] Isabella's reference to the passage in Genesis in which God brings Adam to life by breathing into his nostrils reinforces this sense of "man new made," since regeneration was understood as the beginning of purification from Adam's sin. By contrast, Angelo's private recognition, "Blood, thou art blood" (2.4.15), suggests the kind of entrapment in the body associated with the old Adam. The specific terms of Angelo's insistence that Isabella capitulate to his "sensual race," "sharp appetite," and "will" corroborate his fleshly unregeneracy (2.4.159, 160, 163).

The effect of Angelo's vile proposition to Isabella is to disorient spectators of all religious persuasions with the discovery of what has already been revealed to them: Angelo's wickedness. That theatergoers might experience surprise at the manifestation of the deputy's depravity, even after it has been described to them at length by Angelo himself, highlights the extent to which the play embroils mixed-faith audiences in the problematic of predestinarian spiritual assessment. The exposed subjectivity presented by the first two soliloquies *impairs* theatergoers' ability to interpret Angelo. Intimate access to his romantic twitterpation allows mixed-faith spectators to sympathize with Angelo's fear of reprobation. But when Angelo's sudden willingness to rape, torture, and murder seems to substantiate his own assumption that he is damned, playgoers of all religious groups may be alienated by their error of emotional judgment.

Moreover, Angelo's predestinarian crisis does not have an affective or confessional monopoly on the scene. Isabella appeals to Calvinist Angelo to spare her brother in a Catholic idiom of intercession.[60] She offers to "bribe" the deputy "with true prayers" (2.2.146–52); and she believes the devotions of nuns to be particularly efficacious:

That shall be up at heaven and enter there
Ere sunrise: prayers from preserved souls
From fasting maids, those minds are dedicate
To nothing temporal. (2.2.147–56)

She asks for the potential sin of Angelo's clemency to be "added to the faults of mine, / And nothing of your answer" (2.4.73–74). The lines articulate an alternative, Catholic paradigm in which grace is a gift that can be solicited. Isabella operates in a theological economy of commutable sin and redemptive supplication: Angelo does not. This religious tension is the dramatic impasse of the scene. The implied blocking of the novitiate on her knees, begging grace from an implacable predestinarian, is a *gestus* of their conflicting eschatological systems. Yet Protestant and Catholic audience members did not watch scenes such as this encamped in opposite affective corners, rooting for their respective ideological avatars. Theater is an emotional process, not a position statement. If his preceding soliloquies ask mixed-faith audiences to share predestinarian feeling, the godly magistrate's assault on Isabella reorients attention to the subjectivity of his Catholic supplicant. This shift is clear when Angelo exits and the novitiate assumes the privileged position of soliloquist, appealing to ideologically diverse audiences as sympathetic witnesses to the attempted rape:

To whom should I complain? Did I tell this,
Who would believe me? (2.4.170–71)

Yet the closing couplet of this speech reminds playgoers across the religious spectrum that Isabella's spiritual high ground rests on Claudio's dead body:

Isabel live chaste, and brother, die:
More than our brother is our chastity. (2.4.183–84)[61]

Playgoers' sympathetic engagements with characters in *Measure for Measure* are not static forms of identification but a series of ongoing, unstable shifts between attachment and affective irony.[62] The point is not which model of the holy emerges from the plot least scathed but the emotional and ideological exercise that the process of theatrical response gives mixed-faith audiences.

When the play rejoins Angelo, he is remorseful, prompting confessionally diverse playgoers to again reevaluate his inner being.[63] Despite the fact that at this point he believes he has coercively raped Isabella, executed Claudio, and gotten away with it all, surprisingly, Angelo reappears onstage not as the sex-crazed tyrant exulting in his wickedness who was last seen with Isabella but rather full of self-recrimination. His final soliloquy begins, "This deed unshapes me quite," returning to the vulnerability evident in his earlier speeches (4.4.18). He oscillates between his sense of guilt for the crime and his fear of detection and punishment.[64] Caesuras twice mark breaks from sentences rehearsing reasons he will not be caught, showing Claudio's death intruding on Angelo's thoughts: "He should have liv'd" (4.4.26) and "Would yet he had lived" (4.4.30). Angelo interprets this divided contrition as evidence of his damnation:

> Alack, when once our grace we have forgot,
> Nothing goes right; we would, and we would not. (4.4.31–32)

He understands both his sin and his inability to fully repent as "backsliding," the disappearance of false or temporary grace.[65] Since it was a familiar doctrinal point that the truly elect could not fully fall from grace, a principle referred to as the "perseverance of the saints," theatergoers of various religious persuasions would have recognized Angelo's implicit, overhasty logic, and the conclusion to which he leaps: the elect cannot fall from grace; I have; therefore, I am a reprobate. Angelo's rash assessment of his own soul is delivered in a rhyming couplet that ends the scene, giving it the apparent moral authority of an adage. However, the validity of Angelo's religious despair is qualified by the scene's dramatic irony. Playgoers know, as Angelo does not, that the bed trick and head switch have spared Isabella's virginity and Claudio's life, so that the rape and murder he intended were (as Isabella points out later) crimes never actually committed. The Duke's ruse cues mixed-faith audiences to anticipate a comic resolution to tragic circumstances, leaving open the possibility of Angelo's spiritual recuperation by the structures of the plot.

Measure for Measure insists on the opacity of souls, even Angelo's. While the deputy is implied to be a secret reprobate for most of the first four acts, in the final scene Angelo's spiritual condition is left ambiguous. When his crimes are discovered, Angelo asks for death, not mercy:

> O my dread lord,
> I should be guiltier than my guiltiness
> To think I can be undiscernible,

When I perceive your Grace, like power divine,
Hath looked upon all my passes. Then, good prince,
No longer session hold upon my shame,
But let my trial be mine own confession.
Immediate sentence, then, and sequent death
Is all the grace I beg. (5.1.364–72)

The speech establishes a parallel between the Duke's clandestine surveillance
of his crimes and God's total knowledge of his soul. Theologically, the closing phrase, "Death is all the grace I beg," is a contradiction in terms. Angelo's
desire to die is a sign of despair, a state into which those with grace (the elect)
cannot fall. When Escalus expresses pity that such a man should sin so grossly,
Angelo responds:

I am sorry that such sorrow I procure
And so deep sticks it in my penitent heart
That I crave death more willingly than mercy. (5.1.472–74)

As for Wallington earlier, while Angelo is still suicidal, these lines suggest another possible spiritual condition: the abject repentance of a soul not lost to
God. In one sense, the Duke's reprieve invites audiences to presume that God
extends Angelo the same mercy. But this assumption is complicated by the
Duke's lines:

By this Lord Angelo perceives he's safe;
Methinks I see a quickening in his eye.
Well, Angelo, your evil quits you well. (5.1.492–94)

The remark implies that Angelo's penitence was simply another holy pretense.
Yet "quickening" also suggests regeneration, a sign of the "new man." "Your
evil quits you well" might read either as "Your evil serves you well" or "Your
evil leaves you well." The play reveals Angelo's secret sins only to leave his real
spiritual state undetermined.[66]

Measure for Measure's attention to Angelo's interiority entangles mixed-
faith audiences in the problems of predestinarian assessment. The play inducts
playgoers of various religious persuasions into a Calvinist hermeneutic that
conflates social respectability with salvation. The unfolding drama involves
the shared expectations and responses of ideologically diverse audiences in the

contradictions of this confessional system. Angelo's cultural identity as a godly man is shown to be an unreliable indicator of the predestined condition of his soul. Yet, instead of revealing his true state, Angelo's self-diagnosis as one of the damned is itself undermined by the play's comic resolution. The intimacy and vulnerability of his soliloquies invite mixed-faith audiences to sympathize with Angelo, precisely when he is most convinced he is, to paraphrase Calvin, no better than a devil. The process of continually calling on confessionally diverse playgoers to revise what they think they know—and feel— about Angelo's soul does not replace a misperception of his election with an accurate understanding of his reprobation but rather confounds the possibility of discerning souls from either external or internal signs. Though immersed in the categories of reprobation and election, the play does not affirm Calvinist eschatological claims. Rather, it leads mixed-faith playgoers into the maze of predestinarian confusion.

Back to the State; or, How to Rule (Potential) Reprobates

Having argued that the play invokes, and destabilizes, one of the most quotidian and pervasive interpretive practices of Calvinist culture, I return now to the macropolitical implications of this uncertain hermeneutic for the state's relationship to its sinner-subjects. Through the figure of Barnardine the Bohemian murderer, pardoned by the Duke despite his own confession to the crime, *Measure for Measure* confronts the limits of secular justice over unknowable, already-judged souls. The play marks Barnardine as a reprobate, but it also insists on the dubiousness of that label. His pardon in the closing scene models the ne plus ultra of earthly law.[67]

The Provost who oversees the prison refers to Barnardine as "this reprobate." The word appears only four times in extant Shakespeare and only once, here, as a noun referring to a person.[68] An entirely superfluous character in terms of plot, Barnardine embodies a set of metaphors that describe reprobation as a drunken sleep from which one wakes to die. Imprisoned nine years awaiting execution, Barnardine stays alive in jail by staying drunk: "Drunk many times a day, if not many days entirely drunk" (4.2.147–48). He is, in the Provost's words, "a man that apprehends death no more dreadfully but as a drunken sleep; careless, reckless, and fearless of what's past, present or to come: insensible of mortality and desperately mortal" (4.2.140–43). This account of Barnardine builds on the common injunction in sermons and devotional texts to be watchful Christians, to await Christ's return attentively like the wise virgins of the parable, and unlike the unregenerate "[who] slept in sinne . . . not minding God nor their owne salvation."[69] When Pompey summons him, calling, "Master Barnardine! You must rise and be hanged, Master Barnardine!" (4.3.22–23), Barnardine replies, "Away, you rogue away; I am sleepy," and, "I have been drinking all night; I am not fitted for it" (4.3.29, 42–43). This exchange literalizes a set of tropes that describe the reprobate on the Day of Judgment as sleepers waking to death. As the Scottish minister Robert Rollock writes, "The bodie of the elect shall rise [to glory]. . . . The body of the reprobate is not said to sleep, as it is, to ly dead; for, the rising of it is but to death."[70] Archbishop of York Edwin Sandys also speaks of the predestined damned as sleepers who will only wake to their destruction: "As for the reprobate they . . . are so hard and fast a sleepe, that they will never stirre, untill fire out of heaven flee about their eares to waken them."[71] Sleepy, drunk, spiritually unprepared, and summoned to death, Barnardine is an emblem of reprobation.

However, if the play classifies Barnardine as a reprobate, it undermines the certainty of that label by also identifying him as a faker, or not what he seems. The name Barnardine is the term for a trick for cheating at cards in which the mark is distracted by a partner, the barnard, who feigns drunkenness.[72] Just before Barnardine first appears onstage, Pompey delivers a monologue describing the many young men in prison he recognizes from his former employment with Mistress Overdone the bawd, all twelve of whom have symbolic names, for example, "Master Shoe-tie the great traveller" (4.3.17), most of them suggestive of a louche milieu, such as "Master Deep-vow" (4.3.13) and "young Drop-heir that killed lusty Pudding" (4.3.15–16). This list of seedy monikers attunes auditors to the confidence game reference in Barnardine's name, immediately reinforced by the fact that appearing drunk is precisely the trick that keeps him alive. Barnardine's drunkenness is both the symbol of his reprobation and a false sign.

This figure, both a personification of the predestined damned and a walking wink-and-nudge, prompts conflicting responses. Barnardine is a disturbing character, unconcerned with his own mortality. As the Duke puts it, "Unfit to live or die! O gravel heart" (4.3.63). However, he is also extremely funny, pleading a hangover to get out of hanging, and casually chatting with the executioner: "How now, Abhorson? What's the news with you?" (4.3.39). Barnardine, the man too drunk to die, is likely to appeal to pleasure-seeking theatergoers. Yet we cannot assume that playgoers' responses to the reprobate con man would be divided by their degree of religiosity. Pious audience members did not necessarily take Barnardine only as a serious spiritual warning, nor were less virtuous theatergoers only capable of being entertained by the irreverent joke. Godly and wicked audience members alike could feel either, or both, ends of the affective range that Barnardine opens. Theater recalibrates religious differences of temperature as well as kind. A devout playgoer could delight in the reprobate's blasé impiety, while a prostitute picking up clients could feel chilled by the macabre memento mori. The mixed feelings produced by this figure illustrate the impossibility of neatly separating collective and individual responses to theater. Irreverent and religious responses to Barnardine participate in the same structure of feeling: the grim warning of death and its cheeky evasion are two sides of the same emotional coin. Drunken humor and sober fear produce each other; their effects are mutually entwined and mutually dependent. Divergent reactions to the reprobate grifter are not a matter of playgoers choosing A or B but rather one of sharing affective dissonance. Such variations in response were determined not merely by individuals' religious dispositions but rather by the tonal complexity of the scene.

Unable to execute or release him, the Provost proposes to "omit / This reprobate till he were well inclined," and instead use the head of the dead pirate Ragozine as a decoy (4.3.72–73). Despite the irony that "well inclined" reprobates are still reprobates, the Provost's apparent willingness to indefinitely defer Barnardine's sentence suggests the legal system's inadequacy to the task of regulating souls that remain inscrutable even when labeled. Like Angelo, Barnardine the "reprobate" is given a reprieve in the play's closing scene. The Duke addresses the prisoner:

> Sirrah, thou art said to have a stubborn soul
> That apprehends no further than this world,
> And squar'st thy life according. Thou'rt condemn'd;
> But, for those earthly faults, I quit them all,
> And pray thee take this mercy to provide
> For better times to come. Friar, advise him;
> I leave him to your hand. (5.1.478–84)

The Duke's speech distinguishes between the failings of Barnardine's "stubborn soul" and his "earthly faults." The phrasing implies that Barnardine is condemned for more than falls under the Duke's purview to "quit." While the scene as a whole establishes a parallel between the Duke's judgment and God's— "your Grace, like power divine / Hath looked upon all my passes"—this closing acknowledgment of sins beyond the Duke's power to forgive suggests a view of human judgments as at best provisional and imperfect rehearsals of unknowable judgments already made by God. The play's opening imagines a rigid system of justice operating in a world in which the saved can be distinguished from the wicked, its ending an extended deferral to the ultimate judge.

Whereas *A Game at Chess* hardens Protestant hegemony into its crudest form (a mob), dividing audiences by denomination, *Measure for Measure* allows mixed-faith playgoers to share a complex experience of the internal instability of dominant ideology. The play inducts confessionally diverse theatergoers—Pelagians, papists, prayer-book Protestants, and puritans—into a hypothetical world in which predestinarian rubrics of spiritual and social judgment are operative but do not work.

Measure for Measure does not endorse or clarify the Calvinist interpretive framework it establishes. Instead, the play draws theatergoers of various religious positions into predestinarian judgments that are then subverted. One of the special opportunities post-Reformation theater offered mixed-faith audiences was the chance to emotionally occupy the internal contradictions of different theological paradigms. This was valuable for playgoers regardless of their degree of proximity to the confessional world onstage. Catholic spectators of *Measure for Measure* are invited into the affective position of Calvinists, not in a secure state of faith but in spiritual crisis. Believers in predestination are allowed to aerate an insider's experience of these social and spiritual paradoxes against the perspectives of characters with a different degree of piety or a different doctrine of salvation. Sharing the experiential process of the play does not turn confessionally mixed audiences into ideological clones. However, the simultaneous apprehension of *Measure for Measure*'s plot reversals and subjectivity effects involves spectators of all faith positions in the troubled activity of predestinarian judgment. Through some of the most basic mechanisms of drama—plot twists, dramatic irony, and soliloquies—*Measure for Measure* destabilizes one of the most ubiquitous and deeply entrenched practices of Calvinist culture. The play offers ideologically diverse audiences a more flexible encounter with the rigid categories of election and reprobation than was usually afforded post-Reformation English people in their daily lives. *Measure for Measure* embroils theatergoers across the confessional spectrum in the dangers of making spiritual assumptions on cultural grounds. Unraveling its own confessional hermeneutic, *Measure for Measure* asks mixed-faith audiences to suspend religious judgment, and to stay open to unexpected shifts in sympathy.

Epilogue: Pity in the Public Sphere

Commercial theater drew mixed-faith Londoners into an imaginative space in which to explore the tangle of post-Reformation life. Playgoing—gathering with diverse groups of strangers to engage with refracted versions of a shared, messy culture—was a dynamic process of public formation.[1] Historians of emerging, early modern public spheres rightly recognize the importance of forms of communication, beyond the content they circulate, in organizing publics. Attention to the medium itself is particularly necessary in the case of theatrical public formation. As Richard Schechner observes, "Drama is that art whose subject, structure and action is social process."[2] Unlike the top-down "pitch making" described by Peter Lake and Steven Pincus, in which elite factions attempt to enlist popular support on particular issues through print, manuscript, or pulpit appeals, commercial theater's mediations of religious and political matters are more commonly elliptical rather than explicit, suggestive and exploratory rather than narrowly directed toward changing opinions on particular issues.[3] Turning his attention to the specific conditions of theatrical production, Lake acknowledges the centrality of both ambiguity and audience experience to the stage's social work. He rightly recognizes the interpretive work of playgoers (what happens "between the ears . . . of spectators") as the engine and site of public formation.[4] That an exemplary, archival historian such as Lake identifies live theater as playing a major, constitutive role in the development of a post-Reformation public sphere is a testament to the power of representation to shape culture. Nevertheless, the limitation of Lake's approach is the reduction of theatrical process to plot. This is a serious methodological problem, not simply an aesthetic or technical failure. Any close reading that flattens emotional change and exchange into narrative, or claims, or discursive fossils, erases theater's most potent, and venturesome, ideological work. Plays do not perform the "same educative or hermeneutic functions" as their print sources.[5] The culturally formative mental and emotional activities of playgoers are not limited to rational-critical deliberation. As Steven Mullaney writes, "Theater [is] a significant kind of social thought—a phenomenal, affective, and embodied form of social cognition . . . a public place where audiences could experience, exacerbate, or salve the cognitive and affective conditions of their own possibility."[6] If commercial plays often lacked doctrinal coherence, or clear confessional politics, what they offered instead was a sophisticated technology of virtual experience, through which mixed-faith collectives could wrangle, fear, mock, invent, mourn, and wonder their way through the lived, ideological contradictions of the English Reformation. Here, in closing, I linger on one crucial and distinctive resource of theatrical public making: the flexibility of affective thinking.

Feelings are theater's stock-in-trade, its first and most fluent language. Early modern commercial plays do not usually advance propositions but instead induce emotions. It is through, and not in spite of, this dependence on what Paul Yachnin calls "affective-critical" response that the stage fosters publics.[7] As Michael Warner urges, we need not embrace a "hierarchy of faculties that elevates rational-critical reflection as the self-image of humanity" and limits what activities "count as public" to what can be summarized in propositions, to the exclusion of practices that make "affect and expressivity . . . and embodied sociability" central.[8] Feeling is not less than, or separate from, thinking. Emotion is as powerful and perceptive a tool of social life as reason.[9] Early modern theater's autochthonous techniques of orchestrating collective and divided emotional responses made live drama better suited than rational-critical, print debate for some kinds of cultural processing, better at entertaining the possibilities of alternative paradigms, better at grasping half-formed ideas and ways of being, structures of feeling still "in solution" and not yet precipitated into easily namable forms.[10] As Bronwen Wilson and Paul Yachnin write, "We miss something fundamental about the formation of public life around shared works of art . . . if we fold their various practices into an account of particular rational debates about matters of public concern (just as we mistake their nature if we view them as outside of politics altogether)."[11] The religious and political impact of theatrical feeling is no less powerful because it is often ambiguous or indirect. To the contrary, ideology often manifests most potently at the level of unconscious, embodied, emotional response. Cultures do not re-form themselves only through debate, or analytical thought. The nonrational activities of the social imaginary, the idle questions, wet dreams, half-articulated fears, and nonsense jokes are still all constitutive and generative parts of the ongoing process of culture. The emotional and imaginative faculties that are theater's most basic material resources are adept at making the erratic, associative jumps through which people understand and remix their world at the ground level of lived experience.

For example, in Henry Wotton's famous account of the fire at the Globe, theater does not advance the claim that sacred kingship is a fraud but instead works as a form of background processing that erodes a social sensibility. Yet this perceptual and emotional shift is an important form of collective religious and political thinking. As Raymond William writes, "Not feeling against thought: but thought as felt and feeling as thought."[12] Wotton describes the disastrous performance of *All Is True*:

> [The play's] circumstances of pomp and majesty, even to the matting of the stage; the Knights of the Order with their Georges and garters, the guards with their embroidered coats, and the like [are] sufficient in truth within a while to make greatness very familiar, if not ridiculous. Now, King Henry making a masque at Cardinal Wolsey's house, and certain chambers being shot off at his entry, some of the paper, or other stuff, wherewith one of them was stopped, did light on the thatch, where being thought at first but an idle smoke, and their eyes more attentive to the show, it kindled inwardly, and ran round like a train, consuming within less than an hour the whole house to the very grounds.[13]

In this account, the desacralization of royal power is not experienced as a realization but is as much a hidden conflagration as the undetected playhouse fire, something that kindles inwardly while eyes are attentive to the show. Making familiar, or ridiculous, is not the same as making an argument. As Gina Bloom, Anston Bosman, and William N. West write, "Familiarity is less momentary and less binary than recognition; it does not require a before and an after or a critical moment of change from one state to another. Unlike recognition, familiarity need not even be conscious to be theatrically effective; it is an attentive response that is felt rather than precisely named, and capable of happening below the horizon of conscious cognition."[14] The point is not that creeping changes in perception eventually "get to the same place" as outright revelations. Both unmasking and making familiar demystify kingship; however, these different modes of communication cultivate in their audiences distinctive faculties for participation in public life.[15] Such qualitative differences between forms of religious and political perception are themselves culturally shaping.[16] In contrast to print debates that ask readers to accept or reject propositions about matters of religious doctrine, plays invite simultaneous, emotional apprehension of competing ideological paradigms. Theatrical mediation tends to avoid the "either/or" exigencies of polemic, to offer audiences "both/and" experiences of confessional controversies. Rather than treating the usual absence of explicit doctrinal choice in early modern theater as an evasion, or evacuation, of religious politics, we might instead consider the medium's capacity for ideological ambiguity as a valuable resource for emotional experimentation with the complex contradictions of post-Reformation life—a way of moving around, inside and out of, between, or aslant of rigid confessional binaries. That is to say, commercial theater gave mixed-faith Londoners a form of public art as complicated, malleable, and polyvocal as they were.

Mixed Emotions and the Remix of Religious Debate

Godly playwright John Ford's 1630 'Tis Pity She's a Whore offers audiences an experience of confessional controversy that does not demand playgoers take sides but instead allows them to dwell in religious tension.[17] The play presents a tragic romance between the brilliant Giovanni and his beautiful sister Annabella. On the one hand, 'Tis Pity She's a Whore grounds playgoers' disgust at the protagonists' incest in a dominant, gynophobic, and iconophobic Calvinist discourse, which figures the Roman Church as the Antichristian Whore of Babylon. On the other, the play links audiences' sympathy for the incestuous lovers with an emerging, Laudian understanding of the Roman Church as a corrupt but true Church. These networks of association need not operate at a conscious level to do their cultural work. Playgoers who did not explicitly identify the play's ecclesiological subtext could still feel the way it complicates the dramatic convention in which outwardly beautiful but inwardly corrupt femmes fatales embody the spiritually dangerous allure of Catholic idolatry.[18] The play garners sympathy for its romantic heroine. Through engaging audiences' expectations and emotional competencies, 'Tis Pity She's a Whore establishes Annabella as a significant variation on a familiar cultural and theatrical figure—the seductive Whore of Babylon. Yet the play is not a vindication of incest, or of the Roman Church. Rather than endorsing either a Calvinist or a Laudian position through its confessional coding of the incest plot, the play instead reframes the religious debate as a taut, unresolved, emotional paradox: pure love for an impure object.[19] Through affective contradiction, *'Tis Pity She's a Whore* enables ideological double vision.

Yet the conflicting feelings the play elicits vis-à-vis popish incest are too raw and queasy to be called protoecumenical understanding. *'Tis Pity She's a Whore* enables experimentation with alternative emotional postures toward a dominant discourse of gynophobic antipopery. This is not utopian. The commercial theater's revisions of the mixed materials of confessional life are too erratic and fitful to be "progressive." The indeterminable reprobates and lovable Antichrists that appeared on English stages were not marching teleologically toward a recognizable future of Anglicanism, or ecumenicalism, or secularism. This does not mean that the theater was not an agent of change, only that it conducted its deepest and most generative cultural work moment to moment, in attentional shifts, lovesick sighs, and roars of laughter. At this experiential scale, *longue durée* historical changes are hard to see, just as they were difficult to foresee for the people who lived them. Theater puts multiple cultural possibilities in play simultaneously, versions of the world suspended "in solution."

'Tis Pity She's a Whore appeared onstage just as the pamphlet war over whether the Roman Church was a true Church or Antichristian had come to a point of crisis.[20] In the mid-1620s, rising Laudian bishops, such as Richard Montague and John Cosin, broke from the long-standing Calvinist orthodoxy that held the Church of Rome to be Antichristian: the Whore of Babylon described in Revelations.[21] Instead, these divines maintained two new propositions: that the Roman Church was a true Church (albeit a corrupt one), and that because Rome was a true Church, there should be rapprochement between the Church of Rome and the Church of England. By rejecting the shared anti-Catholicism that had for decades united ceremonialist and reforming English Protestants, these avant-garde ideas shattered the Calvinist consensus. After 1629, when Charles I banned the publication of further tracts on the issue, the question of the status of the Roman Church migrated into the theater. However, the complex characterization of Annabella in *'Tis Pity She's a Whore* is not simply reflective of the way the figure of the Whore of Babylon had been destabilized by Laudian recuperations of the Roman Church in the six years preceding the play's first performance. Annabella revises the anti-Catholic and misogynist theatrical convention to which she belongs by accentuating the more sympathetic elements already within it. The play's emotionally conflicted treatment of Roman "Whoredom" is produced not only

by the shifting external pressures of post-Reformation religious culture but also by the evolving internal logic of theatrical form.

Certainly, Annabella participates in the early modern English stage tradition in which seductive women personify the sensory temptations of Catholic worship. As Alison Shell writes of the Whore of Babylon, "She epitomized the favorite Protestant theme of how idolatry was akin to spiritual whoredom. . . . Within drama, her presence is ubiquitous . . . invoked by much of the language of decadence and female depravity typical of Italianate tragedy, and that invocation, sometimes only an innuendo, is enough to spark off a gunpowder-train of pre-existing association."[22] As Huston Diehl observes, characters continually describe Annabella in the idiom of love idolatry. Giovanni declares that "the gods / Would make a god of [Annabella's beauty] . . . And kneel to it."[23] The Friar calls her "this idol thou ador'st" (1.1.61). Giovanni cries out, "O that it were not in religion sin / To make our love a god, and worship it" (1.2.140–41). Soranzo, her cuckolded husband, laments, "I did too superstitiously adore thee" (4.3.118). Diehl rightly recognizes that such femmes fatales embody the Roman Church not only through their depravity but equally through their sensory allure.[24]

'Tis Pity She's a Whore reparatively recasts the terms of Babylonian ornamentation in which it locates its heroine. A contemporary theatergoer writes of Ford's play:

> With admiration I beheld this Whore
> Adorned with beauty, such as might restore
> . . . .
> Her Giovanni, in his love unblamed.[25]

The seductive, feminized, and popish aesthetics that in Diehl's account provoke iconophobic and symbolic violence can be innocently embraced in this play by a puritan author. By comparison, the prologue to *The Devil's Charter* (1606) introduces the Antichristian pope and his incestuous daughter Lucrezia Borgia by calling on audiences to "behold the Strumpet of proud *Babylon* / Her cup with fornication foaming full."[26] The paradox of a whore that one might love unblamed (the core of the debate between Calvinists and Laudians over the nature of the Roman Church) is the emotional crux of Ford's play.

Yet Annabella's appeal is not simply the physical beauty that in Diehl's account creates the danger of idolatrous love. Annabella modifies the figure of the Babylonian femme fatale by intensifying elements already present in the characterization of her theatrical predecessors. Located in complex fictional worlds and in other dramatic conventions that complicate misogynist discourses of Roman Antichristianity, such resourceful and theatrically compelling characters as Vittoria Corombona and Lucrezia Borgia are always already in excess of their type. In the specific cases of Vittoria and Lucrezia, as later with Annabella, the Catholic heroines are humanized partly through their damaging relationships to sexually or emotionally incestuous brothers. These women are not reducible to the eponymous, allegorical figure that appears in Thomas Dekker's *Whore of Babylon*, riding a seven-headed dragon.[27] Nor is Annabella a mere emblem of the Antichristian seductions of the Roman Church. *'Tis Pity She's a Whore* individuates Annabella, marking a difference between her penitence and the narcissistic violence of her increasingly unhinged brother. Annabella's soliloquy of repentance includes an explicit rejection of seductive exteriors, in favor of an inward faith:

> Now I confess,
> Beauty that clothes the outside of the face
> Is cursed if it be not clothed with grace. (5.1.11–13)

The monologue gives her an internal spirituality that resists reducing the incestuous heroine to a flat figure of the Babylonian Whore.[28]

'Tis Pity She's a Whore devotes considerable theatrical energy to redeeming Giovanni and Annabella's romance. With its bawdy nurse and meddling Friar, the play would have been recognizable to theatergoers as an incestuous reboot of William Shakespeare's *Romeo and Juliet*. Recasting the star-crossed lovers as brother and sister lends Annabella and Giovanni's relationship some of the prestige, and sympathy, attached to its theatrical model. The play validates their attraction by presenting both brother and sister as good-looking, clever, and virtuous. Compared to Annabella's other suitors—an idiot, a murderer, and a womanizer—Giovanni is an appealing love interest. When they speak to each other, the two are nearly always alone. They often metrically complete each other's lines or share stichomythic dialogue. For example, when Giovanni declares his love, the two create a single "closed circuit" epanadiplosic line:

> *Annabella: You* are my brother, Giovanni.
> *Giovanni:*   *You*
>   My sister, Annabella. (1.2.226–28, italics mine)

Annabella and Giovanni's deepening relationship is relatively removed from the sordid revenge subplots that fill much of the play's action. Between themselves, the very consanguinity that makes their relationship monstrous to others justifies, and even naturalizes, their bond. Giovanni tells his sister:

> Nearness in birth or blood doth but persuade
> a nearer nearness in affection. (1.2.234–35)

They vow their love by their mother's ashes; her ring seals their mutual commitment (1.2.249–52, 2.6.37–42). The play creates a private world for Annabella and Giovanni, in which their love is not an abomination but an intimate romance.

'Tis Pity She's a Whore opens a gap between religious judgment and emotional response. "Dispute no more": these first words, spoken onstage by the Friar to his spiritual charge, open a play about an emotional truth (incestuous love) that exceeds theological debate (1.1.1). Giovanni offers several elaborate philosophical defenses of incest, which the Friar rejects as sophistry. His logic leads him to atheism and murder. The play's partial recuperation of the siblings' romance is not through argumentation but through affect. Giovanni expresses a conflict between disputation and feeling when he stabs Annabella, declaring:

> When thou art dead
> I'll give my reasons for it; for to dispute
> With thy . . . most lovely beauty
> Would make me stagger to perform this act. (5.5.87–90)

The analytical case for sleeping with one's sister is treated as dangerous bunk in 'Tis Pity She's a Whore, but the emotional connection between its protagonists exceeds the condemnation of incest.

'Tis Pity She's a Whore calls metatheatrical attention to the tension it creates between pity and religious principle. The constant visibility of the play's title, hung on a placard during performance, foregrounds the emotional judgments not only of characters within the drama but also of playgoers themselves.[29] In his final scene with Annabella, Giovanni makes an implicit appeal to the audience for their sympathetic judgment:

> If ever after-times should hear
> Of our fast-knit affections, though perhaps

The laws of conscience and of civil use
May justly blame us, yet when they but know
Our loves, that love will wipe away that rigour
Which would in other incests be abhorred. (5.5.68–73)

The speech sets "affections" against religious law. The pun on "abhorred" insists on their love as something more than whoredom. Positioned immediately before the climactic sequence of killings that conclude the tragedy, these lines call audiences' attention to their own responses. Pleas for and refusals of "pity" run through the play. Adopting the role of Petrarchan lover, Giovanni woos his sister, "For pity's sake I beg 'ee" (1.2.248). Revealing their mutual love, he begs the Friar's understanding:

Then you will know what pity 'twere we two
Should have been sundered from each other's arms. (2.5.47–48)

These appeals compete with denials of pity. The Friar threatens Annabella with a vision of hell in which "damned souls / Roar without pity" (3.6.15–16). Hippolita curses Annabella to die "hated, scorned, and unpitied!" (4.1.97). While the play regularly models appropriately horrified reactions to the couple's incest from the Friar, Vasques, and the siblings' father, Florio (who dies with grief at the discovery), it often generates sympathy for the incestuous lovers by provoking emotional responses that run counter to the reactions presented onstage. Attempting to beat the name of her lover out of her, Annabella's cuckolded husband, Soranzo, reviles her as "famous whore!" (4.3.1), "cunning whoredom" (4.3.7), "quean" (4.3.25), "strumpet" (4.3.53), and "Whore of whores!" (4.3.20). Despite Annabella's obvious guilt, the dialogue and stage directions specify a level of violence that shifts sympathy from the wronged man to the pregnant woman he threatens with a sword and drags by the hair. The line that closes this assault—"Such a damned whore / Deserves no pity" (4.3.77–78)—foregrounds this affective irony.[30]

The final stage moment crystallizes the tension between pity and abhorrence. When Annabella's bloody body in a bridal gown is brought onstage, the red-robed Cardinal offers the backhanded eulogy:

Of one so young, so rich in Nature's store,
Who could not say, 'Tis pity she's a whore? (5.6.158–59)

The speaker's identity intensifies the affective alienation of the final line. Already established as both the pope's representative and the corrupt protector of a murderer, the Cardinal, as much as the corpse, embodies the Roman Whore. Yet, even at the end of the tragedy, pity for Annabella is complicated by her terrible sin, a kind of "inverted sympathy."[31]

Commercial plays gave early modern Londoners a capacious, affective technology through which to grapple with the lived contradictions of post-Reformation culture. This affective, embodied thinking did not usually produce answers. But the sophisticated techniques of theatrical orchestration cultivated collective, ideological stretching. In the playhouses, mixed-faith audiences came together to participate in an ongoing, provisional remixing of their religious culture, in ways that were not predetermined by their religious identities. Commercial drama created new modes of association among confessionally diverse Londoners. Theater refracted existing structures of religious life and gave post-Reformation playgoers what they badly needed: a forum for continual, emotional reorientation in an ideologically restless world.

NOTES

INTRODUCTION

1. Examples of recent works that filter discussion of the broader religious culture primarily or exclusively through Shakespeare or focus on dramatic treatments of one aspect of the mixed confessional landscape in relative isolation include Gillian Woods, *Shakespeare's Unreformed Fictions* (Oxford: Oxford University Press, 2013); Richard McCoy, *Faith in Shakespeare* (Oxford: Oxford University Press, 2013); Sarah Beckwith, *Shakespeare and the Grammar of Forgiveness* (Ithaca, NY: Cornell University Press, 2011); David Kastan, *A Will to Believe: Shakespeare and Religion* (Oxford: Oxford University Press, 2014); Hannibal Hamlin, *The Bible in Shakespeare* (Oxford: Oxford University Press, 2013); Daniel Swift, *Shakespeare's Common Prayers: The Book of Common Prayer and the Elizabethan Age* (Oxford: Oxford University Press, 2012); Richard Dutton, Alison Findlay, and Richard Wilson, eds., *Theatre and Religion: Lancastrian Shakespeare* (Manchester: Manchester University Press, 2003); and Jean-Christophe Mayer, *Shakespeare's Hybrid Faith: History, Religion and the Stage* (Basingstoke, UK: Palgrave Macmillan, 2006). For an excellent example of a book that looks both to the intersection of multiple faith positions and to the widespread practices of the theater business, see Daniel Vitkus, *Turning Turk: English Theater and the Multicultural Mediterranean, 1570–1630* (New York: Palgrave Macmillan, 2003).

2. Ethan Shagan, "Introduction: English Catholic History in Context," in *Catholics and the "Protestant Nation": Religious Politics and Identity in Early Modern England*, ed. Ethan Shagan (Manchester: Manchester University Press, 2005), 2.

3. Jeffrey Knapp bases his influential claim that early modern theater creates a culture of Erasmian "good-fellowship" largely on evidence that takes seemingly ecumenical statements out of their actual divisive, polemical contexts; see Knapp, *Shakespeare's Tribe: Church, Nation, and Theater in Renaissance England* (Chicago: University of Chicago Press, 2002). For a full refutation, see Chapter 1.

4. Steven Mullaney, *The Reformation of Emotions in the Age of Shakespeare* (Chicago: University of Chicago Press, 2015), 6, 23.

5. Raymond Williams, *Marxism and Literature* (Oxford: Oxford University Press, 1977), 112–13.

6. Louis Montrose, *The Purpose of Playing: Shakespeare and the Cultural Politics of Elizabethan Theatre* (Chicago: University of Chicago Press, 1996), 1–16.

7. Judith Butler, "Performative Acts and Gender Constitution: An Essay in Phenomenology and Feminist Theory," *Theatre Journal* 40, no. 4 (December 1988): 520.

8. Peter Brook, *The Empty Space: Deadly, Holy, Rough, Immediate* (New York: Touchstone, 1968), 9.

9. For discussions of historical formalism's continuities with new historicism, see Stephen Cohen, introduction to *Shakespeare and Historical Formalism*, ed. Stephen Cohen (Aldershot, UK: Ashgate, 2007), 1–30. See also Stephen Cohen, "Between Form and Culture: New Historicism and the Promise of a Historical Formalism," in *Renaissance Literature and Its Formal Engagements*, ed. Mark David Rasmussen (New York: Palgrave, 2002), 17–42. For the distinction between historical formalism (or "activist new formalism") and a reactionary formalism that seeks to reify the splendid isolation of the literary text, see Marjorie Levinson, "What Is New Formalism?," *PMLA* 122, no. 2 (March 2007): 558–69.

10. Georg Lukács, *History and Class Consciousness*, trans. Rodney Livingstone (London: Merlin Press, 1971), 24.

11. For an articulation of a materialist critical practice that attends to social relationships rather than things, see Erika T. Lin, *Shakespeare and the Materiality of Performance* (New York: Palgrave Macmillan, 2012); see also Jonathan Gil Harris, *Untimely Matter in the Time of Shakespeare* (Philadelphia: University of Pennsylvania Press, 2009).

12. The historiography on post-Reformation religious heterogeneity is widely canvassed in Chapter 1. For a magisterial treatment of the complexity and diversity of early modern London's confessional culture, particularly in relation to popular media, see Peter Lake, *The Antichrist's Lewd Hat: Protestants, Papists, and Players in Post-Reformation England*, with Michael Questier (New Haven, CT: Yale University Press, 2002).

13. For playgoer appropriations of early modern drama, see Charles Whitney, *Early Responses to Renaissance Drama* (Cambridge: Cambridge University Press, 2006). For rowdy audience behavior independent of the drama, see Richard Preiss, *Clowning and Authorship in Early Modern Theatre* (Cambridge: Cambridge University Press, 2014).

CHAPTER 1. MIXED FAITH

1. The rich body of scholarship on the intersection of early modern England's theatrical and religious cultures that has emerged over the last two decades has paid productive attention to the heterogeneous religious discourses that the drama absorbs. To give just a few recent examples of valuable work that attends to the heterodoxy of post-Reformation English religious culture, and the circulation of these diverse confessional discourses in the drama, see Lake, *Antichrist's Lewd Hat*; Mayer, *Shakespeare's Hybrid Faith*; and Elizabeth Williamson, *The Materiality of Religion in Early Modern English Drama* (Burlington, VT: Ashgate, 2009). Similarly, while the individual essays in two recent collections on early modern religion and drama focus largely on particular strands of confessional discourse, rather than heterodoxy per se, the breadth of religious positions represented signals the rise of a more nuanced understanding of religious polyvocality in the period;

see, for example, Ken Jackson and Arthur F. Marotti, eds., *Shakespeare and Religion: Early Modern and Postmodern Perspectives* (Notre Dame, IN: University of Notre Dame Press, 2011); and Jane Hwang Degenhardt and Elizabeth Williamson, eds., *Religion and Drama in Early Modern England: The Performance of Religion on the Renaissance Stage* (Burlington, VT: Ashgate, 2011). However, this has not translated into more than a passing recognition of the confessional diversity of audiences themselves. Certainly, valuable work on early modern Catholic reception of plays has expanded our understanding of the drama's interpretive contexts and impact; see, for example, the two excellent essay collections edited by Richard Dutton, Alison Findlay, and Richard Wilson: *Region, Religion and Patronage: Lancastrian Shakespeare* (Manchester: Manchester University Press, 2003) and *Theatre and Religion*. The limitation of this work is that it sometimes treats Catholic reception in isolation from other theatrical and religious contexts. The practice of dividing post-Reformation confessional life into the reductive, denominational binary "Catholic or Protestant" is so widespread it would be gratuitous to cite. However, this tendency toward monolithic classification is not merely due to the sheer difficulty of keeping the actual complexity of post-Reformation religious identities in play; it is also because these were the categories that early modern people themselves turned to and mobilized to understand and shape their world. For an excellent example of dramatic scholarship that recognizes the diversity of post-Reformation religious life, while also demonstrating the necessity of placing that confessional complexity in the context of the crude opposition between the two Churches, see Susannah Brietz Monta, *Martyrdom and Literature in Early Modern England* (Cambridge: Cambridge University Press, 2005), 2. Peter Lake, whose work has defined the field's understanding of the intense heterogeneity of post-Reformation English religious culture, of course, recognizes the confessional diversity of playgoers; see Lake, *How Shakespeare Put Politics on the Stage: Power and Succession in the History Plays* (New Haven, CT: Yale University Press, 2016).

2. Judith Maltby, *Prayer Book and People in Elizabethan and Early Stuart England* (Cambridge: Cambridge University Press, 1998), 60.

3. Peter Lake, "Religious Identities in Shakespeare's England," in *A Companion to Shakespeare*, ed. David Scott Kastan (Malden, MA: Blackwell, 1999), 79.

4. Judith Butler, *Gender Trouble: Feminism and the Subversion of Identity*, 2nd ed. (New York: Routledge, 2006), 44.

5. Thomas Cartelli, *Marlowe, Shakespeare, and the Economy of Theatrical Experience* (Philadelphia: University of Pennsylvania Press, 1991), 34. Cartelli deftly balances the tension between socially mixed audiences and the audience unified by its responses to performance, by tracking the way a shared theatrical experience of transgressive aspiration fans out into multiple class-interested applications.

6. "Cultural systems [and] individual horizons of expectations [inform how an audience decodes a play], but, in turn, the direct experience of that production feeds back to revise a spectator's expectations, to establish or challenge conventions, and, occasionally, to reform the boundaries of culture." Susan Bennett, *Theatre Audiences: A Theory of Production and Reception* (New York: Routledge, 1990), 180.

7. John Donne, "The Ecstasy," in *John Donne*, ed. John Carey (Oxford: Oxford University Press, 1990), 122, line 35.

8. Regarding this and other visits to the theater, see Humphrey Mildmay, "The Records of Sir Humphrey Mildmay," in Gerald Eades Bentley, *The Jacobean and Caroline Stage*, vol. 2, *Dramatic Companies and Players* (Oxford: Clarendon Press, 1941), 678. For evidence of Sir Humphrey's Catholic leanings, see Herbert A. St. John Mildmay, *Brief Memoir of the Mildmay Family* (New York: John Lane, 1913), 78–94. For a discussion of the puritan commitments of Sir Humphrey's brothers, see Andrew Gurr, *Playgoing in Shakespeare's London*, 3rd ed. (Cambridge: Cambridge University Press, 2004), 237–38. For Sir Francis Wortley's religious commitments in his own words, see Wortley, *Eleutherosis tes Aletheias, Truth Asserted by the Doctrine and Practice of the Apostles, Seconded by the Testimony of Synods, Fathers, and Doctors, from the Apostles to This Day viz. that Episcopacie Is Jure Divino* (London, 1641).

9. Ben Jonson, *Volpone*, ed. Brian Parker and David Bevington (Manchester: Manchester University Press, 1999), 1.2.29–30. For a discussion of anti-Catholic traces in *Volpone* despite (or, in the aftermath of the Gunpowder Plot, because of) Jonson's own Catholicism, see Alizon Brunning, "Jonson's Romish Foxe: Anti-Catholic Discourse in *Volpone*," *Early Modern Literary Studies* 6, no. 2 (September 2000): 1–32.

10. For an excellent overview of discussions of "audiences" and "the audience" in early modern drama criticism, see Jennifer A. Low and Nova Myhill's introduction to *Imagining the Audience in Early Modern Drama, 1558–1642*, ed. Jennifer A. Low and Nova Myhill (New York: Palgrave Macmillan, 2011), 1–17.

11. With some additions, these playgoers are drawn from those identified in Gurr, "Appendix 1," in *Playgoing in Shakespeare's London*, 224–46.

12. Andrew Gurr, *The Shakespearean Stage, 1574–1642* (Cambridge: Cambridge University, 1992), 212–13.

13. For examples of the difficult and uneven enforcement of conformity, see Kenneth Fincham, ed., *Visitation Articles and Injunctions of the Early Stuart Church*, 2 vols. (Woodbridge, UK: Boydell Press, 1994).

14. Patrick Collinson, conclusion to *The Sixteenth Century: 1485–1603*, ed. Patrick Collinson (Oxford: Oxford University Press, 2002), 225.

15. Maltby, *Prayer Book and People*, 14.

16. While Patrick Collinson's *The Elizabethan Puritan Movement* (Berkeley: University of California Press, 1967) tends to emphasize the politically disruptive aspects of puritanism, it also demonstrates the degree to which godly people and ideas were embedded in the Church establishment, a view developed more fully in his later work; see Collinson, *The Religion of Protestants: The Church in English Society, 1559–1625* (Oxford: Clarendon Press, 1982).

17. For connections between nonconforming puritans and their conforming brethren, see Peter Lake, *Moderate Puritans and the Elizabethan Church* (Cambridge: Cambridge University Press, 1982).

18. Peter Lake, *The Boxmaker's Revenge: "Orthodoxy," "Heterodoxy" and the Politics of the Parish in Early Stuart London* (Stanford, CA: Stanford University Press, 2001), 179.

See also David R. Como, *Blown by the Spirit: Puritanism and the Emergence of an Antinomian Underground in Pre-Civil-War England* (Stanford, CA: Stanford University Press, 2004).

19. Anthony Milton, "'Anglicanism' by Stealth: The Career and Influence of John Overall," in *Religious Politics in Post-Reformation England: Essays in Honor of Nicholas Tyacke*, ed. Kenneth Fincham and Peter Lake (Woodbridge, UK: Boydell Press, 2006), 159–76. See also Peter Lake, "Lancelot Andrewes, John Buckeridge and Avant-Garde Conformity at the Court of James I," in *The Mental World of the Jacobean Court*, ed. Linda Levy Peck (Cambridge: Cambridge University Press, 1991), 113–33.

20. Nicholas Tyacke, *Anti-Calvinists: The Rise of English Arminianism, c. 1590–1640* (Oxford: Clarendon Press, 1987).

21. For an overview of revisionist and postrevisionist Catholic historiography, see Shagan, "Introduction," 1–21.

22. Brian Magee, *The English Recusants: A Study of the Post-Reformation Catholic Survival and the Operation of the Recusancy Laws* (London: Burns, Oates and Washbourne, 1938), 200.

23. Alexandra Walsham, *Church Papists: Catholicism, Conformity, and Confessional Polemic in Early Modern England* (Woodbridge, UK: Boydell Press, 1993).

24. Christopher Haigh, *The Plain Man's Pathways to Heaven: Kinds of Christianity in Post-Reformation England, 1570–1640* (Oxford: Oxford University Press, 2007).

25. For a discussion of the way the Reformation challenged many of the popular "superstitions" attached to Catholicism but also generated or adapted its own forms of folk magic, see Keith Thomas, *Religion and the Decline of Magic* (New York: Charles Scribner's Sons, 1971). For further excellent demonstrations of ideas about the supernatural that crossed religious boundaries, see Alexandra Walsham, *Providence in Early Modern England* (Oxford: Oxford University Press, 1999), and Alexandra Walsham, *The Reformation of the Landscape: Religion, Identity, and Memory in Early Modern Britain and Ireland* (Oxford: Oxford University Press, 2011).

26. "And even if the miracle occurred, if we could mingle with Shakespeare's audience reincarnate, its secret would prove no more penetrable than the secret of audiences now. What occurs within the minds and hearts of some thousand men and women is not casually revealed." Alfred Harbage, *Shakespeare's Audience* (New York: Columbia University Press, 1941), 3.

27. For a seminal discussion of the social mixture of early modern public theater audiences, see Harbage, *Shakespeare's Audience*. While Harbage likely overestimates the relative numbers of lower-income audience members, this demographic was nonetheless substantial. Ann Jennalie Cook's argument in *The Privileged Playgoers of Shakespeare's London, 1576–1642* (Princeton, NJ: Princeton University Press, 1981) for a predominantly elite theatergoing public has been persuasively refuted by Gurr, *Playgoing in Shakespeare's London*. There is a general critical consensus that even after the adult companies started playing in upscale private playhouses such as Blackfriars around 1609, and while some amphitheater playhouses drew a clientele of mostly working people, other public playhouses such as the Globe continued to attract the most mixed-class audience there has

ever been for commercial English theater. For the impact of paying female spectators, see Jean E. Howard, *The Stage and Social Struggle in Early Modern England* (New York: Routledge, 1994).

28. The narrative that puritans fundamentally opposed theater begins in the early modern period itself. For a foundational early twentieth-century articulation, see Elbert N. S. Thompson, *The Controversy Between the Puritans and the Stage* (New York: Henry Holt, 1903).

29. George Walker, *Puritan Salt: The Story of Richard Madox, Elizabethan Venturer* (London: Lutterworth Press, 1935), 157.

30. Knapp, *Shakespeare's Tribe*; Alison Shell, *Shakespeare and Religion* (London: Bloomsbury Arden Shakespeare, 2010).

31. Knapp, *Shakespeare's Tribe*, 23.

32. Knapp habitually treats Arminian arguments for reconciliation between the Protestant and Roman Churches, appeals that were understood in context as inflammatory sectarian polemic, as evidence of Erasmian toleration. To give just one representative example, Knapp cites Richard Montague's extremely controversial 1624 Arminian tract, *A New Gagg for an Old Goose*—arguably one of the most divisive polemics of the seventeenth century, one regularly identified by historians as opening a visible rift between Calvinists and anti-Calvinists (discussed further in the epilogue)—as an example of "moderate English theologians [following] the lead of Erasmus"; Knapp, *Shakespeare's Tribe*, 45. For a demonstration of struggle between confessional groups to claim the authoritative position of moderation, see Ethan Shagan, *The Rule of Moderation: Violence, Religion and the Politics of Restraint in Early Modern England* (Cambridge: Cambridge University Press, 2011).

33. While too vast a body of work to cite, major trends in post-Reformation revisionist scholarship are synthesized in John Spurr, "The English 'Post-Reformation'?," *Journal of Modern History* 74, no. 1 (March 2002): 101–19.

34. Shell, *Shakespeare and Religion*, 9, 202.

35. Dale B. J. Randall, *Winter Fruit: English Drama, 1642–1660* (Lexington: University Press of Kentucky, 1995), 41.

36. Tanya Louise Pollard, introduction to *Shakespeare's Theater: A Sourcebook*, ed. Tanya Louise Pollard (Malden, MA: Blackwell, 2004), xvi–xvii.

37. For evidence of not only the poet John Milton's playgoing but also his father's involvement with the management of Blackfriars, see Herbert Berry, "The Miltons and the Blackfriars Playhouse," *Modern Philology* 89, no. 4 (May 1992): 510–14.

38. The idea that puritans generally avoided the theater derives partly from Collinson's claim that around 1580 the godly became increasingly iconophobic and hostile to popular culture; however, this argument has been effectively challenged by Peter Lake and others who see puritan preoccupations seeping through a range of popular media from ballads and cheap print to plays. For Patrick Collinson's claim, see Collinson, *From Iconoclasm to Iconophobia: The Cultural Impact of the Second English Reformation* (Reading: University of Reading, 1986), and Collinson, *The Birthpangs of Protestant England: Religious*

and Cultural Change in the Sixteenth and Seventeenth Centuries (New York: St. Martin's Press, 1988). For demonstrations of continued puritan involvement with popular media forms after 1580, see Lake, *Antichrist's Lewd Hat*; Tessa Watt, *Cheap Print and Popular Piety, 1550–1640* (Cambridge: Cambridge University Press, 1991); Walsham, *Providence in Early Modern England*; and Julie Crawford, *Marvelous Protestantism: Monstrous Births in Post-Reformation England* (Baltimore: Johns Hopkins University Press, 2005).

39. Scott McMillin and Sally-Beth MacLean, *The Queen's Men and Their Plays* (Cambridge: Cambridge University Press, 1998).

40. Michael O'Connell sees these Henslowe plays as an abandoned or failed attempt to attract a godly audience, and he therefore understands their appearance to be compatible with the historical claim that puritans withdrew from popular culture in the later decades of the sixteenth century. O'Connell, *The Idolatrous Eye: Iconoclasm and Theater in Early Modern England* (Oxford: Oxford University Press, 2000).

41. Margot Heinemann, *Puritanism and Theatre: Thomas Middleton and Opposition Drama Under the Early Stuarts* (Cambridge: Cambridge University Press, 1980), 15. For a more recent discussion of tolerant stage treatments of puritanism, see Brian Walsh, *Unsettled Toleration: Religious Difference on the Shakespearean Stage* (Oxford: Oxford University Press, 2016).

42. Martin Butler, *Theatre and Crisis, 1632–1642* (Cambridge: Cambridge University Press, 1984).

43. For a discussion of anti-Martinist plays as an opportunity for the stage to demonstrate establishment credentials, see Lake, *Antichrist's Lewd Hat*, 558–60. It is widely recognized among theater scholars that much "antipuritan" satire in the drama is in fact directed not toward the mainstream godly but toward more radical groups such as the Family of Love. Even here the stage's position is not simple disapproval or hostility. For a discussion of anti-Martinist plays as inviting not confessional animosity but carnivalesque celebration of Martin as a figure of misrule, and attention to Middleton's salacious dramatic celebration of the Family and popular "nonchalance" toward the sect, see Kristen Poole, *Radical Religion from Shakespeare to Milton: Figures of Nonconformity in Early Modern England* (Cambridge: Cambridge University Press, 2000), 93–104.

44. Huston Diehl, *Staging Reform, Reforming the Stage: Protestantism and Popular Theater in Early Modern England* (Ithaca, NY: Cornell University Press, 1997); see also Alison Shell, *Catholicism, Controversy, and the English Literary Imagination, 1558–1660* (Cambridge: Cambridge University Press, 1999); Arthur Marotti, *Religious Ideology and Cultural Fantasy: Catholic and Anti-Catholic Discourses in Early Modern England* (Notre Dame, IN: University of Notre Dame Press, 2005); and Frances Dolan, *Whores of Babylon: Catholicism, Gender, and Seventeenth-Century Print Culture* (Ithaca, NY: Cornell University Press, 1999).

45. Similarly, E. M. Symonds prefaces the diary of playgoer John Greene by declaring that "[Greene was] almost certainly royalist in [his] sympathies, but owing to [his] . . . circumstances [was] compelled to throw in [his] lot with the parliament [and puritans]"; Symonds, "The Diary of John Greene (1635–57)," *English Historical Review* 43, no. 171

(July 1928): 390. This claim seems predicated on the assumption that godly parliamentarian sympathies are incompatible with playgoing, rather than on the evidence of Greene's private journal itself, which consistently refers to the parliamentary forces as "our" side and uses faction-specific terminology in referring to the King's supporters as "malignants"; Symonds, "The Diary of John Greene (1635–57). III," *English Historical Review* 44, no. 173 (January 1929): 109. While he opposed a "Warre merely for religion," the diary also shows Greene's participation in godly forms of voluntary spiritual exercise such as frequenting weekday sermons; Symonds, "Diary of John Greene" (1928), 391–92.

46. Patrick Collinson, "A Comment: Concerning the Name Puritan," *Journal of Ecclesiastical History* 31, no. 4 (October 1980): 484. See also Collinson, *Elizabethan Puritan Movement*, 26–27.

47. For a demonstration of the ideological and interpersonal bonds between Calvinists who held different positions toward presbyterianism and questions of ceremony, see Lake, *Moderate Puritans*. For a demonstration of how the rise of Laudianism broke the Calvinist consensus, see Tyacke, *Anti-Calvinists*.

48. For a discussion of the relative nature of religious categories, in particular how "puritan" has heuristic value less as a label for a type of person than for indexing conflicts over what constituted correct worship in the Church of England, or, in other words, how "[puritanism] was not a thing definable in itself but only one half of a stressful relationship," see Collinson, *Birthpangs of Protestant England*, 143.

49. Benjamin Rudyerd, *Five Speeches in the High and Honourable Court of Parliament* (London, 1641), C1r.

50. Benjamin Rudyerd, *The Speeches of Sr. Benjamin Rudyer in the High Court of Parliament* (London, 1641), A4r.

51. Richard Baker, *Theatrum Redivivum, or the Theatre Vindicated* (London, 1662), E2r.

52. My claim here is not that Prynne was not a puritan: he was. Rather, my point is to stop treating puritanism and antitheatricalism as effectively synonymous.

53. Baker, *Theatrum Redivivum*, B1r–B1v.

54. For Gosson's conformity, see Arthur F. Kinney, *Markets of Bawdrie: The Dramatic Criticism of Stephen Gosson* (Salzburg: Universität Salzburg, Institut für Englische Sprache und Literatur, 1974), 22. Kinney himself rejects the description of Gosson's tracts as "puritan" and instead foregrounds their secular and humanist arguments. As Jonas Barish has demonstrated, antitheatrical prejudice has a long classical and early Christian history and should not be considered solely in the context of post-Reformation confessional politics; Barish, *The Antitheatrical Prejudice* (Berkeley: University of California Press, 1981). Augustine, for example, makes essentially the same objection to the morally overpowering effects of spectacle as Gosson. Nevertheless, for a discussion of Gosson's tracts as a series of appeals to the godly, see Lake, *Antichrist's Lewd Hat*, 430–45.

55. Samuel Rowlands, *The Four Knaves: A Series of Satirical Tracts*, ed. E. F. Rimbault, Percy Society, no. 34 (London: Percy Society, June 1843), 22–23. Similarly, in his Calvinist polemic John Gee draws an extended damning analogy between Catholicism

and theater, all the while demonstrating a play buff's detailed knowledge of striking stage effects; Gee, *New Shreds of the Old Snare* (London, 1624).

56. Rowlands wrote both satirical jest books and godly tracts; Rowlands, *Heavens Glory, Seeke It; Earts Vanitie, Flye It; Hell's Horror, Fere It* (London, 1628). For an explanation of the importance of the vestarian controversy to the puritan movement, see Collinson, *Elizabethan Puritan Movement*, 71–77.

57. For a discussion of Madox's patronage connections, see John Bennell, "Madox, Richard (1546–1583)," in *Oxford Dictionary of National Biography*, ed. H. C. G. Matthew and Brian Harrison (Oxford: Oxford University Press, 2004), http://www.oxforddnb.com /view/article/64595. For a discussion of the evangelical aspirations of his voyage, see Beth Quitslund, "The Virginia Company, 1606–1624: Anglicanism's Millenial Adventure," in *Anglo-American Millennialism, from Milton to the Millerites*, ed. Richard Connors and Andrew Colin Gow (Leiden: Brill, 2004), 51.

58. Richard Madox and Elizabeth Story Donno, *An Elizabethan in 1582: The Diary of Richard Madox*, Works Issued by the Hakluyt Society, 2nd ser., no. 147 (London: Hakluyt Society, 1976), 83, 88. Later in the diary, while at sea, Madox complains that the other godly chaplain attached to the voyage is excessively precise. It seems that Madox had agreed to carry some beads to trade in the Moluccas on behalf of a lady in England, and his fellow puritan minister objected to the errand on the grounds of idolatry. Apparently, Madox was also in other contexts capable of distinguishing between harmless engagements with material culture and a commitment to purity in worship.

59. Compare to Samuel Pepys's expression of moral disapprobation toward forms of cultural expression, such as pornography, that he clearly enjoys; see *The Diary of Samuel Pepys*, ed. Richard Le Gallienne (New York: Modern Library, 2001). Identifying something as immoral does not preclude taking pleasure in it.

60. *OED Online*, s.v. "freemartin, n.," accessed February 21, 2015, http://www.oed .com/view/Entry/74416.

61. Martin Butler, *Theatre and Crisis, 1632–1642*, 94.

62. "The Players have a Play, where they bring in a Tinker, and make him believe himself a Lord, and when they have satisfied their humour, they made him a plain Tinker again. . . . If ever two cases were alike, 'tis the *Tinkers* and mine"; Henry Cromwell, "The Lord Henry Cromwel's Speach to the House . . . 1659," in *Some Seventeenth-Century Allusions to Shakespeare and His Works: Not Hitherto Collected*, ed. George Thorn-Drury (London: Dobell, 1920), 11. Cromwell made conciliatory concessions to several confessional groups, but his personal godly piety is evident from the diary of his nonconforming chaplain Isaac Archer; Archer, *Two East Anglian Diaries, 1641–1729*, ed. Matthew Storey (Woodbridge, UK: Boydell Press, 1994), 93, 97.

63. Paul C.-H. Lim, "Wells, Samuel (1614–1678)," in Matthew and Harrison, *Oxford Dictionary of National Biography*, http://www.oxforddnb.com.huntington.idm.oclc.org /view/article/29017.

64. For Richard Newdigate's godly leanings, see Vivienne Larminie, *Wealth, Kinship and Culture: The 17th-Century Newdigates and Their World* (Woodbridge, UK: Boydell

Press, 1995), 176–81, 183–84, 188–90. For his regular playgoing (seven plays in two years), see John Newdigate, "The Undergraduate Account Book of John and Richard Newdigate, 1618–1621," ed. Vivienne Larminie, *Camden Miscellany XXX*, 4th ser., 39, no. 1 (July 1990): 149–269.

65. For Robert Rich's support of nonconforming clergy and involvement with the Massachusetts Bay Colony, see John Louis Beatty, *Warwick and Holland: Being the Lives of Robert and Henry Rich* (Denver: Alan Swallow, 1965), 220–29.

66. For Henry Rich's puritanism, see R. M. Smuts, "The Puritan Followers of Henrietta Maria in the 1630s," *English Historical Review* 93, no. 366 (January 1978): 32–33.

67. The National Archives (TNA), State Papers (SP) 16/240/25. For expressions of Smith's religious and political sympathies, see John Mennes, *Wit Restor'd* (London, 1658), 4, 7, 46, 54, 56–57, 62–63.

68. Richard Norwood, *The Journal of Richard Norwood, Surveyor of Bermuda*, ed. Wesley Frank Craven and Walter B. Hayward (New York: Scholars' Facsimiles and Reprints, 1945).

69. William Prynne, *Mr William Prynn His Defence of Stage-Plays, or, a Retraction of a Former Book of His Called "Histrio-Mastix"* (London, 1649), A3r–A3v.

70. Shagan, *Rule of Moderation*, 112, 19.

71. The polemical edge of this seemingly conciliatory tract becomes clear in the full title: Joseph Hall, *Via Media: The Way of Peace in the Five Busy Articles, Commonly Known by the Name of Arminius*, in *The Works of the Right Reverend Joseph Hall*, ed. Philip Wynter (New York: AMS Press, 1969), 9:488–519. For a fuller discussion of the controversial context of *Via Media*, see Peter Lake, "Joseph Hall, Robert Skinner and the Rhetoric of Moderation at the Early Stuart Court," in *The English Sermon Revised: Religion, Literature and History, 1600–1750*, ed. Lori Anne Ferrell and Peter McCullough (Manchester: Manchester University Press, 2000), 167–85. For a discussion of Hall's career in the context of the division between Calvinist and Arminian divines, see Kenneth Fincham and Peter Lake, "Prelacy and Puritanism in the 1630s: Joseph Hall Explains Himself," *English Historical Review* 111, no. 443 (September 1996): 856–81. Pace Peter White, "The *Via Media* in the Early Stuart Church," in *The Early Stuart Church, 1603–1642*, ed. Kenneth Fincham (Stanford, CA: Stanford University Press, 1993), 211–30.

72. John Marston, "Satire 2: *Quedam sunt, et non videntur*," in *The Metamorphosis of Pigmalions Image and Certaine Satyres* (London, 1598), D2v. For the identification of Marston's target as Hall, see Frank Livingstone Huntley, *Bishop Joseph Hall, 1576–1656: A Biographical and Critical Study* (Cambridge, UK: D.S. Brewer, 1979), 39.

73. John Milton, *An Apology Against a Pamphlet Call'd "A Modest Confutation of the Animadversions upon the Remonstrant Against Smectymnuus"* (London, 1642), D3v, A1r. Milton brushes off the criticism that he frequents the playhouse—"what difficulty was there in that?" (i.e., so what?)—and turns the discussion away from professional players to university acting, which he mocks as both unskillful and unseemly for future ministers; ibid., B3v.

74. Whereas his playgoing puritan brother Richard participated in the impeachment of William Laud, John Newdigate exchanged New Year's gifts with the archbishop; see Larminie, *Wealth, Kinship and Culture*, 182, 165.

75. Francis Bacon to Toby Matthew, London, October 10, 1609, in *The Works of Francis Bacon*, ed. James Spedding, Robert Leslie Ellis, and Douglas Denon Heath (London, 1861–79), 11:138.

76. Lucius Cary Falkland, *Of the Infallibilitie of the Church of Rome* (Oxford, 1645), B3v. Although Cary's tract is a work of controversy against the Catholic doctrine of infallibility, the tone is remarkably latitudinarian. On the skeptical, Erasmian ethos of the Great Tew circle, see Hugh Trevor-Roper, *Catholics, Anglicans and Puritans: Seventeenth Century Essays* (Chicago: University of Chicago Press, 1988), 166–230.

77. James Howell, *Familiar Letters, Domestic and Forren* (London, 1673), 475. While Howell was particularly critical of Presbyterians, his writings and public life are generally characterized by a broadminded attitude to religious difference.

78. D. R. Woolf, "Howell, James (1594?–1666)," in Matthew and Harrison, *Oxford Dictionary of National Biography*, http://www.oxforddnb.com/view/article/13974.

79. B. Whitelocke, *Memorials of the English Affairs* (1732), 73–74, quoted in David L. Smith, "Cary, Lucius, Second Viscount Falkland (1609/10–1643)," in Matthew and Harrison, *Oxford Dictionary of National Biography*, http://www.oxforddnb.com/view/article/4841.

80. Christopher Hill, "The Protestant Nation," in *The Collected Essays of Christopher Hill*, vol. 2, *Religion and Politics in 17th Century England* (Amherst: University of Massachusetts Press, 1986), 30.

81. J. D. Alsop, "Lambarde, William (1536–1601)," in Matthew and Harrison, *Oxford Dictionary of National Biography*, http://www.oxforddnb.com/view/article/15921. Rebecca Brackman emphasizes the role of Lambarde's work in establishing national, rather than primarily religious, identity. But the two are mutually reinforcing. Brackman, *The Elizabethan Invention of Anglo-Saxon England: Laurence Nowell, William Lambarde and the Study of Old English* (Cambridge, UK: D. S. Brewer, 2012).

82. For a demonstration of how antipapal polemic could unite otherwise divided divines within the Church of England, see Anthony Milton, *Catholic and Reformed: The Roman and Protestant Churches in English Protestant Thought, 1600–1640* (Cambridge: Cambridge University Press, 1995). For a discussion of the "othering" of Catholics in English culture, see Marotti, *Religious Ideology and Cultural Fantasy*. For an authoritative account of the way antipopery could be used both to assert Church solidarity and to critique residual "superstitious" practices, see Peter Lake, "Anti-Popery: The Structure of a Prejudice," in *Conflict in Early Stuart England: Studies in Religion and Politics, 1603–1642*, ed. Richard Cust and Ann Hughes (London: Longman, 1989), 72–106.

83. Michael J. Braddick, "Cranfield, Lionel, First Earl of Middlesex (1575–1645)," in Matthew and Harrison, *Oxford Dictionary of National Biography*, http://www.oxforddnb.com/view/article/6609.

84. Maltby, *Prayer Book and People*, 14.

85. George Sedgwick, "A Summary or Memorial of My Own Life, Written by Me, December 10, 1682," in *The History and Antiquities of the Counties of Westmorland and Cumberland*, ed. Joseph Nicolson and Richard Burn (London, 1777), 1:302. On Clifford's continued use of the prayer book in her private chapel during the interregnum, see also

Richard T. Spence, *Lady Anne Clifford, Countess of Pembroke, Dorset and Montgomery (1590–1676)* (Stroud, UK: Sutton, 1997), 221.

86. Maltby, *Prayer Book and People*, 8.

87. For a history of the Book of Common Prayer as "a struggle between those who would further reform English worship after the pattern of Protestant orders of worship and those who would reform it after the patterns of medieval worship," see John Booty, "History of the 1559 Book of Common Prayer," in *The Book of Common Prayer, 1559: The Elizabethan Prayer Book*, ed. John Booty and Judith Maltby (Charlottesville: University of Virginia Press, 2005), 346. For further discussions of controversies surrounding the liturgy, see Natalie Mears and Alec Ryrie, eds., *Worship and the Parish Church in Early Modern Britain* (Farnham, UK: Ashgate, 2013).

88. Admittedly, we only know for certain that Bishop Overall's wife attended the playhouse; however, if we believe John Aubrey's gossip that the bishop was so in love he was a wittol ("willing she should enjoy what she had a mind to"), perhaps it is not too much to suppose the smitten divine sometimes accompanied his wife when her desire was to see a play; John Aubrey, *Aubrey's Brief Lives*, ed. Oliver Lawson Dick (Jaffrey, NH: David R. Godine, 1999), 226. For Overall's avant-garde conformity to and influence on the Laudian Church, see Anthony Milton, "'Anglicanism' by Stealth." See also Fincham, *Visitation Articles and Injunctions*.

89. Edward Rainbow, *A Sermon Preached at the Funeral of the Right Honorable Anne, Countess of Pembroke*, in Anne Clifford, *The Memoir of 1603 and the Diary of 1616–1619*, ed. Katherine O. Acheson (Peterborough, ON: Broadview Editions, 2007), 260.

90. Julie Crawford, "Lady Anne Clifford and the Uses of Christian Warfare," in *English Women, Religion, and Textual Production, 1500–1625*, ed. Micheline White (Burlington, VT: Ashgate, 2011), 110–12.

91. The title page signals Meres' orthodoxy as a "Master of Artes & student in divinity." Louis de Granada, *Granados Devotion* (London, 1598). Technically, Meres was only ordained in 1599, the year following the publication of this book.

92. Richard Brathwaite, *A Spiritual Spicerie* (London, 1638), K5v.

93. Brad S. Gregory, "The 'True and Zealous Service of God': Robert Parsons, Edmund Bunny, and *The First Booke of the Christian Exercise*," *Journal of Ecclesiastical History* 45, no. 2 (April 1994): 236–68.

94. For the formative role of anti-Catholic prejudice in shaping English Protestant identity, see Marotti, *Religious Ideology and Cultural Fantasy*; and Lake, "Anti-Popery."

95. John Melton, *A Sixe-folde Politician Together with a Sixe-folde Precept of Policy* (London, 1609), G1v.

96. Shagan, "Introduction," 15.

97. His grandfather Sir Walter Mildmay (1520–89) founded Emmanuel College, Cambridge, for the advancement of godly, evangelical preaching. Sir Humphrey's younger brother Anthony, a self-described "great opposer of tyranny and Popery," served as Charles I's jailer in 1648. The third Mildmay brother, Henry (1594–1664/5), himself a zealous persecutor of Catholics and opponent of Arminianism through the 1620s, later sat briefly as a judge at the king's trial; L. L. Ford, "Mildmay, Sir Walter (1520/21–1589)," in Matthew

and Harrison, *Oxford Dictionary of National Biography*, http://www.oxforddnb.com/view/article/18696.

98. Mildmay, *Brief Memoir*, 79.

99. Ibid., 94, 88.

100. Ibid., 92.

101. For a Catholic reading of Harington's writing, see Gerard Kilroy, *Edmund Campion: Memory and Transcription* (Aldershot, UK: Ashgate, 2005), 89–120.

102. Alison Shell, "The Epigrams of Sir John Harington," *Recusant History* 30, no. 4 (October 2011): 591.

103. Most notably, see Walsham, *Church Papists*; Christopher Haigh, *English Reformations: Religion, Politics and Society Under the Tudors* (Oxford: Clarendon Press, 1993).

104. Walsham, *Church Papists*, 9.

105. John Davies of Hereford is identified as a Catholic by one of his writing pupils (a Protestant) sent to live and study with him; see Arthur Wilson, "The Life of Mr. Arthur Wilson," in *Desiderata Curiosa*, ed. Francis Peck (London, 1732), vol. 2, bk. 12, 7.

106. For ideas of Christian community among the early modern English, see Haigh, *Plain Man's Pathways*.

107. Walsham, *Church Papists*, 85.

108. While a larger number of recusants in fact came from the lower social orders, complete refusal to participate in Protestant services was in some ways a more readily available option for elite Catholics, such as recusant playgoers Ambrose Vaux and Elizabeth Wybarn, who could afford the fines and were more likely to have access to priests. Because their higher status often protected them from prosecution, upper-class Catholics were sometimes able to flaunt their religious affiliation more openly. For examples of elite playgoing recusants, see Mary A. Blackstone and Cameron Lewis, "Towards 'A Full and Understanding Auditory': New Evidence of Playgoers at the First Globe Theatre," *Modern Language Review* 90, no. 3 (July 1995): 556–71. For a seminal discussion of English Catholic identity, see Michael Questier, *Catholicism and Community in Early Modern England: Politics, Aristocratic Patronage and Religion, c. 1550–1640* (Cambridge: Cambridge University Press, 2006).

109. John Earle, *Micro-cosmographie, or a Peece of the World Discovered in Essayes and Characters* (London, 1628), B7r. While Gurr's index in *Playgoing* does not identify Earle as a playgoer, his book's description of "a player" suggests direct observation.

110. Elizabeth Read Foster, ed., *Proceedings in Parliament, 1610* (New Haven, CT: Yale University Press, 1966), 1:206–7.

111. Ibid.

112. Ibid.

113. Ibid. The bill to restore Davies to the blood passed the House of Lords but was rejected in the House of Commons, underscoring the divided assessment of his political and religious loyalty. J. J. N. McGurk, "Davies, Sir John (1560x63–1625)," in Matthew and Harrison, *Oxford Dictionary of National Biography*, http://www.oxforddnb.com/view/article/7242.

114. For a version of this common expression explicitly identifying domestic Catholics as a security threat, "Yee that beneath an English face, doe hood / A Spanish heart,

preferring forraine good, / Before your Englands health," see Ralph Knevet, *Stratiotikon, or A Discourse of Militarie Discipline: Shewing the Necessitie Therof According to These Perillous Times* (London, 1628), H1r.

115. See Peter Holmes, *Resistance and Compromise: The Political Thought of the Elizabethan Catholics* (Cambridge: Cambridge University Press, 1982).

116. For Sir Charles Percy's connections to the Gunpowder Plot, see Mark Nicholls, "Sir Charles Percy," *Recusant History* 18, no. 3 (1987): 237–50. For a full account of the networks of Catholic families connected, see Antonia Fraser, *Faith and Treason: The Story of the Gunpowder Plot* (New York: Anchor Books, 1996).

117. Quoted in Harbage, *Shakespeare's Audience*, 72.

118. In 1641 Roman Catholics made up an estimated 20 percent of the peerage; Lawrence Stone, *The Crisis of the Aristocracy, 1558–1641* (Oxford: Clarendon Press, 1965), 742.

119. John Bossy claims that "the actual condition of a domestic priest was not so much that of a private chaplain as that of a priest serving a proprietary church whose limits were roughly defined by the boundaries of an estate"; Bossy, *The English Catholic Community, 1570–1850* (London: Darton, Longman and Todd, 1975), 259. For networks of Catholic patronage, see Questier, *Catholicism and Community*. Pace Christopher Haigh, who argues that the concentration of missionary efforts around elite households alienated the clergy from ordinary Catholic people; Haigh, "From Monopoly to Minority: Catholicism in Early Modern England," *Transactions of the Royal Historical Society*, 5th ser., 31 (1981): 129–47.

120. See Marie B. Rowlands, "Hidden People: Catholic Commoners, 1558–1625," in *English Catholics of Parish and Town, 1558–1778*, ed. Marie B. Rowlands (London: Catholic Record Society, 1999), 10–35.

121. Questier points out that Montague House in Southwark was "open to a large number of [Catholic] people"; *Catholicism and Community*, 518–19. For further discussions of prison proselytization, see Lake, *Antichrist's Lewd Hat*.

122. Lisa McClain, *Lest We Be Damned: Practical Innovation and Lived Experience Among Catholics in Protestant England, 1559–1642* (New York: Routledge, 2004), 65.

123. Mark Bayer, *Theatre, Community, and Civic Engagement in Jacobean London* (Iowa City: University of Iowa Press, 2011), 121–23. For a refutation of Bayer's claims about the relationship between confessionally diverse communities and theater repertory, see Chapter 2.

124. For Catholic practice in the Inns of Court, see McClain, *Lest We Be Damned*, 142–44. For student playgoers from the Inns of Court, see Gurr, *Playgoing in Shakespeare's London*, 60, 82, 90.

125. McClain, *Lest We Be Damned*, 147. *A Game at Chess* also mentions Jesuits around Holborn; see Chapter 4.

126. For the concentration of Catholics on Fleet Street, see McClain, *Lest We Be Damned*, 147. For Fleet Street's proximity to these several theaters, see "Locations," ShaLT: Shakespearean London Theatres, accessed August 26, 2014, http://shalt.dmu.ac.uk /locations.html.

127. McClain, *Lest We Be Damned*, 37.

128. Helen Hackett, "Women and Catholic Manuscript Networks in Seventeenth-Century England: New Research on Constance Aston Fowler's Miscellany of Sacred and Secular Verse," *Renaissance Quarterly* 65, no. 4 (Winter 2012): 1094–124. For a discussion of Catholic print culture, see Alexandra Walsham, " 'Domme Preachers'? Post-Reformation English Catholicism and the Culture of Print," *Past and Present*, no. 168 (August 2000): 72–123.

129. Brad S. Gregory, *Salvation at Stake: Christian Martyrdom in Early Modern Europe* (Cambridge, MA: Harvard University Press, 1999).

130. Eamon Duffy, *Stripping of the Altars: Traditional Religion in England, c. 1400–1580*, 2nd ed. (New Haven, CT: Yale University Press, 2005).

131. Bossy, *English Catholic Community*, 110.

132. "*The Lady Falkland: Her Life*, by One of Her Daughters," in Elizabeth Cary, *Tragedy of Mariam, the Fair Queen of Jewry*, ed. Barry Weller and Margaret W. Ferguson (Berkeley: University of California Press, 1994), 224–25.

133. Michael Questier, *Conversion, Politics and Religion in England, 1580–1625* (Cambridge: Cambridge University Press, 1996), 9.

134. John Gee, *The Foot out of the Snare* (London, 1624), A4v. For a discussion of Gee's wavering and the polemical context of his narrative, see Michael C. Questier, "John Gee, Archbishop Abbot, and the Use of Converts from Rome in Jacobean Anti-Catholicism," *Recusant History* 21, no. 3 (May 1993): 347–60.

135. Millar MacLure, *The Paul's Cross Sermons, 1534–1642* (Toronto: University of Toronto Press, 1958), 245–46. The preface to the printed edition of the sermon preached that day interprets the fatal accident as God's "fearfull Comment on this his own Text"; Thomas Adams, *The Barren Tree* (London, 1623), A4r.

136. Arthur Wilson, "Life of Mr. Arthur Wilson," 7.

137. Ibid.

138. Ibid.

139. Ibid., 9.

140. Ibid., 21.

141. Arthur Wilson, *The History of Great Britain* (London, 1653).

142. Arthur Wilson, "Life of Mr. Arthur Wilson," 23.

143. Leander Pritchard, "The Second Treatise Concerning the Life and Writings of the Venerable Father, F. Augustin Baker," in *Memorials of Father Augustine Baker and Other Documents Relating to the English Benedictines*, ed. Justin McCann and Hugh Connelly (London: Catholic Record Society, 1933), 72–75.

144. For Heylyn's religious education, see George Vernon, *The Life of the Learned and Reverend Dr. Peter Heylyn* (London, 1682), 9, 15, 17. For examples of Heylyn's mature Laudian beliefs, see his defense of altars, *A Coale from the Altar* (London, 1636); and his account of Laud's execution as martyrdom, *Breif Relation of the Death and Sufferings of . . . L. Archbishop of Canterbury* (London, 1644).

145. Questier, *Conversion, Politics and Religion*, 3.

146. A. J. Perrett, "The Blounts of Kidderminster," *Transactions of the Worcester Ar-cheological Society* 19 (1942): 14–15. For a discussion of the ways that politics and religion were inseparable in the period, see Brad S. Gregory, *The Unintended Reformation: How a Religious Revolution Secularized Society* (Cambridge, MA: Harvard University Press, 2012), 129–79.

147. T. B. Howell, ed., *A Complete Collection of State Trials and Proceedings for High Treason and Other Crimes and Misdemeanors* (London, 1816), 1:1346, 1415.

148. As one observer wrote in that year, "Much ado we have here both in Town and Country about the Increase of and a general fear conceived of bringing in Popery"; Rev. Mr. Garrard to Thomas Wentworth, first Earl of Strafford, Lord Deputy of Ireland, London, April 28, 1637, quoted in William Knowler, ed., *The Earl of Strafforde's Letters and Dispatches* (London: William Bowyer, 1739), 2:74. Lady Newport's husband, Mountjoy Blount (1597–666), demanded that Archbishop William Laud punish those responsible. Queen Henrietta Maria interceded on behalf of those accused and escalated the conflict by encouraging Lady Newport and other recent converts to celebrate Mass in her private chapel, despite Charles I's attempts to curb this practice. The *Calendar of State Papers* records the King's frustration "that the Roman Catholic party upon that ease they have lately enjoyed had forgotten themselves, and had taken that liberty to themselves that his Majesty never intended and is directly against the laws"; John Bruce, ed., "Charles I—Volume 370: October 19–31, 1637," in *Calendar of State Papers Domestic: Charles I, 1637* (London: Her Majesty's Stationery Office, 1868), http://www.british-history.ac.uk/report.aspx?compid=52753.

149. Tobie Matthew, *A True Historical Relation of the Conversion of Sir Tobie Matthew to the Holy Catholic Faith* (London: Burns and Oates, 1904), 123–24.

150. Quoted in Deborah Kuller Shuger, "A Protesting Catholic Puritan in Elizabethan England," *Journal of British Studies* 48, no. 3 (July 2009): 601.

151. Matthew, *Conversion of Sir Tobie Matthew*, 131–32.

152. Alexandra Walsham, *Charitable Hatred: Tolerance and Intolerance in England, 1500–1700* (Manchester: Manchester University Press, 2006).

153. Molly Murray, *The Poetics of Conversion in Early Modern Literature: Verse and Change from Donne to Dryden* (Cambridge: Cambridge University Press, 2009).

154. *The Petition and Articles Exhibited . . . Against Dr Fuller* (London, 1641).

155. J. W. Stoye, "The Whereabouts of Thomas Killigrew, 1639–41," *Review of English Studies* 25 (July 1949): 245.

156. This criticism is from Mary Boyle, Elizabeth's sister-in-law, quoted in Alfred Harbage, *Thomas Killigrew: Cavalier Dramatist, 1612–83* (Philadelphia: University of Pennsylvania Press, 1930), 47.

157. Cynthia B. Herrup, "Touchet, Mervin, Second Earl of Castlehaven (1593–1631)," in Matthew and Harrison, *Oxford Dictionary of National Biography*, http://www.oxforddnb.com/view/article/66794.

158. This Nathaniel Tomkins is the son of the musician Thomas Tomkins, not to be confused with the Nathaniel Tomkyns in Chapter 2. For Tomkins's alliance with Laud,

for whom he spied on a resistant bishop, see Paul Vining, "Nathaniel Tomkins: A Bishop's Pawn," *Musical Times* 133, no. 1796 (October 1992): 538–40. For his turning church vestments into costumes, see SP 16/298/43 and Calendar of State Papers (C.S.P.) Dom., 1635, 395.

159. Charles Nicholls, *The Lodger Shakespeare: His Life on Silver Street* (New York: Viking, 2008), 112–27.

160. Thomas, *Religion and the Decline*; see also Walsham, *Providence in Early Modern England* and Walsham, *Reformation of the Landscape*.

161. Patrick Collinson estimates the total foreign population of Elizabethan London at four thousand, with half being members of the Dutch and French Churches; Collinson, "Calvinism with an Anglican Face: The Stranger Churches of Early Elizabethan London and Their Superintendent," in *Godly People: Essays on English Protestantism and Puritanism* (London: Hambledon Press, 1983), 214. Andrew Pettegree estimates ten thousand foreigners in London by the end of the sixteenth century, but he agrees that about half were Dutch and French; Pettegree, *Foreign Protestant Communities in Sixteenth-Century London* (Oxford: Clarendon Press, 1986), 78.

162. Charles Nicholls, *Lodger Shakespeare*.

163. Symonds, "Diary of John Greene" (1928), 391.

164. Collinson, "The Elizabethan Puritans and the Foreign Reformed Churches in London," in *Godly People*, 248. For further discussion of the relationship between reformed stranger churches and the Church of England, see Andrew Spicer, "'A Place of Refuge and Sanctuary of a Holy Temple': Exile Communities and the Stranger Churches," in *Immigrants in Tudor and Early Stuart England*, ed. Nigel Goose and Lien Luu (Brighton: Sussex Academic Press, 2005), 91–109; see also Charles G. D. Littleton, "The Strangers, Their Churches and the Continent: Continuing and Changing Connexions," in Goose and Luu, *Immigrants*, 177–91; as well as David Trim, "Immigrants, the Indigenous Community and International Calvinism," in Goose and Luu, *Immigrants*, 211–22.

165. For a discussion of the organization and practices of the stranger churches, as well as Laud's attempt to dissolve them, see Ole Peter Grell, "The French and Dutch Congregations in London in the Early 17th Century," *Proceedings of the Huguenot Society of Great Britain and Ireland* 24, no. 5 (January 1987): 362–77.

166. Claire S. Schen, "Greeks and 'Grecians' in London: The 'Other' Strangers," in *From Strangers to Citizens: The Integration of Immigrant Communities in Britain, Ireland and Colonial America, 1550–1750*, ed. Randolph Vigne and Charles Littleton (Brighton: Sussex Academic Press, 2001), 268–75.

167. Nabil Matar, *Islam in Britain, 1558–1685* (Cambridge: Cambridge University Press, 1998); Nabil Matar, *Turks, Moors, and Englishmen in the Age of Discovery* (New York: Columbia University Press, 1999); Nabil Matar, *Britain and Barbary, 1558–1689* (Gainesville: University Press of Florida, 2005). See also Daniel Vitkus, ed., *Piracy, Slavery, and Redemption: Barbary Captivity Narratives from Early Modern England* (New York: Columbia University Press, 2001). For Judaism and anti-Semitism in early modern England, see James Shapiro, *Shakespeare and the Jews* (New York: Columbia University Press, 1996).

168. Vitkus, *Turning Turk*.

169. Corinne Zeman, "Domesticating the Turk: Islamic Acculturation in Seventeenth-Century England" (PhD diss., Washington University in Saint Louis, forthcoming).

170. Cartelli, *Economy of Theatrical Experience*, 10.

171. Antimo Galli to Andrea Cioli, undated correspondence, quoted in *English Professional Theatre, 1530–1660*, ed. Glynne Wickham, Herbert Berry, and William Ingram (Cambridge: Cambridge University Press, 2000), 415.

172. While plays often had nicknames unrelated to their titles, the likeliest guess would be a revival of Robert Greene's *The Honorable Historie of Frier Bacon, and Frier Bongay* (London, 1594).

173. Francis Bacon, *The Advancement of Learning and Novum Organum* (New York: Colonial Press, 1899), 63.

CHAPTER 2. SHARED FEELING

1. Whitney, *Early Responses*, 3. This summary assessment is not an accurate representation of "the last sixty years" of scholarship on early modern English drama and is particularly unfair to much historicist work (both "new" and later) that emphatically attends to the diverse cultural contexts that informed the uses of playgoing and the possible meanings of plays for differently socially situated spectators.

2. While David McInnis usefully insists on theater as a tool for imaginative departure from the everyday, he embraces a more verisimilar model of early modern performance than I do. McInnis, *Mind-Travelling and Voyage Drama in Early Modern England* (London: Palgrave Macmillan, 2013).

3. McCoy, *Faith in Shakespeare*.

4. For an important discussion of the ways that overtly didactic and polemic early Tudor religious drama provoked resistant reactions from its audiences, see Paul Whitfield White, "Politics, Topical Meaning, and English Theater Audiences, 1485–1575," *Research Opportunities in Renaissance Drama* 34 (1995): 41–54.

5. Philip Sidney, *An Apologie for Poetrie* (London, 1595), G4v.

6. For the counterfactual "as if" of dramatic worlds, see Keir Elam, *The Semiotics of Theatre and Drama*, 2nd ed. (London: Routledge, 2002). For a discussion of the "magic *if*" of acting, see Konstantin Stanislavsky, *An Actor Prepares*, trans. Elizabeth Reynolds Hapgood (New York: Routledge, 1964).

7. For an account of individuals' applications of plays beyond the theater, see Whitney, *Early Responses*. For the claim that the play itself was secondary to the rowdy and disruptive self-creation of the audience, see Preiss, *Clowning and Authorship*. For a discussion of playhouse collectivity as the product of theories of humoral contagion, see Allison P. Hobgood, *Passionate Playgoing in Early Modern England* (Cambridge: Cambridge University Press, 2014). For an account of conjoined audience experience as modeled on Eucharistic collectivity, see Anthony B. Dawson, "Performance and Participation," in *The*

Culture of Playgoing in Shakespeare's England: A Collaborative Debate, ed. Anthony B. Dawson and Paul Yachnin (Cambridge: Cambridge University Press, 2001), 11–37. For a description of docile playgoers, enervated by habituation to theater attendance and made passive by spectacle, see Paul Menzer, "Crowd Control," in Low and Myhill, *Imagining the Audience*, 19–36. For an overview of the discussion regarding the relationship between "audiences" and "the audience," see Low and Myhill, introduction to *Imagining the Audience*. My project does not engage with arguments about collective emotion grounded in cognitive psychology. I reject Amy Cook's claim that "theatre scholars need emotion researchers to study the dynamics of emotion in the theatre," on the grounds that while emotion in the broadest sense may be produced by transhistorical, biological processes of perception and somatization, the lived reality of emotion, and the social and aesthetic pressures that shape and mobilize it, is culturally specific; Amy Cook, "For Hecuba or for Hamlet: Rethinking Emotion and Empathy in the Theatre," *Journal of Dramatic Theory and Criticism* 25, no. 2 (Spring 2011): 82.

8. For a sophisticated discussion of the ways early modern optic regimes shaped theatrical spectatorship, see Lin, *Shakespeare and the Materiality of Performance*.

9. Hobgood, *Passionate Playgoing*, 8, 24.

10. For a critique of Gail Kern Paster's reading of Galenic discourse in relation to early modern theater, see Mullaney, *Reformation of Emotions*, 54–62, 61.

11. Dawson, "Performance and Participation." Dawson takes Richard Hooker's discussion of communion as if it were descriptive of an undisputed and united attitude to the sacrament, which fails to recognize actual variations in parishioners' behaviors and beliefs. As Keith Thomas observes of church behavior on the parish level, "Presentments made before the ecclesiastical courts show that virtually every kind of irreverent (and irrelevant) activity took place during divine worship. Members of the congregation jostled for pews, nudged their neighbors, howled and spat, knitted, made coarse remarks, told jokes, fell asleep, and even let off guns"; Thomas, *Religion and the Decline*, 161. For an overview of Reformation debates over Eucharistic theology and its liturgical expression, see Lee Palmer Wandel, *The Eucharist in the Reformation* (Cambridge: Cambridge University Press, 2006).

12. For a seminal discussion of the social mixture of early modern theater audiences, see Harbage, *Shakespeare's Audience*. See also Ann Jennalie Cook, *Privileged Playgoers*, whose argument for a predominantly elite demographic of theatergoers has been persuasively refuted by Gurr, *Playgoing in Shakespeare's London*.

13. Jeremy Lopez, *Theatrical Convention and Audience Response in Early Modern Drama* (Cambridge: Cambridge University Press, 2003), 55.

14. For a discussion of posted playbills as a widespread form of advertising in London, as well as their concentration in particular neighborhoods, see Tiffany Stern, *Documents of Performance in Early Modern England* (Cambridge: Cambridge University Press, 2009), 50–51. These bills advertised the next day's play, making them a limited guide for planning excursions to the playhouse. Moreover, the advertised play was not the only form of entertainment on stage.

15. Sidney, *Apologie for Poetrie*, K2r.

16. For a discussion of on-stage audience reactions to plays-within-plays, see Stanley Wells, "Shakespeare's Onstage Audiences," in *The Show Within: Dramatic and Other Insets; English Renaissance Drama (1550–1642)*, ed. François Laroque, Collection Astraea 2, no. 4 (Montpellier: Publications de l'Université Paul-Valéry, 1990), 89–108. For a list of early modern plays involving plays-within-plays and other kinds of metatheatrical insets, see Jean Fuzier, comp., "Forms of Metadramatic Insertions in Renaissance English Drama, 1580–1642," in Laroque, *Show Within*, 461–67.

17. For examples, see Jeff Doty, *Shakespeare, Popularity, and the Public Sphere* (Cambridge: Cambridge University Press, 2017); Jean E. Howard, *Theater of a City: The Places of London Comedy, 1598–1642* (Philadelphia: University of Pennsylvania Press, 2007); and McInnis, *Mind-Travelling*.

18. See Stephen Greenblatt, *Hamlet in Purgatory* (Princeton, NJ: Princeton University Press, 2001). For Greenblatt, this theatrical flexibility evacuates the play's religious content.

19. William Shakespeare, *Hamlet*, ed. Ann Thompson and Neil Taylor, Arden Shakespeare, 3rd ser. (London: Thomson Learning, 2006), 1.5.751–52.

20. Thomas Wright, *The Passions of the Minde in Generall* (London, 1604), H1r (italics mine).

21. Roslyn Lander Knutson, *Playing Companies and Commerce in Shakespeare's Time* (Cambridge: Cambridge University Press, 2001), 19.

22. Andrew Gurr and Karoline Szatek, "Women and Crowds at the Theater," *Medieval and Renaissance Drama in England* 21 (2008): 163.

23. Henry Jackson, quoted in *Eyewitnesses of Shakespeare: First Hand Accounts of Performances, 1590–1890*, comp. Gāmini Salgādo (London: Sussex University Press, 1975), 30 (italics mine). Jackson is describing a performance by the King's Men at Oxford, not in London.

24. Wright, *Passions of the Minde*, I1v.

25. Barnabe Riche, *Greenes Newes both from Heaven and Hell*, ed. R. B. McKerrow (Stratford-upon-Avon: Shakespeare Head Press, 1922), 56.

26. Ibid., 58.

27. Lake, *How Shakespeare Put Politics*. Lake himself insists that plays are not tracts, and that their polyvocality is central to their political work. However, while Lake is remarkable for his openness to representational ambiguity, there remains a vast disciplinary divide between what a historian such as Lake and a literary scholar such as Mullaney mean by theatrical "indirection."

28. Stephen Gosson, *Playes Confuted in Five Actions* (London, 1582), C6r (italics mine).

29. For the original full transcription of Tomkyns's account and the circumstances of the Lancaster witchcraft case, see Herbert Berry, "The Globe Bewitched and *El Hombre Fiel*," *Medieval and Renaissance Drama in England* 1 (January 1984): 211–30.

30. The company performed *The Late Lancashire Witches* in a three-day run and seems to have successfully petitioned the Master of the Revels to prevent their competitors from

scooping them with a new witchcraft play before their own was ready; see Gerald Eades Bentley, *The Jacobean and Caroline Stage*, vol. 3, *Plays and Playwrights* (Oxford: Clarendon Press, 1956), 73. These tactics index the commercial appeal of dramatized news.

31. Critical opinion is in broad agreement that the play takes an ambiguous position as to whether witchcraft is real. Herbert Berry rightly observes that Tomkyns himself cannot draw a conclusion; Berry, "The Globe Bewitched." Meg Pearson argues that in contrast to other witch plays of the period, *The Late Lancashire Witches* does not judge its witches but rather undermines certainty in sight, on which judgment depends; Pearson, "Vision on Trial in *The Late Lancashire Witches*," in *Staging the Superstitions of Early Modern Europe*, ed. Verena Theile and Andrew D. McCarthy (Aldershot, UK: Ashgate, 2012), 107–27. For a similar argument as to the ways the play's spectacle undermines epistemological certainty, see Diane Purkiss, *The Witch in History: Early Modern and Twentieth-Century Representations* (London: Routledge, 1996), 231–49. For the argument that the festive nature of the witches' magic circumvents the question of their guilt or innocence, see Heather Anne Hirschfeld, "Collaborating Across Generations: Thomas Heywood, Richard Brome, and the Production of *The Late Lancashire Witches*," *Journal of Medieval and Early Modern Studies* 30, no. 2 (Spring 2000): 339–74. For similar claims and a discussion of the subversions of gender and religious order in the witches' pranks, see Alison Findlay, "Sexual and Spiritual Politics in the Events of 1633–34 and *The Late Lancashire Witches*," in *The Lancashire Witches: Histories and Stories*, ed. Robert Poole (Manchester: Manchester University Press, 2002), 146–65.

32. Thomas Heywood and Richard Brome, *The Late Lancashire Witches* (London, 1634), B1r. Subsequent references in text by page signature.

33. Forman's descriptions of *Macbeth*, *Cymbeline*, and *The Winter's Tale* have no explicit application beyond the repeated injunction to "observe" and "remember," typical of commonplacing for instructive use but used by Forman simply to mark striking stage moments, except for the lesson drawn at the end of the account of *The Winter's Tale*: "Beware of trusting feigned beggars or fawning fellows." His remarks on an unknown play about Richard II occasion more extensive application; see Salgādo, *Eyewitnesses*, 31–33.

34. Tomkyns, quoted in Herbert Berry, "Globe Bewitched," 212–13 (italics mine).

35. Findlay, "Sexual and Spiritual Politics."

36. The comparison between theater and oratory is often observed in the period, perhaps most explicitly in the shared term "action," which denotes both the gestures and voice modulation proper to effective oratory and the actor's physicalization and vocalization on stage.

37. Thomas Overbury, *New and Choise Characters* (London, 1615), M5v.

38. Matthew Steggle, *Laughing and Weeping in Early Modern Theatres* (Aldershot, UK: Ashgate, 2007).

39. Lopez, *Theatrical Convention*, 4. While Lopez offers the fullest and most explicit recent articulation of the effects of common staging devices, the basic principle that theatrical conventions shape audience response has motivated generations of early modern English theater scholars before us. Although this body of work is too large to cite, important

examples include M. C. Bradbrook, *Elizabethan Stage Conditions: A Study of Their Place in the Interpretation of Shakespeare's Plays* (London: Cambridge University Press, 1932); M. C. Bradbrook, *Themes and Conventions of Elizabethan Tragedy* (London: Cambridge University Press, 1935); Alan C. Dessen, *Elizabethan Drama and the Viewer's Eye* (Chapel Hill: University of North Carolina Press, 1977); and Alan C. Dessen, *Recovering Shakespeare's Theatrical Vocabulary* (Cambridge: Cambridge University Press, 1995). Beyond these explicit discussions of theatrical devices, any close reading that posits a possible way early modern people may have experienced a play depends on the underlying assumption that formal conventions have identifiable effects.

40. Preiss, *Clowning and Authorship*.

41. William Shakespeare, *King Henry V*, ed. T. W. Craik, Arden Shakespeare, 2nd ser. (London: Bloomsbury Arden Shakespeare, 1995), prologue, lines 18, 12–13.

42. Preiss, *Clowning and Authorship*, 27.

43. Jean E. Howard, *Shakespeare's Art of Orchestration: Stage Technique and Audience Response* (Urbana: University of Illinois Press, 1984). See also E. A. J. Honigmann, *Shakespeare: Seven Tragedies Revisited; the Dramatist's Manipulation of Response*, 2nd ed. (Basingstoke, UK: Palgrave Macmillan, 2002); Ralph Berry, *Shakespeare and the Awareness of the Audience* (New York: Macmillan, 1985); David Richman, *Laughter, Pain, and Wonder: Shakespeare's Comedies and the Audience in the Theater* (Cranbury, NJ: Associated University Presses, 1990); Michael E. Mooney, *Shakespeare's Dramatic Transactions* (Durham, NC: Duke University Press, 1990); and Kent Cartwright, *Shakespearean Tragedy and Its Double: The Rhythms of Audience Response* (University Park: Pennsylvania State University Press, 1991).

44. For a formative account of the distribution of performance effects across the whole playing system, see Evelyn B. Tribble, *Cognition in the Globe: Attention and Memory in Shakespeare's Theatre* (New York: Palgrave Macmillan, 2011).

45. Preiss, *Clowning and Authorship*; Paul Yachnin, "The Populuxe Theatre," in Dawson and Yachnin, *Culture of Playgoing*, 38–65.

46. Robert Shaughnessy, "Connecting the Globe: Actors, Audience and Entrainment," *Shakespeare Survey* 68 (2015): 295. Though the use of the term "entrainment" in the natural sciences risks naturalizing or mystifying the phenomenon it describes in theater, Shaughnessy's attention to the rhythms of stage action clarifies that this is a social and representational process.

47. Ibid., 300.

48. Preiss, *Clowning and Authorship*, 26.

49. Hobgood, *Passionate Playgoing*, 27; Whitney, *Early Responses*, 3.

50. Hobgood, *Passionate Playgoing*, 27–28.

51. Whitney, *Early Responses*, 3.

52. For a theoretical discussion of theater's cultural work as "feeling-labor," that is, "the solicitation, management, and display of feelings," see Erin Hurley, *Theater and Feeling* (New York: Palgrave Macmillan, 2010), 4. For shared imaginative involvement in theatrical performance, see Roger Grainger, *Suspending Disbelief: Theater as a Context for Sharing* (Eastbourne, UK: Sussex Academic Press, 2010).

53. Whitney, *Early Responses*, 5.

54. For a foundational discussion of the relationship between collective and individual response, see Bennett, *Theatre Audiences*.

55. As Ludwig Wittgenstein defines it, "family resemblance" describes the relationship between parts of a group that are joined by a set of similarities without having any one of those links common to all members of the group; Wittgenstein, *Philosophical Investigations*, trans. G. E. M. Anscombe (Oxford: Basil Blackwell, 1953), esp. 31e–32e.

56. Diehl, *Staging Reform*.

57. For discussions of playgoer input in the actual revision of scripts, see Tiffany Stern, *Rehearsal from Shakespeare to Sheridan* (Oxford: Oxford University Press, 2000), 113–21; and Stern, *Documents of Performance*, 86–91.

58. N. R. Helms, "'Upon Such Sacrifices': An Ethic of Spectator Risk," *Journal of Dramatic Theory and Criticism* 27, no. 1 (Fall 2012): 93.

59. Keir Elam, *The Semiotics of Theatre and Drama*, 2nd edition (London: Routledge, 2002), 78–87.

60. For a discussion of audiences' participation in the making of plays, see Matteo Pangallo, "'Mayn't a Spectator Write a Comedy?' Playwriting Playgoers in Early Modern Drama," *Review of English Studies* 64, no. 263 (February 2013): 42.

61. For discussions of early modern theorizations of the impact of theater, see Tanya Louise Pollard, *Drugs and Theatre in Early Modern England* (Oxford: Oxford University Press, 2005); Agnes Matuska, "'Masking Players, Painted Sepulchers and Double Dealing Ambidexters' on Duty: Anti-theatricalist Tracts on Audience Involvement and the Transformative Power of Plays," *SEDERI: Journal of the Spanish and Portuguese Society for English Renaissance Studies* 18 (2008): 45–59; and Ellen MacKay, *Persecution, Plague, and Fire: Fugitive Histories of the Stage in Early Modern England* (Chicago: University of Chicago Press, 2011).

62. Thomas Heywood, *An Apology for Actors* (London, 1612), B4r (italics mine).

63. Anthony Munday, *A Second and Third Blast of Retreat from Plaies and Theaters* (London, 1580), A8r.

64. As Robert Ormsby puts it, "Audiences fluctuate between the homogeneity and individuality of their constituents"; Ormsby, "Coriolanus, Antitheatricalism, and Audience Response," *Shakespeare Bulletin* 26, no. 1 (2008): 55. For an overview of recent discussions of shared and individual audience response, see Low and Myhill, introduction to *Imagining the Audience*. For the too-simple assumption that socially recognizable aspects of the drama split their audiences along real-world divisions, whereas more aesthetically remote staging united them, see David Crane, "Patterns of Audience Involvement at the Blackfriars Theatre in the Early Seventeenth Century: Some Moments in Marston's *The Dutch Courtesan*," in *Plotting Early Modern London: New Essays on Jacobean City Comedy*, ed. Dieter Mehl, Angela Stock, and Anne-Julia Zwierlein (Aldershot, UK: Ashgate, 2004), 97–107.

65. Menzer, "Crowd Control," 24. Jacques Rancière rightly objects to such assumed binaries and equivalences and recognizes that interactions between artists and audiences produce a "third thing . . . owned by no one"; see Rancière, *The Emancipated Spectator*,

trans. Gregory Elliott (New York: Verso, 2009), 15. Given Rancière's valuable insights into the spectator's power to select and assemble, it is perhaps surprising that he does not play a larger theoretical role in this project. To me, Rancière's work on the politics of spectatorship speaks most aptly and powerfully to the situation of art in a later phase of capitalism. This strength, however, complicates its application to the specific, emerging conditions of commercial playing, commodity consumption, and theatrical reception in early modern London.

66. Preiss, *Clowning and Authorship*, 32.

67. Thomas Nashe, quoted in Gurr, *Playgoing in Shakespeare's London*, 165.

68. Alexander Leggatt, "The Death of John Talbot," in *Shakespeare's English Histories: A Quest for Form and Genre*, ed. John W. Velz (Binghamton, NY: Center for Medieval and Renaissance Texts and Studies, 1996), 19. For a more recent discussion of Talbot's disappearance from the play, see Brian Walsh, *Shakespeare, the Queen's Men, and the Elizabethan Performance of History* (Cambridge: Cambridge University Press, 2009), 108–38.

69. William Shakespeare, *Henry VI, Part 1*, ed. Edward Burns, Arden Shakespeare, 3rd ser. (London: Thomson Learning, 2000), 4.6.2230. Subsequent references appear parenthetically in the text by act, scene, and line.

70. Rebecca Schneider, *Performing Remains: Art and War in Times of Theatrical Reenactment* (New York: Routledge, 2011), 36–37.

71. Audience priming is a performance-specific form of emotional priming, understood in psychology as the linguistic cueing of cognate emotions. This technique is developed most fully by Shakespeare in *King Lear*, through nesting descriptions and stagings of breaking hearts. However, audience priming is not specific to tragedy. It is used also to build wonder in the multiple speeches reporting miraculous reunions that precede the climactic restoration of Hermione in *The Winter's Tale*.

72. Jacques Derrida, *Of Grammatology*, trans. Gayatri Spivak (Baltimore: Johns Hopkins University Press, 1976), 144–45. My use of this term runs counter to Derrida's own insistence that the supplement is not an instrument of plenitude.

73. As one reddit user describes a screening of the Bruce Lee film *Return of the Dragon*, "My friends and I were mightily entertained by the people shouting at the screen. Many repeated variations of 'Damn, Bruce is gonna FUCK him UP!' and 'Uh oh. Look out. Bruce is mad NOW!' It was a blast. But the high point was at the end when Bruce has killed Chuck Norris in single combat. It was an honorable fight, so Bruce retrieves Norris's gi jacket (that he took off during the fight) and kneels down to respectfully cover his face and upper body with it. It is a solemn moment and the entire audience is silent. Then one cat yells out into the silence, 'Bruce, take his watch!' And the whole damn theater just explodes with laughter, whooping, and hollering. It was insane and beautiful and I doubt could ever be topped." Tensegritydan, comment on Pyronaut44, "Cheering and Shouting Mid-movie, an American Thing?," reddit, April 7, 2014, http://www.reddit.com/r/movies/comments/22ez6c/cheering_and_shouting_midmovie_an_american_thing. This anecdote suggests the variety and fluidity of experiences available to audiences: shouting at the screen can both engross spectators and create distance from the movie's illusions; rowdy vocal participation does not exclude intent silence and emotional seriousness.

74. Thomas Heywood, *Apology for Actors*, B4r (italics mine).

75. John Tatham, *Knavery in All Trades, or, The Coffee-House* (London, 1664), D4v–E1r.

76. Lin, *Shakespeare and the Materiality of Performance*, 16.

77. Mullaney, *Reformation of Emotions*, 62.

78. William N. West, "Understanding in the Elizabethan Theaters," *Renaissance Drama* 35 (2006): 134. Steggle makes similar claims regarding the way audience tears and laughter may have contributed to the illusions or sensory fabric of plays in performance; see Steggle, *Laughing and Weeping*.

79. William Shakespeare, *Othello*, ed. E. A. J. Honigmann, Arden Shakespeare, 3rd ser. (London: Bloomsbury Arden Shakespeare, 2006), 5.2.117.

80. Bacon, *Advancement of Learning*, 63.

81. Mullaney, *Reformation of Emotions*, 50.

82. For an authoritative discussion of the repertory practices of theater companies, see Roslyn Lander Knutson, *The Repertory of Shakespeare's Company, 1594–1613* (Fayetteville: University of Arkansas Press, 1991). The King's Men and the Lady Elizabeth's Men were the primary, though not the sole, companies capitalizing on this trend.

83. Beyond the examples of fatal Spanish marriages discussed later, see also John Fletcher and Philip Massinger, *The Spanish Curate* (London, 1647); and Thomas Middleton and William Rowley, *The Changeling* (London, 1653).

84. Thomas Dekker, *The Noble Spanish Soldier*, in *The Dramatic Works of Thomas Dekker*, ed. Fredson Bowers (Cambridge: Cambridge University Press, 1968), 4:1.1.s.d. All subsequent references are made parenthetically in text to this edition.

85. Of course, many other Protestants considered the crucifix compatible with the devotional practices of the Church of England. Queen Elizabeth used one in her chapel, though this drew some criticism. See Patrick Collinson, *Elizabethan Essays* (London: Hambledon Press, 1994), 111.

86. Diehl, *Staging Reform*.

87. Laura Mulvey, "Visual Pleasure and Narrative Cinema," in *Film Theory and Criticism: Introductory Readings*, 5th ed., ed. Leo Braudy and Marshall Cohen (Oxford: Oxford University Press, 1999), 833–44.

88. Thomas Dekker, *Match Mee in London* (London, 1631). Subsequent references are in the text, parenthetically, by page number.

89. Mark Bayer, "The Curious Case of the Two Audiences: Thomas Dekker's *Match Me in London*," in Low and Myhill, *Imagining the Audience*, 61.

90. For an account of the popular outpouring of spontaneous support that greeted Charles on his return, demonstrating widespread general knowledge of the Spanish Match negotiations, see David Cressy, *Bonfires and Bells: National Memory and the Protestant Calendar in Elizabethan and Stuart England* (Berkeley: University of California Press, 1989). For a fuller account of popular discussion of the match in cheap print and sermons, see Chapter 4.

91. Bayer productively demonstrates the important role theaters played in particular neighborhoods in terms of the contributions they made to the local economy, sense of

neighborhood pride, and community ties. Nevertheless, he massively underestimates the intellectual resources and cultural competencies of working people generally, and in particular he assumes that illiterate apprentice and artisan audiences were able only to receive religious indoctrination from plays, rather than participate in a more sophisticated set of theatrical interactions with confessional culture; see Bayer, *Theatre, Community, and Civic Engagement*.

92. For example, the playwrights lower Preciosa's age from fifteen in the source material to twelve, the age of the infanta at the time of the marriage negotiations. For further instances of the play's references to the match, see Suzanne Gossett, introduction to *The Spanish Gypsy*, by John Ford, Thomas Dekker, Thomas Middleton, and William Rowley, ed. Gary Taylor, in *Thomas Middleton: The Collected Works*, ed. Gary Taylor and John Lavagnino (Oxford: Clarendon Press, 2007), 1723–27, as well as the notes therein provided by Taylor.

93. Thomas Middleton and William Rowley, *The Spanish Gipsie* (London, 1653), F4r. Subsequent references are in the text by page signature.

94. David Cressy, *Birth, Marriage, and Death: Ritual, Religion, and the Life-Cycle in Tudor and Stuart England* (Oxford: Oxford University Press, 2002), 363–64.

95. While tetrameter certainly has other functions, it often appears in early modern English plays as a marker of the supernatural (as with the witches in *Macbeth*) or of popery (as with the nuns in both *Friar Bacon, Friar Bungay* and *The Merry Devil of Edmonton*), sometimes also carrying an old-timey sense of the (Catholic) past. Gary Taylor notes the metrical similarity between the two scenes in *Thomas Middleton and Early Modern Textual Culture: A Companion to the Collected Works*, ed. Gary Taylor and John Lavagnino (Oxford: Clarendon Press, 2007), 1114.

96. Thomas Middleton, *A Game at Chess*, ed. T. H. Howard-Hill (Manchester: Manchester University Press, 1993), 3.3.44–45.

97. Gary Taylor notes the connection of both plays to the Spanish Match but usefully foregrounds their aesthetic differences, as well as the differences in the historical circumstances of their staging. Taylor, "Historicism, Presentism and Time: Middleton's *The Spanish Gypsy* and *A Game at Chess*," *SEDERI: Journal of the Spanish and Portuguese Society for English Renaissance Studies* 18 (2008): 147–70.

CHAPTER 3. IN MIXED COMPANY: COLLABORATION
IN COMMERCIAL THEATER

1. Knapp, *Shakespeare's Tribe*.

2. Knutson, *Playing Companies and Commerce*, 34.

3. For confessional accommodation within guilds, families, and other institutions, see Norman Jones, *The English Reformation: Religion and Cultural Adaptation* (Malden, MA: Blackwell, 2002).

4. Bart Van Es, *Shakespeare in Company* (Oxford: Oxford University Press, 2013).

5. Knutson, *Playing Companies and Commerce*.

6. For discussions of the various circumstances of collaboration, see Heather Anne Hirschfeld, *Joint Enterprises: Collaborative Drama and the Institutionalization of the English Renaissance Theater* (Amherst: University of Massachusetts Press, 2004); see also David Nicol, *Middleton & Rowley: Forms of Collaboration in the Jacobean Playhouse* (Toronto: University of Toronto Press, 2012), 15–35. For discussion of the changeable patchwork of documents that made up the play in the playhouse, see Stern, *Documents of Performance*.

7. Jeffrey Masten, *Textual Intercourse: Collaboration, Authorship, and Sexualities in Renaissance Drama* (Cambridge: Cambridge University Press, 1997), 19.

8. Preiss, *Clowning and Authorship*, 73–75.

9. Stern, *Rehearsal from Shakespeare to Sheridan*, 120–21.

10. For an exemplary discussion of the transportable emotional and confessional valences of stage properties, see Williamson, *Materiality of Religion*.

11. For the argument that it is possible to track Middleton and Rowley's distinctive religious views in *The Changeling*, see Nicol, *Middleton & Rowley*, 36–65. However, this reading rests on an attenuated definition of Calvinism.

12. Jeremy Lopez, "Fitzgrave's Jewel: Audience and Anticlimax in Middleton and Shakespeare," in Low and Myhill, *Imagining the Audience*, 200.

13. For the inaccessibility of Shakespeare's religious beliefs, see Kastan, *Will to Believe*. For some recent discussions of Shakespeare's possible Catholicism, see Richard Wilson, *Secret Shakespeare: Studies in Theatre, Religion, and Resistance* (Manchester: Manchester University Press, 2004); Peter Milward, *Shakespeare the Papist* (Ann Arbor, MI: Sapientia Press, 2005); David N. Beauregard, *Catholic Theology in Shakespeare's Plays* (Newark: University of Delaware Press, 2008); and Claire Asquith, *Shadowplay: The Hidden Beliefs and Coded Politics of William Shakespeare* (London: Perseus, 2005).

14. While Fletcher never became a sharer in the company as Shakespeare had been, after 1614 he wrote exclusively for the King's Men; see Gerald Eades Bentley, *The Jacobean and Caroline Stage*, vol. 4, *Dramatic Companies and Players* (Oxford: Clarendon Press, 1941), 305–433. Beaumont and Fletcher's partnership began in 1606; around 1610 the pair began their association with the King's Men that lasted until 1613. Fletcher and Massinger's writing partnership for the King's Men runs from about 1618 to 1623.

15. Fletcher's grandfather's deprivation under Queen Mary is recorded in John Foxe's *Acts and Monuments*. Fletcher himself expressed to his puritan patron Henry Hastings, fifth Earl of Huntingdon, a zealous Protestant enthusiasm for war with Spain. In contrast, Beaumont's parents sheltered priests. However, Beaumont himself may not have maintained the old religion. An elegy praises the playwright for his ability to "confound, if not convert," Jesuits in debate. Even if Beaumont was a converted Protestant, there remains a striking contrast in the collaborators' religious backgrounds, and in their relationships to the faiths of their birth, family, and education; Philip J. Finkelpearl, *Court and Country Politics in the Plays of Beaumont and Fletcher* (Princeton, NJ: Princeton University Press, 1990), 15, 29, 10–13.

16. George Herbert, comp., *Wits Recreations* (London, 1640), B4r.

17. J. Payne Collier, *Memoirs of the Principal Actors in the Plays of Shakespeare* (London: Shakespeare Society, 1846), xiii, xii. The actor Edmond Shakespeare was buried in the same parish, also paying twenty shillings for the knell; Edmund K. Chambers, *The Elizabethan Stage* (Oxford: Clarendon Press, 1923), 2:338.

18. Since my concern is with audiences' experience of the play in performance, the fine-grained, distinctive patterns of usage that may (or may not) be detectable through stylometrics are irrelevant to my argument.

19. Hopkins's argument is tenuous. She bases her claim that Ford was embedded in a Catholic coterie on the fact that his printed works are dedicated to Catholics, or rumored Catholics, or people who had some connection to a Catholic or putative Catholic. In other words, her criteria for Catholic "association" are so broad they describe almost everyone in the period; Lisa Hopkins, *John Ford's Political Theatre* (Manchester: Manchester University Press, 1994), 3–38. Both the poem and prose tract discussed here were dedicated to committed Protestants, William Herbert and James Hay, respectively. For an influential discussion of Ford's "baroque" aesthetics, see Ronald Huebert, *John Ford: Baroque English Dramatist* (Montreal: McGill-Queen's University Press, 1977).

20. For Ford's contribution to the King's Men, see Bentley, *Jacobean and Caroline Stage*, 3:439.

21. John Ford, *A Line of Life* (London, 1620), reprinted in L. E. Stock et al., eds., *The Nondramatic Works of John Ford* (Binghamton, NY: Renaissance English Text Society, 1991), 85:305. In a devotional poem, he embraces the doctrine of double predestination, expresses assurance of his sanctification, and laments the condition of "silen[ced]" preachers ousted by "hir'd" ministers who only read the scriptures "to compound their own traditions"; John Ford, *Christes Bloodie Sweat* (London, 1613), 57–58, 51, 12.

22. Ford, *Christes Bloodie Sweat*, 18.

23. See Bentley, *Jacobean and Caroline Stage*, 2:584–88. For Swanston's religious persuasion, see James Wright, *Historia Histrionica* (London, 1699), 8. An interregnum pamphlet identifies *"Hillyar Swansted* the Player" in the camp of puritan parliamentarians; see Remembrancer, *A Key to the Cabinet of the Parliament, by Their Remembrancer* (London, 1648), A3r.

24. T. J. King, *Casting Shakespeare's Plays: London Actors and Their Roles, 1590–1642* (Cambridge: Cambridge University Press, 1992), 50–60.

25. Tatham, *Knavery in All Trades*, D4v.

26. John Lowin, *Conclusions upon Dances, Both of This Age, and of the Olde* (London, 1607). Lowin's piety is also evident in his involvement in parish business; see Barbara Wooding, *John Lowin and the English Theatre, 1603–1647: Acting and Cultural Politics on the Jacobean and Caroline Stage* (Farnham, UK: Ashgate, 2013), 67–87.

27. Lowin, *Conclusions upon Dances*, D1v.

28. Ibid., A3v.

29. James Wright, *Historia Histrionica*, 10.

30. Rick Bowers, "John Lowin's *Conclusions upon Dances*: Puritan Conclusions of a Godly Player," *Renaissance and Reformation* 23, no. 2 (1987): 170–71.

31. John Field, *A Godly Exhortation, by Occasion of the Late Judgement of God, Shewed at Parris-Garden* (London, 1583), D1v.

32. Nathan Field, "Field the Players Letter to Mr. Sutton, Preacher att St. Mary Overs," M.S. State Papers, Domestic, James I, LXXXIX (1616), reprinted as "The Remonstrance of Nathan Field," in James Orchard Halliwell-Phillipps, *Illustrations of the Life of Shakespeare* (London: Longmans, Green, 1874), 115–16.

33. Ibid., 116.

34. Ibid., 116–17.

35. Ibid., 117.

36. The fact that John Field was a fierce opponent of the episcopacy and the stage—and that one of his sons (Theophilus) became a bishop and the other an actor—does not necessarily mean that Nathan Field maintained religious views entirely opposed to his father's. While the two clearly disagreed about theater, Nathan was only a year old when his father died, which undercuts the tempting assumption that this difference emerged from some bitter family psychodrama. Nathan's insistent use of a godly idiom may come from a sense of inheritance or birthright as the son of a major figure in the Elizabethan puritan movement. For detailed background on Field's family and career, see Roberta Florence Brinkley, *Nathan Field, the Actor-Playwright* (New Haven, CT: Yale University Press, 1928). For a discussion of Nathan Field's role in *Bartholomew Fair* in relation to his father and his conflict with Sutton, see Nora Johnson, *The Actor as Playwright in Early Modern Drama* (Cambridge: Cambridge University Press, 2003).

37. During his two-week incarceration in Newgate in 1598 awaiting possible execution for killing Gabriel Spencer, the Protestant minister's son embraced Catholicism. Jonson remained "12 yeares a Papist," but extremist violence alienated the playwright from the Roman Church. In 1610, in the aftermath of François Ravaillac's assassination of Henry IV in France, Jonson returned to the Church of England; David Riggs, *Ben Jonson: A Life* (Cambridge, MA: Harvard University Press, 1989), 50–54. Although William Drummond's assessment of Jonson as "for any religion, as being versed in both," hints at an irreligious or opportunist changeability, his account of Jonson's second conversion suggests deeper commitment: "After he was reconciled with the Church, and left of to be a recusant, at his first communion, in token of true reconciliation, he drank out all the full cup of wine." This description is of course complicated by Jonson's reputation for prodigious worldly drinking; William Drummond, "Ben Jonson's Conversations with William Drummond of Hawthornden," in *Inigo Jones and Ben Jonson*, ed. David Laing (London: Bradbury and Evans, 1853), 19, 40, 22. There were other Catholics among the King's Men. Jacobean actor William Ecclestone, who was with the company in 1610–11 and performed in *The Alchemist*, was charged with recusancy. For Ecclestone's career, see Bentley, *Jacobean and Caroline Stage*, 2:429–30. For his recusancy, see *Middlesex County Records: Indictments, Recognizances, Coroner's Inquisitions-Post-Mortem, Orders and Memoranda, temp. James I* vol. 2, ed. John Cordy Jeaffreson (Middlesex County Records Office: Clerkenwell Sessions House, 1887), 87. See also Mark Eccles, "Elizabethan Actors II: E–J," *Notes and Queries* 38, no. 4 (December 1991): 454. There were also other converts in the company.

William Trigg, a boy player with the King's Men in the late 1620s and early 1630s, later experienced a turn toward godly piety: "Trigg having turn'd his sute he struts in state, / And tells the world he's now regenerate"; Bentley, *Jacobean and Caroline Stage*, 2:604. Trigg at one point served in the King's army; the verse may signal a public change in party allegiance (with a possible "turncoat" pun), as well as the growth of personal piety. For his Royalist military service, see Leslie Hotson, *The Commonwealth and Restoration Stage* (Cambridge, MA: Harvard University Press, 1928), 13.

38. Compare to *The Sparagus Garden* by Jonsonian playwright Richard Brome, which features a booze-up between two biological brothers, one a zealous soul among the brethren and the other a carousing member of the Brothers of the Blade. Brome, *The Sparagus Garden* (London, 1640).

39. Thomas May, *The Character of a Right Malignant* (London, 1645). Compare to Ben Jonson, *Every Man Out of His Humour*, ed. Randall Martin, in *The Cambridge Edition of the Works of Ben Jonson*, ed. David Bevington, Martin Butler, and Ian Donaldson (Cambridge: Cambridge University Press, 2012), 1:249–427. Though Jonson did not invent the kind of "character" writing that appears in the prefatory material to his play, his interest in humoral personality strengthened his association with the genre. Since May was part of Jonson's circle, the line of influence is clear.

40. May, *Character of a Right Malignant*, 1, 5.

41. See Samuel Rowlands, *Humors Ordinarie* (London, 1605); and Samuel Rowlands, *Humors Looking Glasse* (London, 1608).

42. Robinson may have been Burbage's apprentice and after his death married his widow. Bentley, *Jacobean and Caroline Stage*, 2:550–53.

43. John Squier, *An Answer to a Printed Paper Entitled "Articles Exhibited in Parliament, Against Mr. John Squier Viccar of Saint Leonard Shoreditch"* (London, 1641), 2–3, 6. While the pamphlet insists on John Squier's conformity, his practices are clearly Laudian innovations.

44. For a reading of *Sejanus* as developing a line of Elizabethan Catholic critiques, see Peter Lake, "From *Leicester His Commonwealth* to *Sejanus His Fall*: Ben Jonson and the Politics of Roman (Catholic) Virtue," in *Catholics and the "Protestant Nation,"* ed. Ethan Shagan (Manchester: Manchester University Press, 2005), 128–61. For a reading of the play as a defense of Catholic ritual, see Holly Crawford Pickett, "The Idolatrous Nose: Incense on the Early Modern Stage," in Degenhardt and Williamson, *Religion and Drama*, 19–38. For the apparent discrepancy between Jonson's religious orientation and the complex treatment of idolatry in *Volpone*, see Katharine Eisaman Maus, "Idol and Gift in *Volpone*," *English Literary Renaissance* 35, no. 3 (Autumn 2005): 429–53.

45. Williamson, *Materiality of Religion*, 13–14.

46. John Kuhn, "Making Pagans: Theatrical Practice and Comparative Religion from Marlowe to Southerne" (PhD diss., Columbia University, 2016).

47. Williamson, *Materiality of Religion*, 66.

48. Paul Yachnin, "*Hamlet* and the Social Thing in Early Modern England," in *Making Publics in Early Modern Europe: People, Things, Forms of Knowledge*, ed. Bronwen Wilson and Paul Yachnin (New York: Routledge, 2010), 83.

49. Musa Gurnis, "Martyr Acts: Playing with Foxe's Martyrs on the Public Stage," in Degenhardt and Williamson, *Religion and Drama*, 175–93. I argue that while an early modern theatergoer buying a ticket for a play based on John Foxe's *Acts and Monuments* would have expected to see onstage pious Protestant martyrs, bad Catholics, and the triumphant onward march of providential English history, the Protestant martyr plays that appeared between 1599 and 1606 baffle these expectations. This subgenre includes *Sir John Oldcastle* (1599), *Thomas Lord Cromwell* (1600), *The Famous History of Sir Thomas Wyatt* (1602), *When You See Me You Know Me* (1605), and *1 and 2 If You Know Not Me You Know Nobody* (1605 and 1606).

50. For a discussion of the association of Lollardy with puritanism in *1 and 2 Henry IV*, see David Kastan, "'Killed with Hard Opinions': Oldcastle and Falstaff and the Reformed Text of *1 Henry IV*," in *Shakespeare After Theory* (New York: Routledge, 1999), 93–108. For extended readings of Oldcastle as a puritan figure, see Peter Corbin and Douglas Sedge, introduction to *The Oldcastle Controversy: "Sir John Oldcastle, Part 1" and "The Famous Victories of Henry V"* (Manchester: Manchester University Press, 1991), 1–35; see also Mary Grace Muse Adkins, "Sixteenth-Century Religious and Political Implications in *Sir John Oldcastle*," *University of Texas Studies in English*, no. 22 (1942): 86–104.

51. [Michael Drayton, Richard Hathway, Robert Wilson, and] Anthony Munday, *The First Part of the True and Honorable Historie, of the Life of Sir John Old-castle, the Good Lord Cobham* (London, 1600), A2r. All subsequent citations will appear by page signature parenthetically in the text.

52. Michael Drayton, *The Harmonie of the Church* (London, 1591), A1r.

53. R. W., *Martine Mar-Sixtus* (London, 1591).

54. For the loose syndicates involving these and other playwrights working on martyr plays and their generic cognates, see Knutson, *Playing Companies and Commerce*, 50–52.

55. James Marino, *Owning William Shakespeare: The King's Men and Their Intellectual Property* (Philadelphia: University of Pennsylvania Press, 2011), 124.

56. For cluster marketing, see Knutson, *Playing Companies and Commerce*, 31–36. For duplicates, serials, and character spin-offs as common repertory strategies, see ibid., 57–59; see also Knutson, *Repertory of Shakespeare's Company*.

57. Marino, *Owning William Shakespeare*, 124.

58. *Oldcastle* and *Henry V* both appear in 1599. My assumption here is that the Admiral's Men imitate the Chamberlain's Men's play *Henry V*, just as they clearly borrow heavily from the earlier plays *1 and 2 Henry IV*. Of course all four plays draw material from the anonymous *Famous Victories of Henry V*, and it is equally possible that Shakespeare's *Henry V* was a knockoff of the Chamberlain's Men's *Oldcastle*. Recognizing the recursive and multidirectional quality of the interrelationships between these plays is more important than establishing unilateral lines of influence.

59. Many of the Protestant martyr plays cited here use scenes of merriness and hospitality as devices that consolidate a nostalgic sense of English community. Other examples include Robin Hood plays such as Robert Greene's *A Pleasant and Conceyted Comedie of George a Green, the Pinner of Wakefield* (London, 1599).

60. For a discussion of plays marked with the anxiety that English Catholics dangerously blur the line between "the English and foreigners, loyal subjects and traitors, us and them," see Dolan, *Whores of Babylon*, 5.

61. For a discussion of ways that the English history plays that were fashionable from the mid-1580s to the early 1600s were a means through which a normative, English, masculine, Protestant identity was imagined into being through the exclusion, demonization, or mockery of its others, see Jean E. Howard and Phyllis Rackin, *Engendering a Nation: A Feminist Account of Shakespeare's History Plays* (London: Routledge, 1997).

62. In the text of *Oldcastle*, Henry's speech headings change from "King" to "Harry" for the duration of the dice game to register the informality of his persona in the scene.

63. The play presents Lollard rebel Murley as a sinister, failed version of this trope of merry, old-timey hospitality and fellowship. The malt maker addresses the rebels: "Meal and salt, wheat and mault, fire and tow, frost and snow, why Tom . . . and Robin and Hodge holding my owne two horses, proper men, hansom men, tall men, true men" (E4r). Murley's troops are only his apprentices, described in the stage directions as *"prepared in some filthy order for warre"* (ibid.). This iteration of folksy good humor among soldiers is deadly treason. Fighting for a religion he does not understand, willing to kill a king but obsessed with obtaining a knighthood, Murley's degraded language marks him apart from the loyal community of English good fellows. His coconspirators mock him and criticize his idle speech: "Talke not of trifles" (F1r). Murley's "merry" speech tics make him incapable of successfully pleading for his life when he is arraigned for treason, making his failed performance of good fellowship the mark of his irredeemability as a religious traitor.

64. Similar scenarios appear in other roughly contemporary plays. In Samuel Rowley's 1604 *When You See Me You Know Me*, staged by Prince Henry's Men, Henry VIII runs across Black Will, a thief, pimp, and murderer, but also a strapping English man. King and commoner wrestle to test Black Will's "man-hood," and the thief is then released to fight in the King's wars "because ye shall know King Harrie loves a man." Black Will embraces loyal military service: "The wars sweet King, tis my delight . . . I'll live and dye with thee sweet King"; Samuel Rowley, *When You See Me, You Know Me* (London, 1605), E1r, E4v, E4r–E4v. Manliness here is the sign of Englishness and loyalty, as well as the device through which social problems (e.g., Will's criminality) are resolved.

65. Harry and Falstaff's extradramatic robbery of Oldcastle draws a plot line through both plays. The theft belongs to the world of the Henriad but affects the dynamics of Wrotham's robbery of Harry (making his crime tit for tat and therefore more easily pardoned).

66. Gina Bloom, Anston Bosman, and William N. West, "Ophelia's Intertheatricality, or, How Performance Is History," *Theatre Journal* 65, no. 2 (May 2013): 169. See also William N. West, "Intertheatricality," in *Early Modern Theatricality*, ed. Henry Turner (Oxford: Oxford University Press, 2013), 151–72.

67. Because the green costume is associated with Robin Hood, this reference opens out toward a wider group of cognate, contemporary, stage good fellows.

68. Van Es, *Shakespeare in Company*, 85–87.

69. This is, of course, not to treat Kemp's physicality as a point of origin, or ultimate referent. The clown's own style of masculinity clearly draws on preexisting festive conventions, and other contemporary stylizations of the body. Falstaff himself seems also to have been a particularly transportable character, starring in his own company's spin-off *The Merry Wives of Windsor*, in addition to his duplication in the Admiral Men's play, and later appearing detached from the full play of his origin in Restoration jigs.

70. Peter Lake recognizes only the play's anticlerical content, ignoring the inclusive recuperation of Catholic loyalty achieved by the comic, generic conventions in which Sir John of Wrotham is located. Lake, *How Shakespeare Put Politics*, 418–19.

71. For a full discussion of the play's composition, censorship, revision, and possible performance, including the attribution of hands, see John Jowett, introduction to *Sir Thomas More*, by Anthony Munday and Henry Chettle, Arden Shakespeare, 3rd ser. (London: Bloomsbury Arden Shakespeare, 2011). All subsequent citations will appear parenthetically in the text and refer to this edition.

72. For the argument that the play was in fact performed, see Scott McMillin, *The Elizabethan Theatre and "The Book of Sir Thomas More"* (Ithaca, NY: Cornell University Press, 1987).

73. Addressing the problem of why Shakespeare would add a speech to the insurrection scene after Tilney had ordered that the riot be cut from the play entirely and only described briefly, Arthur Kinney points out that Shakespeare had previously written licensed plays with insurrections that include rhetorically persuasive speeches defending social order of the kind delivered by More in Shakespeare's addition. In other words, the revision may not be flouting Tilney's instructions so much as finding another, previously successful strategy of compliance. See Arthur F. Kinney, "Text, Context, and Authorship of *The Booke of Sir Thomas Moore*," in *Pilgrimage for Love: Essays in Early Modern Literature in Honor of Josephine A. Roberts*, ed. Sigrid King (Tempe: Arizona Center for Medieval and Renaissance Studies, 1999), 133–60.

74. Susannah Brietz Monta, *Martyrdom and Literature in Early Modern Literature* (Cambridge: Cambridge University Press, 2005), 158–72.

75. Monta does discuss More's metatheatrical performance on the scaffold as a device that opens up the self-conscious gap between appearance and inner being that runs through English Renaissance theater. However, this reading invokes the split between outward show and "that within" almost as an automatically operative, theatrical constant. Yet, in the more specific dynamics of the script, More's final appearance on the scaffold, rather than obscuring his soul with its metatheatricality, in fact recalls his earlier performance in the morality play, which gives a direct allegory of the lord chancellor's objections to the King's divorce and remarriage to Anne Boleyn, sympathetically presenting More as "Good Counsel" who warns against embracing "Lady Vanity." In this play, metatheatricality makes More's conscience more visible. For further discussion of the play's metatheatricality, see Lucy Munro, "Archaism, the 'Middle Age' and the Morality Play in Shakespearean Drama," *Shakespeare* 8, no. 4 (December 2012): 356–67; see

also John Jowett, "Sir Thomas More and the Play of Body," *Actes des Congrès de la Société Française Shakespeare* 23 (2005): 75–89.

76. Eamon Duffy, "Bare Ruined Choirs: Remembering Catholicism in Shakespeare's England," in Dutton, Findlay, and Wilson, *Theatre and Religion*, 40–57.

77. Mullaney, *Reformation of Emotions*, 74, 78.

78. Thomas Dekker, *The Double PP* (London, 1606), B1v.

79. Henry Chettle, *Englands Mourning Garment* (London, 1603), D3r.

80. Thomas Heywood, *Troia Britanica* (London, 1609), 463.

81. For a discussion of broader industry conditions affecting this collaboration, as well as the claim that Shakespeare did not contribute to *Sir Thomas More*, see Carol Chillington, "Playwrights at Work: Henslowe's, Not Shakespeare's, *Book of Sir Thomas More*," *English Literary Renaissance* 10, no. 3 (September 1980): 439–79.

82. This lost version of the play was likely adapted or absorbed into *Sir Thomas Wyatt*.

83. For the speculation that Munday's "Puritan sympathies" and commitment to "freedom of conscience" drew him to write a "vindication" of More, see Giorgio Melchiori, "*The Book of Sir Thomas More*: Dramatic Unity," in *Shakespeare and Sir Thomas More: Essays on the Play and Its Shakespearean Interest*, ed. T. H. Howard-Hill (Cambridge: Cambridge University Press, 1989), 77–100. For an attempt to make Munday a coherent Catholic, see Donna B. Hamilton, *Anthony Munday and the Catholics, 1560–1633* (Burlington, VT: Ashgate, 2005). For a discussion of Munday's "egregious" confessional and professional life, see Lake, *Antichrist's Lewd Hat*.

CHAPTER 4. MAKING A PUBLIC THROUGH *A GAME AT CHESS*

1. Ian Munro recognizes the work of the play in creating a kind of public sphere, but he argues that by "excoriating the Black House . . . in commodified terms, the play is registering its ambivalence about its own commercial status"; Ian Munro, "Making Publics: Secrecy and Publication in *A Game at Chess*," *Medieval and Renaissance Drama in England* 14 (2001): 219–20. Christine Marie Carlson detects a troubling similarity between the White and Black Houses, claiming that Middleton "conceives of [anti-Catholic polemic]" and "Machiavellian scheming, as similar strategies . . . that [threaten to] undermine the moral high ground of the true Protestant national cause"; Carlson, "The Rhetoric of Providence: Thomas Middleton's *A Game at Chess* (1624) and Seventeenth-Century Political Engraving," *Renaissance Quarterly* 67, no. 4 (Winter 2014): 1246. Caroline Bicks claims that the Black Queen's Pawn and the White Queen's Pawn share a destabilizing theatricality; Bicks, "Staging the Jesuitess in *A Game at Chess*," *Studies in English Literature* 49, no. 2 (Spring 2009): 475–79. Despite the fact that duplicitous characters are flagged as treacherous as soon as they are introduced, Barbara Fuchs claims that the White House characters who change allegiance "[remind] viewers of the indeterminacy and illegibility of religious and political allegiance"; Fuchs, "Middleton and Spain," in *The Oxford Hand-*

book of Thomas Middleton, ed. Gary Taylor and Trish Thomas Henley (Oxford: Oxford University Press, 2012), 404–17. Paul Yachnin claims that the play "has two faces: it looks one way in praise of the king, the other way in derision; it manages to be both a glowing idealization *and* an uproarious satire of the fiasco of Prince Charles and Buckingham's trip to Spain," with these interpretive alternatives geared toward different demographics of playgoers; Yachnin, "*A Game at Chess*: Thomas Middleton's 'Praise of Folly,'" *Modern Language Quarterly: A Journal of Literary History* 48, no. 2 (June 1987): 108.

2. For the caveat that poststructuralist reading practices tend to create the fragmentation they seek, as well as the observation that *A Game at Chess*, unlike other English history plays that revolve around dynastic faction, makes ideological difference central, see Gary Taylor, "Historicism, Presentism and Time."

3. Thomas Scott, *Vox Dei* (Utrecht [London], 1624), 98–99.

4. Thomas Scott, *The Second Part of Vox Populi* (Goricom [London], 1624), D2v–D3r.

5. For an account of the enthusiastic Protestant unity that characterized 1623–24, as well as the conflict that preceded and followed it, see Thomas Cogswell, *The Blessed Revolution: English Politics and the Coming of War, 1621–1624* (Cambridge: Cambridge University Press, 1989).

6. Writing midway through the play's run, the Spanish ambassador who replaced Gondomar wrote, "During these last four days more than 12,000 persons have all heard the play of *A Game at Chess*, for so they call it, including all the nobility still in London." Performances continued for another five days. Don Carlos Colomna to the Conde-Duque Olivares, London, August 20 [10], 1624, in Thomas Middleton, *A Game at Chess*, ed. T. H. Howard-Hill (Manchester: Manchester University Press, 1993), 197. All subsequent references to the play are to this edition and appear parenthetically in the text by act, scene, and line. All references to contemporary correspondence regarding the play in the notes are also to this edition.

7. John Chamberlain to Sir Dudley Carleton, London, August 21, 1624, in Middleton, *Game at Chess*, 205 (italics mine).

8. John Woolley to William Trumbull, London, August 11, 1624, in Middleton, *Game at Chess*, 198. For a discussion of the exchange of political knowledge as a form of competitive sociability, see András Kiséry, *Hamlet's Moment: Drama and Political Knowledge in Early Modern England* (Oxford: Oxford University Press, 2016).

9. For a concise, authoritative discussion of the way the play's wild popularity created demand for scribal copies, see Gary Taylor, "*A Game at Chess*: General Textual Introduction," in Taylor and Lavagnino, *Thomas Middleton*, 842–47.

10. For identifications of historical people represented by allegorical figures, see Edgar C. Morris, "The Allegory in Middleton's *A Game at Chess*," *Englische Studien* 38 (1907): 39–52; Martin Butler, "William Prynne and the Allegory of Middleton's *Game at Chess*," *Notes and Queries* 30, no. 2 (April 1983): 153–54; T. H. Howard-Hill, "More on 'William Prynne and the Allegory of Middleton's *Game at Chess*,'" *Notes and Queries* 36, no. 3 (September 1989): 349–51; Bicks, "Staging the Jesuitess"; and James Doelman, "Claimed by Two Religions: The Elegy on Thomas Washington, 1623, and Middleton's *A Game at*

Chesse," *Studies in Philology* 110, no. 2 (Spring 2013): 318–49. For identification of the play's sources, see Jerzy Limon, "The 'Missing Source' for Thomas Middleton's *A Game at Chess* (V.iii.141–7) Found," *Notes and Queries* 33, no. 3 (September 1986): 386–87; Paul Yachnin, "A New Source for Thomas Middleton's *A Game at Chess,*" *Notes and Queries* 27 (April 1980): 157–58; Jeanne Shami, "Thomas Middleton's *A Game at Chesse*: A Sermon Analogue," *Notes and Queries* 42, no. 3 (September 1995): 236–39; and James Doelman, "Another Analogue for Middleton's *A Game at Chesse,*" *Notes and Queries* 57, no. 3 (September 2010): 418–19.

11. Important exceptions that productively attend to aspects of the play's form include Roussel Sargent, "Theme and Structure in Middleton's *A Game at Chess,*" *Modern Language Review* 66, no. 4 (October 1971): 721–30; Jane Sherman, "The Pawns' Allegory in Middleton's *A Game at Chesse,*" *Review of English Studies*, n.s., 29, no. 114 (May 1978): 147–59; Paul Yachnin, "*A Game at Chess* and Chess Allegory," *Studies in English Literature* 22, no. 2 (Spring 1982): 317–30; and Robert I. Lublin, *Costuming the Shakespearean Stage: Visual Codes of Representation in Early Modern Theatre and Culture* (Farnham, UK: Ashgate, 2011). However, much of this valuable work focuses on the play's form as it relates to the allegory, i.e., the ways theatrical devices establish the dramatic fiction, rather than the ways theatrical devices affect audiences.

12. In an authoritative essay collection, Richard Dutton acknowledges that *A Game at Chess* is "an effective stage-piece" but treats the play's theatricality largely as incidental to its religious and political importance; Dutton, "Thomas Middleton's *A Game at Chess*: A Case Study," in *The Cambridge History of British Theatre*, vol. 1, *Origins to 1660*, ed. Jane Milling and Peter Thomson (Cambridge: Cambridge University Press, 2004), 426. T. H. Howard-Hill argues that the addition of comic material attenuated Middleton's more serious intentions; Howard-Hill, *Middleton's "Vulgar Pasquin": Essays on "A Game at Chess"* (Newark: University of Delaware Press, 1995).

13. For example, James Doelman resists "slippage between vehicle and tenor [because it] . . . erase[s] the allegorical distinction"; Doelman, "Claimed by Two Religions," 339. In contrast, I maintain that slippage between vehicle and tenor is metaphor's modus operandi.

14. Raymond Williams, "Communications and Community," in *Resources of Hope: Culture, Democracy, and Socialism*, ed. Robin Gable (London: Verso, 1989), 22–23.

15. Amerigo Salvetti to Picchena, London, August 23 [13], 1624, in Middleton, *Game at Chess*, 201.

16. Paul Yachnin, "Playing with Space: Making a Public in Middleton's Theatre," in Taylor and Henley, *Oxford Handbook of Thomas Middleton*, 38.

17. George Lowe to Sir Arthur Ingram, London, August 7, 1624, in Middleton, *Game at Chess*, 193.

18. For an extended discussion of James's investment in the peaceful reconciliation of Christendom, see W. B. Patterson, *James VI and I and the Reunion of Christendom* (Cambridge: Cambridge University Press, 1997). For James's desire to establish an ecumenical peace and Charles's infatuation with the infanta, see Glyn Redworth, "Of Pimps and Princes: Three Unpublished Letters from James I and the Prince of Wales Relating to the Spanish Match," *Historical Journal* 37, no. 2 (1994): 401–9.

19. For a concise account of the breakdown of negotiations in Spain, see Brennan C. Pursell, "The End of the Spanish Match," *Historical Journal* 45, no. 4 (2002): 699–726; see also Glyn Redworth, *The Prince and the Infanta: The Cultural Politics of the Spanish Match* (New Haven, CT: Yale University Press, 2003).

20. Thomas Cogswell, "Thomas Middleton and the Court, 1624: *A Game at Chess* in Context," *Huntington Library Quarterly* 47, no. 4 (Autumn 1984): 283. For the foundational argument that the Spanish were only using the match negotiations to manipulate the English and had no intention of going through with the union, see S. R. Gardiner, *Prince Charles and the Spanish Marriage, 1617–1623*, 2 vols. (London: Hurst and Blackett, 1869). For the view that Buckingham was the key figure able to see through the Spanish deception, see Roger Lockyer, *Buckingham: The Life and Political Career of George Villiers, First Duke of Buckingham, 1592–1628* (London: Longman, 1981).

21. For an account of the ecstatic and widespread popular support that greeted Charles on his return, see Cressy, *Bonfires and Bells*.

22. John Woolley to William Trumbull, London, August 6, 1624, in Middleton, *Game at Chess*, 193.

23. Margot Heinemann fails to recognize that the match was no longer a possibility by the time of the play's staging and therefore wrongly identifies this play as an example of "opposition drama"; Heinemann, *Puritanism and Theatre*. For a seminal discussion locating the play in the relative harmony among Protestants in August 1624, see Cogswell, "Thomas Middleton and the Court"; see as well Howard-Hill, *"Vulgar Pasquin,"* 87–90. Indeed, the production and reception history of *A Game at Chess* is an object lesson in the way that "puritan" attitudes can shade off imperceptibly into the mainstream Calvinist consensus. As Peter Lake writes, "The incorporation of attitudes central to the puritan world-view into the contemporary establishment enabled zealots like Scott to present an activist puritan case as but the natural development of premises and principals generally held to be true. Scott was operating within what he and certainly most of his contemporaries assumed to be an ideological consensus"; Lake, "Constitutional Consensus and Puritan Opposition in the 1620s: Thomas Scott and the Spanish Match," *Historical Journal* 25, no. 4 (December 1982): 807. For a broader discussion of anti-Catholicism as the glue holding together the Calvinist consensus, see Lake, "Anti-Popery."

24. John Holles, Lord Haughton, to the Earl of Somerset, London, August 11, 1624, in Middleton, *Game at Chess*, 198–99.

25. Sherman, "Pawns' Allegory," 154.

26. As the public face of Charles (sharing his court status and gender), the White Knight is never duped or tempted by the Black House. However, partial displacement onto the figure of the White Queen's Pawn (a nonnoble woman) allows the players a discreet remove from which to stage Charles wavering spiritually under Catholic influence, as well as romantically vulnerable in a duplicitous marriage contract. It is no contradiction for the White Queen's Pawn to represent both Charles and true faith, since her plot dramatizes the possible personal conversion of the head of the Church of England. This

public-private psychomachia would be complicated to diagram but easy to understand (whether consciously articulated or not) in watching a performance.

27. Alvise Valaresso, Venetian Ambassador, to the Doge and Senate, August 30 [20], 1624, in Middleton, *Game at Chess*, 204. The emphatic intelligibility of the topical allegory is not always produced by neat one-to-one correspondences but rather by muddling or doubling some of the identifications while bringing others into sharp focus. Pace T. H. Howard-Hill, who declares, "One thing certain is that a piece on the stage could not have borne at one and the same time . . . multiple identifications"; Howard-Hill, *"Vulgar Pasquin,"* 114. Why not?

28. For a discussion of this emphasis, see Howard-Hill, *"Vulgar Pasquin,"* 114.

29. Don Carlos Coloma to the Conde-Duque Olivares, London, August 20 [10], 1624, in Middleton, *Game at Chess*, 195.

30. John Woolley to William Trumbull, London, August 11, 1624, in Middleton, *Game as Chess*, 198.

31. John Chamberlain to Sir Dudley Carleton, London, August 21, 1624, in Middleton, *Game at Chess*, 205. Although it is in no way a direct record of the actor's performance, a description of Gondomar in one of Scott's later pamphlets gives one possible idea of how this character, or some Spanish characters more generally, may have been physicalized: "For the Spaniard is not of our dull English qualitie, to let his words passe from him as neglected strangers or thoughts out of the compasse of his dearest familiaritie, but rather as deare children or choicest friends, to lend them admiration with his eyes and hands, to adorne them with expectation in the shrugge of shoulders, and with a thousand other minicke gestures, to make a speech that is as triviall and unseasoned as folly it selfe, to appeare as serious as if it were a *Delphan* Oracle: upon some one or other of these Spanish disgusts the Fox [Gondomar] . . . unkennels himselfe . . . his anticke postures, mumps, moes, and Munkey-like wrye faces might drawe laughter or scorne"; Scott, *Sir Walter Rawleighs Ghost* (Utrecht [London], 1626), B1r–B1v. As a further instance of the highly personalized satire of Black House figures, the Spanish ambassador complains that "the king of the blacks has easily been taken for our lord the King, because of his youth, dress, and other details"; Don Carlos Coloma to the Conde-Duque Olivares, London, August 20 [10], 1624, in Middleton, *Game at Chess*, 194.

32. In terms of the size of individual parts, Gondomar speaks the most lines and the White Queen's Pawn the second most; however, as a group the Black House characters have far more to say and do onstage than the White House characters collectively. Heinemann makes much of the fact that five of the White Duke's lines may mock Buckingham as an overweight sodomite. Even if this is so, it is beside the point. Buckingham is not the focus of the play's dramatic energy.

33. John Holles, Lord Haughton, to the Earl of Somerset, London, August 11, 1624, in Middleton, *Game at Chess*, 199.

34. "Chess was, first and foremost, a war game . . . [that] came down ultimately to politics"; Daniel E. O'Sullivan, "Introduction: 'Le beau jeu nottable,'" in *Chess in the Middle Ages and Early Modern Age: A Fundamental Thought Paradigm of the Premodern World*, ed. Daniel E. O'Sullivan (Boston: De Gruyter, 2012), 7.

35. In a workshop on scenes from the play in 2015 at the Folger Shakespeare Library, the first observation from the actors was that the script suggested "very broad comedy."

36. Dessen, *Shakespeare's Theatrical Vocabulary*, 88–108.

37. Lopez, *Theatrical Convention and Audience Response*, 57.

38. Howard, *Shakespeare's Art of Orchestration*, 74.

39. Lopez, *Theatrical Convention and Audience Response*, 57.

40. Dessen, *Shakespeare's Theatrical Vocabulary*, 65.

41. For a discussion of antitheatrical descriptions of the theater as a kind of drug, see Pollard, *Drugs and Theatre*. For a discussion of food metaphors in antitheatrical writing, see Lopez, *Theatrical Convention and Audience Response*.

42. Stephen Gosson, *The Schoole of Abuse* (London, 1579), A2r.

43. Gosson, *Playes Confuted in Five Actions*, B5r.

44. There is a possibility that the chair was painted gold (paid for with money Gondomar extracted from English courtiers with promises of court advancement after the prince's marriage to the infanta): "I love o'life to sit upon a bank / Of heretic gold" (4.2.3–4). This does not affect the basic design element—the hole in the seat—that makes the chair signify as a toilet onstage.

45. Scott, *Rawleighs Ghost*, B1v. The illustration featuring Gondomar's stool appears on the title page to Scott's *Second Part of Vox Populi*.

46. Lena Orlin, *Locating Privacy in Tudor London* (Oxford: Oxford University Press, 2007).

47. Don Carlos Coloma to the Conde-Duque Olivares, London, August 20 [10], 1624, in Middleton, *Game at Chess*, 195.

48. For women's leakiness in this and other plays, see Gail Kern Paster, *The Body Embarrassed: Drama and the Disciplines of Shame in Early Modern England* (Ithaca, NY: Cornell University Press, 1993).

49. Paracelsus, *Paracelsus His Dispensatory and Chirurgery* (London, 1656), 122.

50. Don Carlos Coloma to the Conde-Duque Olivares, London, August 20 [10], 1624, in Middleton, *Game at Chess*, 195.

51. "Bum" appears in Q1, elsewhere replaced by "drum."

52. The scene also literalizes a cluster of imagery in the play in which Gondomar's brain full of secrets is a dunghill. Earlier the Black Knight proposes scorching the letters past legibility so that

> 'Twill mock the adversary strangely
> . . . .
> When [they come] all spectacled
> To pick syllables out of the dung of treason
> As children pick their cherry-stones, yet [find] none
> But what they made themselves with ends of letters. (2.1.218–25)

Later, he recycles this language to describe his own mind, declaring that, if opened, his brains would resemble a globe, so thick with secrets that "sharp state eyes will . . . [need spectacles to] pick out / The plots" (3.1.136–43). As Yachnin writes, "The relationship between the play and the globe, which epitomizes the mastery of space for the powerful, is larger and more telling, especially since the playhouse where the brain and globe are figured as instruments of geographical domination is itself called the Globe—the very building in which a very large, heterogeneous gathering of playgoers are making a public by taking in the world at a look"; Yachnin, "Playing with Space," 46.

53. For example, Jerzy Limon claims that White House figures are in the dark as to Black House plots until the play's final scene of discovery exposes to them the secrets that have been revealed to audiences all along. Limon, *Dangerous Matter: English Drama and Politics, 1623/24* (Cambridge: Cambridge University Press, 1986), 106.

54. Earlier too, when the attempted rape of the White Queen's Pawn is brought to light, the undeceived White King assesses Gondomar:

> That Black Knight
> Will never take an answer; 'tis a victory
> To make him understand he does amiss
> When he knows in his own clear understanding
> That he does nothing else. (3.3.192–96)

55. Amerigo Salvetti to Picchena, London, August 23 [13], 1624, in Middleton, *Game at Chess*, 201. In a similar vein, marking both the play's emphasis and its contrary side effect, he elsewhere writes, "In going about to discouer his trickes, me thinkes they make him a man of understanding with a great reflection / upon them that he daylie treated with . . . but the main runs all together upon [Gondomar] and his phistula"; Amerigo Salvetti to Sir John Scudamore, London, August 14, 1624, in Middleton, *Game at Chess*, 202.

56. John Holles, Lord Haughton, to the Earl of Somerset, London, August 11, 1624, in Middleton, *Game at Chess*, 199.

57. Don Carlos Coloma to the Conde-Duque Olivares, London, August 20 [10], 1624, in Middleton, *Game at Chess*, 194. While Loyola does observe the Black Bishop's Pawn take his place on the chessboard in the induction, the pawn does not speak any lines and could be played in the induction by another actor in the costume (or a backstage supernumerary filling in as the induction brings both houses onstage).

58. The Black Queen's Pawn alone knows a way to help the Jesuit escape unseen through "a secret vault" (2.1.90). It is possible that the Black Queen Pawn's line, "*There lies a secret vault,*" is deictic and indicates an imagined place below the stage (2.1.90). The possibility that the Jesuit exits by descending through the trapdoor is suggested later in the scene when the Black Knight's Pawn asks, "Where's my confessor? / Why dost thou point to the ground?" To this the Black Queen's Pawn replies, "'Cause he went that way" (2.1.233). Howard-Hill's footnote rightly reads the joke as a reference to the phrase "gone to ground." However, if the Jesuit does exit through the trap, this punch line joins several others in the play that pun on both verbal and visual levels. Furthermore, this early use of the trap as a Black House trick may resonate ironically later in the play, as Black House characters are tossed into the "bag" through the trap, creating a sense that the Black

House pieces are hoisted by their own petard by being confined in a space they originally used for escape.

59. As Lopez points out, through an aside a character may stand next to another character and yet occupy "the same theatrical space as the audience"; Lopez, *Theatrical Convention and Audience Response*, 66. This claim does not assume that the fiction of the play occurs in a separate illusionistic "world" from which asides "cross over" to the audience. My point is the porousness between stage and playhouse.

60. The exception is in 2.1 when the Black Bishop's Pawn directly assaults the White Queen's Pawn; however, that she is undeceived by his attempt to convert or seduce her and that she escapes the rape attempt unharmed is consistent with the connection the play maintains between awareness and safety.

61. In Q1 the image of Gondomar delivering "a letter from his Holynes" to the Fat Bishop, who warns, "Keepe yr distance," appears in the lower panel of the frontispiece, in a composite engraving with the climactic scene, in which the White Knight defeats the Black House "by discovery!" The image is expanded to fill the whole frontispiece in Q2 and Q3.

62. The dialogue suggests he may approach the Black Knight after the others exit ("I rest upon you, Knight, for my advancement"), only to be seized by Gondomar and brought offstage. The Black Knight responds to his appeal, "O, for the staff, the strong staff that will hold . . . Into the bag know thy first way" (3.1.304–7). Since Gondomar is represented pictorially with a staff in the frontispieces of both the second and third editions of *A Game at Chess* and *The Second Part of Vox Populi*, which also refers to his "little Brasill staffe," the verisimilitudinous personal props of the Black Knight may have included a staff; Scott, *Second Part*, B1r. If so, there seems an opportunity for stage business in which the violence of the real staff makes a visual pun on the staff of office the White King's Pawn had hoped to receive, thus physicalizing the dramatic irony of the scene.

63. This is the case even though the title illustration on Q2 and Q3 shows a specific line of dialogue from a specific scene, because Q1 shows the same figures and same line of dialogue without the chessboard beneath them (although a chessboard appears on a table in the image above).

64. John Holles, Lord Haughton, to the Earl of Somerset, London, August 11, 1624, in Middleton, *Game at Chess*, 199.

65. *Arden of Faversham* creates similar effects. In the scene in which Arden is murdered, a game board is set on the table. In a 2015 production by the company Brave Spirits in Washington, DC, the gesture had a quality of fixity, creating a sense that Arden was trapped. This effect of enclosure was intensified by the unusual concentration of asides from the murderers in the scene. For a fuller discussion of the relationship between the backgammon table and spatial mastery in the play, see Gina Bloom, " 'My Feet See Better than My Eyes': Spatial Mastery and the Game of Masculinity in *Arden of Faversham*'s Amphitheatre," *Theatre Survey* 53, no. 1 (April 2012): 5–28.

66. Gina Bloom, "Games," in Turner, *Early Modern Theatricality*, 192.

67. Jerzy Limon makes the similar observation that "[sometimes the] chess conceit comes into play with stage action as when the Black Bishop's Pawn wants the White

Queen's Pawn to come 'nearer'; Limon, *Dangerous Matter*, 100. However, Limon does not connect this effect to the possibility of a visible chessboard. In some moments of the play, such as the Jesuit's eroticized encroachment, protective attention to the White Queen's Pawn's chastity is mixed with a prurient pleasure in her sexual endangerment. However, this is regulated by the devices described previously.

68. It is not clear when this line is spoken that she is planning to reintroduce the Black Bishop's Pawn as another character. The Jesuitess says, "Since all's come out, I'll bring him strangely in again" (3.1.207), just before denouncing his rape attempt. In the context of the scene, her line may be understood to mean something like, "Since the whole story is out, I will get him further into trouble with my unexpected revelation."

69. Editor R. C. Bald asserts in an endnote that "the Black Bishop's Pawn came onto the stage behind the White Queen's Pawn and stood so that she could see him reflected in the mirror," pointing to Rowley's *A Shoo-Maker a Gentleman* as a model; Thomas Middleton, *A Game at Chesse*, ed. R. C. Bald (Cambridge: Cambridge University Press, 1929), 150. Later editors follow Bald, taking the Jesuitess's injunction against "looking back or questioning the spectre" as confirmation that "the Jesuit comes onto the stage behind the White Queen's Pawn so that she sees him reflected in the mirror"; however, this line refers to the fictional mirror and does not indicate a technique for its theatrical staging; Thomas Middleton, *A Game at Chess*, ed. J. W. Harper (New York: Hill and Wang, 1967), 3.3.51.s.d.n. Richard Dutton similarly claims that the Jesuit "enters behind the White Queen's Pawn who, forbidden to turn round . . . sees him only in the mirror"; Thomas Middleton, *Women Beware Women and Other Plays*, ed. Richard Dutton (Oxford: Oxford University Press, 1999), 3.3.s.d.n. Gary Taylor similarly references the scene in *A Shoo-Maker a Gentleman*; Thomas Middleton, *A Game at Chess: An Early Form*, ed. Gary Taylor, in Taylor and Lavagnino, *Thomas Middleton: The Collected Works*, 3.1.328n.

70. Alan C. Dessen, *Elizabethan Stage Conventions and Modern Interpreters* (Cambridge: Cambridge University Press, 1984), 87.

71. These are the Lansdowne manuscript in the British Library (MS Lansdowne 690) and the Malone manuscript in the Bodleian Library (MS Malone 25). For the uninterrupted blended scene (3.1), see Thomas Middleton, *A Game at Chess: A Later Form*, ed. Gary Taylor, in Taylor and Lavagnino, *Collected Works*, 1825–85.

72. Kuhn, "Making Pagans."

73. Given the sophistication of the script and the company, the fact that this is a more theatrically complex configuration should make it a more likely, and not a less likely, alternative.

74. The variant phrasing "*stands before the glass*" in Q1 and the Bridgewater-Huntington manuscript conveys a similar sense of the actor orienting himself in relation to a fixed mirror. By contrast, in an earlier Rowley play, *A Shoo-Maker a Gentleman*, Crispinus must move the mirror to catch the reflection. In that play, Leodice uses a hand mirror to "magically" reveal to Crispinus his future wife—herself, reflected from behind him. However, this is a contrasting dramatic example, not a model for the conjuring scene in *A Game at Chess*. Leodice's "speculatory magick" is a pickup, or meet-cute, only nominally disguised as an enchantment. It makes sense in *A Shoo-Maker a Gentleman* to use a hand prop because

the pleasure of the scene is that the mirror is not magical at all but simply part of Leo-dice's flirtation. The joke is that she is no specter, but she is standing there proposing, "Away with shadowes, and imbrace / The substance, introth I love thee"; William Rowley, *A Shoo-Maker a Gentleman* (London, 1638), E2r. The opposite is true of *A Game at Chess*, where both the Jesuit's physical reality and emotional fidelity are dubious.

75. Bicks recognizes this as a stagey scene in which the Jesuitess is both director and performer; however, she argues that the Black Queen's Pawn instructs the White Queen's Pawn's theatricality in a way that threatens to conflate the two women; Bicks, "Staging the Jesuitess," 467, 475, 477.

76. The switch in meter begins midway through the penultimate couplet—"By the lustre of the grace / By all these thou art summoned to this place"—perhaps making a more conspicuous shift in aural gears (3.3.48–49).

77. A later scene in the discovery space similarly oscillates between Catholic magic and theatrical show. When the White Knight (Prince Charles) and White Duke (Buck-ingham) travel to the Black House, they are greeted with a display of dancing statues: "*Music. An altar discovered and statues with a song*" (5.1.35.s.d.). This spectacle is framed as both religious and theatrical. The Black Knight presents the dance as idolatrous wor-ship ("yond altar . . . seems to adore [you]") and as a court entertainment ("those brazen statues move . . . to show our love") (5.1.31–34, 43–45). He comments on the music ("Hark . . . sweet sounding airs") and the mysterious nature of the spectacle ("abstruse things open"), just as the Jesuitess glosses the mirror trick she orchestrates from the same discovery space (5.1.31–32). The two scenes sound alike. Both feature music, and both the Jesuitess's incantation and the statues' welcome are delivered in tetrameter, which was often used in early modern English plays for magic spells (such as the witches' in *Macbeth*) or to mark Catholic speech as archaic. The aural similarity between the two discovery space scenes of theatrical, Catholic enchantment is registered typographically, as the quartos italicize both passages. The link the play draws between Catholic worship and theatrical spectacle is a staple of Protestant attacks on the Roman Church. What matters is not that the play makes this familiar connection per se, but that by leaving undetermined whether the statues are idols or actors in a masque—just as the mirror scene leaves unresolved the relationship between the Jesuitess's deceptive enchantment and the Jesuit's change of clothes—*A Game at Chess* puts religious pressure on playgoers' discernment of the stage.

78. I read this line in the stage directions of the Rosenbach manuscript as having the same logic as a backstage "plot," in which a box or line separates theatrical units of the play (not always identical to scene divisions). As Henry Turner writes, "The platt provides a structural translation of the actor's movement through space, since each box designates a discrete episode in the mimetic action"; Turner, *The English Renaissance Stage: Geome-try, Poetics, and the Practical Spatial Art, 1580–1630* (Oxford: Oxford University Press, 2006), 173. See also Stern, *Documents of Performance*, 209–14.

79. Gee, *Foot out of the Snare*, G4r–H2r (italics mine). Gee's book ends with a list of "the Names of Romish Priests and Jesuits now resident about the City of London" that gives specific addresses and physical descriptions: "F. Palmer . . . lodging about

Fleet Street, very rich in apparell . . . useth to weare a scarlet cloake over a crimsin Sattin suit"; ibid., P2r.

80. For a discussion of the play's development of the common cultural link between Jesuits and theatricality, see Swapan Chakravorty, *Society and Politics in the Plays of Thomas Middleton* (Oxford: Clarendon Press, 1996), 166–81.

81. The induction establishing the chess frame reverses vehicle and tenor:

> *Ignatius*: Were any of my sons placed for the game?
> *Error*: Yes, and a daughter too, a secular daughter
> That plays the Black Queen's Pawn, he the Black Bishop's. (Induction, lines
>   45–47)

In this allegorical tautology, a Jesuit plays the role of a chess piece that represents a Jesuit.

82. Extinguishing the light makes a visual pun on the Black Bishop's Pawn's ignorance. Jokes on "light" and "knowledge" run through the play, keeping the already easily available connection especially close to the surface. To give a couple of examples, the Catholic Black Knight's Pawn jokes, "I scarce can read; I was brought up in darkness" (3.1.134); and with chromic irony the Black Knight declares of his lies, "Light is not clearer" (2.2.212). In the most literal sense, putting out the taper before entering the chamber means he will not be able to see that it is her. Part of the joke is that because she is "Black," the pawn will be invisible without the light. The Jesuit's lack of sexual awareness is cheekily underscored, as the extinguished candle at the end of the dumb show bed trick enacts the familiar dirty proverb, "All Cats be grey in the darke"; John Taylor, *A Juniper Lecture* (London, 1639), 88. Compare to "To take lacke of beauty but as an eye sore / The faire and the foule by darke are lyke store"; John Heywood, *A Dialogue Conteinyng the Number in Effect of All Proverbes in the Englishe Tongue* (London, 1546), B2r. For an early recognition that bed tricks often involve black characters, see William R. Bowden, "The Bed-Trick, 1603–1642: Its Mechanics, Ethics, and Effects," *Shakespeare Studies* 5 (1969): 112–23. For a discussion of the degraded sexualization of black women's bodies through the bed trick, see Louise Denmead, "The Discovery of Blackness in the Early-Modern Bed-Trick," in *The Invention of Discovery, 1500–1700*, ed. James Dougal Fleming (Farnham, UK: Ashgate, 2011), 153–67.

83. Like almost any claim about blocking, this can only be speculative. However, having the Jesuitess speak unseen from the same space in act 1, at the beginning of her plot, and in act 5, at its conclusion, has more than symbolic resonance. It also simplifies staging for the actors, as the two scenes require the same characters doing similar basic actions (the Jesuitess interrupts the Jesuit's threat to the White Queen's Pawn).

84. Dramatic irony is never only about audiences' knowledge; it is also about their emotional orientation toward the scene. Since dramatic irony is not all of one affective kind, it makes sense to speak of playgoers' superior knowledge "entrapping" Gondomar but "protecting" the White Queen's Pawn.

85. S. R. Gardiner, *History of England: From the Accession of James I. to the Outbreak of the Civil War 1603–1642* (London: Longmans, Green, and Co., 1896), 4:118–19.

86. Stephen Greenblatt, *Shakespearean Negotiations: The Circulation of Social Energy in Renaissance England* (Berkeley: University of California Press, 1988), 7.

87. William Mason, *A Handful of Essaies* (London, 1621), 124–25.

88. Compare to

Ignatius eldest sonne . . .
Proteus in doctrine . . .
A wolfe in wooll; a glow-worme that doth shine
Most in the darke: a Sainted feind at best:
Rome in a Surplice, ranck hypocrisie,
Rotten, but painted o're divinitie. (A. B. C. D. E., *Novembris monstrum*
  [London, 1641], 120)

89. "Prohibition forbidding Catholic priests to attend plays," March 9, 1617/18, Folger MS V.a.244, fol. 21, 28, 11. Folger Shakespeare Library.

90. For a discussion of epilogues as a liminal space of renegotiation "between the world-in-the-play and the playing-in-the-world," see Robert Weimann, *Author's Pen and Actor's Voice: Playing and Writing in Shakespeare's Theatre*, ed. Helen Higbee and William N. West (Cambridge: Cambridge University Press, 2000), 216. However, Weimann's model of a "threshold" suggests a greater separation between the dramatic fiction and world of playgoers than is applicable in the case of *A Game at Chess* (or, I would argue, in early modern theater generally).

91. Don Carlos Coloma to the Conde-Duque Olivares, London, August 20 [10], 1624, in Middleton, *Game at Chess*, 197.

92. John Holles, Lord Haughton, to the Earl of Somerset, London, August 11, 1624, in Middleton, *Game at Chess*, 198; Amerigo Salvetti to Picchena, London, August 23 [13], 1624, in Middleton, *Game at Chess*, 201; Amerigo Salvetti to Sir John Scudamore, London, August 14, 1624, in Middleton, *Game at Chess*, 202.

93. Don Carlos Coloma to the Conde-Duque Olivares, London, August 20 [10], 1624, in Middleton, *Game at Chess*, 194.

94. Don Carlos Coloma to the Conde-Duque Olivares, London, August 28 [18], 1624, in Middleton, *Game at Chess*, 203.

95. I am grateful to Jean Howard for this insight.

96. Paul Overton to Dr. William Bishop, Bishop of Chalcedon, [August] 23 [13], 1624, in Middleton, *Game at Chess*, 201.

CHAPTER 5. *MEASURE FOR MEASURE*: THEATRICAL CUES
AND CONFESSIONAL CODES

1. Williams, *Marxism and Literature*, 112–13.

2. William Shakespeare, *Measure for Measure*, ed. J. W. Lever, Arden Shakespeare, 2nd ser. (London: Bloomsbury Arden Shakespeare, 2006). All citations will

appear parenthetically in the main body of the text; references are to act, scene, and line.

3. Making a related claim, Huston Diehl calls attention to *Measure for Measure*'s emphasis on the hermeneutic problem of mistaking signs for the spiritual things they represent; Diehl, " 'Infinite Space': Representation and Reformation in *Measure for Measure*," *Shakespeare Quarterly* 49, no. 4 (Winter 1998): 393–410. My argument differs from Diehl's both in content (as Diehl does not attach the problem of knowing to predestinarian theology) and more broadly in terms of the impact of theater on religious discourse. Whereas Diehl describes the play as deploying Calvinist representational paradigms to draw its audiences into a reformed mode of seeing and moral judgment, I claim that the play's dramatic strategies disrupt interpretive practices endemic to Calvinist culture. Claire Griffiths-Osborne similarly notes *Measure for Measure*'s preoccupation with distinguishing outward appearances from inward spiritual truths in her discussion of the way the play juxtaposes Catholic auricular confession against Calvinist casuistry and public penance; Griffiths-Osborne, " 'The Terms for Common Justice': Performing and Reforming Confession in *Measure for Measure*," *Shakespeare* 5, no. 1 (April 2009): 36–51. Certainly, the gap between interiority and exteriority has long been understood as a ubiquitous obsession of early modern English drama; see Katharine Eisaman Maus, *Inwardness and Theater in the English Renaissance* (Chicago: University of Chicago Press, 1995). However, my interest is in the particular work this theatrical preoccupation does in the context of predestinarian culture. For a broader discussion of how English theater practitioners and the clergy shared an engagement with epistemological problems fundamental to Christianity, see Bryan Crockett, *The Play of Paradox: Stage and Sermon in Renaissance England* (Philadelphia: University of Pennsylvania Press, 1995).

4. For an example of earlier readings of the play as a Christian allegory, see Roy W. Battenhouse, "*Measure for Measure* and the Christian Doctrine of Atonement," *PMLA* 61, no. 4 (December 1946): 1029–59. For a deflation of Christian allegorical readings, with a short discussion of the play's inclusion of biblical references to election and reprobation, see Howard C. Cole, "The 'Christian' Context of *Measure for Measure*," *Journal of English and Germanic Philology* 64, no. 3 (July 1965): 447–48, 451. For a less rigid allegorical reading and a discussion of the play's engagement with antimonastic literature, see Darryl Gless, *"Measure for Measure," the Law and the Convent* (Princeton, NJ: Princeton University Press, 1979). For an alternative thread of political readings of the play as particularly engaged with the issues related to the rule of the newly crowned James I, see Richard Levin, "The King James Version of *Measure for Measure*," *Clio* 3, no. 2 (February 1974): 129–63; Jonathan Goldberg, *James I and the Politics of Literature* (Stanford, CA: Stanford University Press, 1989); Andrew Barnaby and Joan Wry, "Authorized Versions: *Measure for Measure* and the Politics of Biblical Translation," *Renaissance Quarterly* 51, no. 4 (December 1998): 1225–54; and Robert N. Watson, "False Immortality in *Measure for Measure*: Comic Means, Tragic Ends," *Shakespeare Quarterly* 41, no. 4 (December 1990): 411–32.

5. Lake, *Antichrist's Lewd Hat*, 668, 672. For a related reading of the play in the context of puritan projects of moral reform, particularly the regulation of social behavior,

with an acknowledgment of the desire of the godly to distinguish themselves from reprobates, see Martha Widmayer, "'To Sin in Loving Virtue': Angelo of *Measure for Measure*," *Texas Studies in Literature and Language* 49, no. 2 (Summer 2007): 156. For a reading of the play as critical of excessively rigorous puritan enforcements of common law, see Maurice Hunt, "Being Precise in *Measure for Measure*," *Renascence: Essays on Values in Literature* 58, no. 4 (Summer 2006): 243–67. For a discussion of the way the play deploys theatrical pleasure to align the audience with more tolerant forms of regulating sexual behavior against extremely punitive puritan proposals, see Victoria Hayne, "Performing Social Practice: The Example of *Measure for Measure*," *Shakespeare Quarterly* 44, no. 1 (April 1993): 1–29. For an earlier discussion of the way the play's biblical references establish a parallel between the Duke and God, but one that functions ironically to underscore the limits of that comparison, see Louise Schleiner, "Providential Improvisation in *Measure for Measure*," *PMLA* 97, no. 2 (March 1982): 227–36. Deborah Kuller Shuger's important study of the play's negotiation of competing puritan and "Anglican" forms of Christian justice, *Political Theologies in Shakespeare's England: The Sacred and the State in "Measure for Measure"* (New York: Palgrave, 2001), deals with the soul only insofar as it is subject to punitive or penitential discipline in these respective models of Christian rule. For a discussion of the play as mediating a different intra-Protestant dispute between Lutherans and Anabaptists regarding conflicting relationships of justice and mercy, see Stacy Magedanz, "Public Justice and Private Mercy in *Measure for Measure*," *Studies in English Literature, 1500–1900* 44, no. 2 (Spring 2004): 317–32. For the argument that the play carves a domain of citizenship out from sacramentality, see Julia Reinhard Lupton, *Citizen-Saints: Shakespeare and Political Theology* (Chicago: University of Chicago Press, 2005), 127–57. For a discussion of the way the play's economic language mediates between the older Christian model of a *corpus mysticum* and the idea of a body politic in a post-Reformation commonwealth, see Jennifer R. Rust, "'Coining God's Image': The Fiscal Theology of the Mystical Body in *Measure for Measure*," in *The Body in Mystery: The Political Theology of the* Corpus Mysticum *in the Literature of Reformation England* (Evanston, IL: Northwestern University Press, 2013), 103–38.

6. While Catholic theology does maintain a complex doctrine of predestination, just as Calvinism includes a concept of free will, for post-Reformation believers the practical difference was between negotiable and nonnegotiable personal salvation.

7. Lake, *Moderate Puritans*, 227–42.

8. As John Calvin summarizes, "God, by His eternal goodwill, which has no cause outside itself, destined those whom He pleased to salvation, rejecting the rest"; Calvin, *Concerning the Eternal Predestination of God*, trans. John Kelman Sutherland Reid (Louisville, KY: Westminster John Knox Press, 1997), 58.

9. William Perkins, *A Golden Chaine, or The Description of Theologie* (London, 1591), V8r. For an articulation of Perkins's centrality to the theological development of the Church of England, see Bryan D. Spinks, *Two Faces of Elizabethan Anglican Theology: Sacraments and Salvation in the Thought of William Perkins and Richard Hooker* (Lanham, MD: Scarecrow Press, 1999), 2–5.

10. For a discussion of the self-confirming nature of godly communities, see Lake, *Boxmaker's Revenge*, 35–40. Arthur Dent lists eight "infallible" signs of salvation, the very first of which is "a love to the children of God"; Dent, *The Plaine Mans Path-Way to Heaven* (London, 1601), C8r–C8v.

11. *OED Online*, s.v. "assurance," accessed July 5, 2013, http://www.oed.com/view /Entry/12057. William Barrett's claim, in his 1595 sermon at Cambridge, that no one could be certain of his or her salvation was one of the key points that William Whittaker, and the other Calvinist heads of the college, found so objectionable as to require a clarification of the doctrine in the Lambeth Articles; Lake, *Moderate Puritans*, 210. For Barrett's subsequent retraction, see Thomas Fuller, *History of the University of Cambridge from the Conquest to the Year 1634*, ed. Marmaduke Prickett and Thomas Wright (Cambridge: Cambridge University Press, 1840), 283.

12. Thomas Adams, *The Happiness of the Church* (London, 1619), 331–32.

13. George Chapman, "To His Ingenuous, and Much Lov'd Friend, the Author," in Christopher Brooke, *The Ghost of Richard the Third* (London, 1614), A2v. For early Jacobean libels accusing puritans of presumption, see Haigh, *Plain Man's Pathways*, 126–27.

14. Theodore Dwight Bozeman, *The Precisianist Strain: Disciplinary Religion and Antinomian Backlash in Puritanism to 1638* (Chapel Hill: University of North Carolina Press, 2004), 105–80.

15. See Laurence Chaderton, *An Excellent and Godly Sermon, Most Needefull for This Time, Wherein We Live in All Securitie and Sinne, to the Great Dishonour of God, and Contempt of His Holy Word* (London, 1578); Thomas Wilson, *Saints by Calling: Or Called to Be Saints, a Godly Treatise of Our Holy Calling to Christ, by the Gospell, with the Severall Gifts Proper unto the Called: And Their Counterfeits in the Hypocrites Which Are Not Partakers of This Effectuall Calling* ([London], 1620); Samuel Crook, *Ta Diapheronta, or Divine Characters in Two Parts, Acutely Distinguishing the More Secret and Undiscerned Differences between 1. The Hypocrite in His Best Dresse of Seeming Virtues and Formal Duties, and the True Christian in His Real Graces and Sincere Obedience as Also Between 2. The Blackest Weeds of Dayly Infirmities of the Truly Godly, Eclipsing Saving Grace, and the Reigning Sinnes of the Unregenerate That Pretend unto That Godlinesse They Never Had* (London, 1658); Thomas Adams, *The White Devil, or the Hypocrite Uncased: In a Sermon Preached at Pauls Crosse* (London, 1613); and Thomas Cooper, *The Estates of the Hypocrite and Syncere Christian, Containing, Certaine Lively Differences, Betweene Synceritie and Hypocrisie; Very Necessarie, for the Tryall of Our Estates in Grace* (London, 1613).

16. Daniel Dyke, *The Mystery of Selfe-Deceiving, or a Discourse and Discovery of the Deceitfullnesse of Mans Heart* (London, 1614), 66.

17. Perkins, *Golden Chaine*, V3v.

18. John Calvin, *Institutes of the Christian Religion*, ed. John T. McNeill, trans. Ford Lewis Battles (Philadelphia: Westminster Press, 1960), 1:3.2.10.

19. David Booy, ed., *The Notebooks of Nehemiah Wallington, 1618–1654: A Selection* (Burlington, VT: Ashgate, 2007), 38. For a discussion of the potential of the doctrine of predestination to induce suicidal despair in the faithful, see John Stachniewski, *The Per-*

secutory Imagination: English Puritanism and the Literature of Religious Despair (Oxford: Clarendon Press, 1991). While richly documented, Stachniewski's book is imbalanced in the emphasis it places on despair to the exclusion of other affective states generated by the search for signs of election. He focuses on Wallington's suicidal tendencies rather than his vacillation between despair and comfort; ibid., 50.

20. Walsham, *Providence*, 15–17. For a discussion of the different meanings of affliction for the elect and damned, see Lake, *Moderate Puritans*, 124–25. For a description of how the injunction not to "vainly judge" the secret workings of God sometimes checked Wallington's habitual practice of reading violent accidents and narrow escapes as signs of God's judgments, see Paul S. Seaver, *Wallington's World: A Puritan Artisan in Seventeenth-Century London* (Stanford, CA: Stanford University Press, 1985), 46. While Peter G. Platt's discussion of *Measure for Measure* in particular focuses on the relationship between justice and equity, his broader discussion of paradoxical both/and formulations as a pervasive mode of early modern English thought resonates with the hermeneutics of predestinarian signs, which can point simultaneously to opposite spiritual extremes; Platt, *Shakespeare and the Culture of Paradox* (Burlington, VT: Ashgate, 2009).

21. For example, in the commentary on the story of Jacob and Esau (typological figures of election and reprobation, respectively), one marginal note glosses Esau's sale of his birthright with "the *reprobate* esteem not God's benefits," while the very next annotation reads, "Thus the *wicked* preferred their worldelie commodities to God's spiritual graces"; William Whittingham et al., eds. and trans., *The Geneva Bible: A Facsimile of the 1560 Edition* (Peabody, MA: Hendrickson, 2007), Gen. 25:32–33. All subsequent biblical references are to this edition.

22. John Gore, *The Poore Mans Hope* (London, 1646), D1r–D1v.

23. Puritans had a special investment in teaching the doctrine more explicitly, but this does not mean that the godly had a monopoly on these softer forms of predestinarian thinking. For puritan spokesman John Reynolds's failed attempt at the Hampton Court Conference to have the Lambeth Articles, which spelled out the doctrine of double predestination more explicitly, appended to the Thirty-Nine Articles, see Edward Cardwell, *A History of Conferences and Other Proceedings Connected with the Revision of the Book of Common Prayer; from the Year 1558 to the Year 1690* (Oxford: Oxford University Press, 1849), 180. For puritan enthusiasm for preaching on predestination, see Haigh, *Plain Man's Pathways*, 24–26.

24. For examples, see Dent, *Plaine Mans Path-Way*, C3v, C1r.

25. Anthony Milton, *Catholic and Reformed*, 160–69.

26. For a discussion of the coexistence of confessional groups at the parish level, see Haigh, *Plain Man's Pathways*.

27. Walsham, *Providence*, 107. For a further discussion of the ways cheap-print accounts of providential judgments—such as monstrous births—could transmit a range of cultural attacks, see Crawford, *Marvelous Protestantism*. While self-separation from the wicked was of particular importance to the godly, the condemnatory implication of reprobation was available to be deployed by people in a wider range of social and economic

positions than Keith Wrightson and David Levine allow when they claim that puritan disdain for the ungodly was simply a mechanism of social differentiation for an upwardly mobile middling sort; Wrightson and Levine, *Poverty and Piety in an English Village: Terling, 1525–1700*, 2nd ed. (Oxford: Clarendon Press, 1995). For critiques of this position, see Eamon Duffy, "The Godly and the Multitude in Stuart England," *Seventeenth Century* 1, no. 1 (January 1986): 31–55; and Nicholas Tyacke, *Aspects of English Protestantism, c. 1530–1700* (Manchester: Manchester University Press, 2001), 16–17, 90–110. As Patrick Collinson puts it, "The friction between the godly and the ungodly . . . could arise *within* and not necessarily *between* social classes"; Collinson, *Religion of Protestants*, 194.

28. Dent, *Plaine Mans Path-Way*, D1r.

29. Ibid., D6v.

30. Ibid., E1r.

31. Ibid., E3v.

32. For discussions of the place of predestination in popular culture, see Walsham, *Providence*; and Lake, *Antichrist's Lewd Hat*. For a ripping example of a heavily predestinarian Paul's Cross sermon, see Chaderton, *Excellent and Godly Sermon*. For further examples of Paul's Cross sermons on predestination, see MacLure, *Paul's Cross Sermons*.

33. T. B. Howell, *Complete Collection of State Trials*, 1:1346, 1415.

34. Mullaney, *Reformation of Emotions*, 76.

35. Elam, *Semiotics of Theatre*, 100.

36. William Shakespeare, *As You Like It*, ed. Juliet Dusinberre, Arden Shakespeare, 3rd ser. (London: Bloomsbury Arden Shakespeare, 2006), 2.4.14.

37. For a discussion of the mixed confessional valences of this scene, see Diehl, *Staging Reform*, 208–12.

38. John Webster, *The Duchess of Malfi*, ed. Leah S. Marcus, Arden Early Modern Drama (London: Bloomsbury Arden Shakespeare, 2009), 3.2.321.

39. For more on the Catholic valences in *Measure for Measure*, see Rust, "'Coining God's Image.'" For a reading of the play as a response to King James's anti-Catholic policies, see James Ellison, "*Measure for Measure* and the Executions of Catholics in 1604," *English Literary Renaissance* 33, no. 1 (December 2003): 44–87. For an investigation of *Measure for Measure*'s critique of Catholic confession, see Griffiths-Osborne, "'Terms for Common Justice.'" For the use of *Measure for Measure* in support of the argument that Shakespeare was a Catholic, see Beauregard, *Catholic Theology*.

40. Elam, *Semiotics of Theatre*, 105.

41. For discussions of Angelo's puritanism, see Donald J. McGinn, "The Precise Angelo," in *Joseph Quincy Adams Memorial Studies*, ed. James G. McManaway, Giles E. Dawson, and Edwin E. Willoughby (Washington, DC: Folger Shakespeare Library, 1948), 129–39; Robert G. Hunter, *Shakespeare and the Comedy of Forgiveness* (New York: Columbia University Press, 1965), 210–13; Harold Fisch, "Shakespeare and the Puritan Dynamic," *Shakespeare Survey* 27 (1974): 81–92; and Schleiner, "Providential Improvisation."

42. Lake, *Moderate Puritans*, 85–86; Patrick Collinson, *From Cranmer to Sancroft: Essays on English Religion in the Sixteenth and Seventeenth Centuries* (New York: Hamble-

don Continuum, 2006), 166–67; see also Collinson, *Elizabethan Puritan Movement*, 24–25.

43. *OED Online*, s.v. "fantastic," accessed July 5, 2013, http://www.oed.com/view /Entry/68107. For a description of the difference between profane and puritan dress in a contemporary play, see Thomas Heywood, *How a Man May Chuse a Good Wife from a Bad* (London, 1602), G2v–G3r. Independent of how common plain bands and short hair-cuts may have been among actual godly people, it seems reasonable to suppose that the-ater companies would have used their primary visual resource, costume, to mark cultural differences between characters.

44. Compare to Shakespeare's *Othello*, in which Michael Cassio drunkenly declares that election follows rank: generals and men of quality are saved before lieutenants; lieu-tenants are saved before ancients. His sudden wish to change the subject and his benign, inclusive platitude ("God forgive us our sins!") suggest an awareness that he has said something wrong, and an attempt to palliate the impropriety of so directly equating spiritual value with military rank, which, in the context of Iago's resentment toward posh Cassio's promotion to lieutenant, serves as a shorthand for class difference. Overall, the effect is that Cassio has rudely blurted out an assumption that usually goes unspoken. Shakespeare, *Othello*, 2.3.98–109.

45. Isabella uses "abhor" three times in the play (2.2.779, 2.4.1215, 3.1.1334) before Ab-horson first appears to express disapprobation of sexual vice.

46. For a reading of the Duke's proposal as an attempted reformation of Catholic celibacy to Protestant marriage, see Daniel Salerno, "Isabella's Silence: Staging Asceticism in *Measure for Measure*," in *Shakespeare in Performance*, ed. Eric C. Brown and Estelle Rivier (Newcastle upon Tyne: Cambridge Scholars Publishing, 2013), 2–23. While Salerno's cultural framing is persuasive, he makes an a priori assumption of the ideological limita-tions of post-Reformation audiences, claiming that Isabella's silence must be read as "en-thusiastic acceptance" because this ideological correction would have been "socially necessary" for "Protestant" playgoers; ibid., 23. In contrast, I would stress the internal cues of the play. As Salerno himself recognizes, Isabella's silence breaks the conventions of ro-mantic comedy. This disruption of generic convention effects an ideological interruption of the Duke's attempt to impose heteronormative Protestantism. For the view that Isa-bella's silence ends the play with Catholic resistance to Protestant matrimony, see Bar-bara J. Baines, "Assaying the Power of Chastity in *Measure for Measure*," *Studies in English Literature, 1500–1900* 30, no. 2 (April 1990): 284–98.

47. For the argument that the play suggests a critique of the Calvinist God as a ty-rant precisely because of the seemingly arbitrary nature of predestination, see Lake, *Anti-christ's Lewd Hat*, 656–58.

48. William Burton, *An Exposition of the Lords Prayer* (London, 1594), B4r.

49. See Poole, *Radical Religion*.

50. Hayne argues that "Angelo's hypocrisy *differs in quality, though not in kind*, from more superficial portraits of puritan hypocrites because it is an attempt to imagine—and to portray—what they feel"; Hayne, "Performing Social Practice," 18–19 (italics mine).

While I share her interest in the strong subjectivity effects produced in Angelo's soliloquies, my claim is that Angelo's unwitting spiritual hypocrisy does in fact constitute a different "kind" of subjective state from the merely social hypocrisy expressed by other stage puritans.

51. Griffiths-Osborne suggests that the flower and flesh in this passage correspond to the elect and reprobate in Calvinist theology, but she presents this as her own observation without demonstrating that the metaphor was used in this way in the period; Griffiths-Osborne, "'Terms for Common Justice,'" 42.

52. Burton, *Lords Prayer*, I8r.

53. Gervase Babington, *A Profitable Exposition of the Lords Prayer* (London, 1588), D4v–D5r.

54. See also Enoch Clapham, who writes, "The unregeneration of our nature . . . is uncleane and as a polluted Carrion: but it can no more defile the giftes and operations of the Holy-ghost in a new-man, then a stinking carrion can defile the glorious rayes or beames of the Sun shining theron"; Clapham, *Three Partes of Salomon His Song of Songs, Expounded* (London, 1603), O5r.

55. Julia Reinhard Lupton, *Afterlives of the Saints: Hagiography, Typology, and Renaissance Literature* (Stanford, CA: Stanford University Press, 1996), 110–142.

56. For an excellent analysis of the rhetorical production of internality effects in this soliloquy, see Karen Newman, *Shakespeare's Rhetoric of Comic Character* (London: Routledge, 1985), 12–14. Admittedly, a few of these caesuras are questionable; my count errs on the side of inclusion.

57. William Shakespeare, *Richard III*, ed. James R. Siemon, Arden Shakespeare, 3rd ser. (London: Bloomsbury Arden Shakespeare, 2009), 1.1.154.

58. John Bridges, *The Supremacie of Christian Princes* (London, 1573), 1030.

59. Spinks, *Two Faces*, 65; Dewey D. Wallace, *Puritans and Predestination: Grace in English Protestant Theology, 1525–1695* (Chapel Hill: University of North Carolina Press, 1982), 7. As the puritan minister William Burton writes, "It is needfull that we be regenerated and made new men by the Spirite of God"; Burton, *Ten Sermons* (London, 1602), I3r.

60. For a discussion of the theme of intercession in the play, see Devin Byker, "Bent Speech and Borrowed Selves: Substitutionary Logic and Intercessory Acts in *Measure for Measure*," *Journal of Medieval and Early Modern Studies* 46, no. 2 (May 2016): 405–32.

61. Whatever opinions early modern playgoers or later critics may have formed about the legitimacy of Isabella's preservation of her body, it is clear from the fact that two central characters (Claudio and Isabella) spend an emotional scene arguing about it that the play makes it a question.

62. Mullaney, *Reformation of Emotions*, 74.

63. Certainly, other characters in the play undergo sudden internal shifts. Claudio, for example, vacillates between fear of death and resignation. His spiritual oscillation, however, draws more on classical discussions of death than on specifically predestinarian discourse. The Duke, as discussed later, reverses his opening position on godly rule. And Isabella's spiritual and sexual future is left a conspicuously open question at the end.

64. Compare to Claudius's inability to repent for the murder he continues to profit from in Shakespeare's *Hamlet*, 3.3.36–72, 3.3.97–98.

65. "Backsliding" is a sixteenth-century neologism that refers specifically to lapses of faith; *OED Online*, s.v. "backsliding," accessed June 23, 2011, http://www.oed.com/view /Entry/14453. Doctrinally, the Church of England held that the elect may continue to struggle with sin and doubt, even after they have achieved a sense of assurance, but could not "finally or totally" fall from grace. Again, like so many predestinarian signs, what constituted a "total" fall from grace was highly subjective.

66. Tellingly, critical opinion is divided as to Angelo's repentance. G. M. Pinciss reads Angelo's final state as a form of productive despair that brings him to total dependence on God in "The 'Heavenly Comforts of Despair' and *Measure for Measure*," *Studies in English Literature, 1500–1900* 30, no. 2 (1990): 308–9. Similarly, Diehl understands Angelo as penitently seeking forgiveness at the end of the play in "'Infinite Space,'" 408–9. In contrast, Griffiths-Osborne takes the final scene to "repeat and emphasize Angelo's hypocrisy" and insists that he remains unpenitent, refusing to ask for pardon, in "'Terms for Common Justice,'" 45–46.

67. Barnardine has indeed been read as a figure that points up the limitations of state power. For a reading of Barnardine as a resistant subject who marks the limit of the Duke's power to have his subjects internalize the state's disciplinary regimes, see David Lindley, "The Stubbornness of Barnardine: Justice and Mercy in *Measure for Measure*," *Shakespeare Yearbook* 7 (1996): 333–51. For a discussion of how Barnardine's ability to evade punishment for his crime makes the Duke appear a negligent ruler, and how the absence of a response from Barnardine to his pardon can be read as one of the play's "open silences," see Kaori Ashizu, "'Pardon Me?'—Judging Barnardine's Judge," *English Studies* 78, no. 5 (September 1997): 417–29. However, neither study relates Barnardine's predestinarian status to the problem he poses for the legal apparatus of the state.

68. William Shakespeare, *Love's Labor's Lost*, ed. H. R. Woudhuysen, Arden Shakespeare, 3rd ser. (London: Arden Shakespeare, 1998), 1.2.362; William Shakespeare, *Rape of Lucrece*, in *Shakespeare's Poems: Venus and Adonis, the Rape of Lucrece, and the Shorter Poems*, ed. Katherine Duncan-Jones and H. R. Woudhuysen (London: Bloomsbury Arden Shakespeare, 2007), 300. I include in this group the close cognate "reprobance," which appears in *Othello*, 5.2.207.

69. Thomas Wilson, *A Commentarie upon the Most Diuine Epistle of S. Paul to the Romanes* (London, 1614), 1116.

70. Robert Rollock, *Lectures upon the First and Second Epistles of Paul to the Thessalonians* (Edinburgh, 1606), P1r.

71. Edwin Sandys, *Sermons Made by the Most Reverende Father in God, Edwin, Archbishop of Yorke* (London, 1585), Z1r.

72. For an observation of this meaning of Barnardine, see J. J. M. Tobin, "How Drunk Was Barnardine?," *Notes and Queries* 50, no. 1 (March 2003): 46–47. See also *OED Online*, s.v. "barnard," accessed July 5, 2013, http://www.oed.com/view/Entry/15629.

EPILOGUE: PITY IN THE PUBLIC SPHERE

1. Scholars have made important historical revisions, and political objections, to the model of public life as a consensus-oriented practice of rational deliberation that Jürgen Habermas articulates in *The Structural Transformation of the Public Sphere: An Inquiry into a Category of Bourgeois Society*, trans. Thomas Burger and Frederick Lawrence (Cambridge, MA: MIT Press, 1991). For a seminal critique of the Habermasian misrecognition of publics as defined by rational-critical debate, and a call for an expanded vocabulary of public expression that includes affective and embodied exchange as well as argumentation, see Michael Warner, *Publics and Counterpublics* (New York: Zone Books, 2002). For a discussion of the importance of the embodied audience in the theatrical formation of a virtual commons, see Elizabeth Maddock Dillon, *New World Drama: The Performative Commons in the Atlantic World, 1649–1849* (Durham, NC: Duke University Press, 2014). For the insistence that a radical politics cannot be achieved through the rational agreement of all parties but rather requires the identification of an adversary, see Ernesto Laclau and Chantal Mouffe, *Hegemony and Socialist Strategy: Towards a Radical Democratic Politics*, 2nd ed. (London: Verso, 2001).

2. Richard Schechner, *Essays on Performance Theory* (New York: Drama Book Specialists, 1977), 121. All communication—language itself—is a social process. Yet this is most overtly so in the case of theater, where the real-time interactions of live actors and audiences are themselves the basic medium.

3. Peter Lake and Steven Pincus, *The Politics of the Public Sphere in Early Modern England* (Manchester: Manchester University Press, 2007). For the claim that early modern theater falls outside the public sphere because it lacks the privacy Habermas considers so crucial to public formation, see Alexandra Halasz, *The Marketplace of Print: Pamphlets and the Public Sphere in Early Modern England* (Cambridge: Cambridge University Press, 1997). For a critique of the Habermasian exclusions of theater publics, see Steven Mullaney, "What's Hamlet to Habermas? Spatial Literacy, Theatrical Production and the Publics of the Early Modern Public Stage," in *Making Space Public in Early Modern Europe: Performance, Geography, Privacy*, ed. Angela Vanhaelen and Joseph P. Ward (New York: Routledge, 2013), 17–40.

4. Lake, *How Shakespeare Put Politics*, 57.

5. Ibid., 38. While Lake repeatedly, and admirably, insists that "plays are not tracts" and acknowledges the polyvocality and ambiguity of theater, his close readings limit spectators' imaginative involvement with plays to the same narrow range of rational-critical responses elicited in print debates.

6. Mullaney, *Reformation of Emotions*, 85, 4.

7. Paul Yachnin, "Performing Publicity," *Shakespeare Bulletin* 28, no. 2 (2010): 216.

8. Michael Warner, "Publics and Counterpublics," *Public Culture* 14, no. 1 (2002): 83–84, 88.

9. For a brilliant discussion of the role of emotion in early modern public life, see Doty, *Shakespeare, Popularity*. For an account of early modern theatrical spectatorship as including a corporeal as well as a cognitive form of understanding, see West, "Understanding."

10. Certainly, works of religious controversy address themselves to the undecided and heavily reference the arguments of their opponents in debate, thus allowing in the possibility of alternative views. Nevertheless, it was a common strategy for polemicists to undermine the counterargument in advance, by defining key religious terms and principles in accordance with their own confessional positions and then showing the conclusions other groups allegedly drew to be false; see Walsham, *Church Papists*. Ultimately, the point of polemic is, by definition, to persuade readers to agree with a set of propositions. For structures of feeling, see Williams, *Marxism and Literature*, 133–34.

11. Bronwen Wilson and Paul Yachnin, introduction to *Making Publics in Early Modern Europe: People, Things, and Forms of Knowledge*, ed. Bronwen Wilson and Paul Yachnin (New York: Routledge, 2010), 6. Christopher B. Balme acknowledges that a theory of the theatrical public sphere must account for emotion as well as rational-critical thought. However, in stressing the relative independence of the theatrical public sphere from specific performance events, and locating theater's public impact outside actual theaters, primarily in terms of a play's ability to generate debate, Balme implicitly prioritizes rational critical discussion over affective exchange; Balme, *The Theatrical Public Sphere* (Cambridge: Cambridge University Press, 2014).

12. Williams, *Marxism and Literature*, 132. Brian Massumi similarly observes that "[affect] cannot be reduced to 'feeling' as opposed to thinking. It has to be understood as feeling involving thinking and *vice versa*"; Massumi, *The Politics of Affect* (Cambridge, UK: Polity Press, 2015), 91.

13. Sir Henry Wotton to Sir Edmond Bacon, July 2, 1613, in *The Life and Letters of Henry Wotton*, ed. Logan Pearsall Smith (Oxford: Clarendon Press, 1907), 2:32–33.

14. Bloom, Bosman, and West, "Ophelia's Intertheatricality," 177.

15. For a discussion of the "means of communication as a means of production," see Raymond Williams, *Culture and Materialism* (London: Verso, 2005), 56–72.

16. As Wilson and Yachnin write, "At the far end of this range [of more or less overtly political activities] public formation does not engage with politics at the level of ideology or action but rather achieves its sociopolitical effects by way of changing available and normative forms of speech, practice, and association"; Wilson and Yachnin, introduction to *Making Publics*, 7.

17. Several scholars identify other plays that redraw the binaries of polemic into more elliptical shapes. For discussion of Falstaff's complex relationship to the Marprelate debates, see Poole, *Radical Religion*. For the argument that *Hamlet* adopts a skeptical distance from the culture of polemic, see Jesse M. Lander, *Inventing Polemic: Religion, Print, and Literary Culture in Early Modern England* (Cambridge: Cambridge University Press, 2006), 110–44.

18. For seminal work on anti-Catholic misogyny in early modern English drama, see Diehl, *Staging Reform*; Dolan, *Whores of Babylon*; and Shell, *Catholicism, Controversy*.

19. Critics have not considered *'Tis Pity She's a Whore* in relation to Laudian recuperations of the Roman Church. For a discussion of the way the theatrical display of Annabella's heart overwhelms specific (Eucharistic and other) discursive inscriptions, see Michael Neill, "'What Strange Riddle's This?': Deciphering *'Tis Pity She's a Whore*," in

Revenge Tragedy, ed. Stevie Simkin (Basingstoke, UK: Palgrave, 2001), 229–54. For a discussion of the way the play's language of courtly love resists dominant discourses of incest, see Susan J. Wiseman, "*'Tis Pity She's a Whore*: Representing the Incestuous Body," in Simkin, *Revenge Tragedy*, 208–28; for the social stakes of the incest taboo the play challenges, see Richard A. McCabe, "*'Tis Pity She's a Whore* and Incest," in *Early Modern English Drama: A Critical Companion*, ed. Garrett A Sullivan Jr., Patrick Cheney, and Andrew Hadfield (New York: Oxford University Press, 2006), 309–20.

20. The exact dating of the play's first performance by the Queen Henrietta's Men at the Phoenix is uncertain, falling sometime between 1629 and the play's publication in 1633; see Bentley, *Jacobean and Caroline Stage*, 3:462–64.

21. For the opening salvo, see Richard Montague, *A New Gagg for an Old Goose* (London, 1624). The tract to which Montague responds exemplifies the standard treatment of the Roman Church as Antichristian in Protestant works of controversy; see *A Gagge for the Pope, and the Jesuits* (London, 1624). For an excellent account of the controversy over papal Antichristianity, see Anthony Milton, *Catholic and Reformed*. For further discussions of Antichristianity in English Protestant thought, see Richard Bauckham, *Tudor Apocalypse: Sixteenth Century Apocalypticism, Millenarianism, and the English Reformation; from John Bale to John Foxe and Thomas Brightman* (Oxford: Sutton Courtenay Press, 1978); Katharine R. Firth, *The Apocalyptic Tradition in Reformation Britain, 1530–1645* (Oxford: Oxford University Press, 1979); Paul Christianson, *Reformers and Babylon: English Apocalyptic Visions from the Reformation to the Eve of the Civil War* (Toronto: University of Toronto Press, 1978); and Christopher Hill, *Antichrist in Seventeenth-Century England* (London: Oxford University Press, 1971).

22. Shell, *Catholicism, Controversy*, 31.

23. John Ford, *'Tis Pity She's a Whore*, ed. Martin Wiggins (London: Methuen Drama, 2003), 1.1.21–23. All subsequent references to this edition of the play are in text by act, scene, and line.

24. Diehl, *Staging Reform*, 156–81.

25. Thomas Ellice, "To My Friend, the Author," in Ford, *'Tis Pity She's a Whore*, 42.

26. Barnabe Barnes, *The Divils Charter: A Tragædie, Conteining the Life and Death of Pope Alexander the Sixt* (London, 1607), A2r.

27. "*Dumb shew: Empresse on the Beast.*" Thomas Dekker, *The Whore of Babylon* (London, 1607), H3r. Though significantly closer to Dekker's Antichristian Empress than Ford's ill-fated lover Annabella, Lucrezia the incestuous murderess makes claims on the audience's sympathies beyond her beauty. In her first scene, she delivers a powerful soliloquy that establishes her bravery and positions her in the theatrical role of revenger. Later, she demonstrates impressive histrionic skills in her false mourning for the husband she stabs. After her death, she assumes the role of wronged ghost haunting the papal father who corrupted her. Before his death, Pope Alexander VI is excoriated by his son for the spiritual ruin of their family. Collectively, these dramatic features establish a compelling character whose personal guilt is partly mitigated.

28. Arguably, the play here maintains the traditional opposition between true and false Churches, by coding Annabella's final repentance in the language of Protestant grace.

However, I would stress the cohabitation of conflicting confessional markings within a single character.

29. Matthew Steggle, *Digital Humanities and the Lost Drama of Early Modern England: Ten Case Studies* (New York: Routledge, 2015), 16. To draw a contemporary comparison, the title of Spike Lee's 1989 film *Do the Right Thing* similarly asks audiences to evaluate characters' political actions, as well as their own.

30. For affective irony, see Mullaney, *Reformation of Emotions*, 74.

31. Ibid., 78.

BIBLIOGRAPHY

PRIMARY SOURCES

A. B. C. D. E. *Novembris monstrum*. London, 1641.

Adams, Thomas. *The Barren Tree*. London, 1623.

———. *The Happiness of the Church*. London, 1619.

———. *The White Devil, or the Hypocrite Uncased: In a Sermon Preached at Pauls Crosse*. London, 1613.

Archer, Isaac. *Two East Anglian Diaries, 1641–1729*. Edited by Matthew Storey. Woodbridge, UK: Boydell Press, 1994.

Aubrey, John. *Aubrey's Brief Lives*. Edited by Oliver Lawson Dick. Jaffrey, NH: David R. Godine, 1999.

Babington, Gervase. *A Profitable Exposition of the Lords Prayer*. London, 1588.

Bacon, Francis. *The Advancement of Learning and Novum Organum*. New York: Colonial Press, 1899.

———. *The Works of Francis Bacon*. Edited by James Spedding, Robert Leslie Ellis, and Douglas Denon Heath. Vol. 11. London, 1861–79.

Baker, Richard. *Theatrum Redivivum, or the Theatre Vindicated*. London, 1662.

Barnes, Barnabe. *The Divils Charter: A Tragædie, Conteining the Life and Death of Pope Alexander the Sixt*. London, 1607.

Brathwaite, Richard. *A Spiritual Spicerie*. London, 1638.

Bridges, John. *The Supremacie of Christian Princes*. London, 1573.

Brome, Richard. *The Sparagus Garden*. London, 1640.

Burton, William. *An Exposition of the Lords Prayer*. London, 1594.

———. *Ten Sermons*. London, 1602.

Chaderton, Laurence. *An Excellent and Godly Sermon, Most Needefull for This Time, Wherein We Live in All Securitie and Sinne, to the Great Dishonour of God, and Contempt of His Holy Word*. London, 1578.

Chapman, George. "To His Ingenuous, and Much Lov'd Friend, the Author." In Christopher Brooke, *The Ghost of Richard the Third*, A2r–A2v. London, 1614.

Chettle, Henry. *Englands Mourning Garment*. London, 1603.

Clapham, Enoch. *Three Partes of Salomon His Song of Songs, Expounded*. London, 1603.

Cooper, Thomas. *The Estates of the Hypocrite and Syncere Christian, Containing, Certaine Lively Differences, Betweene Synceritie and Hypocrisie; Very Necessarie, for the Tryall of Our Estates in Grace*. London, 1613.

Cromwell, Henry. "The Lord Henry Cromwel's Speach to the House . . . 1659." In *Some Seventeenth-Century Allusions to Shakespeare and His Works: Not Hitherto Collected*, edited by George Thorn-Drury, 11. London: Dobell, 1920.

Crook, Samuel. *Ta Diapheronta, or Divine Characters in Two Parts, Acutely Distinguishing the More Secret and Undiscerned Differences Between 1. The Hypocrite in His Best Dresse of Seeming Virtues and Formal Duties, and the True Christian in His Real Graces and Sincere Obedience as Also Between 2. The Blackest Weeds of Dayly Infirmities of the Truly Godly, Eclipsing Saving Grace, and the Reigning Sinnes of the Unregenerate That Pretend unto That Godlinesse They Never Had*. London, 1658.

de Granada, Louis. *Granados Devotion*. London, 1598.

Dekker, Thomas. *The Double PP*. London, 1606.

———. *Match Mee in London*. London, 1631.

———. *The Noble Spanish Soldier*. In *The Dramatic Works of Thomas Dekker*, edited by Fredson Bowers, 4:231–300. Cambridge: Cambridge University Press, 1968.

———. *The Whore of Babylon*. London, 1607.

Dent, Arthur. *The Plaine Mans Path-Way to Heaven, Wherein every man may clearly see whether he shall be saved or damned*. London, 1601.

Donne, John. *John Donne*. Edited by John Carey. Oxford: Oxford University Press, 1990.

Drayton, Michael. *The Harmonie of the Church*. London, 1591.

[Drayton, Michael, Richard Hathway, Robert Wilson, and] Anthony Munday. *The First Part of the True and Honorable Historie, of the Life of Sir John Old-castle, the Good Lord Cobham*. London, 1600.

Drummond, William. "Ben Jonson's Conversations with William Drummond of Hawthornden." In *Inigo Jones and Ben Jonson*, edited by David Laing, section 2, 1–54. London: Bradbury and Evans, 1853.

Dyke, Daniel. *The Mystery of Selfe-Deceiving, or a Discourse and Discovery of the Deceitfullnesse of Mans Heart*. London, 1614.

Earle, John. *Micro-cosmographie, or a Peece of the World Discovered in Essayes and Characters*. London, 1628.

Falkland, Lucius Cary. *Of the Infallibilitie of the Church of Rome*. Oxford, 1645.

Field, John. *A Godly Exhortation, by Occasion of the Late Judgement of God, Shewed at Parris-Garden*. London, 1583.

Field, Nathan. "Field the Players Letter to Mr. Sutton, Preacher att St. Mary Overs." M.S. State Papers, Domestic, James I, LXXXIX (1616), reprinted as "The Remonstrance of Nathan Field," in James Orchard Halliwell-Phillipps, *Illustrations of the Life of Shakespeare*, 115–17. London: Longmans, Green, 1874.

Fletcher, John, and Philip Massinger. *The Spanish Curate*. London, 1647.

Ford, John. *Christes Bloodie Sweat*. London, 1613.

———. *A Gagge for the Pope, and the Jesuits*. London, 1624.

———. *A Line of Life.* London, 1620.

———. *'Tis Pity She's a Whore.* Edited by Martin Wiggins. London: Methuen Drama, 2003.

Gee, John. *The Foot out of the Snare.* London, 1624.

———. *New Shreds of the Old Snare.* London, 1624.

Gore, John. *The Poore Mans Hope.* London, 1646.

Gosson, Stephen. *Playes Confuted in Five Actions.* London, 1582.

———. *The Schoole of Abuse.* London, 1579.

Greene, Robert. *The Honorable Historie of Frier Bacon, and Frier Bongay.* London, 1594.

———. *A Pleasant and Conceyted Comedie of George a Green, the Pinner of Wakefield.* London, 1599.

Hall, Joseph. *Via Media: The Way of Peace in the Five Busy Articles, Commonly Known by the Name of Arminius.* In *The Works of the Right Reverend Joseph Hall,* edited by Philip Wynter, 9:488–519. New York: AMS Press, 1969.

Herbert, George, comp. *Wits Recreations.* London, 1640.

Heylyn, Peter. *Breif Relation of the Death and Sufferings of . . . L. Archbishop of Canterbury.* London, 1644.

———. *A Coale from the Altar.* London, 1636.

Heywood, John. *A Dialogue Conteinyng the Number in Effect of All Proverbes in the Englishe Tongue.* London, 1546.

Heywood, Thomas. *An Apology for Actors.* London, 1612.

———. *How a Man May Chuse a Good Wife from a Bad.* London, 1602.

———. *Troia Britanica.* London, 1609.

Heywood, Thomas, and Richard Brome. *The Late Lancashire Witches.* London, 1634.

Howell, James. *Familiar Letters, Domestic and Forren.* London, 1673.

Howell, T. B., ed. *A Complete Collection of State Trials and Proceedings for High Treason and Other Crimes and Misdemeanors.* Vol. 1. London, 1816.

Jeaffreson, John Cordy, ed. *Middlesex County Records: Indictments, Recognizqnces, Coroners' Inquisitions-Post-Mortem Orders and Memoranda, temp. James I.* Vol. 2. Clerkenwell Sessions House: Middlesex County Records Society, 1887.

Jonson, Ben. *Every Man Out of His Humour.* Edited by Randall Martin. In *The Cambridge Edition of the Works of Ben Jonson,* edited by David Bevington, Martin Butler, and Ian Donaldson, 1:249–427. Cambridge: Cambridge University Press, 2012.

———. *Volpone.* Edited by Brian Parker and David Bevington. Manchester: Manchester University Press, 1999.

Knevet, Ralph. *Stratiotikon, or A Discourse of Militarie Discipline: Shewing the Necessitie Therof According to These Perillous Times.* London, 1628.

Knowler, William, ed. *The Earl of Strafforde's Letters and Dispatches.* Vol. 2. London: William Bowyer, 1739.

"*The Lady Falkland: Her Life,* by One of Her Daughters." In Elizabeth Cary, *Tragedy of Mariam, the Fair Queen of Jewry,* edited by Barry Weller and Margaret W. Ferguson, 224–25. Berkeley: University of California Press, 1994.

Lowin, John. *Conclusions upon Dances, Both of This Age, and of the Olde*. London, 1607.

Marston, John. "Satire 2: *Quedam sunt, et non videntur*." In *The Metamorphosis of Pigmalions Image and Certaine Satyres*, 38–49. London, 1598.

Mason, William. *A Handful of Essaies*. London, 1621.

May, Thomas. *The Character of a Right Malignant*. London, 1645.

Melton, John. *A Sixe-folde Politician Together with a Sixe-folde Precept of Policy*. London, 1609.

Mennes, John. *Wit Restor'd*. London, 1658.

Middleton, Thomas. *A Game at Chess*. Edited by J. W. Harper. New York: Hill and Wang, 1967.

———. *A Game at Chess*. Edited by T. H. Howard-Hill. Manchester: Manchester University Press, 1993.

———. *A Game at Chess: A Later Form*. Edited by Gary Taylor. In *Thomas Middleton: The Collected Works*, edited by Gary Taylor and John Lavagnino, 1825–85. Oxford: Clarendon Press, 2007.

———. *A Game at Chess: An Early Form*. Edited by Gary Taylor. In *Thomas Middleton: The Collected Works*, edited by Gary Taylor and John Lavagnino, 1773–824. Oxford: Clarendon Press, 2007.

———. *A Game at Chesse*. Edited by R. C. Bald. Cambridge: Cambridge University Press, 1929.

———. *Women Beware Women and Other Plays*. Edited by Richard Dutton. Oxford: Oxford University Press, 1999.

Middleton, Thomas, and William Rowley. *The Changeling*. London, 1653.

———. *The Spanish Gipsie*. London, 1653.

Mildmay, Herbert A. St. John. *Brief Memoir of the Mildmay Family*. New York: John Lane, 1913.

Milton, John. *An Apology Against a Pamphlet Call'd "A Modest Confutation of the Animadversions upon the Remonstrant Against Smectymnuus."* London, 1642.

Montague, Richard. *A New Gagg for an Old Goose*. London, 1624.

Munday, Anthony. *A Second and Third Blast of Retrait from Plaies and Theaters*. London, 1580.

Newdigate, John. "The Undergraduate Account Book of John and Richard Newdigate, 1618–1621." Edited by Vivienne Larminie. *Camden Miscellany XXX*, 4th ser., 39, no. 1 (July 1990): 149–269.

Norwood, Richard. *The Journal of Richard Norwood, Surveyor of Bermuda*. Edited by Wesley Frank Craven and Walter B. Hayward. New York: Scholars' Facsimiles and Reprints, 1945.

Overbury, Thomas. *New and Choise Characters*. London, 1615.

Paracelsus. *Paracelsus His Dispensatory and Chirurgery*. London, 1656.

Pepys, Samuel. *The Diary of Samuel Pepys*. Edited by Richard Le Gallienne. New York: Modern Library, 2001.

Perkins, William. *A Golden Chaine, or The Description of Theologie*. London, 1591.

———. *The Petition and Articles Exhibited . . . Against Dr Fuller*. London, 1641.

Prynne, William. *Mr William Prynn His Defence of Stage-Plays, or, a Retraction of a Former Book of His Called "Histrio-Mastix."* London, 1649.

Rainbow, Edward. *A Sermon Preached at the Funeral of the Right Honorable Anne, Countess of Pembroke*. In Anne Clifford, *The Memoir of 1603 and the Diary of 1616–1619*, edited by Katherine O. Acheson, 233–70. Peterborough, ON: Broadview Editions, 2007.

Remembrancer. *A Key to the Cabinet of the Parliament, by Their Remembrancer*. London, 1648.

Riche, Barnabe. *Greenes Newes both from Heaven and Hell*. Edited by R. B. McKerrow. Stratford-upon-Avon: Shakespeare Head Press, 1922.

Rollock, Robert. *Lectures upon the First and Second Epistles of Paul to the Thessalonians*. Edinburgh, 1606.

Rowlands, Samuel. *The Four Knaves: A Series of Satirical Tracts*. Edited by E. F. Rimbault. Percy Society, no. 34. London: Percy Society, June 1843.

———. *Heavens Glory, Seeke It; Earts Vanitie, Flye It; Hell's Horror, Fere It*. London, 1628.

———. *Humors Looking Glasse*. London, 1608.

———. *Humors Ordinarie*. London, 1605.

Rowley, Samuel. *When You See Me, You Know Me*. London, 1605.

Rowley, William. *A Shoo-Maker a Gentleman*. London, 1638.

Rudyerd, Benjamin. *Five Speeches in the High and Honourable Court of Parliament*. London, 1641.

———. *The Speeches of Sr. Benjamin Rudyer in the High Court of Parliament*. London, 1641.

R. W. *Martine Mar-Sixtus*. London, 1591.

Sandys, Edwin. *Sermons Made by the Most Reverende Father in God, Edwin, Archbishop of Yorke*. London, 1585.

Scott, Thomas. *The Second Part of Vox Populi*. Goricom [London], 1624.

———. *Sir Walter Rawleighs Ghost*. Utrecht [London], 1626.

———. *Vox Dei*. Utrecht [London], 1624.

Sedgwick, George. "A Summary or Memorial of My Own Life, Written by Me, December 10, 1682." In *The History and Antiquities of the Counties of Westmorland and Cumberland*, edited by Joseph Nicolson and Richard Burn, 1:294–303. London, 1777.

Shakespeare, William. *As You Like It*. Edited by Juliet Dusinberre. Arden Shakespeare, 3rd ser. London: Bloomsbury Arden Shakespeare, 2006.

———. *Hamlet*. Edited by Ann Thompson and Neil Taylor. Arden Shakespeare, 3rd ser. London: Thomson Learning, 2006.

———. *Henry VI, Part 1*. Edited by Edward Burns. Arden Shakespeare, 3rd ser. London: Thomson Learning, 2000.

———. *King Henry V*. Edited by T. W. Craik. Arden Shakespeare, 2nd ser. London: Bloomsbury Arden Shakespeare, 1995.

————. *Love's Labor's Lost*. Edited by H. R. Woudhuysen. Arden Shakespeare, 3rd ser. London: Arden Shakespeare, 1998.

————. *Measure for Measure*. Edited by J. W. Lever. Arden Shakespeare, 2nd ser. London: Bloomsbury Arden Shakespeare, 2006.

————. *Othello*. Edited by E. A. J. Honigmann. Arden Shakespeare, 3rd ser. London: Bloomsbury Arden Shakespeare, 2006.

————. *Rape of Lucrece*. In *Shakespeare's Poems: Venus and Adonis, the Rape of Lucrece, and the Shorter Poems*, edited by Katherine Duncan-Jones and H. R. Woudhuysen, 231–384. London: Bloomsbury Arden Shakespeare, 2007.

————. *Richard III*. Edited by James R. Siemon. Arden Shakespeare, 3rd ser. London: Bloomsbury Arden Shakespeare, 2009.

Sidney, Philip. *An Apologie for Poetrie*. London, 1595.

Smith, Logan Pearsall, ed. *The Life and Letters of Henry Wotton*. Vol. 2. Oxford: Clarendon Press, 1907.

Squier, John. *An Answer to a Printed Paper Entitled "Articles Exhibited in Parliament, Against Mr. John Squier Viccar of Saint Leonard Shoreditch."* London, 1641.

Stock, L. E., Gilles D. Monsarrat, Judith M. Kennedy, and Dennis Danielson, eds. *The Nondramatic Works of John Ford*. Vol. 85. Binghamton, NY: Renaissance English Text Society, 1991.

Tatham, John. *Knavery in All Trades, or, The Coffee-House*. London, 1664.

Taylor, John. *A Juniper Lecture*. London, 1639.

Vernon, George. *The Life of the Learned and Reverend Dr. Peter Heylyn*. London, 1682.

Webster, John. *The Duchess of Malfi*. Edited by Leah S. Marcus. Arden Early Modern Drama. London: Bloomsbury Arden Shakespeare, 2009.

Whittingham, William, and Lloyd E. Berry, eds. and trans. *The Geneva Bible: A Facsimile of the 1560 Edition*. Peabody, MA: Hendrickson, 2007.

Wilson, Arthur. *The History of Great Britain*. London, 1653.

————. "The Life of Mr. Arthur Wilson." In *Desiderata Curiosa*, edited by Francis Peck. Vol. 2, bk. 12, 6–35. London, 1732.

Wilson, Thomas. *A Commentarie upon the Most Diuine Epistle of S. Paul to the Romanes*. London, 1614.

————. *Saints by Calling: Or Called to Be Saints, a Godly Treatise of Our Holy Calling to Christ, by the Gospell, with the Severall Gifts Proper unto the Called: And Their Counterfeits in the Hypocrites Which Are Not Partakers of This Effectuall Calling*. [London], 1620.

Wortley, Francis. *Eleutherosis tes Aletheias, Truth Asserted by the Doctrine and Practice of the Apostles, Seconded by the Testimony of Synods, Fathers, and Doctors, from the Apostles to This Day viz. that Episcopacie Is Jure Divino*. London, 1641.

Wright, James. *Historia Histrionica*. London, 1699.

Wright, Thomas. *The Passions of the Minde in Generall*. London, 1604.

SECONDARY SOURCES

Adkins, Mary Grace Muse. "Sixteenth-Century Religious and Political Implications in *Sir John Oldcastle*." *University of Texas Studies in English*, no. 22 (1942): 86–104.

Alsop, J. D. "Lambarde, William (1536–1601)." In *Oxford Dictionary of National Biography*, edited by H. C. G. Matthew and Brian Harrison. Oxford: Oxford University Press, 2004. http://www.oxforddnb.com/view/article/15921.

Ashizu, Kaori. "'Pardon Me?'—Judging Barnardine's Judge." *English Studies* 78, no. 5 (September 1997): 417–29.

Asquith, Claire. *Shadowplay: The Hidden Beliefs and Coded Politics of William Shakespeare*. London: Perseus, 2005.

Baines, Barbara J. "Assaying the Power of Chastity in *Measure for Measure*." *Studies in English Literature, 1500–1900* 30, no. 2 (April 1990): 284–98.

Balme, Christopher B. *The Theatrical Public Sphere*. Cambridge: Cambridge University Press, 2014.

Barish, Jonas. *The Antitheatrical Prejudice*. Berkeley: University of California Press, 1981.

Barnaby, Andrew, and Joan Wry. "Authorized Versions: *Measure for Measure* and the Politics of Biblical Translation." *Renaissance Quarterly* 51, no. 4 (December 1998): 1225–54.

Battenhouse, Roy W. "*Measure for Measure* and the Christian Doctrine of Atonement." *PMLA* 61, no. 4 (December 1946): 1029–59.

Bauckham, Richard. *Tudor Apocalypse: Sixteenth Century Apocalypticism, Millenarianism, and the English Reformation; from John Bale to John Foxe and Thomas Brightman*. Oxford: Sutton Courtenay Press, 1978.

Bayer, Mark. "The Curious Case of the Two Audiences: Thomas Dekker's *Match Me in London*." In *Imagining the Audience in Early Modern Drama, 1558–1642*, edited by Jennifer A. Low and Nova Myhill, 55–70. New York: Palgrave Macmillan, 2011.

———. *Theatre, Community, and Civic Engagement in Jacobean London*. Iowa City: University of Iowa Press, 2011.

Beatty, John Louis. *Warwick and Holland: Being the Lives of Robert and Henry Rich*. Denver: Alan Swallow, 1965.

Beauregard, David N. *Catholic Theology in Shakespeare's Plays*. Newark: University of Delaware Press, 2008.

Beckwith, Sarah. *Shakespeare and the Grammar of Forgiveness*. Ithaca, NY: Cornell University Press, 2011.

Bennell, John. "Madox, Richard (1546–1583)." In *Oxford Dictionary of National Biography*, edited by H. C. G. Matthew and Brian Harrison. Oxford: Oxford University Press, 2004. http://www.oxforddnb.com/view/article/64595.

Bennett, Susan. *Theatre Audiences: A Theory of Production and Reception*. New York: Routledge, 1990.

Bentley, Gerald Eades. *The Jacobean and Caroline Stage*. Vol. 2, *Dramatic Companies and Players*. Oxford: Clarendon Press, 1941.

——. *The Jacobean and Caroline Stage*. Vol. 3, *Plays and Playwrights*. Oxford: Clarendon Press, 1956.

——. *The Jacobean and Caroline Stage*. Vol. 4, *Dramatic Companies and Players*. Oxford: Clarendon Press, 1941.

Berry, Herbert. "The Globe Bewitched and *El Hombre Fiel*." *Medieval and Renaissance Drama in England* 1 (January 1984): 211–30.

——. "The Miltons and the Blackfriars Playhouse." *Modern Philology* 89, no. 4 (May 1992): 510–14.

Berry, Ralph. *Shakespeare and the Awareness of the Audience*. New York: Macmillan, 1985.

Bicks, Caroline. "Staging the Jesuitess in *A Game at Chess*." *Studies in English Literature* 49, no. 2 (Spring 2009): 463–84.

Blackstone, Mary A., and Cameron Lewis. "Towards 'A Full and Understanding Auditory': New Evidence of Playgoers at the First Globe Theatre." *Modern Language Review* 90, no. 3 (July 1995): 556–71.

Bloom, Gina. "Games." In *Early Modern Theatricality*, edited by Henry S. Turner, 189–211. Oxford: Oxford University Press, 2013.

——. "'My Feet See Better than My Eyes': Spatial Mastery and the Game of Masculinity in *Arden of Faversham*'s Amphitheatre." *Theatre Survey* 53, no. 1 (April 2012): 5–28.

Bloom, Gina, Anston Bosman, and William N. West. "Ophelia's Intertheatricality, or, How Performance Is History." *Theatre Journal* 65, no. 2 (May 2013): 165–82.

Booty, John. "History of the 1559 Book of Common Prayer." In *The Book of Common Prayer, 1559: The Elizabethan Prayer Book*, edited by John Booty and Judith Maltby, 327–84. Charlottesville: University of Virginia Press, 2005.

Booy, David, ed. *The Notebooks of Nehemiah Wallington, 1618–1654: A Selection*. Burlington, VT: Ashgate, 2007.

Bossy, John. *The English Catholic Community, 1570–1850*. London: Darton, Longman and Todd, 1975.

Bowden, William R. "The Bed-Trick, 1603–1642: Its Mechanics, Ethics, and Effects." *Shakespeare Studies* 5 (1969): 112–23.

Bowers, Rick. "John Lowin's *Conclusions upon Dances*: Puritan Conclusions of a Godly Player." *Renaissance and Reformation* 23, no. 2 (1987): 163–73.

Bozeman, Theodore Dwight. *The Precisianist Strain: Disciplinary Religion and Antinomian Backlash in Puritanism to 1638*. Chapel Hill: University of North Carolina Press, 2004.

Brackman, Rebecca. *The Elizabethan Invention of Anglo-Saxon England: Laurence Nowell, William Lambarde and the Study of Old English*. Cambridge, UK: D. S. Brewer, 2012.

Bradbrook, M. C. *Elizabethan Stage Conditions: A Study of Their Place in the Interpretation of Shakespeare's Plays*. London: Cambridge University Press, 1932.

——. *Themes and Conventions of Elizabethan Tragedy*. London: Cambridge University Press, 1935.

Braddick, Michael J. "Cranfield, Lionel, First Earl of Middlesex (1575–1645)." In *Oxford Dictionary of National Biography*, edited by H. C. G. Matthew and Brian Harrison.

Oxford: Oxford University Press, 2004. http://www.oxforddnb.com/view/article /6609.

Brinkley, Roberta Florence. *Nathan Field, the Actor-Playwright*. New Haven, CT: Yale University Press, 1928.

Brook, Peter. *The Empty Space: Deadly, Holy, Rough, Immediate*. New York: Touchstone, 1968.

Bruce, John, ed. "Charles I—Volume 370: October 19–31, 1637." In *Calendar of State Papers Domestic: Charles I, 1637*. London: Her Majesty's Stationery Office, 1868. http://www.british-history.ac.uk/report.aspx?compid=52753.

Brunning, Alizon. "Jonson's Romish Foxe: Anti-Catholic Discourse in *Volpone*." *Early Modern Literary Studies* 6, no. 2 (September 2000): 1–32.

Butler, Judith. *Gender Trouble: Feminism and the Subversion of Identity*. 2nd ed. New York: Routledge, 2006.

———. "Performative Acts and Gender Constitution: An Essay in Phenomenology and Feminist Theory." *Theatre Journal* 40, no. 4 (December 1988): 519–31.

Butler, Martin. *Theatre and Crisis, 1632–1642*. Cambridge: Cambridge University Press, 1984.

———. "William Prynne and the Allegory of Middleton's *Game at Chess*." *Notes and Queries* 30, no. 2 (April 1983): 153–54.

Byker, Devin. "Bent Speech and Borrowed Selves: Substitutionary Logic and Intercessory Acts in *Measure for Measure*." *Journal of Medieval and Early Modern Studies* 46, no. 2 (May 2016): 405–32.

Calvin, John. *Concerning the Eternal Predestination of God*. Translated by John Kelman Sutherland Reid. Louisville, KY: Westminster John Knox Press, 1997.

———. *Institutes of the Christian Religion*. Edited by John T. McNeill. Translated by Ford Lewis Battles. 2 vols. Philadelphia: Westminster Press, 1960.

Cardwell, Edward. *A History of Conferences and Other Proceedings Connected with the Revision of the Book of Common Prayer; from the Year 1558 to the Year 1690*. Oxford: Oxford University Press, 1849.

Carlson, Christine Marie. "The Rhetoric of Providence: Thomas Middleton's *A Game at Chess* (1624) and Seventeenth-Century Political Engraving." *Renaissance Quarterly* 67, no. 4 (Winter 2014): 1224–64.

Cartelli, Thomas. *Marlowe, Shakespeare, and the Economy of Theatrical Experience*. Philadelphia: University of Pennsylvania Press, 1991.

Cartwright, Kent. *Shakespearean Tragedy and Its Double: The Rhythms of Audience Response*. University Park: Pennsylvania State University Press, 1991.

Chakravorty, Swapan. *Society and Politics in the Plays of Thomas Middleton*. Oxford: Clarendon Press, 1996.

Chambers, Edmund K. *The Elizabethan Stage*. Vol. 2. Oxford: Clarendon Press, 1923.

Chillington, Carol. "Playwrights at Work: Henslowe's, Not Shakespeare's, *Book of Sir Thomas More*." *English Literary Renaissance* 10, no. 3 (September 1980): 439–79.

Christianson, Paul. *Reformers and Babylon: English Apocalyptic Visions from the Reformation to the Eve of the Civil War*. Toronto: University of Toronto Press, 1978.

Cogswell, Thomas. *The Blessed Revolution: English Politics and the Coming of War, 1621–1624*. Cambridge: Cambridge University Press, 1989.

———. "Thomas Middleton and the Court, 1624: *A Game at Chess* in Context." *Huntington Library Quarterly* 47, no. 4 (Autumn 1984): 273–88.

Cohen, Stephen. "Between Form and Culture: New Historicism and the Promise of a Historical Formalism." In *Renaissance Literature and Its Formal Engagements*, edited by Mark David Rasmussen, 17–42. New York: Palgrave, 2002.

———. Introduction to *Shakespeare and Historical Formalism*, edited by Stephen Cohen, 1–30. Aldershot, UK: Ashgate, 2007.

Cole, Howard C. "The 'Christian' Context of *Measure for Measure*." *Journal of English and Germanic Philology* 64, no. 3 (July 1965): 425–51.

Collier, J. Payne. *Memoirs of the Principal Actors in the Plays of Shakespeare*. London: Shakespeare Society, 1846.

Collinson, Patrick. *The Birthpangs of Protestant England: Religious and Cultural Change in the Sixteenth and Seventeenth Centuries*. New York: St. Martin's Press, 1988.

———. "A Comment: Concerning the Name Puritan." *Journal of Ecclesiastical History* 31, no. 4 (October 1980): 483–88.

———. Conclusion to *The Sixteenth Century: 1485–1603*, edited by Patrick Collinson, 217–242. Oxford: Oxford University Press, 2002.

———. *Elizabethan Essays*. London: Hambledon Press, 1994.

———. *The Elizabethan Puritan Movement*. Berkeley: University of California Press, 1967.

———. *From Cranmer to Sancroft: Essays on English Religion in the Sixteenth and Seventeenth Centuries*. New York: Hambledon Continuum, 2006.

———. *From Iconoclasm to Iconophobia: The Cultural Impact of the Second English Reformation*. Reading: University of Reading, 1986.

———. *Godly People: Essays on English Protestantism and Puritanism*. London: Hambledon Press, 1983.

———. *The Religion of Protestants: The Church in English Society, 1559–1625*. Oxford: Clarendon Press, 1982.

Como, David R. *Blown by the Spirit: Puritanism and the Emergence of an Antinomian Underground in Pre-Civil-War England*. Stanford, CA: Stanford University Press, 2004.

Cook, Amy. "For Hecuba or for Hamlet: Rethinking Emotion and Empathy in the Theatre." *Journal of Dramatic Theory and Criticism* 25, no. 2 (Spring 2011): 71–87.

Cook, Ann Jennalie. *The Privileged Playgoers of Shakespeare's London, 1576–1642*. Princeton, NJ: Princeton University Press, 1981.

Corbin, Peter, and Douglas Sedge. Introduction to *The Oldcastle Controversy: "Sir John Oldcastle, Part 1" and "The Famous Victories of Henry V,"* 1–35. Manchester: Manchester University Press, 1991.

Crane, David. "Patterns of Audience Involvement at the Blackfriars Theatre in the Early Seventeenth Century: Some Moments in Marston's *The Dutch Courtesan*." In *Plot-*

ting Early Modern London: New Essays on Jacobean City Comedy, edited by Dieter Mehl, Angela Stock, and Anne-Julia Zwierlein, 97–107. Aldershot, UK: Ashgate, 2004.

Crawford, Julie. "Lady Anne Clifford and the Uses of Christian Warfare." In *English Women, Religion, and Textual Production, 1500–1625*, edited by Micheline White, 101–26. Burlington, VT: Ashgate, 2011.

———. *Marvelous Protestantism: Monstrous Births in Post-Reformation England*. Baltimore: Johns Hopkins University Press, 2005.

Cressy, David. *Birth, Marriage, and Death: Ritual, Religion, and the Life-Cycle in Tudor and Stuart England*. Oxford: Oxford University Press, 2002.

———. *Bonfires and Bells: National Memory and the Protestant Calendar in Elizabethan and Stuart England*. Berkeley: University of California Press, 1989.

Crockett, Bryan. *The Play of Paradox: Stage and Sermon in Renaissance England*. Philadelphia: University of Pennsylvania Press, 1995.

Dawson, Anthony B., and Paul Yachnin. *The Culture of Playgoing in Shakespeare's England: A Collaborative Debate*. Cambridge: Cambridge University Press, 2001. See esp. Dawson, "Performance and Participation," 11–37, and Yachnin, "The Populuxe Theatre," 38–65.

Degenhardt, Jane Hwang, and Elizabeth Williamson, eds. *Religion and Drama in Early Modern England: The Performance of Religion on the Renaissance Stage*. Burlington, VT: Ashgate, 2011.

Denmead, Louise. "The Discovery of Blackness in the Early-Modern Bed-Trick." In *The Invention of Discovery, 1500–1700*, edited by James Dougal Fleming, 153–67. Farnham, UK: Ashgate, 2011.

Derrida, Jacques. *Of Grammatology*. Translated by Gayatri Spivak. Baltimore: Johns Hopkins University Press, 1976.

Dessen, Alan C. *Elizabethan Drama and the Viewer's Eye*. Chapel Hill: University of North Carolina Press, 1977.

———. *Elizabethan Stage Conventions and Modern Interpreters*. Cambridge: Cambridge University Press, 1984.

———. *Recovering Shakespeare's Theatrical Vocabulary*. Cambridge: Cambridge University Press, 1995.

Diehl, Huston. "'Infinite Space': Representation and Reformation in *Measure for Measure*." *Shakespeare Quarterly* 49, no. 4 (Winter 1998): 393–410.

———. *Staging Reform, Reforming the Stage: Protestantism and Popular Theater in Early Modern England*. Ithaca, NY: Cornell University Press, 1997.

Dillon, Elizabeth Maddock. *New World Drama: The Performative Commons in the Atlantic World, 1649–1849*. Durham, NC: Duke University Press, 2014.

Doelman, James. "Another Analogue for Middleton's *A Game at Chesse*." *Notes and Queries* 57, no. 3 (September 2010): 418–19.

———. "Claimed by Two Religions: The Elegy on Thomas Washington, 1623, and Middleton's *A Game at Chesse*." *Studies in Philology* 110, no. 2 (Spring 2013): 318–49.

Dolan, Frances. *Whores of Babylon: Catholicism, Gender, and Seventeenth-Century Print Culture*. Ithaca, NY: Cornell University Press, 1999.

Doty, Jeff. *Shakespeare, Popularity, and the Public Sphere*. Cambridge: Cambridge University Press, 2017.

Duffy, Eamon. "Bare Ruined Choirs: Remembering Catholicism in Shakespeare's England." In *Theatre and Religion: Lancastrian Shakespeare*, edited by Richard Dutton, Alison Findlay, and Richard Wilson, 40–57. Manchester: Manchester University Press, 2003.

———. "The Godly and the Multitude in Stuart England." *Seventeenth Century* 1, no. 1 (January 1986): 31–55.

———. *Stripping of the Altars: Traditional Religion in England, c. 1400–1580*. 2nd ed. New Haven, CT: Yale University Press, 2005.

Dutton, Richard. "Thomas Middleton's *A Game at Chess*: A Case Study." In *The Cambridge History of British Theatre*, vol. 1, *Origins to 1660*, edited by Jane Milling and Peter Thomson, 424–38. Cambridge: Cambridge University Press, 2004.

Dutton, Richard, Alison Findlay, and Richard Wilson, eds. *Region, Religion and Patronage: Lancastrian Shakespeare*. Manchester: Manchester University Press, 2003.

———, eds. *Theatre and Religion: Lancastrian Shakespeare*. Manchester: Manchester University Press, 2003.

Eccles, Mark. "Elizabethan Actors II: E–J." *Notes and Queries* 38, no. 4 (December 1991): 454–61.

Elam, Keir. *The Semiotics of Theatre and Drama*. 2nd ed. London: Routledge, 2002.

Ellison, James. "*Measure for Measure* and the Executions of Catholics in 1604." *English Literary Renaissance* 33, no. 1 (December 2003): 44–87.

Fincham, Kenneth, ed. *Visitation Articles and Injunctions of the Early Stuart Church*. 2 vols. Woodbridge, UK: Boydell Press, 1994.

Fincham, Kenneth, and Peter Lake. "Prelacy and Puritanism in the 1630s: Joseph Hall Explains Himself." *English Historical Review* 111, no. 443 (September 1996): 856–81.

Findlay, Alison. "Sexual and Spiritual Politics in the Events of 1633–34 and *The Late Lancashire Witches*." In *The Lancashire Witches: Histories and Stories*, edited by Robert Poole, 146–65. Manchester: Manchester University Press, 2002.

Finkelpearl, Philip J. *Court and Country Politics in the Plays of Beaumont and Fletcher*. Princeton, NJ: Princeton University Press, 1990.

Firth, Katharine R. *The Apocalyptic Tradition in Reformation Britain, 1530–1645*. Oxford: Oxford University Press, 1979.

Fisch, Harold. "Shakespeare and the Puritan Dynamic." *Shakespeare Survey* 27 (1974): 81–92.

Ford, L. L. "Mildmay, Sir Walter (1520/21–1589)." In *Oxford Dictionary of National Biography*, edited by H. C. G. Matthew and Brian Harrison. Oxford: Oxford University Press, 2004. http://www.oxforddnb.com/view/article/18696.

Foster, Elizabeth Read, ed. *Proceedings in Parliament, 1610*. Vol. 1. New Haven, CT: Yale University Press, 1966.

Fraser, Antonia. *Faith and Treason: The Story of the Gunpowder Plot*. New York: Anchor Books, 1996.

Fuchs, Barbara. "Middleton and Spain." In *The Oxford Handbook of Thomas Middleton*, edited by Gary Taylor and Trish Thomas Henley, 404–17. Oxford: Oxford University Press, 2012.

Fuller, Thomas. *History of the University of Cambridge from the Conquest to the Year 1634*. Edited by Marmaduke Prickett and Thomas Wright. Cambridge: Cambridge University Press, 1840.

Fuzier, Jean, comp. "Forms of Metadramatic Insertions in Renaissance English Drama, 1580–1642." In *The Show Within: Dramatic and Other Insets; English Renaissance Drama (1550–1642)*, edited by Francois Laroque, 461–67. Collection Astraea 2, no. 4. Montpellier: Publications de l'Université Paul-Valéry, 1990.

Gardiner, S. R. *History of England: From the Accession of James I. to the Outbreak of the Civil War 1603–1642*. 10 vols. London: Longmans, Green, and Co., 1896.

———. *Prince Charles and the Spanish Marriage, 1617–1623*. 2 vols. London: Hurst and Blackett, 1869.

Gless, Darryl. *"Measure for Measure," the Law and the Convent*. Princeton, NJ: Princeton University Press, 1979.

Goldberg, Jonathan. *James I and the Politics of Literature*. Stanford, CA: Stanford University Press, 1989.

Gossett, Suzanne. Introduction to *The Spanish Gypsy*, by John Ford, Thomas Dekker, Thomas Middleton, and William Rowley. Edited by Gary Taylor. In *Thomas Middleton: The Collected Works*, edited by Gary Taylor and John Lavagnino, 1723–27. Oxford: Clarendon Press, 2007.

Grainger, Roger. *Suspending Disbelief: Theater as a Context for Sharing*. Eastbourne, UK: Sussex Academic Press, 2010.

Greenblatt, Stephen. *Hamlet in Purgatory*. Princeton, NJ: Princeton University Press, 2001.

———. *Shakespearean Negotiations: The Circulation of Social Energy in Renaissance England*. Berkeley: University of California Press, 1988.

Gregory, Brad S. *Salvation at Stake: Christian Martyrdom in Early Modern Europe*. Cambridge, MA: Harvard University Press, 1999.

———. "The 'True and Zealous Service of God': Robert Parsons, Edmund Bunny, and *The First Booke of the Christian Exercise*." *Journal of Ecclesiastical History* 45, no. 2 (April 1994): 236–68.

———. *The Unintended Reformation: How a Religious Revolution Secularized Society*. Cambridge, MA: Harvard University Press, 2012.

Grell, Ole Peter. "The French and Dutch Congregations in London in the Early 17th Century." *Proceedings of the Huguenot Society of Great Britain and Ireland* 24, no. 5 (January 1987): 362–77.

Griffiths-Osborne, Claire. "'The Terms for Common Justice': Performing and Reforming Confession in *Measure for Measure*." *Shakespeare* 5, no. 1 (April 2009): 36–51.

Gurnis, Musa. "Martyr Acts: Playing with Foxe's Martyrs on the Public Stage." In *Religion and Drama in Early Modern England: The Performance of Religion on the Renaissance Stage*, edited by Jane Hwang Degenhardt and Elizabeth Williamson, 175–93. Burlington, VT: Ashgate, 2011.

Gurr, Andrew. *Playgoing in Shakespeare's London*. 3rd ed. Cambridge: Cambridge University Press, 2004.

———. *The Shakespearean Stage, 1574–1642*. Cambridge: Cambridge University Press, 1992.

Gurr, Andrew, and Karoline Szatek. "Women and Crowds at the Theater." *Medieval and Renaissance Drama in England* 21 (2008): 157–69.

Habermas, Jürgen. *The Structural Transformation of the Public Sphere: An Inquiry into a Category of Bourgeois Society*. Translated by Thomas Burger and Frederick Lawrence. Cambridge, MA: MIT Press, 1991.

Hackett, Helen. "Women and Catholic Manuscript Networks in Seventeenth-Century England: New Research on Constance Aston Fowler's Miscellany of Sacred and Secular Verse." *Renaissance Quarterly* 65, no. 4 (Winter 2012): 1094–124.

Haigh, Christopher. *English Reformations: Religion, Politics and Society Under the Tudors*. Oxford: Clarendon Press, 1993.

———. "From Monopoly to Minority: Catholicism in Early Modern England." *Transactions of the Royal Historical Society*, 5th ser., 31 (1981): 129–47.

———. *The Plain Man's Pathways to Heaven: Kinds of Christianity in Post-Reformation England, 1570–1640*. Oxford: Oxford University Press, 2007.

Halasz, Alexandra. *The Marketplace of Print: Pamphlets and the Public Sphere in Early Modern England*. Cambridge: Cambridge University Press, 1997.

Hamilton, Donna B. *Anthony Munday and the Catholics, 1560–1633*. Burlington, VT: Ashgate, 2005.

Hamlin, Hannibal. *The Bible in Shakespeare*. Oxford: Oxford University Press, 2013.

Harbage, Alfred. *Shakespeare's Audience*. New York: Columbia University Press, 1941.

———. *Thomas Killigrew: Cavalier Dramatist, 1612–83*. Philadelphia: University of Pennsylvania Press, 1930.

Harris, Jonathan Gil. *Untimely Matter in the Time of Shakespeare*. Philadelphia: University of Pennsylvania Press, 2009.

Hayne, Victoria. "Performing Social Practice: The Example of *Measure for Measure*." *Shakespeare Quarterly* 44, no. 1 (April 1993): 1–29.

Heinemann, Margot. *Puritanism and Theatre: Thomas Middleton and Opposition Drama Under the Early Stuarts*. Cambridge: Cambridge University Press, 1980.

Helms, N. R. "'Upon Such Sacrifices': An Ethic of Spectator Risk." *Journal of Dramatic Theory and Criticism* 27, no. 1 (Fall 2012): 91–107.

Herrup, Cynthia B. "Touchet, Mervin, Second Earl of Castlehaven (1593–1631)." In *Oxford Dictionary of National Biography*, edited by H. C. G. Matthew and Brian Harrison. Oxford: Oxford University Press, 2004. http://www.oxforddnb.com/view/article/66794.

Hill, Christopher. *Antichrist in Seventeenth-Century England*. London: Oxford University Press, 1971.

———. "The Protestant Nation." In *The Collected Essays of Christopher Hill*, vol. 2, *Religion and Politics in 17th Century England*, 21–36. Amherst: University of Massachusetts Press, 1986.

Hirschfeld, Heather Anne. "Collaborating Across Generations: Thomas Heywood, Richard Brome, and the Production of *The Late Lancashire Witches*." *Journal of Medieval and Early Modern Studies* 30, no. 2 (Spring 2000): 339–74.

———. *Joint Enterprises: Collaborative Drama and the Institutionalization of the English Renaissance Theater*. Amherst: University of Massachusetts Press, 2004.

Hobgood, Allison P. *Passionate Playgoing in Early Modern England*. Cambridge: Cambridge University Press, 2014.

Holmes, Peter. *Resistance and Compromise: The Political Thought of the Elizabethan Catholics*. Cambridge: Cambridge University Press, 1982.

Honigmann, E. A. J. *Shakespeare: Seven Tragedies Revisited; the Dramatist's Manipulation of Response*. 2nd ed. Basingstoke, UK: Palgrave Macmillan, 2002.

Hopkins, Lisa. *John Ford's Political Theatre*. Manchester: Manchester University Press, 1994.

Hotson, Leslie. *The Commonwealth and Restoration Stage*. Cambridge, MA: Harvard University Press, 1928.

Howard, Jean E. *Shakespeare's Art of Orchestration: Stage Technique and Audience Response*. Urbana: University of Illinois Press, 1984.

———. *The Stage and Social Struggle in Early Modern England*. New York: Routledge, 1994.

———. *Theater of a City: The Places of London Comedy, 1598–1642*. Philadelphia: University of Pennsylvania Press, 2007.

Howard, Jean E., and Phyllis Rackin. *Engendering a Nation: A Feminist Account of Shakespeare's History Plays*. London: Routledge, 1997.

Howard-Hill, T. H. *Middleton's "Vulgar Pasquin": Essays on "A Game at Chess."* Newark: University of Delaware Press, 1995.

———. "More on 'William Prynne and the Allegory of Middleton's *Game at Chess*.'" *Notes and Queries* 36, no. 3 (September 1989): 349–51.

Huebert, Ronald. *John Ford: Baroque English Dramatist*. Montreal: McGill-Queen's University Press, 1977.

Hunt, Maurice. "Being Precise in *Measure for Measure*." *Renascence: Essays on Values in Literature* 58, no. 4 (Summer 2006): 243–67.

Hunter, Robert G. *Shakespeare and the Comedy of Forgiveness*. New York: Columbia University Press, 1965.

Huntley, Frank Livingstone. *Bishop Joseph Hall, 1576–1656: A Biographical and Critical Study*. Cambridge, UK: D. S. Brewer, 1979.

Hurley, Erin. *Theater and Feeling*. New York: Palgrave Macmillan, 2010.

Jackson, Ken, and Arthur F. Marotti, eds. *Shakespeare and Religion: Early Modern and Postmodern Perspectives*. Notre Dame, IN: University of Notre Dame Press, 2011.

Johnson, Nora. *The Actor as Playwright in Early Modern Drama*. Cambridge: Cambridge University Press, 2003.

Jones, Norman. *The English Reformation: Religion and Cultural Adaptation*. Malden, MA: Blackwell, 2002.

Jowett, John. Introduction to *Sir Thomas More*, by Anthony Munday and Henry Chettle. Arden Shakespeare, 3rd ser. London: Bloomsbury Arden Shakespeare, 2011.

———. "Sir Thomas More and the Play of Body." *Actes des Congrès de la Société Française Shakespeare* 23 (2005): 75–89.

Kastan, David. "'Killed with Hard Opinions': Oldcastle and Falstaff and the Reformed Text of *1 Henry IV*." In *Shakespeare After Theory*, 93–108. New York: Routledge, 1999.

———. *A Will to Believe: Shakespeare and Religion*. Oxford: Oxford University Press, 2014.

Kilroy, Gerard. *Edmund Campion: Memory and Transcription*. Aldershot, UK: Ashgate, 2005.

King, T. J. *Casting Shakespeare's Plays: London Actors and Their Roles, 1590–1642*. Cambridge: Cambridge University Press, 1992.

Kinney, Arthur F. *Markets of Bawdrie: The Dramatic Criticism of Stephen Gosson*. Salzburg: Universität Salzburg, Institut für Englische Sprache und Literatur, 1974.

———. "Text, Context, and Authorship of *The Booke of Sir Thomas Moore*." In *Pilgrimage for Love: Essays in Early Modern Literature in Honor of Josephine A. Roberts*, edited by Sigrid King, 133–60. Tempe: Arizona Center for Medieval and Renaissance Studies, 1999.

Kiséry, András. *Hamlet's Moment: Drama and Political Knowledge in Early Modern England*. Oxford: Oxford University Press, 2016.

Knapp, Jeffrey. *Shakespeare's Tribe: Church, Nation, and Theater in Renaissance England*. Chicago: University of Chicago Press, 2002.

Knutson, Roslyn Lander. *Playing Companies and Commerce in Shakespeare's Time*. Cambridge: Cambridge University Press, 2001.

———. *The Repertory of Shakespeare's Company, 1594–1613*. Fayetteville: University of Arkansas Press, 1991.

Kuhn, John. "Making Pagans: Theatrical Practice and Comparative Religion from Marlowe to Southerne." PhD diss., Columbia University, 2016.

Laclau, Ernesto, and Chantal Mouffe. *Hegemony and Socialist Strategy: Towards a Radical Democratic Politics*. 2nd ed. London: Verso, 2001.

Lake, Peter. *The Antichrist's Lewd Hat: Protestants, Papists, and Players in Post-Reformation England*. With Michael Questier. New Haven, CT: Yale University Press, 2002.

———. "Anti-Popery: The Structure of a Prejudice." In *Conflict in Early Stuart England: Studies in Religion and Politics, 1603–1642*, edited by Richard Cust and Ann Hughes, 72–106. London: Longman, 1989.

———. *The Boxmaker's Revenge: "Orthodoxy," "Heterodoxy" and the Politics of the Parish in Early Stuart London*. Stanford, CA: Stanford University Press, 2001.

———. "Constitutional Consensus and Puritan Opposition in the 1620s: Thomas Scott and the Spanish Match." *Historical Journal* 25, no. 4 (December 1982): 805–25.

———. "From *Leicester His Commonwealth* to *Sejanus His Fall*: Ben Jonson and the Politics of Roman (Catholic) Virtue." In *Catholics and the "Protestant Nation,"* edited by Ethan Shagan, 128–61. Manchester: Manchester University Press, 2005.

———. *How Shakespeare Put Politics on the Stage: Power and Succession in the History Plays*. New Haven, CT: Yale University Press, 2016.

———. "Joseph Hall, Robert Skinner and the Rhetoric of Moderation at the Early Stuart Court." In *The English Sermon Revised: Religion, Literature and History, 1600–1750*, edited by Lori Anne Ferrell and Peter McCullough, 167–85. Manchester: Manchester University Press, 2000.

———. "Lancelot Andrewes, John Buckeridge and Avant-Garde Conformity at the Court of James I." In *The Mental World of the Jacobean Court*, edited by Linda Levy Peck, 113–33. Cambridge: Cambridge University Press, 1991.

———. *Moderate Puritans and the Elizabethan Church*. Cambridge: Cambridge University Press, 1982.

———. "Religious Identities in Shakespeare's England." In *A Companion to Shakespeare*, edited by David Scott Kastan, 57–84. Malden, MA: Blackwell, 1999.

Lake, Peter, and Steven Pincus. *The Politics of the Public Sphere in Early Modern England*. Manchester: Manchester University Press, 2007.

Lander, Jesse M. *Inventing Polemic: Religion, Print, and Literary Culture in Early Modern England*. Cambridge: Cambridge University Press, 2006.

Larminie, Vivienne. *Wealth, Kinship and Culture: The 17th-Century Newdigates and Their World*. Woodbridge, UK: Boydell Press, 1995.

Leggatt, Alexander. "The Death of John Talbot." In *Shakespeare's English Histories: A Quest for Form and Genre*, edited by John W. Velz, 11–30. Binghamton, NY: Center for Medieval and Renaissance Texts and Studies, 1996.

Levin, Richard. "The King James Version of *Measure for Measure*." *Clio* 3, no. 2 (February 1974): 129–63.

Levinson, Marjorie. "What Is New Formalism?" *PMLA* 122, no. 2 (March 2007): 558–69.

Lim, Paul C.-H. "Wells, Samuel (1614–1678)." In *Oxford Dictionary of National Biography*, edited by H. C. G. Matthew and Brian Harrison. Oxford: Oxford University Press, 2004. http://www.oxforddnb.com.huntington.idm.oclc.org/view/article/29017.

Limon, Jerzy. *Dangerous Matter: English Drama and Politics, 1623/24*. Cambridge: Cambridge University Press, 1986.

———. "The 'Missing Source' for Thomas Middleton's *A Game at Chess* (V.iii.141–7) Found." *Notes and Queries* 33, no. 3 (September 1986): 386–87.

Lin, Erika T. *Shakespeare and the Materiality of Performance*. New York: Palgrave Macmillan, 2012.

Lindley, David. "The Stubbornness of Barnardine: Justice and Mercy in *Measure for Measure*." *Shakespeare Yearbook* 7 (1996): 333–51.

Littleton, Charles G. D. "The Strangers, Their Churches and the Continent: Continuing and Changing Connexions." In *Immigrants in Tudor and Early Stuart England*, edited by Nigel Goose and Lien Luu, 177–91. Brighton: Sussex Academic Press, 2005.

Lockyer, Roger. *Buckingham: The Life and Political Career of George Villiers, First Duke of Buckingham, 1592–1628*. London: Longman, 1981.

Lopez, Jeremy. "Fitzgrave's Jewel: Audience and Anticlimax in Middleton and Shakespeare." In *Imagining the Audience in Early Modern Drama, 1558–1642*, edited by Jennifer A. Low and Nova Myhill, 189–203. New York: Palgrave Macmillan, 2011.

———. *Theatrical Convention and Audience Response in Early Modern Drama*. Cambridge: Cambridge University Press, 2003.

Low, Jennifer A., and Nova Myhill. Introduction to *Imagining the Audience in Early Modern Drama, 1558–1642*, edited by Jennifer A. Low and Nova Myhill, 1–17. New York: Palgrave Macmillan, 2011.

Lublin, Robert I. *Costuming the Shakespearean Stage: Visual Codes of Representation in Early Modern Theatre and Culture*. Farnham, UK: Ashgate, 2011.

Lukács, Georg. *History and Class Consciousness*. Translated by Rodney Livingstone. London: Merlin Press, 1971.

Lupton, Julia Reinhard. *Afterlives of the Saints: Hagiography, Typology, and Renaissance Literature*. Stanford, CA: Stanford University Press, 1996.

———. *Citizen-Saints: Shakespeare and Political Theology*. Chicago: University of Chicago Press, 2005.

MacKay, Ellen. *Persecution, Plague, and Fire: Fugitive Histories of the Stage in Early Modern England*. Chicago: University of Chicago Press, 2011.

MacLure, Millar. *The Paul's Cross Sermons, 1534–1642*. Toronto: University of Toronto Press, 1958.

Madox, Richard, and Elizabeth Story Donno. *An Elizabethan in 1582: The Diary of Richard Madox*. Works Issued by the Hakluyt Society, 2nd ser., no. 147. London: Hakluyt Society, 1976.

Magedanz, Stacy. "Public Justice and Private Mercy in *Measure for Measure*." *Studies in English Literature, 1500–1900* 44, no. 2 (Spring 2004): 317–32.

Magee, Brian. *The English Recusants: A Study of the Post-Reformation Catholic Survival and the Operation of the Recusancy Laws*. London: Burns, Oates and Washbourne, 1938.

Maltby, Judith. *Prayer Book and People in Elizabethan and Early Stuart England*. Cambridge: Cambridge University Press, 1998.

Marino, James. *Owning William Shakespeare: The King's Men and Their Intellectual Property*. Philadelphia: University of Pennsylvania Press, 2011.

Marotti, Arthur. *Religious Ideology and Cultural Fantasy: Catholic and Anti-Catholic Discourses in Early Modern England*. Notre Dame, IN: University of Notre Dame Press, 2005.

Massumi, Brian. *The Politics of Affect*. Cambridge, UK: Polity Press, 2015.

Masten, Jeffrey. *Textual Intercourse: Collaboration, Authorship, and Sexualities in Renaissance Drama*. Cambridge: Cambridge University Press, 1997.

Matar, Nabil. *Britain and Barbary, 1558–1689*. Gainesville: University Press of Florida, 2005.

———. *Islam in Britain, 1558–1685*. Cambridge: Cambridge University Press, 1998.

———. *Turks, Moors, and Englishmen in the Age of Discovery*. New York: Columbia University Press, 1999.

Matthew, Tobie. *A True Historical Relation of the Conversion of Sir Tobie Matthew to the Holy Catholic Faith*. London: Burns and Oates, 1904.

Matuska, Agnes. "'Masking Players, Painted Sepulchers and Double Dealing Ambidexters' on Duty: Anti-theatricalist Tracts on Audience Involvement and the Transformative Power of Plays." *SEDERI: Journal of the Spanish and Portuguese Society for English Renaissance Studies* 18 (2008): 45–59.

Maus, Katharine Eisaman. "Idol and Gift in *Volpone*." *English Literary Renaissance* 35, no. 3 (Autumn 2005): 429–53.

———. *Inwardness and Theater in the English Renaissance*. Chicago: University of Chicago Press, 1995.

Mayer, Jean-Christophe. *Shakespeare's Hybrid Faith: History, Religion and the Stage*. Basingstoke, UK: Palgrave Macmillan, 2006.

McCabe, Richard A. "'*Tis Pity She's a Whore* and Incest." In *Early Modern English Drama: A Critical Companion*, edited by Garrett A. Sullivan Jr., Patrick Cheney, and Andrew Hadfield, 309–20. New York: Oxford University Press, 2006.

McClain, Lisa. *Lest We Be Damned: Practical Innovation and Lived Experience Among Catholics in Protestant England, 1559–1642*. New York: Routledge, 2004.

McCoy, Richard. *Faith in Shakespeare*. Oxford: Oxford University Press, 2013.

McGinn, Donald J. "The Precise Angelo." In *Joseph Quincy Adams Memorial Studies*, edited by James G. McManaway, Giles E. Dawson, and Edwin E. Willoughby, 129–39. Washington, DC: Folger Shakespeare Library, 1948.

McGurk, J. J. N. "Davies, Sir John (1560x63–1625)." In *Oxford Dictionary of National Biography*, edited by H. C. G. Matthew and Brian Harrison. Oxford: Oxford University Press, 2004. http://www.oxforddnb.com/view/article/7242.

McInnis, David. *Mind-Travelling and Voyage Drama in Early Modern England*. London: Palgrave Macmillan, 2013.

McMillin, Scott. *The Elizabethan Theatre and "The Book of Sir Thomas More."* Ithaca, NY: Cornell University Press, 1987.

McMillin, Scott, and Sally-Beth MacLean. *The Queen's Men and Their Plays*. Cambridge: Cambridge University Press, 1998.

Mears, Natalie, and Alec Ryrie, eds. *Worship and the Parish Church in Early Modern Britain*. Farnham, UK: Ashgate, 2013.

Melchiori, Giorgio. "*The Book of Sir Thomas More*: Dramatic Unity." In *Shakespeare and Sir Thomas More: Essays on the Play and Its Shakespearean Interest*, edited by T. H. Howard-Hill, 77–100. Cambridge: Cambridge University Press, 1989.

Menzer, Paul. "Crowd Control." In *Imagining the Audience in Early Modern Drama, 1558–1642*, edited by Jennifer A. Low and Nova Myhill, 19–36. New York: Palgrave Macmillan, 2011.

Milton, Anthony. "'Anglicanism' by Stealth: The Career and Influence of John Overall." In *Religious Politics in Post-Reformation England: Essays in Honor of Nicholas Tyacke*, edited by Kenneth Fincham and Peter Lake, 159–76. Woodbridge, UK: Boydell Press, 2006.

————. *Catholic and Reformed: The Roman and Protestant Churches in English Protestant Thought, 1600–1640*. Cambridge: Cambridge University Press, 1995.

Milward, Peter. *Shakespeare the Papist*. Ann Arbor, MI: Sapientia Press, 2005.

Monta, Susannah Brietz. *Martyrdom and Literature in Early Modern England*. Cambridge: Cambridge University Press, 2005.

Montrose, Louis. *The Purpose of Playing: Shakespeare and the Cultural Politics of Elizabethan Theatre*. Chicago: University of Chicago Press, 1996.

Mooney, Michael E. *Shakespeare's Dramatic Transactions*. Durham, NC: Duke University Press, 1990.

Morris, Edgar C. "The Allegory in Middleton's *A Game at Chess*." *Englische Studien* 38 (1907): 39–52.

Mullaney, Steven. *The Reformation of Emotions in the Age of Shakespeare*. Chicago: University of Chicago Press, 2015.

————. "What's Hamlet to Habermas? Spatial Literacy, Theatrical Production and the Publics of the Early Modern Public Stage." In *Making Space Public in Early Modern Europe: Performance, Geography, Privacy*, edited by Angela Vanhaelen and Joseph P. Ward, 17–40. New York: Routledge, 2013.

Mulvey, Laura. "Visual Pleasure and Narrative Cinema." In *Film Theory and Criticism: Introductory Readings*, 5th ed., edited by Leo Braudy and Marshall Cohen, 833–44. Oxford: Oxford University Press, 1999.

Munro, Ian. "Making Publics: Secrecy and Publication in *A Game at Chess*." *Medieval and Renaissance Drama in England* 14 (2001): 207–26.

Munro, Lucy. "Archaism, the 'Middle Age' and the Morality Play in Shakespearean Drama." *Shakespeare* 8, no. 4 (December 2012): 356–67.

Murray, Molly. *The Poetics of Conversion in Early Modern Literature: Verse and Change from Donne to Dryden*. Cambridge: Cambridge University Press, 2009.

Neill, Michael. "'What Strange Riddle's This?': Deciphering *'Tis Pity She's a Whore*." In *Revenge Tragedy*, edited by Stevie Simkin, 229–54. Basingstoke, UK: Palgrave, 2001.

Newman, Karen. *Shakespeare's Rhetoric of Comic Character*. London: Routledge, 1985.

Nicholls, Charles. *The Lodger Shakespeare: His Life on Silver Street*. New York: Viking, 2008.

Nicholls, Mark. "Sir Charles Percy." *Recusant History* 18, no. 3 (1987): 237–50.

Nicol, David. *Middleton & Rowley: Forms of Collaboration in the Jacobean Playhouse*. Toronto: University of Toronto Press, 2012.

O'Connell, Michael. *The Idolatrous Eye: Iconoclasm and Theater in Early Modern England*. Oxford: Oxford University Press, 2000.

Orlin, Lena. *Locating Privacy in Tudor London*. Oxford: Oxford University Press, 2007.

Ormsby, Robert. "Coriolanus, Antitheatricalism, and Audience Response." *Shakespeare Bulletin* 26, no. 1 (2008): 43–62.

O'Sullivan, Daniel E. "Introduction: 'Le beau jeu notable.'" In *Chess in the Middle Ages and Early Modern Age: A Fundamental Thought Paradigm of the Premodern World*, edited by Daniel E. O'Sullivan, 1–16. Boston: De Gruyter, 2012.

Pangallo, Matteo. "'Mayn't a Spectator Write a Comedy?' Playwriting Playgoers in Early Modern Drama." *Review of English Studies* 64, no. 263 (February 2013): 39–69.

Paster, Gail Kern. *The Body Embarrassed: Drama and the Disciplines of Shame in Early Modern England*. Ithaca, NY: Cornell University Press, 1993.

Patterson, W. B. *James VI and I and the Reunion of Christendom*. Cambridge: Cambridge University Press, 1997.

Pearson, Meg. "Vision on Trial in *The Late Lancashire Witches*." In *Staging the Superstitions of Early Modern Europe*, edited by Verena Theile and Andrew D. McCarthy, 107–27. Aldershot, UK: Ashgate, 2012.

Perrett, A. J. "The Blounts of Kidderminster." *Transactions of the Worcester Archeological Society* 19 (1942): 10–18.

Pettegree, Andrew. *Foreign Protestant Communities in Sixteenth-Century London*. Oxford: Clarendon Press, 1986.

Pickett, Holly Crawford. "The Idolatrous Nose: Incense on the Early Modern Stage." In *Religion and Drama in Early Modern England: The Performance of Religion on the Renaissance Stage*, edited by Jane Hwang Degenhardt and Elizabeth Williamson, 19–38. Burlington, VT: Ashgate, 2011.

Pinciss, G. M. "The 'Heavenly Comforts of Despair' and *Measure for Measure*." *Studies in English Literature, 1500–1900* 30, no. 2 (1990): 303–13.

Platt, Peter G. *Shakespeare and the Culture of Paradox*. Burlington, VT: Ashgate, 2009.

Pollard, Tanya Louise. *Drugs and Theatre in Early Modern England*. Oxford: Oxford University Press, 2005.

———. Introduction to *Shakespeare's Theater: A Sourcebook*, edited by Tanya Louise Pollard, xvi–xvii. Malden, MA: Blackwell, 2004.

Poole, Kristen. *Radical Religion from Shakespeare to Milton: Figures of Nonconformity in Early Modern England*. Cambridge: Cambridge University Press, 2000.

Preiss, Richard. *Clowning and Authorship in Early Modern Theatre*. Cambridge: Cambridge University Press, 2014.

Pritchard, Leander. "The Second Treatise Concerning the Life and Writings of the Venerable Father, F. Augustin Baker." In *Memorials of Father Augustine Baker and Other Documents Relating to the English Benedictines*, edited by Justin McCann and Hugh Connelly, 72–75. London: Catholic Record Society, 1933.

Purkiss, Diane. *The Witch in History: Early Modern and Twentieth-Century Representations*. London: Routledge, 1996.

Pursell, Brennan C. "The End of the Spanish Match." *Historical Journal* 45, no. 4 (2002): 699–726.

Questier, Michael. *Catholicism and Community in Early Modern England: Politics, Aristocratic Patronage and Religion, c. 1550–1640*. Cambridge: Cambridge University Press, 2006.

———. *Conversion, Politics and Religion in England, 1580–1625*. Cambridge: Cambridge University Press, 1996.

———. "John Gee, Archbishop Abbot, and the Use of Converts from Rome in Jacobean Anti-Catholicism." *Recusant History* 21, no. 3 (May 1993): 347–60.

Quitslund, Beth. "The Virginia Company, 1606–1624: Anglicanism's Millenial Adventure." In *Anglo-American Millennialism, from Milton to the Millerites*, edited by Richard Connors and Andrew Colin Gow, 43–114. Leiden: Brill, 2004.

Rancière, Jacques. *The Emancipated Spectator.* Translated by Gregory Elliott. New York: Verso, 2009.

Randall, Dale B. J. *Winter Fruit: English Drama, 1642–1660.* Lexington: University Press of Kentucky, 1995.

Redworth, Glyn. "Of Pimps and Princes: Three Unpublished Letters from James I and the Prince of Wales Relating to the Spanish Match." *Historical Journal* 37, no. 2 (1994): 401–9.

———. *The Prince and the Infanta: The Cultural Politics of the Spanish Match.* New Haven, CT: Yale University Press, 2003.

Richman, David. *Laughter, Pain, and Wonder: Shakespeare's Comedies and the Audience in the Theater.* Cranbury, NJ: Associated University Presses, 1990.

Riggs, David. *Ben Jonson: A Life.* Cambridge, MA: Harvard University Press, 1989.

Rowlands, Marie B. "Hidden People: Catholic Commoners, 1558–1625." In *English Catholics of Parish and Town, 1558–1778,* edited by Marie B. Rowlands, 10–35. London: Catholic Record Society, 1999.

Rust, Jennifer R. "'Coining God's Image': The Fiscal Theology of the Mystical Body in *Measure for Measure.*" In *The Body in Mystery: The Political Theology of the* Corpus Mysticum *in the Literature of Reformation England,* 103–38. Evanston, IL: Northwestern University Press, 2013.

Salerno, Daniel. "Isabella's Silence: Staging Asceticism in *Measure for Measure.*" In *Shakespeare in Performance,* edited by Eric C. Brown and Estelle Rivier, 2–23. Newcastle upon Tyne: Cambridge Scholars Publishing, 2013.

Salgādo, Gāmini, comp. *Eyewitnesses of Shakespeare: First Hand Accounts of Performances, 1590–1890.* London: Sussex University Press, 1975.

Sargent, Roussel. "Theme and Structure in Middleton's *A Game at Chess.*" *Modern Language Review* 66, no. 4 (October 1971): 721–30.

Schechner, Richard. *Essays on Performance Theory.* New York: Drama Book Specialists, 1977.

Schen, Claire S. "Greeks and 'Grecians' in London: The 'Other' Strangers." In *From Strangers to Citizens: The Integration of Immigrant Communities in Britain, Ireland and Colonial America, 1550–1750,* edited by Randolph Vigne and Charles Littleton, 268–75. Brighton: Sussex Academic Press, 2001.

Schleiner, Louise. "Providential Improvisation in *Measure for Measure.*" *PMLA* 97, no. 2 (March 1982): 227–36.

Schneider, Rebecca. *Performing Remains: Art and War in Times of Theatrical Reenactment.* New York: Routledge, 2011.

Seaver, Paul S. *Wallington's World: A Puritan Artisan in Seventeenth-Century London.* Stanford, CA: Stanford University Press, 1985.

Shagan, Ethan. "Introduction: English Catholic History in Context." In *Catholics and the "Protestant Nation": Religious Politics and Identity in Early Modern England,* edited by Ethan Shagan, 1–21. Manchester: Manchester University Press, 2005.

———. *The Rule of Moderation: Violence, Religion and the Politics of Restraint in Early Modern England.* Cambridge: Cambridge University Press, 2011.

Shami, Jeanne. "Thomas Middleton's *A Game at Chesse*: A Sermon Analogue." *Notes and Queries* 42, no. 3 (September 1995): 236–39.

Shapiro, James. *Shakespeare and the Jews*. New York: Columbia University Press, 1996.

Shaughnessy, Robert. "Connecting the Globe: Actors, Audience and Entrainment." *Shakespeare Survey* 68 (2015): 294–305.

Shell, Alison. *Catholicism, Controversy, and the English Literary Imagination, 1558–1660*. Cambridge: Cambridge University Press, 1999.

———. "The Epigrams of Sir John Harington." *Recusant History* 30, no. 4 (October 2011): 591–93.

———. *Shakespeare and Religion*. London: Bloomsbury Arden Shakespeare, 2010.

Sherman, Jane. "The Pawns' Allegory in Middleton's *A Game at Chesse*." *Review of English Studies*, n.s., 29, no. 114 (May 1978): 147–59.

Shuger, Deborah Kuller. *Political Theologies in Shakespeare's England: The Sacred and the State in "Measure for Measure."* New York: Palgrave, 2001.

———. "A Protesting Catholic Puritan in Elizabethan England." *Journal of British Studies* 48, no. 3 (July 2009): 587–630.

Smith, David L. "Cary, Lucius, Second Viscount Falkland (1609/10–1643)." In *Oxford Dictionary of National Biography*, edited by H. C. G. Matthew and Brian Harrison. Oxford: Oxford University Press, 2004. http://www.oxforddnb.com/view/article/4841.

Smuts, R. M. "The Puritan Followers of Henrietta Maria in the 1630s." *English Historical Review* 93, no. 366 (January 1978): 26–45.

Spence, Richard T. *Lady Anne Clifford, Countess of Pembroke, Dorset and Montgomery (1590–1676)*. Stroud, UK: Sutton, 1997.

Spicer, Andrew. "'A Place of Refuge and Sanctuary of a Holy Temple': Exile Communities and the Stranger Churches." In *Immigrants in Tudor and Early Stuart England*, edited by Nigel Goose and Lien Luu, 91–109. Brighton: Sussex Academic Press, 2005.

Spinks, Bryan D. *Two Faces of Elizabethan Anglican Theology: Sacraments and Salvation in the Thought of William Perkins and Richard Hooker*. Lanham, MD: Scarecrow Press, 1999.

Spurr, John. "The English 'Post-Reformation'?" *Journal of Modern History* 74, no. 1 (March 2002): 101–19.

Stachniewski, John. *The Persecutory Imagination: English Puritanism and the Literature of Religious Despair*. Oxford: Clarendon Press, 1991.

Stanislavsky, Konstantin. *An Actor Prepares*. Translated by Elizabeth Reynolds Hapgood. New York: Routledge, 1964.

Steggle, Matthew. *Digital Humanities and the Lost Drama of Early Modern England: Ten Case Studies*. New York: Routledge, 2015.

———. *Laughing and Weeping in Early Modern Theatres*. Aldershot, UK: Ashgate, 2007.

Stern, Tiffany. *Documents of Performance in Early Modern England*. Cambridge: Cambridge University Press, 2009.

———. *Rehearsal from Shakespeare to Sheridan*. Oxford: Oxford University Press, 2000.

Stone, Lawrence. *The Crisis of the Aristocracy, 1558–1641*. Oxford: Clarendon Press, 1965.

Stoye, J. W. "The Whereabouts of Thomas Killigrew, 1639–41." *Review of English Studies* 25 (July 1949): 245–48.

Swift, Daniel. *Shakespeare's Common Prayers: The Book of Common Prayer and the Elizabethan Age.* Oxford: Oxford University Press, 2012.

Symonds, E. M. "The Diary of John Greene (1635–57)." *English Historical Review* 43, no. 171 (July 1928): 385–94.

———. "The Diary of John Greene (1635–57). III." *English Historical Review* 44, no. 173 (January 1929): 106–17.

Taylor, Gary. "*A Game at Chess*: General Textual Introduction." In *Thomas Middleton and Early Modern Textual Culture: A Companion to the Collected Works*, edited by Gary Taylor and John Lavagnino, 842–47. Oxford: Clarendon Press, 2007.

———. "Historicism, Presentism and Time: Middleton's *The Spanish Gypsy* and *A Game at Chess.*" *SEDERI: Journal of the Spanish and Portuguese Society for English Renaissance Studies* 18 (2008): 147–70.

Taylor, Gary, and John Lavagnino, eds. *Thomas Middleton and Early Modern Textual Culture: A Companion to the Collected Works.* Oxford: Clarendon Press, 2007.

Thomas, Keith. *Religion and the Decline of Magic.* New York: Charles Scribner's Sons, 1971.

Thompson, Elbert N. S. *The Controversy Between the Puritans and the Stage.* New York: Henry Holt, 1903.

Tobin, J. J. M. "How Drunk Was Barnardine?" *Notes and Queries* 50, no. 1 (March 2003): 46–47.

Trevor-Roper, Hugh. *Catholics, Anglicans and Puritans: Seventeenth Century Essays.* Chicago: University of Chicago Press, 1988.

Tribble, Evelyn B. *Cognition in the Globe: Attention and Memory in Shakespeare's Theatre.* New York: Palgrave Macmillan, 2011.

Trim, David. "Immigrants, the Indigenous Community and International Calvinism." In *Immigrants in Tudor and Early Stuart England*, edited by Nigel Goose and Lien Luu, 211–22. Brighton: Sussex Academic Press, 2005.

Turner, Henry. *The English Renaissance Stage: Geometry, Poetics, and the Practical Spatial Art, 1580–1630.* Oxford: Oxford University Press, 2006.

Tyacke, Nicholas. *Anti-Calvinists: The Rise of English Arminianism, c. 1590–1640.* Oxford: Clarendon Press, 1987.

———. *Aspects of English Protestantism, c. 1530–1700.* Manchester: Manchester University Press, 2001.

Van Es, Bart. *Shakespeare in Company.* Oxford: Oxford University Press, 2013.

Vining, Paul. "Nathaniel Tomkins: A Bishop's Pawn." *Musical Times* 133, no. 1796 (October 1992): 538–40.

Vitkus, Daniel, ed. *Piracy, Slavery, and Redemption: Barbary Captivity Narratives from Early Modern England.* New York: Columbia University Press, 2001.

———. *Turning Turk: English Theater and the Multicultural Mediterranean, 1570–1630.* New York: Palgrave Macmillan, 2003.

Walker, George. *Puritan Salt: The Story of Richard Madox, Elizabethan Venturer.* London: Lutterworth Press, 1935.

Wallace, Dewey D. *Puritans and Predestination: Grace in English Protestant Theology, 1525–1695.* Chapel Hill: University of North Carolina Press, 1982.

Walsh, Brian. *Shakespeare, the Queen's Men, and the Elizabethan Performance of History.* Cambridge: Cambridge University Press, 2009.

———. *Unsettled Toleration: Religious Difference on the Shakespearean Stage.* Oxford: Oxford University Press, 2016.

Walsham, Alexandra. *Charitable Hatred: Tolerance and Intolerance in England, 1500–1700.* Manchester: Manchester University Press, 2006.

———. *Church Papists: Catholicism, Conformity, and Confessional Polemic in Early Modern England.* Woodbridge, UK: Boydell Press, 1993.

———. "'Domme Preachers'? Post-Reformation English Catholicism and the Culture of Print." *Past and Present*, no. 168 (August 2000): 72–123.

———. *Providence in Early Modern England.* Oxford: Oxford University Press, 1999.

———. *The Reformation of the Landscape: Religion, Identity, and Memory in Early Modern Britain and Ireland.* Oxford: Oxford University Press, 2011.

Wandel, Lee Palmer. *The Eucharist in the Reformation.* Cambridge: Cambridge University Press, 2006.

Warner, Michael. *Publics and Counterpublics.* New York: Zone Books, 2002.

———. "Publics and Counterpublics." *Public Culture* 14, no. 1 (2002): 49–90.

Watson, Robert N. "False Immortality in *Measure for Measure*: Comic Means, Tragic Ends." *Shakespeare Quarterly* 41, no. 4 (December 1990): 411–32.

Watt, Tessa. *Cheap Print and Popular Piety, 1550–1640.* Cambridge: Cambridge University Press, 1991.

Weimann, Robert. *Author's Pen and Actor's Voice: Playing and Writing in Shakespeare's Theatre.* Edited by Helen Higbee and William N. West. Cambridge: Cambridge University Press, 2000.

Wells, Stanley. "Shakespeare's Onstage Audiences." In *The Show Within: Dramatic and Other Insets; English Renaissance Drama (1550–1642)*, edited by François Laroque, 89–108. Collection Astraea 2, no. 4. Montpellier: Publications de l'Université Paul-Valéry, 1990.

West, William N. "Intertheatricality." In *Early Modern Theatricality*, edited by Henry Turner, 151–72. Oxford: Oxford University Press, 2013.

———. "Understanding in the Elizabethan Theaters." *Renaissance Drama* 35 (2006): 113–43.

White, Paul Whitfield. "Politics, Topical Meaning, and English Theater Audiences, 1485–1575." *Research Opportunities in Renaissance Drama* 34 (1995): 41–54.

White, Peter. "The *Via Media* in the Early Stuart Church." In *The Early Stuart Church, 1603–1642*, edited by Kenneth Fincham, 211–30. Stanford, CA: Stanford University Press, 1993.

Whitney, Charles. *Early Responses to Renaissance Drama.* Cambridge: Cambridge University Press, 2006.

Wickham, Glynne, Herbert Berry, and William Ingram, eds. *English Professional Theatre, 1530–1660.* Cambridge: Cambridge University Press, 2000.

Widmayer, Martha. "'To Sin in Loving Virtue': Angelo of *Measure for Measure*." *Texas Studies in Literature and Language* 49, no. 2 (Summer 2007): 155–80.

Williams, Raymond. "Communications and Community." In *Resources of Hope: Culture, Democracy, and Socialism*, edited by Robin Gable, 19–31. London: Verso, 1989.

———. *Culture and Materialism*. London: Verso, 2005.

———. *Marxism and Literature*. Oxford: Oxford University Press, 1977.

Williamson, Elizabeth. *The Materiality of Religion in Early Modern English Drama*. Burlington, VT: Ashgate, 2009.

Wilson, Bronwen, and Paul Yachnin. Introduction to *Making Publics in Early Modern Europe: People, Things, and Forms of Knowledge*, edited by Bronwen Wilson and Paul Yachnin, 1–24. New York: Routledge, 2010.

Wilson, Richard. *Secret Shakespeare: Studies in Theatre, Religion, and Resistance*. Manchester: Manchester University Press, 2004.

Wiseman, Susan J. "*'Tis Pity She's a Whore*: Representing the Incestuous Body." *Revenge Tragedy*, edited by Stevie Simkin, 208–28. Basingstoke, UK: Palgrave, 2001.

Wittgenstein, Ludwig. *Philosophical Investigations*. Translated by G. E. M. Anscombe. Oxford: Basil Blackwell, 1953.

Wooding, Barbara. *John Lowin and the English Theatre, 1603–1647: Acting and Cultural Politics on the Jacobean and Caroline Stage*. Farnham, UK: Ashgate, 2013.

Woods, Gillian. *Shakespeare's Unreformed Fictions*. Oxford: Oxford University Press, 2013.

Woolf, D. R. "Howell, James (1594?–1666)." In *Oxford Dictionary of National Biography*, edited by H. C. G. Matthew and Brian Harrison. Oxford: Oxford University Press, 2004. http://www.oxforddnb.com/view/article/13974.

Wrightson, Keith, and David Levine. *Poverty and Piety in an English Village: Terling, 1525–1700*. 2nd ed. Oxford: Clarendon Press, 1995.

Yachnin, Paul. "*A Game at Chess*: Thomas Middleton's 'Praise of Folly.'" *Modern Language Quarterly: A Journal of Literary History* 48, no. 2 (June 1987): 107–23.

———. "*A Game at Chess* and Chess Allegory." *Studies in English Literature* 22, no. 2 (Spring 1982): 317–30.

———. "*Hamlet* and the Social Thing in Early Modern England." In *Making Publics in Early Modern Europe: People, Things, Forms of Knowledge*, edited by Bronwen Wilson and Paul Yachnin, 81–95. New York: Routledge, 2010.

———. "A New Source for Thomas Middleton's *A Game at Chess*." *Notes and Queries* 27 (April 1980): 157–58.

———. "Performing Publicity." *Shakespeare Bulletin* 28, no. 2 (2010): 201–19.

———. "Playing with Space: Making a Public in Middleton's Theatre." In *The Oxford Handbook of Thomas Middleton*, edited by Gary Taylor and Trish Thomas Henley, 32–46. Oxford: Oxford University Press, 2012.

Zeman, Corinne. "Domesticating the Turk: Islamic Acculturation in Seventeenth-Century England." PhD diss., Washington University in Saint Louis, forthcoming.

Active reception, 50–60

Actors, 178n6; action thread recovered by, 58; Alleyn, Edward, 42, 73; audiences and, 41, 44, 54, 183n65; boys playing female parts as, 21; Burbage, Richard, 74; clowns with shticks as, 69; Ecclestone, William, 189n37; Field, Nathan, 73–74, 189n36; Kemp, Will, 80, 193n69; Lowin, John, 13, 73, 188n26; nonhuman actors and, 71–76; Robinson, Richard, 75, 190n42; Shakespeare, Edmond, 188n17; strike without touching, 59; Swanston, Eyllaerdt, 72–73, 188n23; theater and oratory for, 181n36; Trigg, William, 189n37

Admiral's Men, 112; cluster marketing, spin-offs, tropes by, 77–78; Jonson murder and work with, 68

Allegory, 89, 92, 111, 193n75, 206n4

Allen, William, 32

Anti-Catholicism, 171n82, 192n60, 197n23, 216n21; church papists in, 15, 27–28; English Protestant identity and, 24, 172n94; femme fatales and, 53, 61–62, 154, 156; A Game at Chess and, 203n77; Jesuits targeted as, 114–16, 120–21, 204n80; Jonson and Volpone as, 164n9; loyalism doubted in, 28; merriness and hearty masculinity smoothing, 80, 85–86; misogyny and, 215n18; "Protestant gaze" and, 62; puritan caricature and parody of, 83; recusancy as resisting, 14–15, 28; Spanish Match plays as, 40, 61

Anti-Theatre factions, 55, 199n41

Anti-theatricalism: history of, 168n54; puritanism as not, 168n52; Puritans and, 16, 18–23; stage as delicious danger for, 100

Arden of Faversham, 201n65

Arminians, 23, 91, 124–25; Mildmay, Henry, opposing, 172n97; reconciliation

arguments of, 166n32; Roman Church as, 128

Asides, 99–100, 104, 109, 116, 201n59

Attendance: A Game at Chess, 195n6; reasons for theater, 52; of theater during 1576–1642, 14–16, 42–44, 165n27, 183n55

Audience priming: bodies readied for crying in, 57; emotions cued in, 184nn71–72

Audience response, 11; historical figure enlivened by, 56–57; play scripts and, 51; in theater, 52–53, 184n73, 185n78; vocal contrasted with quiet, 55; Whore of Babylon and different, 53

Audiences, 158, 164n10, 165n26, 178n7, 179n8, 214n9; actors exchanging with, 41, 44, 54, 183n65; applause as cohesion for, 120; asides for knowledge gaps of, 99, 104; becoming inner performers, 55–56; collective and individual responses of, 183n54, 183n64; death of More as orchestration of, 86; demographics of, 14–16, 42–44, 165n27, 183n55; didactic drama and resistance from, 178n4; early modern Catholics as, 162n1; emotions and, 36, 41, 43–44, 118; entrainment and emotional contagion with, 52; experience feeds back onto, 163n6; A Game at Chess plot as policing by, 90, 97, 118–21; heroine plea to, 117–18; ideological flexibility of, 11–12, 14, 125; improvised joke demanded by, 58; Machiavel as intimate with, 100; Measure for Measure and mixed-faith, 124–25, 143, 150; as mixed-faith, 1–3, 14–16, 163n5; orchestration of, 3, 11, 38–39, 62, 121, 160; plays-within-plays and, 180n16; predestination and, 125–30, 147; props, space, costumes influencing, 69; publics formed between ears of, 39, 151; puritans as, 16–23; religious spectrum of,

Audiences (*continued*)
129–30; sanctity as experiential for, 87; secrets known in *A Game at Chess*, 98; social mixture of, 179n12; Spanish Match and mixed-faith, 61; theater demanding competency of, 43, 113–15; theater unsettling judgments of, 122; theatricality and response of, 40–41, 160

Baro, Peter, 124
Bayer, Mark, 63, 174n123, 185n91
Bennett, Susan, 11
Blackfriars, 21–22, 29
Bloom, Gina, 81, 111, 153
Bossy, John, 29–30, 174n119
Bunny, Edmund, 25
Burton, William, 137, 139, 212n59
Butler, Judith, 4, 11
Butler, Martin, 18, 21–22

Calvinism, 168n47; Catholic seeping into, 131; piety and clothes of, 124, 128–29, 133, 211n43; predestination judgments of, 122–28, 210n32; puritanism as, 15, 17; theater business and playgoers of, 17; twists, dramatic irony, soliloquies destabilizing, 8, 150
Campion, Edmund, 88
Catholicism, 10, 25, 33, 165n21, 174n121; Calvinism seeping into, 131; coping mechanisms of, 116; English, 26–30; English community and *Sir Thomas More* in, 83, 85; *A Game at Chess* and, 114–16, 118–21; grace as solicited in, 144; heroines and incestuous brothers of, 157; hospitality refused as, 85–86; at Inns of Court and Holborn, 174n124, 174n125; King James on Protestantism and, 196n18; meter implying, 186n95, 210n39; occult and medieval, 34; piecemeal devotional life of, 29; print culture of, 175n128; rapprochement with, 155; as recusant and persistent, 14–15, 28; sensory allure of, 156; theater and, 18, 168n55; *'Tis Pity She's a Whore* and, 155–57; universal monarchy as aim of, 98–99; as Whore of Babylon, 9, 96, 154–55. *See also* Anti-Catholicism; Popery
Catholics, 26, 173n108, 176n148; audiences as early modern, 162n1; English peerage and, 174n118; on Fleet Street, 174n126; *A Game at Chess* endangering, 90, 118–21;

Protestants on damnation and heaven for, 86–87, 128; resistance to Protestant matrimony, 211n46; security threat as, 173n114
Chamberlain's Men, 77–78, 80, 82
A Chaste Maid in Cheapside, 103
Church of England: crucifix and, 185n85; *A Game at Chess* and dangers to, 91, 94–95, 107–16; mixed-faith as normal in, 23–26; as Protestant hegemony, 2, 4, 10, 17, 23, 90, 150; puritanism as conflicts in, 168n48; stranger churches and, 177n164, 177n166
Church papists, 15, 27–28
Clark, Samuel, 21–22
Clothing, 124, 128–29, 133, 211n43
Cockpit, 33, 63
Collaborative authorship, 7–8, 67–72, 87–88, 187n6
Collinson, Patrick, 14, 19, 164n16, 177n161
Comedy: *A Game at Chess* as, 103, 199n35; humoral theory and, 41; *The Late Lancashire Witches* as, 49–50; ridiculous contrasted with religion in, 50
Confessional positions, 1
Conversion, 10, 15, 75; beliefs undergoing, 22–24; between Catholicism and Protestantism, 26; compromises instead of, 28; fatal vespers and Gee in, 30–31; *A Game at Chess* character in, 99; Jonson in multiple, 13, 189n37; mixed-faith families and, 30–34; of Prince Charles, 94–95
Crawford, Julie, 25
Cultural materialism, 1, 5–6
Culture: Catholicism and print, 175n128; emotion power on, 152–53; gasps, tears, laughter creating, 40; plays influence on, 41, 60; religions of mixed-faith, 23; social processes remaking, 90; theater transfiguring mixed-faith, 4–5, 36–37, 160; theatricality and pressures on, 40–42
Curtain, 36

Dawson, Anthony, 41–42, 179n11
Dekker, Thomas, 61–64, 79, 87–88, 96
Dent, Arthur, 129, 208n10
Derrida, Jacques, 57
Dessen, Alan, 100
Devotional practices, 25–26, 30
Diehl, Huston, 18, 53, 61–62, 156
Discovery space, 112–14
Do the Right Thing, 217n29

Drama, 2; actors and audiences exchanging in, 41, 54; audiences reshaped by, 11, 54; emotions evoked with, 11–12, 45–46; mixed-faith creation and viewing of, 11–12; open scenes of, 59–60; religions shown in, 12, 161n1; resistance to didactic, 178n4; shared emotions evoked by, 11–12; as social process, 151; theatricality shaping engagement in, 38

Dudley, Robert, 18, 21, 32, 77

Duffy, Eamon, 29

Dutch Reformed Churches, 35

Dyke, Daniel, 126–27, 140

Elam, Keir, 130, 132, 178n6

Emotions, 3, 76, 144, 149–50, 178n7, 214n9; anti-theatre factions threatened by, 55; audience and actor bond in, 44; audience priming cueing, 184nn71–72; beyond audiences, 36; audiences and, 36, 41, 43–44, 52, 118; clues for, 129–30; culture and power of, 40, 152–53; as disturbing or contributory, 56–58; drama evoking, 11–12, 45–46; feelings as, 41, 50–51, 55–59, 90–94, 152, 182n52, 215nn11–12; genre and, 130–31; humoral theory and, 41; incest overcome by, 157–58; innocence contrasted with, 108; *Measure for Measure* challenging, 122–23; mixed-faith wedding, 64; publics made with, 9; in public sphere, 151–60; religion not predetermining, 14; religions debated with, 154–60; theater as experiment in, 1, 5, 7, 38, 66

English nationalism, 24, 40, 63–64, 92–94; Henry V invoking, 79; *Sir Thomas More* and Catholicism with, 83, 85

Entrainment, 52, 93, 182n46

Epilogues, 205n90

Erasmianism, 2, 12, 16–17, 23–24, 67

Van Es, Bart, 68, 82

Falstaff: antipuritan caricature and anti-Catholic parody with, 83; as irreverence, 73; *I Sir John Oldcastle* answering, 77; Kemp playing both roles of, 81–82

Fatal vespers, 30–31

Femme fatales, 53, 61–62, 154, 156

Field, John, 74

Free will, 207n6

A Game at Chess, 7–8, 40, 60–61, 195n8, 198n27, 200n54, 200n57, 201nn60–63, 202n68; anal fistula and, 101, 103–4, 200n55; anti-Catholicism in, 203n77; applause and experiential cohesion from, 120; asides in, 99, 104; attendance at, 195n6; audience knowing secrets in, 98, 118; audience policing in, 90, 97, 118–21; "bum" replaced by "drum," 199n51; chair implying privy in, 102, 103, 199nn44–45; character as converting, 99; chess and, 97, 111, 198n34, 201n67, 203n81; Church of England in danger in, 91, 94–95, 107–16; climactic scene in, 105; comedy potential in, 199n35; discovery space utilized in, 112–13; dramatic irony in, 106–8, 118; dramatic technique and feeling on, 92–93; "globe" and power in, 199n52; at Globe theater, 108–9, 121; heroine urging Protestant vigilance in, 108, 117–18; historical people represented in, 195n10; historical revision in, 104–5; implied magic and blocking in, 111–13; innocence contrasted with emotional depth in, 108; Jesuits targeted in, 114–16, 120–21, 204n80; King Charles as King of Spain in, 63–64, 197n26; King's Men punishment for, 94–95; knowledge controlling theatrical space in, 108; lack of religious neutrality in, 89–90; levels of awareness in, 100; lurking Catholicism in, 114–16; Machiavel and subversive impressions of, 106–7; from mastery to bore in, 105–6; mirror in, 94, 111–15, 202n69, 202n73, 202n74, 205n88; mixed-faith responses to, 121; number of lines per character in, 198n32; politics limiting run of, 89; Protestant and Spanish plots of, 94–95, 107; Protestant factions softened in, 96; Protestant vigilance orchestrated by, 91; public event beyond playhouse as, 91, 93; scatological humor undercutting character in, 103; secrets and, 97, 109–11, 200n53; social event and fiction fused in, 92, 119; Spanish characters and espionage in, 95–100, 198n31; stage master from control of secrets in, 117; staging and acting as challenge in, 113–15; staging devices in, 89, 200n58, 203n78, 203nn75–76, 204n83; theatrical space showing danger in, 109, 111; views on, 194n1, 195n2; written copies of, 195n9

Globe, 15, 22, 47–49, 52, 72, 153; Catholicism
    close to, 29; Chamberlain's Men at,
    77–78; *Falstaff* roles cited of, 81–82; *A
    Game at Chess* at, 108–9, 121; grave ledger
    stones near, 70
Good fellows, 16, 67, 79–88, 192n67
De Granada, Louis, 25
Greek Orthodox Church, 35
Gunpowder Plot, 28, 64, 164n9, 174n116
Gurr, Andrew, 44, 174n124

Haigh, Christopher, 27, 173n106
Hamlet, 43, 213n64
Harbage, Alfred, 15, 42–43
Hegemony, 61–62; Calvinist, 122; Protes-
    tant, 2–4, 10, 17, 90, 150; theater loosening
    cultural, 4
Heinemann, Margot, 18
Hill, Christopher, 24
Historical formalism, 162n9
Hobgood, Allison, 41
Holles, John, 106–7
Hopkins, Lisa, 72, 188n19
Howard, Jean, 51–52, 205n95
Huguenots, 35
Humoral theory, 41

Ideological flexibility, 11–12, 14, 125
Images, 20–21
Irony, 8; as affective, 87, 159, 217n30;
    dramatic, 106–8, 118, 123, 142, 150,
    204n84
Irreverence, 14–15, 148–49; *Falstaff* as, 73;
    The Late Lancashire Witches, 49–50;
    mixed-faith, 34
I Sir John Oldcastle, 77; Catholicism as
    hospitality refused in, 85–86; Kemp
    playing *Falstaff* role of, 81–82; merriness
    and hearty masculinity in, 80, 85–86
Islam, 35

Judaism, 35

King's Men, 47, 60, 68, 70, 89, 103; Ford as
    playwright of, 188n21; *A Game at Chess*
    punishment of, 94–95; human and
    nonhuman actors in, 71–76; set design
    by, 111
Knapp, Jeffrey, 16–17, 67, 161n3, 166n32
Knutson, Roslyn Lander, 44
Kuhn, John, 112

Lady Elizabeth's Men, 60
Lake, Peter, 11, 46, 124, 151–52, 162n1,
    162n12, 193n70, 214n5
The Late Lancashire Witches, 39–40; current
    news and tactics of, 180n30; Laud allusion
    in phrase of, 49; stage tricks suspending
    magic issue in, 49; witchcraft reality not
    decided in, 47–50, 181n31
Laudianism, 2, 15, 19, 22, 24–25, 53, 154–56,
    168n47; archbishop of Canterbury as, 47,
    170n74; Calvinism contrasted with, 9, 10;
    Heylyn as polemicist of, 32; *The Late
    Lancashire Witches* and, 49; Squier and,
    190n43; stranger churches suppressed by,
    35; Tomkins and, 34, 176n158
Lin, Erika T., 59, 162n11
London: Gee and fatal vespers in, 30–31;
    mixed-faith clearinghouse as, 15, 35–36;
    predestination familiarity in, 124–25;
    Spanish Match and denizens of, 63;
    theater and early modern, 36, 40
Lopez, Jeremy, 43, 51, 71, 99–100
Lukewarmness, 10, 23–24, 128–30, 137–38

Machiavel, 93, 100–107, 109
MacLean, Sally-Beth, 18
Magic, 15, 165n25; *A Game at Chess* mirror
    as, 94, 111–15, 202n69, 202n73, 202n74;
    The Late Lancashire Witches and, 47–50,
    181n31; meter as incantation of, 66,
    186n95; staging device for, 49; ungodly,
    occult, foreign as, 34–36
Maltby, Judith, 10, 15, 25
Manliness: plays forging Protestant, 192n61;
    in *When You See Me You Know Me*,
    192n64
Marino, James, 77–78
Martyr plays, 76–88; English community in,
    191n59; Protestant, 191n49; syndicates
    writing, 191n54
Mary, Queen of Scotts, 32
Masten, Jeffrey, 69, 72
Match Me in London, 7, 40, 62–64
May, Thomas, 75
McClain, Lisa, 29
McCoy, Richard, 39
McInnis, David, 178n2
McMillin, Scott, 18
Measure for Measure, 209n21, 211n45, 212n51,
    212n54, 212n56; attempted rape in, 142,
    212n61; audiences and predestination

confusion in, 122, 147; Barnardine in, 147–50, 213n67, 213n72; Calvinist predestination judgments and, 122–26; Calvinist seeping into Catholic in, 131; Catholic resistance to Protestant matrimony in, 211n46; clothing defining characters in, 133; clues misread in, 130–37; condition of souls exposed in, 123; emotional and ideological exercise in, 122–23, 144; heroine and male depravity in, 135–36; inner struggles in, 138, 212n63, 213n66; intercession in, 212n60; jumbled sentences in, 140–41; from lust to damned in, 139; mixed-faith audience of, 124–25, 143, 150; plot reversals and predestination in, 150; predestination and, 144, 206n3, 209n20; predestination as code of, 133, 137; puritan hypocrite and baffled soul in, 138, 141–42; puritanism and, 206n5; religion established and challenged in, 123, 132–35; reprobate and audience elasticity in, 137–38, 148–49; reprobation staved off in, 145; scripture and predestination in, 136–37; self-complacency as spiritual threat in, 140; soliloquies inviting sympathy in, 147; spiritual state undetermined in, 145–46, 149–50; twists, dramatic irony, soliloquies of, 150; wickedness as disorienting in, 142–43

Meter, 65; implying Catholicism, 186n95, 210n39; jumbled sentences as, 140–41; as magic incantation, 66, 186n95

Middleton, Thomas, 187n11; A Chaste Maid in Cheapside by, 100; A Game at Chess by, 7–8, 40, 60–61, 64–66, 89–121, 150; Roaring Girl by, 59

Misogyny: anti-Catholicism and, 215n18; Measure for Measure attempted rape as, 142, 212n61; The Spanish Gypsy rape as, 64–65

Monta, Susannah Brietz, 85, 193n75

More, Thomas, 33, 83–88

Mullaney, Steven, 3–4, 41, 59–60, 87, 130, 152, 179n10

Murray, Molly, 33–34

News, topical: A Game at Chess as, 92, 119; The Late Lancashire Witches as, 180n30

The Noble Spanish Soldier (1622), 7, 40, 61–62, 131

Nomenclature, 19, 27

Occult, 34

O'Connell, Michael, 18

Open scenes, 59–60

Orchestration, 152; active reception in, 50–60; of audience response, 3, 11, 38–39, 62, 121, 160; death of More and audience reaction as, 86; emotions to mixed-faith with, 64

Othello, 44, 59, 211n44

Overton, Paul, 121

Parson, Robert, 25

Passions of the Minde in Generall, 43–44

Paul's Cross sermons, 30–31, 129, 175n135

Pelagianism, 15, 17, 125, 150

Pepys, Samuel, 169n59

Phelips, Robert, 48

Playgoers: Bacon, Francis, 23, 37, 60; Baker, Augustine, 32; Baker, Richard, 19–20; Bale, John, 17; Barrington, Thomas, 21; Blount, Anne (Lady Newport), 33, 176n148; Blount, Christopher, 32, 129, 176n146; Brathwaite, Richard, 25; Cary, Elizabeth, 30; Cary, Lucius, 23–24, 171n76; Clifford, Anne, 24–25, 171n85; confessional groups as conciliatory in, 23; Corbett, Richard, 22; Cranfield, Lionel, 24; Cromwell, Henry, 22, 169n62; Davies, John (of Hereford), 27, 31, 173n105; Davies, John (of Oxford), 27–28, 173n113; Dering, Edward, 22; Devereaux, Robert (2nd Earl of Essex), 32; Devereaux, Robert (3rd Earl of Essex), 31; Donne, John, 33–34; Earle, John, 27, 173n109; Essex, Charles, 22; Forman, Simon, 34, 48, 181n33; Foscarini, Antonio, 36–37; Foxe, John, 17, 76; Gee, John, 30–31, 168n55, 175n134, 203n79; Gosson, Stephen, 20, 46, 100; Greene, John, 35, 167n45; Habington, William, 29; Hall, Joseph, 23, 170n71; Harington, John, 26–27, 33, 173n101; Heylyn, Peter, 32, 175n144; Howell, James, 24, 171n77; Hutton, Timothy, 34; instability processed by mixed-faith, 12–13; Jackson, Henry, 44, 180n23; Killigrew, Thomas, 34, 176n156; Lambarde, William, 24, 171n81; Leggatt, Alexander, 56; Leke, Thomas, 28; Lucy, Thomas, 21; Madox, Richard, 16, 21, 169n57, 169n58; Marston, John, 23; Matthew, Tobie, 23, 33; Melton, John, 26;

Playgoers (*continued*)

Meres, Francis, 25, 172n91; Mildmay, Anthony, 12–13, 172n97; Mildmay, Humphrey, 12–13, 26, 172n97; Milton, John, 17, 23, 166n37, 170n73; Nashe, Thomas, 56; Newdigate, Richard, 22, 169n64, 170n74; Newdigate (3rd), John, 23, 170n74; Norwood, Richard, 22; Overall, John, 25, 172n88; Overbury, Thomas, 50–51; Parker, William, 28; Percy, Charles, 28; Prynne, William, 19–20, 22–23, 168n52; puritanism and, 16–23; Rich, Henry, 22, 170n66; Rich, Mary, 21; Rich, Robert, 22, 31, 170n65; Rowlands, Samuel, 20–21, 75, 169n56; Rudyerd, Benjamin, 19; script revision by, 183n57, 183n60; Skipwith, Henry, 34; Smith, John, 22; surveillance enlisting, 8; theater response and religion of, 7; Tomkins, Nathaniel, 34, 176n158; Tomkyns, Nathaniel, 47–49, 180n29; Whitelock, Bulstrode, 22; Wilson, Arthur, 31; Wortley, Frank, 12–13

Plays, 59, 178n7, 187n10, 191n58; actors interpreting, 69; advertising for, 179n14; audience response and scripts of, 51; collaboration percentage on, 68–69; culture influences and, 41, 60; on current news, 92, 119, 180n30; ideological outcomes in, 71; leakiness of women portrayed in, 199n48; linguistic stylometrics for, 188n18; manly Protestant identity from, 192n61; on martyrs, 76–88; as not religious tracts, 46–50, 180n27; within plays, 180n16; public feeling reorganized by, 41, 90; religion into characters, settings, dialogue, props in, 131; religious matter as changing in, 3; religious sensibilities of, 130; space, props, costumes influencing, 69; on Spanish Match in 1620s, 7, 40, 60–66, 89–121, 131; written copies of, 195n9

Playwrights, 2; Beaumont, Francis, 71, 187n15; Brome, Richard, 190n38; changing fashions influencing, 68; Chettle, Henry, 84, 87; collaboration and, 67, 69, 187n6; Drayton, Michael, 77; Eyre, Simon, 79; Fletcher, John, 70–72, 187nn14–15; Ford, John, 64, 72, 154, 188n19, 188n21; Greene, Robert, 178n172; Hathway, Richard, 77; Henslowe, Philip, 18, 78, 167, 194n81;

Heywood, Thomas, 54–58, 62, 88; Jonson, Ben, 12–13, 68, 74–75, 164n9, 189n37, 190n39; Massinger, Philip, 70–72; Middleton, Thomas, 7–8, 40, 59–61, 64–66, 89–121, 187n11; mixed-faith collaborators as, 7–8, 87–88; Munday, Anthony, 55, 77, 82–84, 88, 194n83; Perkins, William, 126, 207n9; religion and, 67, 69, 77; Riche, Barnabe, 45; Rowley, William, 64; Wilson, Robert, 77

Plot devices: anal fistula as, 101, 103–4, 200n55; dramatic irony as, 106–8, 118, 123, 142, 150, 204n84; soliloquies as, 8, 123, 147, 150; twists as, 44, 123, 150; visceral clues and theatrical cues as, 131

Polemics, 215n10

Politics: Catholics at Protestant services as, 28; *A Game at Chess* limited by, 89; *The Late Lancashire Witches* as case of, 47, 49

Poole, Kristen, 138

Popery, 12, 20–21, 24, 78

Post-Reformation scholarship, 166n33

Predestination, 208n11, 211n47; assurance or security in, 126; audiences and, 125–30, 147; backsliding in, 213n65; Calvinism and judgments on, 122–26; clothing defining godliness in, 124, 128–29, 133, 135; comfort, despair, suicide in, 208n19; free will and salvation in, 207n6; lack of self knowledge in, 126–27; London familiar with, 124–25; *Measure for Measure* and, 206n3, 209n20; negotiable and nonnegotiable salvation in, 207n6, 207n8; *Othello and*, 211n44; poorness and lifestyle vilified in, 128–29; practical impossibility of determining, 134–35; ruling reprobates of, 147–50; scripture similarity and, 136–37; sermons and judgments of, 127–28, 210n32; sympathy for reprobate of, 137–47; from will of God, 125

Preiss, Richard, 51–52, 56, 69, 162n13

Props, 69; discovery space instead of, 112–13; nonhuman actors as, 76

Protestantism, 172n87, 172n94, 195n5; anti-Catholicism and, 24, 62; Calvinist consensus in, 15, 17; on Catholic damnation or heaven, 86–87, 128; Catholic resistance to matrimony in, 211n46; Catholics attending services in, 28; ceremonial conformity of, 20, 25; Church of England as, 10, 17, 23; church papists and, 28; continental, 34–35; *A Game at Chess* and protection of, 91, 94–95, 107–16; hegemony of, 2–4, 10, 17, 90, 150; King James on Catholicism and, 196n18; martyr plays of, 191n49; nomenclature struggles in, 27; occult and, 34; plays forging manly identity of, 192n61; "prayer-book" as committed, 15, 24–25; Spanish Match failure consolidating, 90–91, 96; Spanish Match fears by, 40; *'Tis Pity She's a Whore* and coding as, 216n28. *See also* Puritanism

Protestants, 26; heroine urging vigilance of, 108, 118; Spanish hero coded as, 62–63

Publics, 3, 46, 89–93; audience reactions forming, 151; communications in, 215nn15–16; as developing experience, 151–54; emotions in sphere of, 151–60; *A Game at Chess* as event of, 91, 93; making of, 9, 14, 214n1, 214n3; multitude swayed in, 50–51; polemics in, 215n10, 215n17

Puritanism, 164n17, 169n56, 191n50, 208n13, 209n23, 210n41; anti-Catholic parody and caricature of, 83; antipuritan satire and, 18; anti-theatricalism and, 16, 18–23, 168n52; Calvinism as continuum with, 15, 17; Church of England conflicts as, 168n48; clothing and costumes of, 211n43; as conflict within social classes, 209n27; hypocrisies of, 138, 142, 211n50; *I Sir John Oldcastle* as, 77; Judaism and, 35; Lollardy as precursor to, 77; Martinism as radical group in, 167n43; *Measure for Measure* and, 206n5; nomenclature on, 19; outsider characterization of, 19; playgoers from, 16–23; theater and, 18–19, 166n28, 166n38, 167nn40–41

Queen Anne's Men, 62–63
Queen's Men touring company, 15, 18
Questier, Michael, 30, 32, 174n121

Red Bull, 29, 63
Religions, 1, 2, 7, 162n1, 209n26; audiences and, 42, 129–30; believers modifying beliefs in, 22–23, 30; Catholicism as illegal, 27; into characters, settings, dialogue, props, 131; devices undermining judgment on, 123; dramatic treatments of, 12, 161n1; early modern theater and, 13–14, 131, 154; emotions and, 14, 154–60;

enforcement of, 164n13; established and challenged, 132–35; Eucharistic participation in, 179n11; lack of neutrality on, 89–90; *The Late Lancashire Witches* and, 49; in London, 15, 35–36; mixed-faith culture and, 23, 34; plays not tracts of, 46–50, 180n27; playwrights alignment with, 67, 69, 77; theater reconfiguring, 42; theatricality and, 39, 180n18; tropes and agendas of, 78

Religious culture, 3, 80, 161n1; opinion changing labels of, 10–11; soliloquies unsettling Calvinist, 8, 150; theater expanding mixed-faith, 7, 89

Religious diversity, 1–2, 10–11, 14–17, 30–31; cross-confessional, 25–26; in London, 15, 35–36; mixed-faith families, 33–34; in theater companies, 71–76

Religious identity, 4, 82; Shakespeare beliefs as, 187n13; theatricality and alternative, 3

Reprobation, 123–24, 126–29, 133, 143, 213n68; anxiety, 122, 125, 138; Barnardine and, 147–50; character as hero in, 141; sympathy for, 137–40; trick and switch staving, 145

Rowley, William, 187n11

Salisbury Court, 29
Salvetti, Amerigo, 106
Schneider, Rebecca, 56–57
Scott, Thomas, 91, 93
Secrets: audience knowing, 98; *A Game at Chess* and, 200n53; plot and theatrical process as, 97, 109–11; stage mastery as control of, 117

Sejanus, 190n44
Shagan, Ethan, 2, 23, 26
Shakespeare, William, 1, 17, 35, 67, 71; conventions with influence on, 68; *Henry IV, Parts 1 and 2*, 77–83; *Henry V*, 78–80; *Measure for Measure*, 8, 122–50; religious beliefs of, 187n13; religious culture discussions through, 161n1; *Sir Thomas More*, 83–88, 193n73; *Taming of the Shrew*, 22

Shaughnessy, Robert, 52
Shell, Allison, 16–19
Sherman, Jane, 95
Sidney, Philip, 39
Sir John Oldcastle, 191n58, 192n65, 192nn62–63

Sir Thomas More, 193nn71–73, 194n82; Catholic martyr and English community in, 83, 85, 191n59; Catholic spiritual condition assessed in, 86–87; experiential evidence of sanctity of, 87; governmental revisions on, 83–84; Henslowe and, 194n81; lack of performance evidence on, 85; merriness, hospitality and charity in, 85–86; metatheatricality in, 193n75

Soliloquies: Calvinist culture unsettled by, 8, 150; plot devices as, 123, 150; sympathy invited with, 147

The Spanish Gypsy, 40, 66; current events in, 186n92; gypsy marriage and Spanish rape in, 64–65

Spanish Match, 197n19; anti-Catholic and anti-Spanish stereotypes of, 40, 61; denominational or mixed-faith audiences of, 61; disastrous weddings in plays of, 61, 185n83; English and Spanish marriage alliance as, 90, 93–94; London denizens interested in, 40, 63, 185n90; play companies capitalizing on, 185n82; plays in 1620s on, 7, 40, 60–66, 89–121, 131; Prince Charles after, 197n21; Protestants consolidated in failure of, 90–91; Spanish intentions for, 197n20

Spin-offs, 77–78, 88, 191n56

Staging devices, 196nn11–13; antipuritan satire as, 18; audiences challenged by, 43, 113–15; bed tricks as, 204n82; blocking as, 111–13, 201n67, 203n81; caricature and parody as, 47–48, 83; chair as privy as, 102, 103, 199nn44–45; commentary on, 181n39; couplets satirizing *Volpone* as, 13; discovery space as, 112–13; effects in, 182n44; *A Game at Chess* with, 89, 97, 109–11, 203n78, 203nn75–76, 204n83; magic issue suspended with, 49; plot reversals as, 150; props, space, costumes as, 69; secrets as, 97, 109–11; set design as, 111; theatergrams and, 78; theatrical illusions as, 39; trap door as, 200n58. *See also* Plot devices

Steggle, Matthew, 51

St. Paul's, 29, 33

Stranger churches, 35, 177n164, 177n166

Surveillance, 8, 118–21

Sutton, Thomas, 74–75

Szatek, Karoline, 44

Taylor, Gary, 112, 186n97

Theater, 6, 20–21, 55–56, 154, 214n2; affective thinking and feeling in, 152, 215nn11–12; audience demands by, 43, 113–15; audience judgments unsettled in, 122; audience response in, 39, 52–53, 184n73, 185n78; Catholicism and, 168n55; Church of England as dominant in, 17; cluster marketing, spin-offs, tropes used by, 77–78, 88; cultural adaptation mechanism as, 4–5, 90, 155; emotional and mental experiments as, 1, 5, 7, 11–12, 38–39, 45–46, 66; feelings and, 152, 182n52; ideas, skills, foreign travel from, 43; ideology reassembled by, 66; imagination cultivated by, 42–46; London and commercial, 36, 40; merry English past represented in, 78–79; mixed-faith culture transfigured by, 36–37, 160; puritanism and, 17–19, 22, 166n28, 166n38, 167n40; puritanism tolerance by, 167n41; religion reconfigured by, 7, 42; social impact of, 12, 36–37; Spanish Match capitalized on by, 185n82; suspension of belief and, 12, 39; theatergrams and stage business in, 78

Theater, early modern, 183n61; attendance during 1576–1642, 14; genres of, 43; imaginative flexibility from, 7, 160; martyr plays and, 76–88; mixed-faith playgoers to, 10, 39; religion grafted to form in, 13–14, 131, 154; religious culture and, 7, 89; 1642 closures of, 17; thoughts and feelings orchestrated in, 50–51, 55–59, 152

Theater business: Calvinist playgoers and, 17; cluster marketing, spin-offs, tropes as, 77–78; financially crucial character for, 79; ideology reconfigured by, 68; mixed-faith and, 161n1; religious diversity in, 71–76

Theatricality, 18, 42; asides in, 99, 104, 109, 116, 201n59; audience response from, 40–41; bodies readied for crying in, 57; early entrance as, 100, 105; imagination and ideology stretched by, 3, 38, 160; meter for opposite tones in, 65–66; religion and, 39, 180n18; *Sir Thomas More* and meta, 193n75; spacial distance and plot as, 107–18; theatrical italics as hyper-, 99

Thomas, Keith, 34

Tilney, Edmund, 83–84

'Tis Pity She's a Whore, 216n20; audience reminded with title in, 158; Catholicism

sympathetic elements in, 155–57; final line in, 159–60; ideological double vision of, 154–55; incest in, 9, 154–59, 215n19; pity requested and denied in, 159–60; Protestant coding in, 216n28
Topcliff, Richard, 88
Tyacke, Nicholas, 19

Ungodly, occult, foreign, 34–36

Villiers, George, 91, 93
Volpone, 12–13, 74–75, 164n9, 190n44

Walsham, Alexandra, 27, 209n20
Walsingham, Francis, 18–20, 32

West, William, 59
When You See Me You Know Me, 192n64
Whitney, Charles, 38, 53, 162n13, 178n1
Whore of Babylon: audience responses to, 53; Catholic Church as, 9, 96, 154–55; *'Tis Pity She's a Whore* as, 155–56
The Whore of Babylon, 156–57, 216n27
Williams, Raymond, 4, 6, 92, 122
Williamson, Elizabeth, 76
Worcester's Men, 80
Wright, Thomas, 43–45

Yachnin, Paul, 52, 76, 93, 152

Zemar, Corinne, 35

ACKNOWLEDGMENTS

No book has only one author. The best parts of this one are those in which you can hear the voices of the people here, and many unnamed others, to whom I owe great thanks.

From Trinity College Dublin: my undergraduate mentor Amanda Piesse and friend Wayne Jordan.

From Columbia: my excellent mentors and even better friends Julie Crawford, Molly Murray, and Alan Stewart; and my crew, Jenny Davidson, Andras Kisery, Anjuli Raza Kolb, John Kuhn, Bryan Lowrance, Julie Peters, Christine Varnado, Atticus Zavaleta, and the inimitable Allison Deutermann.

At Washington University: the Mellon Vertical Seminar gave feedback on Chapter 5, and the Early Modern Reading Group on Chapters 1 and 2. I am grateful for the support of many colleagues there and at Saint Louis University: Jami Ake, Mary Jo Bang, Anupam Basu, Daniel Bornstein, Dillon Brown, Rob Henke, Long Le-Khac, Bill Maxwell, Mel Micir, Jessica Rosenfeld, Ignacio Sanchez Prado, Jonathan Sawday, Julia Walker, and Rebecca Wanzo. Jen Rust and Abram Van Engen offered helpful feedback on Chapter 5. I hope that my students hear themselves in this book, particularly David Davidson and Lydia Zoells, who helped prepare the manuscript. Jonathan Koch, Lauren Robertson, and Corinne Zeman gave valuable advice on Chapter 2.

A Myers Fellowship supported several months' work at the Huntington Library, where I was made welcome by Steve Hindle. Ari Freidlander, with his usual clarity, gave me timely self-knowledge when he pointed out, correctly, "Oh, you're an unreconstructed cultural materialist." Urvashi Chakravarty, Jessica Rosenberg, and Marjorie Rubright, brilliant women whom I had just met, held an impromptu dinner workshop of Chapter 2. The extraordinary Dympna Callaghan nurtured this project over daily tea in the garden. With astonishing care and generosity she read drafts of Chapters 1, 2, and 4, and helped clarify and deepen my methodological commitments.

The Folger Shakespeare Library has supported this project at every phase of its development. I owe a tremendous debt to Mike Witmore, Owen Williams, and especially the wonderful Kathleen Lynch. As a graduate student, the yearlong research seminar gave me the archival skills for Chapters 1 and 3. At a weekend symposium on publics, I began a long and generative conversation with Paul Yachnin that became the epilogue. An O. B. Hardison Fellowship supported several months' research in that paradise of scholars. Brad Gregory rigorously read Chapters 1 and 2. Claire Bourne inspired us all daily in the reading room. Kathleen's enthusiasm for the project enabled me to experiment with live actors (the talented Jenna Burke, Megan Dominy, and Daniel Yabut) on the material that became Chapter 4.

The Blackfriars' Conference facilitated further work with actors on the "privy scene" in Chapter 4.

At the Renaissance Society of America conference, I once gave a paper to an audience of three, among them Alison Shell, at whose work the intervention of my talk was primarily directed. Her gracious and generous reception of my critique reflects the quality of her character and scholarship.

Many have encouraged this project from its earliest stages onward: Kim Coles, Jane Hwang Degenhardt, Hannibal Hamlin, Richard McCoy, Dan Vitkus, Will West, and Elizabeth Williamson.

On Chapter 2, I received incredibly helpful feedback from Erika Lin, Jeremy Lopez, and Richard Preiss.

The angelically patient Jerry Singerman let me take the time I needed.

Peter Lake taught me everything I know about post-Reformation England, the most interesting bits over beers. I owe him more than a pint.

Tom Cartelli inspired much, and read all, of this book. His insight, advice, and fearless example have been invaluable.

Jeff Doty talked out and read this whole book from its conception to last paragraph so thoroughly and generously that it feels as though we wrote it together. Jeff's unfailing support made it possible for me to hear my own voice when I felt most besieged by naysayers.

The debt I owe Steven Mullaney goes back to 1998, my first year of college, when reading the introduction to *The Place of the Stage* sent me racing out of the library with the hair standing up on the back of my neck. His beautiful mind, friendship, and support for this project over the last decade have been a great gift in my life.

Jean Howard's example, the best and most challenging to follow, has inspired growth in the field for the last thirty years. All her many students have felt her clarity of thought, strength of purpose, kindness, and tireless generosity. We internalize the voices of our mentors. Jean, your voice in my head is the bravest.

Family, I owe the greatest debt to my family, for their love and constant support.

9 780812 250251